The Memoirs of
Constable Jeremiah Mee, RIC

THE MEMOIRS OF CONSTABLE JEREMIAH MEE, RIC

J. ANTHONY GAUGHAN

MERCIER PRESS
IRISH PUBLISHER – IRISH STORY

MERCIER PRESS

Cork

www.mercierpress.ie

First published in hardback in 1975

This edition published by Mercier Press, 2012

© J. Anthony Gaughan, 1975, 2012

ISBN: 978 1 85635 884 2

10 9 8 7 6 5 4 3 2 1

A CIP record for this title is available from the British Library

Printed and bound in the EU.

CONTENTS

ACKNOWLEDGEMENTS

In connection with the preparation of this book, I wish to thank the library staffs of the National Library of Ireland, the Royal Irish Academy, Trinity College Dublin, the British Museum Newspaper Library and the New York City Public Library for their courtesy and help; the librarians of the various institutions and the private individuals mentioned on pp. 403–4 for allowing me to consult papers in their charge; all who gave me information, especially those whose names appear on pp. 409–10; Eamonn de Barra, Richard Hawkins, Seán Mac Cormaic, Maurice O'Connell, Prof. Maurice R. O'Connell and Dr Christopher J. Woods for much helpful criticism; Colonel David Neligan for his kind foreword; and Mrs Eileen Mee Doyle for her constant encouragement, for her co-operation in the research necessitated by this book.

I am grateful also to John Burgess of Lafayette for successfully reproducing from very worn prints some of the early photographs which appear in this book.

I must thank especially James R. W. Goulden who was most generous in sharing with me his extensive knowledge of the RIC, which is derived from a fairly comprehensive set of Constabulary Lists and a lifelong interest in the force. Mr Goulden, however, wishes it to be stated that he is not in accord with some of the views of the late Jeremiah Mee.

Finally I wish to thank the Controller of Her Majesty's Stationery Office for permission to reproduce PRO London CAB 24/109, CP 1693, pp. 445–65, which appears as the Addendum.

FOREWORD

This is the story of ex-Constable Jeremiah Mee of the Royal Irish Constabulary.

In June 1920, when the struggle for Irish freedom was at its height, Mee was stationed at Listowel, County Kerry. On 16 June, Mee and his comrades were instructed to hand over their barracks to the British army. This they refused to do. The barracks was visited on 19 June by the newly appointed Divisional Commissioner Smyth, an ex-colonel of the British army and a native of Banbridge, County Down. Among other things, he told the assembled policemen that they were to shoot down IRA suspects and that he would ensure that none of them would get into trouble for mistakenly shooting an innocent person. Mee, who had been elected spokesman by his comrades, threw his belt on the table and in a spirited speech refused there and then to carry out Smyth's orders. Soon afterwards, he and a number of his comrades resigned from the police force. The subsequent publicity which was given to this incident prevented the full implementation of the military strategy which the British had worked out at that time. It also quickened the growing demoralisation of the RIC. Mee tells his story with modesty and with no attempt at dramatics. He did not join the IRA yet he emerges as a man of great moral and physical courage. Like many men and women in Ireland at that time, he accepted the danger and hardship which the course he had taken presented both to himself and to his family. As a result of his courageous stand at Listowel, his father's home was burned by the British. In my opinion, this book is a valuable contribution to the literature on the Anglo-Irish War and, besides, is delightful reading. Father J. Anthony Gaughan is to be congratulated for placing it before the public.

David Neligan

MAP KEY

A North Entrance
B Parade Ring
C Hall of Fame Entrance
D Centaur Entrance
E Finishing Post
F Best Mate Entrance

Best Mate Enclosure
Club Enclosure
Tattersalls Enclosure

On Open Saturday and The Festival there are separate Club and Tattersalls enclosures. For all other meetings the Club and Tattersalls enclosures are combined.

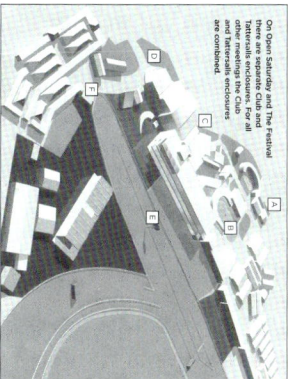

Venue :Cheltenham Racecourse

Tuesday 15 March 2016

Event :Champion Day

Club

Admission Type:Adult

Ticket No: 31500

Booking Ref :1976865

Mr Paul Terry

CHELTENHAM
A Jockey Club Racecourse

CHELTENHAM RACECOURSE, Cheltenham Gloucestershire GL50 4SH
WWW.CHELTENHAM.CO.UK

THE JOCKEY CLUB
Since 1750

CHELTENHAM
A Jockey Club Racecourse

Introduction

Jeremiah (Jerry) Mee was born on 29 March 1889 at Knickanes, Glenamaddy, County Galway. His father was John Mee and his mother's maiden name was Ellen Mee. He had four brothers and four sisters, and he was the fourth child in the family. His home was a twenty-acre farm some two miles north of Glenamaddy village. From 1893 to 1901 he attended Stonetown National School, whose principal was the national-minded John O'Keeffe, NT. After leaving school he worked on his father's farm for eight years. In the early 1950s he prepared some memoirs with a view to having them published. These concerned his life as a member of the Royal Irish Constabulary and later as an official in the ministry of labour of the First Dáil. They also contained interesting information on the time he spent as an organiser of the Belfast Boycott campaign and subsequently as an agent of the White Cross Fund. The papers containing these memoirs were in the possession of his eldest daughter, the late Mrs Eileen Mee Doyle. I have extensively rewritten Mee's memoirs, but I have not significantly altered their content. I have also added chapter headings, subtitles, footnotes, appendices and an addendum which I hope will prove useful to the reader. Readers of the section on the Anglo-Irish War period will be inclined to agree with the French proverb: *plus ça change, plus c'est la même chose.*

J. Anthony Gaughan

1

BEGINNINGS:
AUGUST 1909–FEBRUARY 1911

Had my father complied with the law and paid the licence for our dog in August 1909, this story would never have been written and the whole course of my life would have been different. At the age of twenty I was anxious to leave home, but there seemed to be no place to go to. It was at that critical period in my life that a policeman called at our home and found that we had an unlicensed dog. That same evening I set out for the village of Williamstown, County Galway, to take out a dog licence and present it for inspection at the police barracks. There I joined the sergeant and two constables in a game of 'Nap'.[1] It must have been my knowledge of 'Nap' that impressed the sergeant, as before I left the barracks that night he suggested that I join the Royal Irish Constabulary.[2] This was the last thought in my head, but when he produced a tape and took my chest measurements I knew that he was taking the matter seriously. Having satisfied himself that my chest was up to standard, he set me some papers in mathematics and other subjects which I managed without any great effort. He then assured me that I was a 'likely recruit' and that he would forward my application and let me know the result later. The night was well advanced when I got home. On the following morning when I reported to my father what had happened he was well pleased with my evening's work. He also considered that I was a likely recruit and he readily agreed to my joining the police force.

I JOIN THE RIC: THE POLICE DEPOT

After the usual period of waiting, and having passed at least three medical examinations, I was called for training to the police depot[3] at Phoenix Park in August 1910, just twelve months after my game with the sergeant and his two constables.[4] At the depot I settled down for a six-month course of training which included foot drill, carbine and revolver exercises, physical culture, swimming, rope climbing, ju-jitsu, first aid, firefighting, criminal law and police duties. At that time there were at the depot about 400 men on the 'reserve' in addition to about 100 recruits in training. The reserve were kept 'standing-to' in case of emergency when they were rushed to districts to quell disturbances such as cattle driving, at that time the principal source of trouble. To qualify for the reserve one had to be at least six feet in height and have less than eight years service. The average height of the reserve men was well over six feet, many of them being up to six foot four and five, while one, Thomas (Tom) Shannon, a drill instructor, was six foot seven. Physically the RIC was one of the finest police forces in the world and its members always attracted attention as they marched on Sundays from the depot to Mass at Aughrim Street church wearing their spiked helmets, which added a few inches to their height. The recruits marched with the reserve men to divine service and, being only the bare five foot ten, I felt like a mascot marching with these huge men.

The depot tug-of-war team was famous and unbeaten. Indeed, with the Dublin Metropolitan Police (DMP) and Guinness' horses it was one of the sights of Dublin.[5] The RIC boxing team at the depot included such big men as the Glennon brothers,[6] Begley and Forde, all of whom taught boxing, physical culture and drill so that they were always more or less in training. Boxing had not then attained the popularity that it has today so that the RIC boxers were generally matched only against those in the British army and navy. Against this competition, they gave a good account of themselves. We looked forward to the various boxing matches and took a keen interest in the preparations of our heroes. I attended many of their training sessions and I often found myself donning the gloves to help these giants in what they called 'warming up exercises'. Stripped to the waist, one of the boxers would fold his arms while I hammered away at his powerful body until I became exhausted when another recruit would take my place and continue with the slogging without seemingly having the least effect.

In addition to the ordinary foot police there was also a 'mounted force' of about fifty men at the depot, where they had a riding and training school. These 'mounted' men were inclined to despise the ordinary police.

The first thing that struck the new recruit was the absolute orderliness of everything both inside and outside the depot buildings. One had to notice the creased pants of the men, the neat uniforms and the shining horses. The entire barrack square was spotless, not even a cigarette end or match could be found on it.

Each morning by nine o'clock all beds were neatly folded, boots polished and put carefully away, the floors cleaned and every room dusted. While the nine o'clock parade was on, the sergeants inspected the rooms and woe betide the man who had left even a handkerchief out of place. There was no parade on Saturday, that whole morning up to one o'clock being given over to scrubbing floors and cleaning the cookhouse. Once a week every room in the barracks was disinfected, and twice a week new sheets were supplied for each bed. Cleanliness and orderliness were a kind of religion. The change which the six-month course of training at the depot effected in a young country boy was almost unbelievable.

After six weeks in the depot I was supplied with my first uniform, which included a bottle-green tunic and trousers, a shining peak cap and black cane stick – for in those days a man was not regarded as being properly dressed if he had not a walking stick. The day I donned my first uniform was one of the happiest in my life, and I felt that 'Dublin belonged to me' as I swaggered down Grafton Street with my black cane stick, gloves neatly under my shoulder strap and my whistle chain across my breast.

The police force then offered great attractions to the young man who was anxious for an active, outdoor life and had the required physical and educational qualifications. The policeman's salary was, on the whole, equal to that of the bank clerk, the civil servant and the schoolteacher, and his prospects of advancement were much better.[7] Moreover, while the young schoolteacher and bank clerk would be confined within the narrow space of a classroom or behind a bank counter, the RIC constable would be out in the open air. There were also other advantages such as the fact that uniforms and boots were supplied free, and married men received a lodging allowance.[8]

I spent six happy months at the depot, and, after receiving certificates of merit in first aid, swimming, firefighting, physical culture and drill, I was ready for the road as a fully fledged policeman whose duty was the 'prevention and detection of crime and the security of life and property'. And so on a very bleak day at the end of February 1911, I bade farewell to the depot and set out for the police barracks at Kesh, County Sligo, to which I had been posted.[9]

2

KESH:
FEBRUARY 1911–AUGUST 1913

Kesh is on the main road from Ballymote to Boyle, about four miles from the former and eight from the latter. The little roadside police barracks stood amid a cluster of trees at the foot of Keshcorran Hill. It was the first roadside police barracks which I had seen and I wondered why it should have been located in such an out of the way place. The only other houses in the neighbourhood were the curate's residence and the local pub. Apart from the pub beside the barracks, there were two other pubs in the sub-district, and beyond keeping a watchful eye on these there was nothing whatever to do in the line of police work.

After the excitement of the city and the 500 policemen who were my comrades in the depot, the sergeant and his three constables who came out to greet me looked forlorn. The barracks servant had gone home before I arrived and one of the constables set about getting my tea. I soon learned that to be able to cook was one of the important qualifications for this police barracks, since the servant often took extended holidays with pay. The little police barracks was very neat and tidy. The sergeant and his three men were all single, and there was a distinct air of homeliness about my new station which pleased me.

After tea the local curate called in, a pack of cards was produced and the curate joined us in a game of 'Nap'. I noticed that the sergeant was an expert at the game and even the presence of the curate did not deter him from 'setting' the cards to suit himself! The curate was a regular caller as well as one or two locals. It was late that night when I went to bed rather pleased with my new surroundings.

On the following morning, while cooking the breakfast, the barracks servant regaled me with the history of the barracks, including the recent dismissal of 'poor Mr McCormack who was the nicest man in Ireland but a little fond of drink'. She confided that 'the sergeant is all right but a little hard to put up with at times, and especially in the mornings. The other men understand him, of course,' she added, 'and take no notice of him in the mornings and after that he is the grandest man in Ireland.' She was sure I would like Kesh. 'God be with poor Mr Barton, did he not cry his fill the day he was transferred from Kesh?' At this stage she left the frying pan, went to the foot of the stairs and shouted up: 'It's after nine o'clock and it's the price of ye if he comes out and catches ye all in bed. Are ye going to get up at all today?' The district inspector, I was to learn later, was always referred to as 'he'.

One by one, the sergeant and his men came down to breakfast, which was eaten in silence except for an occasional remark directed to me. During breakfast I began to become familiar with the features of my new comrades. Sergeant Anthony McManamon, who had about twenty years' service, was a hardy-looking man with close-cropped, dark hair turning grey, and a short moustache. He was 'just one of the boys' and did not appear to ask for or get any special attention because of his rank. Constable John Browne also had twenty years' service and had the baldest head I ever saw. He was over sixteen-stone in weight, was broad-faced and had a long, fair moustache, which was waxed at the ends. I was later to discover that he had been passed over for promotion.[1] Some remarks that he made during breakfast were obviously intended to annoy the sergeant who ignored them in a superior kind of way. I could see that there was no love lost between these two. Constable Martin Walsh was a fine specimen and was eight years in the force. His hair was jet black, as was his moustache, which, like Browne's, was waxed at the ends. Constable Higgins was fair-haired, rather small for a policeman, had a rather sad expression and also sported the customary moustache. He had only four years' service and struck me as the most intelligent of the group. Conversation came easily to him and he spoke in a rather low, subdued voice.

After breakfast the sergeant made an entry in the diary showing that the barracks orderly paraded at 8 a.m. and that the general parade took place at 9 a.m. Then he and the rest of us headed for the washhouse where all shaved, and in less than an hour both men and barracks were spick and span.

I spent my first day in Kesh putting my clothes and equipment in order and getting the feel of things. The barracks was in the shade of Keshcorran Hill. The hill is a prominent landmark and is clearly visible for miles around. Each year a 'gathering' was held here and thousands came from all over Counties Sligo and Roscommon. Tinkers also came in great numbers and these festive assemblies often ended in large-scale, drunken fighting. This was anticipated and we usually had extra police drafted in to cope with the situation.

At the bottom of the barracks garden was a beautiful shrubbery surrounded by trees, which in winter provided good shelter and in summer was a good hiding place for men too lazy to do the daily patrol. It was also a favourite retreat for our sergeant. Two public houses at Carrowcrory and Culfadda respectively were two miles away and in different directions from the barracks. All our patrols led directly or indirectly to one or other of these, which must have been the best inspected public houses in Ireland.

LAND AGITATION

The second day after my arrival at Kesh was Sunday and Higgins and I were directed to go to a place near Ballaghaderreen where there was to be a demonstration in connection with a boycotted farm. At that time there was an outbreak of land agitation in the west of Ireland. Land-hungry people began to harass not only the agents of absentee landlords but even local resident landlords. 'The land for the people and the road for the bullock' was the popular, somewhat menacing catchcry.

As Higgins and I cycled on that beautiful Sunday morning to the point at which we were instructed to assemble, we passed many of the demonstrators who were also repairing to their meeting place. They were armed with 'ash plants', seemed to be in high spirits and almost invariably greeted us in a friendly manner. I asked Higgins if he thought there was going to be serious trouble. He replied briefly, 'You'd never know.'

About midday we came to a handball alley beside which there was a narrow lane leading to the boycotted farm. Here about thirty or forty fully armed, helmeted policemen were already assembled. In charge was a district inspector.[2] He was six feet three inches in height and of very large proportions. He was made to appear larger still by the tall, spiked helmet on his head. When I learned that he was the district inspector in charge of Kesh barracks I realised why he was always referred to as 'he'.

Along the roads and across the little fields the demonstrators streamed to their meeting place, less than half a mile away from where we had assembled. An occasional cheer broke the silence of that fine afternoon as we rested on our Martini carbines awaiting the first move from the enemy.

After about an hour the sound of drums told us that the demonstrators were now approaching. Our chief brought us to 'attention' and gave the command 'fix swords'. In a flash all swords were drawn from their scabbards and firmly fixed to the carbine barrels. As the procession slowly approached I marvelled at the coolness of the district inspector who produced a huge, crooked pipe which he lit and began to puff as if the whole world was at peace. Soon, round the bend of the road the procession made its appearance, headed by a young man well over six feet in height, wearing a large green sash across his left shoulder and tied at the waist in bandolier fashion. He was many years younger than our district inspector, yet with his green sash and ash plant he was almost as imposing a figure. On and on came the procession, uncoiling itself around the bend of the road in ever-increasing numbers and headed by two bands playing 'A Nation Once Again'. By this time we were drawn up in lines in front of the narrow laneway with our swords pointing outwards. With our spiked helmets, polished buckles and bright, glittering swords we must have presented a formidable-looking barrier to the young men armed only with their ash plants. Our chief gave us some last-minute instructions and concluded with the words: 'No man shall go down that laneway except across our dead bodies.' I offered a silent prayer that at the eleventh hour something might happen to prevent serious trouble.

When the processionists were only a hundred yards away I found it difficult to hold my carbine steady and I began to imagine little trickles of blood running down the blade of my sword. It was like some terrible nightmare, and I was beginning to hope that it was all a dream when I was startled by the commanding voice of the district inspector calling upon the leader of the procession to halt his men and advance to meet him.

The procession immediately halted within forty paces from us while our district inspector and their leader advanced to meet each other in 'no man's land'.[3] For a full ten minutes, the two remained in deep conversation. Their serious demeanour gave little indication of what was taking place, but the mere fact that negotiations were in progress reduced the tension. At last the negotiations came to an end. The two saluted each other, made a smart about turn and each returned to his own group. The leader of the processionists mounted a small, grassy bank and called his men to 'attention'. Then he gave the command: 'About turn. Quick march.' The procession marched smartly away to the tune of 'The Wearin' of the Green'. The district inspector pulled himself up smartly and gave the order: 'Unfix swords. Right turn. Dismiss.' He refilled his big crooked pipe in a leisurely fashion, lit up and left a cloud of tobacco smoke behind him as he walked towards the sidecar awaiting him at the handball alley.

I soon became accustomed to these Sunday outings, most of which provided something of a victory to both sides. The *Sligo Champion* would carry a full report of how the local leader marched his men up to the point of the sword, while the district inspector would send a nicely phrased report to Dublin Castle showing how the RIC had saved another landlord from harassment.[4]

MY FIRST INSPECTION

During my first week at Kesh, word was received that the county inspector was coming on his quarterly inspection.[5] The news had the same effect on the barracks staff as the presence of a hawk on a flock of chickens. The resultant confusion extended even to the barracks servant. We immediately began to clean and tidy up the barracks.

In every barracks there were at least fifty copies of different acts of parliament dealing with everything from licensing laws to laws concerning hawkers, pedlars, chimney sweeps, dogs, fish and vehicles. All policemen were expected to have a thorough knowledge of these acts and the county inspector was liable to test our knowledge of any one of them. The neglect of months cannot be made good in a few days, so the sergeant suggested that each man take a different act and read it over carefully so that at least one of us would have a knowledge of any act on which the inspector examined us.

The servant almost turned the place upside down. Buckets, brushes, soap and dishcloths were to be found in every part of the barracks. Wherever there was a dry corner a policeman was to be seen busy polishing and cleaning his buckles, belts and equipment, with an act of parliament spread in front of him which he read aloud the better to grasp its meaning. In the evening we sat around the fire and took turns at explaining and discussing the acts which we had studied.

At last the great day came and the county inspector arrived. He was a low-sized man with rather bulgy eyes and a peculiar accent which was hard to understand. We were marched out to the backyard where the sergeant put us through our paces. He was so excited that more than once he gave us the wrong words of command but we ignored them and did the right thing instead. Then we went into the dayroom for the ordeal on police duties and acts of parliament.

The sergeant was told to examine us on the General Dealers Act, which nobody had studied. I am convinced that the sergeant had not read the act for years but he was capable of meeting all contingencies. He adopted the easy but risky method of asking questions. Unfortunately the success of this depended on our ability to respond. 'For what purpose was this act passed?' he asked. Somebody answered. 'Describe section one,' he continued. This was not answered. Here the county inspector took up the questioning to the great relief of all, as we knew that the sergeant was in deep water and we were unable to get him out of it. From the General Dealers Act the county inspector took up the Poaching Act with which all were familiar, and we came out of the ordeal with flying colours and got a good entry for our smart turnout and for our answering on police duties.

Before the county inspector had turned the corner of the road after leaving the barracks on his way back to Sligo, the barracks servant was sent home and the sergeant led us down to Kelly's pub where we held a lengthy 'post-mortem' on the inspection.

PATROLLING KESH DISTRICT

With the inspection over all were in good cheer and 'Home Rule' was re-established once more. I purchased a new bicycle on what later became known as the instalment system, and Higgins and myself commenced touring the district. There was no crime in the district and patrols were a mere matter of form. In any case we were all single men and there was hardly a place in the district that one of us did not visit each day in our cycling tours for recreation.

The duty list was put up on the wall each morning by the sergeant but nobody took the least notice of it. If an inspector called it proved that we were working to a set programme, but beyond that it served no purpose whatsoever. The barracks orderly kept the diary in such a way that the entries agreed with the contents of the slip on the wall. The patrolling of the district was reduced to a fine art. There were four justices of the peace in the locality and it was an unwritten law that one of us would walk or cycle past each justice's house at least once a week. This would show that we were active and should any question of dereliction of duty ever arise these justices would be powerful witnesses on our side.

On the mornings of fairs at Boyle or Ballymote, the farmers driving their animals before them would be sure to meet two policemen on the road or perhaps sheltering from the rain under a bush. The fact that we were seen prowling around so early in the morning would be discussed at many firesides that night. The sergeant called this kind of duty 'prevention of crime'. In reality it was good propaganda and would keep the people's mind off the true fact that we were doing practically nothing, for indeed there was little for a policeman to do in rural Ireland in those peaceful days.

In addition to the ordinary day patrols, each man was supposed to do at least two patrols each month during the hours between midnight and 8 a.m. These were known as 'Rising Patrols'. In Kesh those who were detailed to do these patrols went to bed. However, the entry of the patrol was not made until somebody took a cycle round next morning. After some discreet enquiries to make sure that all was well the patrol was filled in with the usual entry 'found all regular'.

Our sergeant was an expert at varying the wording of reports of patrols in the patrol book. He always made some special note such as 'saw a light in the window of Ruane's licensed premises. Inspected the premises and found all regular.' For 'Rising Patrols' he also generally showed the direction of the wind as N/E, S/E etc. as evidence that the patrol was out.

On one occasion when his conscience was troubling him about these false entries in the patrol book he consulted the local curate. To his query as to whether his action was sinful or not the curate replied: 'No, it's not a sin, but it will be serious if you are caught at it!'

RECREATION AT KESH

Shortly after my arrival in Kesh, Higgins took me down to the shrubbery at the end of the garden where he had made a clearance for weight-throwing and jumping. He was delighted to find that I was as keen as he was on this kind of pastime. I was able to beat him at the hop-step-and-jump and we were fairly evenly matched at the throwing of the half-hundred-weight. He was able to straighten the half-hundred-weight thirty-six times while I was able to do it about twenty. With practice I improved, but was never able to beat him at this particular exercise.

I was useful on the horizontal bar and suggested to Higgins that we set one up on a tree, which we did by suspending two ropes from an overhanging branch and affixing the handle of a spade to them. In a short time we were both able to circle the bar and to hold on with our toes, while the bar was in a swinging motion.

This gave us further ideas and we paid three guineas to the Sandow Institute for a three-month course in physical culture.[6] We also purchased a set of Sandow developers and found the course both enjoyable and beneficial.

Our equipment included a punchball, the sound of which always attracted the neighbouring youngsters. Among the exercises, recommended by 'Sandow', was a daily cold bath. We fixed up a tub in the washhouse and rarely missed having a cold bath either in summer or winter. This kept us in great physical condition. Also, of course, we often cycled thirty or forty miles each day.

In summer we attended every 'pattern', sports and race meeting for miles around, and in winter we attended country dances and private parties.[7] Occasionally we came back late and were abused by the sergeant. This we took in good part and the sergeant did not remain angry with us for long. The principal punishment we received was a long patrol to the foot of the Curlew mountains which were at the extreme end of our district. To us this was not punishment at all, as we enjoyed long walks and on that particular patrol there were a few nice young ladies who were the best of company.

The district of Kesh ran to within four miles of Boyle and less than two miles from the beautiful village of Ballinafad on the banks of Lough Arrow. From Kesh to Boyle, then on to Ballinafad, and across the Curlew mountains back to Kesh is roughly twenty miles. This was our favourite cycle-spin and we knew every square yard of the Curlew mountains and the wooded shores of Lough Arrow. The people, all of the small-farming class, were as pleasant as the surroundings and were very sociable.

I DO THE TILLAGE CENSUS

The tillage census was made by the police in June each year. Two policemen were assigned to the job in each district and the whole month was given to it. Every house had to be visited, the stock counted and full details of tillage, grazing land, wasteland and shrubbery recorded. When done properly it was hard and laborious work.

I, being the newest arrival in the district, was selected by the sergeant on the grounds that the compilation of the tillage census would enable me to acquire a knowledge of the district. After lots were drawn, Browne was also appointed. He and I then conferred as to the best method of 'working the area'. The first day was devoted to the consulting of old records which Browne had, and which would act as a guide to our operations.

Browne, as already mentioned, was sixteen stone and to quote his own axiom he 'believed in doing the maximum amount of work with the minimum of labour'! He was a splendid penman, was extra good at figures and on more than one occasion had been complimented for the way in which he had furnished the tillage returns. Sitting on the dayroom form and smoking a big crooked pipe he confided in me as follows: 'Young fellow, the first requirement of a good policeman is brains, and only you have brains you would not be here. Therefore, use your brains while you're on the tillage and don't start doing the idiot, looking into mouse holes! Take the case of fowl. I'll guarantee there are not half-a-dozen women in the whole district who can tell you off-hand how many hens they have, and do you mean to tell me that they are going out to count them for you? Even if they tried they could not count them at this time of year with half of them clucking on the hedges and ditches. In order to get shut of you they'll give you a number at random. You may please yourself whether you accept that number or give your own estimate. Of one thing I must caution you, don't accept or enter any figures that do not end in 0 or 5. Any other figures are awkward for totting and anyway a few hens here or there do not make the slightest difference. Suppose for instance that a woman tells you that she has twenty-seven hens, you may take it from me that two of them will be killed or have died from disease by the time you have your forms completed, which means that the correct number would, in any case, be twenty-five. You know what I mean. The same applies in the case of tillage. Suppose that a man had two acres of tillage last year, do you mean to tell me that he will have three acres this year? Not likely. There again you have to use your brains and see that he has the same this year that he had last year. Occasionally you may add on or take off half an acre for appearance sake. Avoid quarter acres for the same reason that you avoid the odd hens. Be careful to get the number of horses correct as a separate list of these has to be kept in case of war. When you come across a decent man he will be able to give you particulars of his neighbour's tillage much better than the farmer himself, so don't be doing the idiot by visiting every farm.'

With this advice fresh in my mind I set off on my bicycle. I carried a haversack which contained the tillage books and my lunch. I made up my mind to ignore most of Browne's instructions, to visit every house and attempt to make an honest return. This I did for the first few days, at the end of which time I was convinced that it would take three months and not one to complete the returns. Practically every farmer was out working in the fields, while his wife and family were busily engaged in household duties and had little time to answer all my questions. When I made too many enquiries they would remark: 'You must be the new man.'

I soon realised the value of Browne's advice, I adopted his method and acquired the art of doing the 'maximum amount of work with the minimum amount of labour'! It had the advantage of giving me more time to get to know the people with whom I made many friends, especially among the young ladies. Only twice did I carry my lunch in the haversack and even on those two occasions I was offered at least four dinners by those sociable people.

Long before the end of the month Browne and myself completed the returns. In due course a Blue Book was issued by the Department of Agriculture showing the tillage returns for Ireland and one could only smile at such round figures as 'Total number of hens: 7,000,000'!

CHRISTMAS IN KESH POLICE BARRACKS

There are two places which few people would select for a Christmas holiday – one is the county jail and the other is a police barracks. Of the two, I would say that the county jail would be the more cheerful. In the barracks the bare white tables and deal forms provided the only furniture, while leather belts, batons, swords and police caps took the place of pictures on the walls. The library consisted of piles of acts of parliament which everybody detested, while the diary and patrol book held a prominent place to remind one that duty was always calling, even at Christmas.

As in many other respects Kesh was the great exception. For a whole week before Christmas presents of geese and turkeys were arriving and Christmas greetings came from far and wide, from friends whom we had met on our long cycling tours during the summer and from tourists whom we had entertained during their trips around Kesh. In the lock-up we had four cases of stout and several bottles of whiskey, which we received from our publican friends. Although stout was then only two pence per pint and whiskey five pence per glass, we accepted the presents for what they were, genuine tokens of friendship and not in any way calculated to be bribes.

On Christmas Eve we had just taken the usual precautionary cycle spins around the district to make sure that all was well and were settling down to enjoy our Christmas when the peace of the district was temporarily disturbed by an old man named Horan, who lived alone about a half mile from the barracks. Returning from Kelly's pub he was well under the influence of drink and halted at the barracks gate. Here he shouted abuse at the top of his voice and, throwing off his coat, challenged the police to come out. At first we ignored him, but this only encouraged him to shout louder. Eventually he attracted the attention of the curate who lived across the road. Reluctantly it was decided that action would have to be taken, but how? We could not arrest him as the lock-up was filled with valuable goods. The sergeant, as usual, came to the rescue. Walsh and myself were instructed to escort Horan home, get him to bed and remain with him until he was asleep. This was rather distasteful work on Christmas Eve night, but anything was preferable to upsetting our improvised canteen.

Leaving Horan home was not as simple as we had expected, as he resisted violently. This we overcame by borrowing an ass-and-cart from the local publican and into the cart went Horan, Walsh and myself. A few people returning home after eleven o'clock on Christmas Eve night enjoyed the spectacle of two of their policemen in the ass-and-cart, one driving and the other holding down Horan, who was shouting at the top of his voice. Horan refused point blank to go to bed and we had to sit in the kitchen for at least two hours until he eventually went to sleep on the chair. Having taken off his boots, we got him into bed and for some time we watched him while he slept peacefully, dreaming, perhaps, of his four fine sons who were far away across the Atlantic. Walsh had very thoughtfully taken a drop of whiskey in his pocket and he left this on a chair beside the bed with a note 'From the RIC with the compliments of the season. Call at the barracks first thing in the morning.' Early on Christmas morning poor old Horan called expecting to get a summons for 'drunk and disorderly behaviour'. Instead he got another glass of whiskey and a good breakfast of turkey and ham with an invitation to call back for his dinner which he did.

During the whole Christmas week all duty was suspended in so far as doing the ordinary patrols were concerned. Each day, of course, we took a spin round on the bicycles and made the usual discreet enquiries and 'found all regular'. The unwritten law in the RIC, the sergeant told me on one occasion, was to 'keep sober and shaved and keep the diary and patrol book up to date and you can't be sacked'. This law was strictly kept at Kesh during Christmas and did not in the least interfere with the dances and card-playing parties which were held during the Christmas period.

INDUSTRIAL UNREST 1912–1913

The blessing of a long term of peace before 1912 was abused by the governing classes who enriched themselves by the labour of the working masses. Though the nations of Europe were at peace, it was an uneasy peace, and the evidence of approaching turmoil was there for those who could read the signs.

In England Labour was on the march and strikes were the order of the day in the industrial areas. Strike-breakers, then known as 'scab labour', were employed by the industrialists in a desperate effort to beat the trade unions. Strike-breakers received double the pay of the ordinary labourer and were recruited from the slums of the industrial cities.

James Larkin[8] made his appearance on the Irish scene and, taking the lead from British Labour, organised strikes throughout the country, including the Sligo dock strike of 1913 which lasted for eight weeks.[9] In that year also there was a 'revolution' within the RIC when they received permission to wear toe-cap boots as part of their uniform. This concession came after an agitation lasting over ten years.

Within the police force there was considerable discontent because of their small pay. Discipline alone prevented them from joining the ranks of Labour in the struggle for better conditions. Schoolteachers were in a similar position and they did throw in their lot with Labour.

A Liberal government held office in England on the strength of the Irish Party vote. A strong Conservative opposition was prepared to use every means to oust the Liberal Party. The Prime Minister, Mr Asquith, held the Irish Party vote on the promise of Home Rule while Sir Edward Carson, backed by the Conservatives, opposed Home Rule tooth and nail.[10]

In the North of Ireland members of Orange Lodges, complete with wooden guns, drilled and paraded in the streets, especially in Belfast. At the end of 1912 their total strength was estimated at 100,000.

Apart from these groups and keenly on the alert were the American-based Clan na Gael and the Irish Republican Brotherhood (IRB). Members of these organisations made no speeches and carried neither banner nor ribbon. They had lost faith in British promises and believed in action rather than flag-waving. They were the advance guard of Sinn Féin and the Irish Republican Army.

KEEPING AN EYE ON 'RETURNED YANKS'

One of the duties of the RIC was to be on the alert for information concerning the IRB and Clan na Gael.[11] Since these were secret organisations we knew nothing whatsoever about them and even when we did receive scraps of information about their activities we did not pass the information on to the authorities, as the tenuous nature of the intelligence would have entailed the writing of endless and vague reports. The authorities probably realised this and about 1911 a directive was issued to all barracks that Irish-Americans on visits to their homeland were to be kept under surveillance and that weekly reports on their movements were to be forwarded to Dublin Castle. At Kesh this aspect of our police-duties gave us an opportunity to mix business with pleasure. After a week at home the average 'returned Yank' would be at a loss for company during the middle of the day, as members of his family would be engaged in household work or on the land. He would then make for one of the local pubs to find himself company. There one of us would contrive to meet him. Generally the visitor and the policeman deputed 'to look after him' would become fast friends and thereafter the visitor would sometimes spend as much of his time in the police barracks, chatting with us, as down in one of the local pubs. In the meantime, innocuous police reports concerning the movements of the visitor would be forwarded each week, under sealed cover, to Dublin Castle. These weekly reports were written by the sergeant. As with his entries in the patrol book, in writing these reports he showed how well he understood the 'official mind'. In every report he mentioned the two organisations whom he knew the authorities were most interested in, and for good measure described all the people who came in contact with the subject of the report as either belonging or not belonging to the Ancient Order of Hibernians (AOH).

Occasionally the district inspector would note in the official book the absence of prosecutions, after which we would keep an eye out for animals wandering on the roads and would bring the owners to justice. Summonses would be issued and the defendants brought to Ballymote court before a bench of five or six magistrates. In each county there was at least one resident magistrate who was appointed to the post not because he had any special qualifications but because he was a man of influence with the government. This important personage attended the court only when there was an unusual case for hearing. In his absence, the senior magistrate would act as chairman of the court and neither he nor the other magistrates would have an extensive knowledge of the law.[12] Their decisions, on the whole, were reasonable and fair, based as they were on common sense rather than on acts of parliament.

Having stated in great detail the charge of allowing the animals to wander on the public road, the policeman would withdraw and the defendant would go into the witness box to take the solemn oath and give his evidence. Rarely was it known for a defendant to dispute the evidence given by a policeman. The usual defence in a case of this kind would be: 'Your worship, I was very busy cutting corn in the field when my little girl came up with my tea. She must have left the gate open and the cattle got out. They could not be more than a few minutes there when the policeman came along and found them on the road.' Here the constable would be recalled and he would verify that this was the defendant's first offence and that the defendant was a decent, hardworking man. After much craning of necks by the bench of magistrates the defendant would get a lecture on the seriousness of the offence and would get off under the First Offenders Act or be fined at most only half-a-crown (12½p). There was never any bad feeling between the police and the defendants over these prosecutions. It was understood, of course, that an occasional prosecution was necessary in order to justify the existence of the force, and there the matter ended. Indeed, it was not unusual to see the policeman travelling to Ballymote on the defendant's sidecar and returning on the same car with the week's groceries for the barracks.

THE PEOPLE OF KESH

A good local knowledge was considered an essential qualification for a good policeman. After two and a half years in Kesh I must therefore have been one of the best policemen in Ireland. Not alone did I know every townland from Battlefield to Carrowmacelnanny and from Carrowcrory to Carrownacreevy, but I knew every house in the district and the people who lived in it. In my cycling tours I became familiar with the beauty spots around Lough Arrow, Lough Key and Lough Gara. These three lakes are convenient to the town of Boyle and, viewed from the Curlew mountains, present a scene equalled only by the lakes of Killarney.

It was, therefore, with a heavy heart that I received the news of my transfer from Kesh to Collooney in August 1913. In my two and a half years at Kesh I had practically forgotten that I was a policeman and I had learned much that many policemen miss. It was true that our sergeant had broken every regulation of the police code but he substituted instead the finest code of all, a Christian outlook towards his fellow man. In the barracks all were treated as equals and this created a wonderful atmosphere.

During those years not one prisoner had entered our lock-up and that at a time when intoxicating drink was within the reach of all. Being the driver of an unlighted vehicle at night or the owner of a cow which wandered on the public road were the only crimes which occurred in the area. This surely was a good record and speaks volumes for the people of that district.

I can recall vividly my transfer in August 1913. I can see myself sitting on the old sidecar, with all my worldly goods packed in its well. At the little barracks gate stand the sergeant and his three men wishing me Godspeed, while the sergeant wipes his nose with a large red handkerchief. At the barracks door stands the old barracks servant wiping her eyes with her apron which she holds with her two hands, as she makes a mental note of another very decent man who cried when he left Kesh.

3

COLLOONEY:
AUGUST 1913–MAY 1914

In 1913 Collooney was a small, tidy town with a population of less than a thousand people. No serious crime had been committed in the town or surrounding district over a period of twenty years. Yet in 1913, this peaceful town had a police district headquarters with a district inspector[1] (with clerk), head constable,[2] two sergeants and ten constables. How the presence of such an imposing force of police could be justified will always remain a mystery to me, as two junior constables could easily have coped with the police work which had to be done in the district.[3]

The police barracks, in the outskirts of the town, was a dark, dismal-looking building of cut stone. If it was dismal-looking from the outside, it was much more so inside. As often happened in barracks where there was a group of men with little or nothing to do, the police code of regulations was adhered to down to the last detail.

CODE OF REGULATIONS
The RIC code of regulations, which remained in force up to the disbandment of the force on 31 August 1922, was stringent. In fact, the policeman who was forced to comply fully with the code had less freedom than a ticket-of-leave suspect. Fortunately most officers and officials had sufficient common sense to turn a blind eye to the more degrading sections of the regulations, and, without impairing the efficiency of the force, made it possible for a policeman to live as an ordinary, self-respecting citizen.

The code was most comprehensive. A policeman's every move, whether on or off duty, had to be recorded in the barracks diary.[4] When walking for recreation his walk was restricted to a radius of two miles from the barracks. When cycling for recreation his absence could not exceed three hours and the time of departure and return to barracks had to be recorded in the diary. After ten o'clock at night he could not leave the barracks without special leave, which was given only on rare occasions. If he wished to attend a dance or other function after midnight a full day's leave would have to be taken for 'private purposes'. He was forbidden to play Gaelic games.[5] When taking up duty as barracks orderly at 8 a.m. he had to be properly dressed and inspected by the senior officer in charge. Each time that he left on or returned off duty he was inspected by the senior officer, unless the senior officer happened to be absent, in which case the next in seniority would do the inspection, and each inspection was entered by the barracks orderly in the diary. An active policeman who took walks and cycle spins and did his two patrols each day would be inspected up to a dozen times a day, whereas a ticket-of-leave suspect generally had to report only once a week to the police.[6]

THE HEAD CONSTABLE

The head constable at Collooney was well past middle age and resided in the police barracks. He was married, but his wife and family resided in Dublin. Enforced isolation from his family probably engendered in him some of the cynicism and bitterness which he generally exhibited. He was particularly severe on the men under his charge. His office was on the ground floor and his bedroom right over the front door. When not inspecting patrols in the town or on country roads, his time was devoted to brooding over the police code or acts of parliament in his office. It was impossible to enter or leave the barracks without attracting his attention. The men spoke in whispers, and there was a depressing atmosphere in the barracks.

Every morning he paraded the sergeants and men in the backyard for at least half an hour. This would then be followed by at least an hour discussing police duties and acts of parliament.

The district inspector was a young cadet officer who had only one year's service, and he and the head constable were not on speaking terms. Although senior in rank to the head constable, it was obvious that he was trying to steer clear of trouble with him and to do so he also had to keep his eye on the code of regulations.[7] However, he made his monthly inspections with the least amount of display and, unlike the head constable, did not seek to make life difficult for the police under his charge.

I APPLY FOR A TRANSFER

At that time most policemen were anxious to be assigned to a barracks in a town and were inclined to look down on their rural-based comrades. Thus, although most of those stationed in Collooney were unhappy there, none of them considered leaving it for a rural station. There was little competition, therefore, for a vacancy which occurred in the spring of 1914 at Geevagh, twelve miles from Collooney and on the border between Counties Sligo and Roscommon. I told the district inspector that I was anxious to go to Geevagh, as Collooney was not agreeing with my health. He asked me if that was the only reason. I assured him that it was, and he smiled and agreed to make the transfer.

After spending nine months in Collooney I can truthfully say that I was not acquainted with twenty people in the entire district. Nor had any of the other men in the barracks a knowledge of the district or its people. They were too busy learning the details of acts of parliament which were of little use either to themselves or the people. They also kept themselves very much apart from the people who, consequently, regarded them with suspicion.

I was not sorry to exchange the gloomy atmosphere of Collooney police barracks for the pure air in the shade of the Arigna mountains.

4

GEEVAGH:
MAY 1914–AUGUST 1915

For a young policeman whose ambition did not extend beyond a good, healthy, outdoor life, Geevagh, because of its situation, was the ideal police barracks. It was within easy cycling distance of the Bricklieve mountains to the north and the Curlew mountains to the south and it was also near Lough Arrow and Lough Key. Moreover, Sergeant Bernard Drum, who was in charge of the barracks, was a devoted family man whose main interest in life was to bring up his children in the fear and love of God.

The barracks was stone built and had accommodation for five single men, as well as the sergeant and his family. The hall, running from the front door to the back, divided the barracks into two self-contained units. On the right were the sergeant's quarters and on the left the dayroom and the men's quarters.

On my arrival at the barracks, the sergeant brought his wife and young family into the dayroom and introduced them to me. He also invited me to have my tea with them, which I did. After the meal, I joined them in the family Rosary.

THE PERFECT SERGEANT
It takes the perfect sergeant to comply with police regulations and at the same time make life pleasant for his family and for the men under his charge. This the Geevagh sergeant did, without any apparent effort on his part. However, he was aided by the fact that in the barracks there were three young constables, one old constable and a married man who

lived out of barracks. This was the perfect blend, as the older men were always available 'to keep house' when the younger men wished to attend 'patterns', sports, race meetings or dances.

Every morning at 9 a.m. the sergeant assembled his men in the dayroom for parade. With his own rifle at the 'shoulder' and looking down at the ground, he would give the one word of command 'right turn, dismiss'. This seemed to ease his conscience and then all was well. The wettest night that ever came he would dress up for patrol and walk about twenty yards away from the barracks, stop and turn back with the remark: 'I think we'll let it clear off.' This too eased his conscience, as he was out on patrol and nobody could dispute that fact.

During the day each man went on patrol at the appointed time, but where he went was his own affair and his own responsibility. The sergeant did his patrols, tilled his garden, helped the children with their school lessons, repaired their shoes and asked no awkward questions.

THE INSPECTION

July 1914 will always remain in my memory as a period of great anxiety and uncertainty. The district and county inspectors were due for the monthly and quarterly inspections respectively, the sergeant's wife was expecting a new addition to the family and the children were all down with measles. Day after day we studied acts of parliament, polished our carbines and bayonets, and studied the *Hue-and-Cry* until we knew the colour of the eyes and the length of the hair of every criminal in Ireland.[1] After some days the children got over the measles but nothing else happened. The sergeant confined his patrols to short circuits around the barracks where he would be within easy reach if required. I had myself in readiness night and day for a quick cycle spin to Ballyfarnon for the nurse and doctor. Still nothing happened until the very last day of the month when the sergeant's wife gave birth to a baby girl. That evening the district and county inspectors called at practically the same time to hold their monthly and quarterly inspections. However, we got over the inspections all right thanks to the sergeant, who was a tower of strength.

The sergeant was a very temperate man, but having surmounted all the difficulties he felt that a little relaxation was due and accompanied us to the local pub where we all forgot our worries during a nice social evening.

Not long afterwards the European war broke out. We felt that this too could not be allowed to pass without due recognition and we all adjourned to the local and, with a very mixed cross-section of Irish life, including the local leaders of the Irish Volunteers,[2] drank toasts to the king, the kaiser, John Redmond[3] and the sergeant.

THE GREAT WAR

The outbreak of war in 1914 surprised but did not alarm the Irish people. The continent then seemed to be very far away and all felt that Ireland would not be involved. The pressing question in the people's minds was what would happen to the Home Rule Bill which by then had been very much discussed in the British House of Commons.

The outbreak of the war was supposed to have taken England by surprise and found her unprepared. Yet, it seemed a strange coincidence that when war broke out the British fleet had been fully mobilised in home waters and within forty-eight hours had the German navy bottled up in German harbours. German ships on the high seas and in foreign ports were rounded up by the British navy and put out of action. The result was that a British Expeditionary Force was landed on the continent without the loss of a single life. Meanwhile the huge German army was trying to steamroll its way through little Belgium, which was putting up a heroic fight against terrific odds. The prophets told us that the war would be over in six months and everybody believed it.

Within a few days of the outbreak of war, posters showing soldiers of the various regiments of the British army were posted up outside every police barracks in Ireland, and appeals were made for recruits for the army. The response from Geevagh district was bad, and few, if any, recruits came forward. In rural Ireland at that time it was considered a family disgrace when one of its members joined the army, so that the few who did join up did so quietly and without any display.

The only effect the war had on the RIC at Geevagh was to increase their work, which up to then had been pretty light. The Aliens Act came into full operation and all aliens had to register at the nearest police barracks. This did not give us much trouble as there was not a single alien in the whole district. 'Dangerous Yanks' were now forgotten and we had to keep a look out for Germans. The only Germans we ever met were those who had visited the police barracks in the past and sold us very good Krupps' razors at a half-a-crown each.

From the commencement of the war the daily newspapers supplied maps of the war front. With one of those on the wall and a supply of flags representing the various armies, it was possible to follow the fortunes of war with reasonable accuracy. As the armies advanced or retreated, the flags were shifted to indicate the new positions. When in doubt as to who had won any particular battle we gave the benefit of the doubt to the Allies.

In the early phases of the fighting in Belgium and France, with the Germans on the offensive, it was always fairly easy to anticipate the downfall of the next stronghold. As I followed the flags of war carefully and had ample leisure to read everything possible about the war, my presence in a hay or cornfield was a 'Godsend' to the local farmers who gathered round me to smoke their pipes and hear the latest news from the front. I became the 'special' war correspondent for the Geevagh district and was being quoted at fireside and pub as an authority on the progress of the war.

The RIC were supposed to be the recruiting agents for the districts in which they served, not directly but indirectly. Although I had no intention of doing anything to prevent recruiting in the district, I am afraid that my eloquence as a war correspondent did not help it among my large circle of small farmers and their families.

As the war dragged on the work of the police became more and more unpleasant. The Defence of the Realm Act came into operation and, though it applied to the whole British Empire, much of it had very little application to Ireland, especially to a remote district like Geevagh. It was a cumbersome act with high-sounding phrases which the average policeman did not understand, much less digest. We were expected to keep an eye on railways, canals, viaducts, harbours, channels, lighthouses, piers, etc. As Geevagh was twelve miles from the nearest railway station and the only thing within miles resembling a river was a little stream, we did not see any necessity for keeping our eyes on viaducts. Indeed it was only after consulting the dictionary that we learned what a viaduct was. To add still further to our difficulties, the original act was amended and extended so often that one could easily get lost in the Defence of the Realm Act and we simply gave it up in despair. A special file was opened for the Defence of the Realm circulars which came by the bundle and which ceased to have any meaning for us. Fortunately our superiors were in the same plight as ourselves and hid their ignorance of the Defence of the Realm Act by confining their inspections to the Lights on Vehicles Act or other simple acts of parliament.

Parcels of recruiting posters arrived daily showing British soldiers from different regiments in attractive uniforms. These posters were put up outside the barracks to catch the eye of the would-be recruit. Recruiting meetings were held from time to time and the speakers generally were well-to-do gentlemen who were too old for military service. All got a good hearing at Geevagh but no recruits came forward.

THE VOLUNTEERS

The Volunteers began to train and drill and we had to keep a watchful eye on them also. Lest we might overlook accompanying them on their parades they usually marched past the barracks, when the sergeant would detail two men on bicycles to keep them under observation. They generally drilled in a field convenient to the barracks until ejected by the owner. They then moved off to another field. Sometimes they drilled on the road.

These manoeuvres were always conducted in a good spirit after which the Volunteers and their police escort would retire to the local pub to compare notes. On one particular occasion Constable Sweeney and myself were on this duty, and, in company with some of the Volunteer leaders, retired for refreshments to a pub in Ballyfarnon. We settled

41

down for a game of 'Nap' which lasted until 7.30 next morning. It was the lowing of cattle arriving for the fair of Ballyfarnon that reminded us that we were both due for fair duty there at 8 a.m. It was after 8 a.m. when we reached the barracks, which was then almost ten hours late returning off duty and already late for duty at the fair.

This was the one and only time that I ever saw Sergeant Drum angry. Standing in the hall outside his own kitchen door, he was pale with rage and indignation. Immediate dismissal and other terrible consequences, he said, would be the price we would have to pay for our dereliction of duty. However, before he continued any further in this vein his wife intervened and we slipped back out on duty.

In August 1915 I again found myself on the move. My destination was Ballintogher, near Lough Gill.

5

BALLINTOGHER:
AUGUST 1915–JUNE 1918

The police barracks at Ballintogher was an imposing, private residence which had been leased from the proprietor in order to house the local guardians of the law.[1] It was situated well back from the road on rising ground and overlooked the village on the north side and the railway station on the south side, each being about 500 yards away.

On viewing the barracks for the first time I noted much that pleased me: the large beech tree standing in front of the barracks door on which I could hang my horizontal bar; the high walls surrounding the vegetable garden which would give me privacy while I practised on my punchball and performed other exercises which had to be neglected at Collooney and Geevagh for want of accommodation; the big field at the back of the barracks where I could take my daily run before breakfast; the big, airy bedroom with its four large windows which I would have all to myself for doing the arm and leg exercises recommended by 'Sandow'; and, finally, the large dayroom, which I would have more or less to myself, as all the other men in the station were married and lived out of barracks, and where I could pursue a course of studies which I had started while in Geevagh.[2]

In addition to these advantages the sergeant had a nice young family ranging in ages from twelve years downwards.[3] The eldest, Milo, was about ten and just the right age at which to commence a course in physical culture, which I decided to give him. Not only he but his little sisters proved to be keen pupils.

I spent my first few days at Ballintogher setting up my various contraptions. I also fixed up a swing from the beech tree for the sergeant's children. The sergeant and his wife were very pleased with the swing as they were anxious to keep their son, Milo, away from the handball alley in the village where he tended to get into bad company!

After making myself comfortable in the barracks I next began to familiarise myself with my new district. This I did by cycling through a different part of it each day.

Ballintogher was a typical west-of-Ireland village, with its Catholic and Protestant churches, Catholic curate, Protestant minister, three schoolteachers, six policemen, three justices of the peace, three publicans, a few small grocery shops and a creamery. This community catered for the district's farmers, most of whose holdings averaged from twenty to thirty acres.

The village is on the road from Dromahair to Collooney, a road which links the Leitrim mountains with the Ox mountains. The land on either side of this ten miles of road is not fertile except for some rich patches around Collooney. Although the district was very thickly populated, it was free from crime of any kind. And yet in that ten miles of barren and peaceful country there were four police barracks and no fewer than thirty armed policemen including myself. At different points the Catholic dioceses of Kilmore, Ardagh, Elphin and Achonry ran across this short stretch of road on their way to the sea. Whether the fact that the small farmers who inhabited this area were both industrious and law abiding was due to the presence of thirty armed policemen or the influence of the four bishops I was unable to decide. Of one thing I was quite satisfied, however – that so far as law and order were concerned, the situation was well in hand.

I was only a week in Ballintogher when I made the acquaintance of three men who were to be lifelong friends of mine. They were Anthony Foody, who taught at Kilross national school, and Charles (Charlie) McMorrow and Cornelius (Con) O'Rourke, the principals of Crossboy and Ballintogher national schools respectively.[4] Each of the teachers had a residence to himself and I received invitations to join them whenever I was at a loose end. I gladly accepted the invitations and hardly a day passed that I did not meet one or more of my newfound friends. As time passed our circle extended until it embraced such fine characters as Francis (Frank) Jeiter, Harold McBrien, Jerry Mulrooney, James McGowan and Thomas (Tom) Dillon. It was hard to imagine that in less than a week I had established myself so well in the barracks and had made such pleasant friends in the neighbourhood.

I MEET THE DISTRICT INSPECTOR

While the first week at Ballintogher was an unqualified success, the second week brought me a crop of accidents and misfortunes. My first trouble started early in the second week when I was barracks orderly. The barracks orderly is expected to be sober, properly dressed, shaved, constantly on the alert, and to remain in the barracks for twenty-four hours at a stretch. It is a monotonous job, especially for an active young man.

Feeling the strain of confinement particularly at about three o'clock in the afternoon, I decided, while all the party were out, to do a few circles on the horizontal bar suspended from the tree in front of the barracks. For this purpose I threw off tunic and shirt and put on a sleeveless singlet and a pair of white canvas shoes. After doing a few circles of the bar I did my favourite stunt of gripping the bar with my legs and allowing my head and body to hang down. I had no sooner done this when to my horror the district inspector suddenly appeared as if from nowhere.[5] Dressed in a cycling suit and a small cycling cap, he stood holding his bicycle and looking straight into my eyes without as much as a smile on his serious face. I nearly fell off the bar with fright but managed to keep my balance and dropped down beside him. I could not salute him as I was not properly dressed and I could not speak until spoken to as a matter of police courtesy. Seeing that he did not speak, I began to move towards the barracks when he called me back.

As I stood to attention before him in my pants and singlet, he looked me up and down before he casually remarked: 'You are good at the horizontal bar.' I could have hugged him for this casual remark which proved that he was not too ill-pleased at what he had seen. 'Would you mind doing that drop act again?' was his next remark. I jumped to the bar and circled it five times while it swayed to and fro and then did the difficult stunt of gripping the bar with my feet and touching the ground with my hands, returning to the original position and again dropping down beside him. 'Splendid,' was all he said as we marched shoulder to shoulder towards the barracks. 'Is the sergeant in?' was his next question. I answered that all the men were out on duty. 'Who is barracks orderly?' he asked. I must have looked very foolish, as I replied: 'I am.' 'Dress', was the only word he spoke, and off I went to my bedroom and returned in quick-time fully dressed.

We went up to the sergeant's office and he took down the inspection book which he commenced to fill in as I sat opposite him at the dayroom table. 'Have you done a course in first aid?' he asked, and when I replied that I held a certificate in first aid he seemed pleased. He regretted, he said, that it was not taught in his time and continued that he would like to have a practical lesson on artificial respiration. He suggested that I fetch a blanket from the bedroom and when I did he spread it out on the floor, lay full length on his back on it and said up to me 'Go ahead.' Positioning myself behind his head I grasped his two arms firmly and went through the motions involved in artificial respiration until he told me to stop. He rose, lit a cigarette, became very friendly and flattered me on my expertise in physical culture and first aid, which he said could be very useful to me, especially in the army where they were in need of men like me. With my training in the use of arms, physical culture and first aid there would be a splendid future for me in the British army where he himself had two sons. He suggested that, being the only single man in Ballintogher barracks, I must have found life monotonous, whereas in the army things would be different. At that stage I realised that his interest in the horizontal bar and first aid were only a means to an end. We parted good friends and he made no mention in the inspection book of my being absent from my post as barracks orderly.

When the sergeant and the other men returned I informed them of all that had happened. The sergeant felt that I had let him down by leaving my post as barracks orderly and 'going out to swing off the trees like a monkey', as he put it. Being somewhat upset at the sergeant's abuse, I gave him and the rest of my comrades to understand that I had made up my mind to join the army. As it was an offence to prevent recruiting, they made no immediate response to this information. Before I went to bed, however, each of them had a private chat with me for the purpose of telling me that I would be most foolish to join the army, and earlier in the evening Mrs Brigid Flynn and the children came into the dayroom when the place was quiet, and, with tears in their eyes, implored me to change my mind. I promised Mrs Flynn for the children's sake to think the matter over and I assured her that I would not do anything without consulting her again. The children need not have wept, as joining the army was the very last thought in my head at the time.

WINTER 1915: THE VOLUNTEERS

1915 found me well prepared for the winter gales. The outdoor life during the summer and autumn had left me strong and fit in body while my mind was at peace with the world. In the turf house I had a pony-cart of turf which I had purchased for 7s 6d (37½p) and which I felt would keep me in firing until the late spring. One did not plan further ahead than that, as single men were liable to transfer at short notice. I also had purchased two pairs of handmade boots for the sum of £2, the war having already advanced the price from 12s 6d (62½p) to £1 per pair. And so, with my worldly wants provided for, my thoughts began to dwell on the millions of unfortunate men then digging themselves into trenches in the battlefields of France and Flanders. The war was dragging its weary way and nobody knew how or when it was going to end. The flags on my war map were in the same positions day after day and the little progress on either side was hardly worth noting. Trench warfare was, of its nature, slow, and the hearts of the Irish people went out to the hapless soldiers, irrespective of which side they fought on.

At home, as each month passed, the Volunteers were becoming more and more like an army. In Ballintogher a Boer War veteran named Charles (Charlie) Somers was in charge of the local company and, although he knew little about field manoeuvres, he was good at foot and rifle drill. The police always accompanied the Volunteers on their route marches. Generally I looked forward to these marches, especially when accompanied by the local band. At that time the police authorities did not take the Volunteers too seriously. For years they had been keeping their eye on secret societies so that the open parades looked less dangerous and, of course, were 'only a passing phase'.

RELAXING WITH MY FRIENDS

Besides my police duties I had ample leisure, much of which I spent in the company of my schoolteacher friends. They also enjoyed my company and especially accounts of my experiences in the North of Ireland. Like most of the police in the north-west I had been drafted into different parts of the North for the annual celebrations of 12 July, 12 August and St Patrick's Day. My friends would sit enthralled as I described for them riots which I had witnessed around the walls of Derry, with bottles flying and batons falling, and how I had drawn my baton to defend the Catholics of Omagh and Dungannon as they marched on St Patrick's Day, and how this exercise was repeated in the case of the Protestants of Portadown as they stepped out on 12 July to curse the pope.

In the meantime the district inspector had not again referred to the question of my joining the British army. However, it seemed to me that he had simply adopted a new method to make me think along these lines. At each inspection with unfailing consistency little faults on my part were found and entered in the inspection book. Sometimes my carbine would allegedly be showing signs of neglect, at other times my answering in police duties would be found unsatisfactory and it was even noted that I neglected to keep my section of the vegetable garden properly tilled. I knew, of course, that there was only one thing I could do to please the district inspector and that one thing I was resolved not to do. I knew also that besides harassing me at inspections the only other way in which he could punish me was by transferring me from post to pillar at the public expense. However, since I was keen for new scenes and fresh experiences, this did not unduly worry me. On one occasion, after I discussed with my schoolteacher friends the way in which I was being harassed by the district inspector, McMorrow suggested that I play a little joke on him. Consequently, the next time that worthy was around on inspection, I confided to him that I was uncomfortable at Ballintogher, found the cost of living there excessive and was anxious for a transfer. Showing a great lack of courtesy, he cut me very short and told me that there was no vacancy and that even if a vacancy did arise more senior men would have first preference. The schoolteachers and myself had a great laugh at McMorrow's joke and one result of it was that I spent longer at Ballintogher than in any other barracks.

THE RISING

Spring or at least the signs of it came early in Ballintogher. The farms were small and the fields difficult to work, as they were hilly and unsuitable for ploughing. From January on the farmers and their families would be turning up the green, or more often the heather-coloured lealand into ridges for the potato crops. This was slow and laborious work and had to be started early in order to have the soil ready for the spring sowing.

It was just when this hard spring work had been completed that news came on Easter Monday 1916 of the rebellion in Dublin. At first the news was taken calmly, but it soon became evident that something out of the ordinary had happened, and as the news of the fighting spread the people left their little fields to gather in groups to discuss the new situation. The great majority of them were keen supporters of John Redmond who was soon to vehemently condemn the rebellion.

Before the people had time to recover from the shock of Easter week, word came of the death at Ashbourne, County Meath, of James Gormley, an RIC constable who was a native of Ballintogher, and whose brother was an active member of the local Volunteers.[6] The Gormley family was very popular in the district and nearly all the people, including the local Volunteers, turned out to attend a Requiem Mass for the dead constable, and to sympathise with his widowed mother and family.

Initially Redmond's condemnation of the Rising and especially the death of young Gormley made it well-nigh impossible for the local people to appreciate the patriotism of the 1916 rebels. They were confused and spoke in quiet tones about the 'goings-on' in Dublin. When, however, the Sinn Féin leaders surrendered and were shot or deported for long terms of penal servitude, the local people began to harden their hearts against the British government. The people had for some years been reading the war news from France and Belgium, knew that the Germans had ruthlessly invaded Belgium, yet they had not read of German soldiers being shot in cold blood after surrendering to the Allies. This would have been against the rules of international warfare. Now the people began to ask why the same rules did not apply in Ireland.

The change in the attitude of the people of the district towards British rule in Ireland between Easter 1916 and June 1918 was astonishing. It was a continual and gradual process and at the beginning was hardly perceptible. There were, however, a number of small indications as to how things were developing, such as the tendency of people, who previously had no interest in politics, to name their children Seán, Éamon, Pearse, etc., and also a distinct coolness on the part of many of the people to members of the RIC.[7]

With the war not going to their satisfaction on the continent and the Republican movement growing in Ireland, the British government was kept under pressure and the RIC also began to feel the pinch. After Easter week the *Hue-and-Cry*, a two-sheet weekly newspaper with descriptions of 'wanted criminals', grew into an eight- or ten-page paper with the names and descriptions of men wanted in connection with the rebellion. We were expected to memorise all these descriptions, which was a physical impossibility. The descriptions in most cases bore no resemblance to the persons referred to, and, in despair, we ceased to be interested in the *Hue-and-Cry* which went the same road as the Defence of the Realm Acts.

I think it was towards the end of 1917 that Arthur Griffith's policy of passive resistance was put into operation. Instructions were issued to the people from Sinn Féin headquarters that they were not to take out dog licences, pay income tax, or, indeed, any other kind of tax to the British government.[8] The policy also involved non-recognition of the ordinary courts of justice. Prisoners brought before the courts would refuse to remove their hats or caps and treated the judges and courts with contempt.[9] The usual decision of the courts in such cases was to send the prisoners to jail for a few weeks for contempt of court.[10] When the prisoners came out of jail they were met by torchlight processions and escorted through the towns by the local bands. In many cases the prisoners had very little interest in politics going into jail but after the torchlight processions there was no turning back and they became dedicated Republicans.

The result of this new move by Sinn Féin was that the British authorities, to avoid humiliation, instructed the RIC to refrain from collecting dog licences or taking up any petty cases which would only result in exposing the judges to contempt and filling the jails.

LAND DIVISION

When, however, the Volunteers began to divide ranches, the British government had to sit up and take notice. It was well for the Volunteers and Sinn Féin that it did so, as otherwise there would have been chaos in the country.[11]

My first experience of land division was at a farm in a place called Toberanania, about a mile from Ballintogher village. The local Sinn Féin club decided to divide a farm among 'deserving small farmers' in the district. Since all the farmers around were 'deserving' and 'small', they all turned up on the appointed day at the farm due for division. The local secretary, who was himself a 'small' farmer, got up on a cart and announced that he was about to divide the farm. 'Hands up,' he said, 'all who want an addition to their farms.' Every hand went up. I was half tempted to put up my own hand so as not to feel odd in that great forest of hands. As there were only about eighty acres to be divided it would have required a miracle almost equal to that of the loaves and fishes to satisfy that crowd of land-hungry men and women. It was at that moment that the secretary showed real leadership. 'Ladies and gentlemen,' he said, 'we did not anticipate so many applications and, as you are all aware, our one ambition is to see that everybody is satisfied. We have decided to take all the names and each case will get our personal and sympathetic attention. In the meantime we shall confine ourselves to marking out the plots with the ploughs and taking over the farm in the name of the Irish Republic.' The cheering in response to this announcement could be heard miles away and, after the secretary had made a few concluding remarks, all present, except the police, shouted in chorus 'Up the Republic' and 'Down with British tyranny'. A few ploughmen then went into action and ploughed single furrows in a very large field to mark off divisions of land. As most of the land in question was of poor quality and too swampy for the horses, the division of the rest of it was deferred to that day week when another 'monster' meeting was to be held at the same time and place. Fortunately for the leader, he was safely behind the bars of Sligo jail that day week. When he came out some months later he was met by the bands and acclaimed a local hero. In the meantime the division of Toberanania farm was postponed indefinitely.[12]

Apart from this agitation over the disputed farm, things drifted peacefully along until the spring of 1918 when the British government moved unsuccessfully to apply conscription to Ireland.[13] It was this act of folly on the part of the British authorities that rekindled the smouldering fires of Easter week and led to the elimination of the Irish Parliamentary Party led by John Redmond and later John Dillon. When the menace of conscription passed the people settled down to the work on their small farms. The summer came and I planned to spend some time around Lough Gill and have a few picnics at Dooney Rock, but the silent hand of fate again beckoned me. This time my destination was Grange in North Sligo.

6

GRANGE:
JUNE 1918–JULY 1919

The village of Grange is on the brow of a hill, half a mile from the sea, and is backed by the mountains of Ballintrillick and Benbulben. The surrounding district was made up of small farms and the people seemed on the whole to be comfortable. Although there was good sea fishing nearby, the people of Grange took no part in this industry, which was keenly pursued by their neighbours at Cliffony and Mullaghmore. From the latter places cartloads of mackerel and herring passed daily through Grange and on to Sligo where the fish were sold. It was possible therefore to get fresh fish each day at ridiculously low prices in the village.

From the beginning of my stay I noticed that the people were more distant and more difficult to make friends with than had been the case in Ballintogher, Geevagh and Kesh. Whether this was due to the political situation, natural reticence on the part of the local people, or to the fact that the police tended to be aloof I could not say. There was no open hostility to the police, and yet I was conscious of something which prevented that easy approach to people to which I had been accustomed.

I soon found that police duties were different from what I had been used to. For instance Inismurray Island, some five miles from the mainland, was a notorious centre in the area for the manufacture of illicit spirits or poteen, and called for police attention.[1] From time to time we had to investigate reports from the British Admiralty that there were lights along the coast which could be signals to German submarines. We also had to cope with wrecks and the occasional body which were washed in from the ocean, consequences of the war at sea. In addition to these we had to report on the Sinn Féin movement in our district, which throughout 1918 was going from strength to strength.

Also, during part of the Great War period there was a threat of a German invasion. This prompted the British government to issue a circular to the RIC stationed along the Irish coast to the effect that, in the event of a German landing they were to get the inhabitants to move twenty miles inland with their livestock. They were then to see that all crops in the vacated area were destroyed by fire or otherwise. Father Michael O'Flanagan, who was an excellent platform orator, often made use of this particular instruction for the purpose of ridiculing the British government.[2] During 1918 I heard him orate in Grange on more than one occasion as follows: 'Men and women of Cliffony and Grange, the Germans may be here any time now. You need not worry as the RIC have the situation well in hand!' He would then read the circular and add, amid great cheers: 'We have twenty policemen in Cliffony, Grange and Drumcliffe who will see that your crops are all destroyed and then with their twenty rifles they will keep back the German army and navy!'

SERGEANT CONNOLLY

Sergeant William Connolly, who was in charge of Grange police barracks, was a big, broad-shouldered man with small, brown eyes, a heavy moustache and thick, dark eyebrows which gave him a forbidding-looking appearance. At our very first meeting I sensed that he regarded me with suspicion, and this put me on the defensive. For the next week or so we were like two strange dogs who, having sniffed each other, kept walking round in circles with hair bristling. I understood the reasons for the sergeant's suspicion. Sergeants were naturally wary of men who were transferred too often, as this was generally an indication that these men had not seen eye to eye with the authorities.

The sergeant and I were still on our guard when, a week later, we went on a 'conference patrol' with the Cliffony police. The purpose of the conference patrol was to enable the sergeants at Cliffony and Grange to compare notes on matters of mutual concern. It was later reported to me that their conversation veered round to myself, and went somewhat as follows:

Perry, the Cliffony sergeant: 'How do you like the new man?'[3]
Sergeant Connolly: 'I'm damned if I know. I have been trying to weigh him up for the past week and I can make nothing of him. He's either a very decent fellow or else a well-conducted blackguard.'

The Cliffony sergeant, who had a wonderful sense of humour, evidently enjoyed this description of me and the story went round the district where I subsequently became known as 'the well-conducted blackguard'. Eventually Connolly heard the story and being serious-minded he 'was not impressed'. After some months, however, he thawed out and he and I became very close friends.

Besides Sergeant Connolly and myself there were four other constables stationed at Grange.

POTEEN HUNTING AT INISMURRAY ISLAND

A few days after my arrival in Grange I was ordered to accompany Sergeant Connolly and Constable Clarke[4] to Inismurray Island on revenue duty, that is, 'poteen hunting'. I was supplied with an official lifebelt. This was a kind of waistcoat, made of squares of cork about the size of half bricks, which were threaded together with thin wire. It was fitted under the police tunic and gave the wearer an ungainly appearance.

Until then I had never been in a boat except on Lough Gill, where I was always within easy reach of one of the islands, and safety. It was, therefore, with some misgivings that I donned the cork waistcoat which was to act as my lifebelt while crossing the five miles of very rough sea which extended between the mainland and Inismurray. Besides the lifebelts, the sergeant, Constable Clarke and myself were equipped with long, pointed steel rods which were to be used for probing hay and corn stacks, and shingle along the strand, in our search for illicit stills.

At Streedagh Point a small boat manned by two hefty Mullaghmore fishermen was waiting for us. The fishermen wore seafaring clothes and had their caps, with the peaks turned back, pulled well down over their foreheads the better to withstand the stiff breezes coming in from the Atlantic. As there was no proper pier and the water was shallow for several yards out from the shore, the boat was at anchor in fairly deep water. With their pants folded well above their knees the two fishermen advanced from the boat to meet us. On reaching the strand, after a peremptory greeting, they turned their backs on the sergeant and Clarke who got up on the fishermen's backs and were carried high and dry to the little boat. The two RIC men took this as a matter of course and the sergeant did not even smile as I sat on the shore laughing at the unusual sight. One of the boatmen returned and I, too, got up on his back, and never in my life did I feel less like a policeman.

The sea was choppy, as the boatmen euphemistically put it, and my cork waistcoat did not prevent my heart thumping as the little boat ploughed through mountainous waves. To add to my discomfort the boatmen regaled us with stories of lucky escapes which they had from sharks while out fishing for herring around Inismurray Island. It seems that the fishermen were guided to the herring shoals by the presence of hundreds of seagulls hovering over them. The sharks, too, kept close to the herring shoals and from time to time made circuits at great speed around the fish. If the nets are set while the shark is making his circuit he is liable to be caught in it, and as he pulls on it the boat can be swamped unless the fishermen are quick enough to cut the net free.

As we seesawed our way through the rough sea we caught sight of three other rowboats two or three miles away. Their progress was so slow that it was difficult to know whether they were coming towards us or going in the opposite direction. I was assured, however, that they were the boats carrying the Cliffony, Magherow and Drumcliffe police to Inismurray on the same mission as ourselves. It soon became evident that the boats were all making for the island and that the timing was 'according to schedule', as, judging by the distance that the boats were from the island, I realised that they should reach it at about the same time that we would.

There were then twelve families on Inismurray Island and when I saw the whole population, men, women and children, assembled on the shore, I thought we were in for a hot reception. In this I was greatly mistaken, as, apart from the fact that there were no flags or bands, we could not have received a warmer welcome. The men actually came down to the water's edge to help us ashore and the women were not far behind in their display of genuine friendship. They knew all the policemen except myself and the police called them by their Christian names. A number of parcels which had been brought from the mainland were then distributed.

On practically every journey that the RIC made to the island, parcels of groceries and messages, including letters, were brought out to the islanders. I later learned from the islanders that these parcels often contained supplies of treacle, yeast and barm for the manufacture of poteen, and that some of the letters would contain orders for poteen from their customers on the mainland. They also informed me that they always knew when the police were due to call and that the illicit stills and poteen would be put on board one or more of their boats and rowed out west of the island where the oarsmen would devote their time to fishing until the RIC left the island.

After about half an hour's conversation with the islanders we got down to business and set off in pairs to search for illicit stills and poteen.

Inismurray, which is twice as long as it is wide, is roughly 200 statute acres with some reasonably good tillage and grazing land. Most of it, however, is barren and infertile. It has neither trees, rivers nor lakes and is completely exposed to the Atlantic gales. There are no proper landing places for boats, except for a few narrow creeks, so that in stormy weather boats cannot enter or leave the island. It is surrounded on all sides by huge boulders of rock, many tons in weight, and piled up in great profusion.

The island is deeply indented and in places there are caves at least twenty feet in height and penetrating in some cases to a depth which it is difficult to ascertain. The floors of the caves are strewn with rocks and up through these rocks the sea lashes its way, throwing up great sheets of water and making a noise which is deafening. Indeed, we might as well have taken lead pencils instead of steel rods to probe for poteen in this difficult terrain, frequented only by hawks, swallows and martins. Never until that day on Inismurray did I realise that police duty could be reduced to such a farce. Not only was it possible to conceal illicit stills and spirits, but even a regiment of soldiers could be hidden in the rocks and caves of this remote island. Needless to say we made no captures that day. Having failed to destroy the sole industry of these friendly people, we returned to the home of Mrs Harte who always provided tea for the police and revenue officers. The tea was excellent and the charge modest even for those days. And, believe it or not, at the end of our meal we were treated to a few glasses of poteen.

While we were having our tea a storm arose with thunder, lightning and torrential rain. As the day advanced the storm continued and the question of our having to remain on the island was discussed. The islanders encouraged us to stay and made preparations for our doing so. The boatmen, when consulted on the advisability of returning to the mainland, shook their heads. Later in the day, however, the storm abated somewhat and we decided against the wishes of the boatmen to return to the mainland.

What I considered was a rough sea on the outward journey was, by comparison with the return journey, quite calm. Instead of high waves and deep ravines, the sea was now a mass of angry water and foam. Before we were half a mile from the island wave after wave swept over our little boat, at times half filling it with water, and keeping two men constantly bailing it out. I made no secret of the fact that I was terribly scared and one of the boatmen took advantage of this to produce a bottle of poteen which was passed around and all had a drink. Between the buffeting of the waves and the strong poteen, I did not care whether the boat went up or down. I was unable even to help with the bailing out of the water. It was well after dark when we reached the mainland, exactly two miles from where we had intended landing. Even the sea-hardened boatmen were immensely relieved at getting ashore and said that it was the worst crossing they had ever experienced. It was the first of many trips which I made to Inismurray on revenue duty.

A DEAD BODY DRIFTS IN FROM THE SEA TO DERNISH ISLAND

In the late autumn of 1918, as the seaweed was drifting on to the shore in great black masses, and farmers were busy carting it away either to use as manure for their crops or to pile it in big stacks along the foreshore with a view to its being burned and made into kelp, the body of a woman was washed ashore at Dernish Island, about a mile from Grange, and half a mile from the mainland. There were one or two families on the island, but neither they nor their neighbours along the shore would go within hailing distance of a dead body washed in from the sea. They simply reported the tragic find to the police barracks and left the rest up to us. We arranged an inquest at which it was established that the body had been in the water for at least two weeks and that it was the body of a person unknown. It was late in the afternoon by the time the formalities of the inquest had been gone through and then a young constable named Boylan and I, accompanied by the relieving officer for the district, set about burying the body.

In many graveyards along the coast there is what is known as 'the stranger's plot', a corner in the graveyard where bodies which have been washed ashore are buried. The graveyard of Ahamlish at Moneygold, on the Cliffony Road, is about half a mile from Grange, and it was in the 'stranger's plot' there that the body was to be buried.

Constable Boylan and I hired an ass-and-cart and a small boy to drive it. We placed a coffin in it and went to the shore where we hired a boat which took us across to the island. We soon got to the body which had been placed well up on the strand for the inquest. It was in a perfect state of preservation. It was the body of a woman of between twenty-five and thirty years of age. It was lying face upwards, and the dead woman's long, auburn hair was being tossed about by the wind. Apart from a mark on the side of the face, evidently caused by contact with a rock, there were no other injuries. We presumed that she had been the victim of a sinking disaster, fairly common during those war years.

By the time we had placed the remains in the coffin and had returned to the mainland, night had fallen, and so we borrowed a lantern from a local farmer and walked behind the ass-and-cart to the graveyard. There in the lantern light we buried the stranger and, having recited the Rosary, left her to the crooning winds and waves that ever sound in that lonely graveyard overlooking Dernish Island. We had a number of such burials in the district, but none made such a lasting impression on me as the burial of that beautiful young stranger, apparently an innocent victim of war.

As we walked back from the graveyard, we heard cheering from Grange where preparations were being made for a big meeting which was to be addressed by Mrs Hanna Sheehy-Skeffington.[5] When we arrived at the village we saw that the local Volunteers were marching in processional order to the meeting which was to be held in the parish hall. Boylan and I slipped into the back of the hall, as the sergeant had directed us to attend the meeting. Much of the address of Mrs Sheehy-Skeffington, the main speaker, was given over to making unflattering comments about the RIC in general and Boylan and me in particular.

THE POLICE UNION

In addition to the fact that I had not complied with the county inspector's wishes by joining the British army, I incurred further official displeasure when, in July 1918, I joined the Police Union, the object of which was to improve the conditions of police service and, above all, to ensure that eventually the RIC would be a civil rather than a paramilitary police force.[6] It was never recognised by the authorities, although a more or less similar type of union existed in Britain. Nevertheless, in spite of the fact that the right of the RIC to meet and discuss their grievances was denied, the union, under the leadership of Thomas J. McElligott ('Pro Patria') who was elected its chairman, continued to function.[7] The union's newssheet came by post to each barracks and, especially in the early days of the union, was a kind of 'untouchable' because to be seen reading it implied membership. It was a study to watch non-members biding their time to get an opportunity to read the 'dangerous paper'. Under the brilliant leadership of McElligott, membership of the union grew to about 4,000. At this stage the authorities became alarmed and decided to crush the union. Their first efforts to this end proved to be counterproductive. To discourage membership, active members were transferred from post to pillar. But the transfers had the very opposite effect to that intended by the authorities, because each member penalised by transfer became a potential organiser in his new barracks. However, the unremitting pressure on the union membership eventually began to tell. In May 1919 the dynamic chairman, Thomas J. McElligott, who was a young sergeant stationed at Trim, County Meath, was forced to resign. The union continued in existence but soon lost vigour and eventually petered out. This was a greater tragedy than most of us realised at that time, as an active union might have saved most members of the RIC from the terrible dilemma in which as a paramilitary force they were soon to find themselves.[8]

Before I was very long in Grange it became evident that the authorities were taking every opportunity to make things unpleasant for me. I was well aware of the causes of their displeasure, but was not prepared to apply the remedy, which was to leave the Police Union or, better still, to join the British army. During most of my time at Grange, I was an open and an enthusiastic member of the Police Union. This did not unduly worry the sergeant or the other four constables. It did, however, cause a great deal of concern to the district inspector, as he repeatedly pointed out to me.[9] Thus I found myself at odds with authority. In Ballintogher and Collooney, it was due to my disinclination to join the British army, in Grange to my membership of the Police Union. Accordingly, I was not surprised when in July 1919, after returning from a long walk near Grange, I was handed my transfer to Kerry, to which place I was instructed to proceed by the first train next morning. I was to report at Tralee RIC barracks where I would receive further instructions and I was to sign on the dotted line as evidence that the instruction would be obeyed. Being by nature of a roving disposition the transfer would, in normal times, have pleased me, but the times were far from normal, especially in the south where the RIC and IRA were in open conflict. As I was considering what I should do one of my comrades, Constable Lynch, came into the dayroom and between us we thrashed the whole thing out. It became clear to me that I had no option other than going on the transfer or leaving the force. So I appended my name on the dotted line. The Constable Lynch who helped me to decide to stay in the RIC was a young man who had a wife and three young children, for one of whom I had acted as sponsor. He and I were very close friends and we had spent pleasant times together. Some fifteen months later he was shot dead in an ambush at Moneygold, near Grange.[10] The members of the IRA who took part in that ambush deeply regretted the shooting of Lynch, who was well known and respected by all.

MY JOURNEY SOUTH

Early on the following morning I set out for Kerry.[11] On my way I was joined at Collooney railway station by Constable John Kealy and Constable Peter J. Raftery, two Galway men who were being transferred to Kerry for basically the same reasons as I was being transferred.

As I travelled south on the train, my carbine lying on the carriage rack over my head assumed a new meaning. I was leaving a peaceful district and heading for a district where anything could happen. The guerrilla war that had flared up at Soloheadbeg and Knocklong was spreading rapidly through Munster, and the RIC were targets for Republican activists.[12] It was to strengthen RIC garrisons in the south that we were being transferred from the comparatively quiet districts of the west. In selecting men for transfer in these circumstances, the authorities chose those who were giving or were likely to give the most trouble in the districts from which they were being transferred, and probably also considered that our loyalty to the crown would be stiffened by the way in which the lines had been drawn by this time in the south-west of the country. Raftery was well known to me as we had served together in Geevagh and Ballintogher. He was a fine type of young fellow who had taken an active part in the Police Union and thereby had proved himself obnoxious to the authorities. With Kealy I was not acquainted. I knew, of course, that he too was an active member of the union and as a result had had more than his quota of transfers. None of us had any illusions as to why we were being sent south.

Although we were travelling in civilian clothes, nobody could mistake us for other than what we were, with our three carbines resting on the rack over our heads. It was amusing to watch the passengers coming into our carriage, make themselves comfortable in the seat facing us, and then, glancing at the carbines, make the flimsiest excuse to leave the carriage. This gave us ample space and an opportunity to discuss the past and the prospects of the future. Strange to say it was not the danger to our own lives that troubled us but the thought that very soon we might be compelled to use those carbines against our own people, even in self-defence.

Before leaving Grange I was presented with a bottle of good Inismurray poteen and by way of turning our thoughts from sordid shootings I produced my bottle and we impartially drank toasts to the king and the republic on Irish whiskey for which neither king nor republic had received duty. The poteen had a most soothing effect and we settled down to talk of more pleasant experiences and of my exploits while poteen hunting in Inismurray. The county and district inspectors came in for a good deal of abuse for having sent us wandering into the unknown far from our peaceful little districts in Sligo.

In this way we travelled pleasantly along until we reached a small station some miles from Ennis. Here two young men in trench coats came into our carriage, took a good look at the carbines above our heads, nudged each other and settled down for a discussion, which soon developed into a heated political argument between Raftery and the man who sat directly opposite to me. Raftery, who had spent the past hour abusing the British authorities, now took up the cudgels on behalf of the king but was clearly no match for our friend, who had all the Sinn Féin propaganda at his fingertips. At Ennis a third man joined us and, though he appeared to be acquainted with one of our companions, he took no part in the argument but contented himself by listening to the discussion which at times seemed to be getting beyond the limits of moderation. A fourth man, who joined us at Limerick, became a perfect nuisance as he was under the influence of drink. He made no secret of the fact that he was anti-Sinn Féin. He seemingly had two brothers in the RIC and his interventions into the argument consisted of the most outrageous charges against Sinn Féin and all it stood for.

At this stage the position seemed to be getting very nasty and I realised for the first time that we had made a mistake in sitting under our carbines instead of opposite them.

As it was impossible for us to leave the carriage for refreshments without the risk of losing our carbines I again produced the poteen bottle and after Raftery, Kealy and myself had refreshed ourselves I passed it round and all drank to the Irish Republic, even our drunken companion who had shown such hostility before. Although the poteen was not by any means meant as a peace offering, it was surprising the change that came over the little party. Even the gentleman who was sitting opposite me and doing all the attacking was now prepared to admit that he knew some decent RIC men and that they were not all as black as they were being painted. To prove that there was no ill feeling, he produced a bottle of whiskey and we drank another toast to the Irish Republic and were careful to leave out the king – on this occasion. The intoxicated gentleman left us at a small station on the way and the remainder of the journey passed rather pleasantly. Two of our companions, including the argumentative one, got off at Listowel and we continued with one remaining companion to Tralee where we bade him goodnight as we had reached our destination.

It was when we reached Tralee police barracks that it first came home to us that all was not quiet on the 'southern front'. The barracks door was closed and barred and we were challenged before being admitted. Two men acting as guards were armed with revolvers and seemed to be taking themselves quite seriously. It was the first time I saw two policemen doing guard in a police barracks and it was the first time I ever saw a policeman wearing his revolver while acting as guard.[13] It was also the first time I saw four policemen going on ordinary patrol duty fully armed with carbines. The prospects did not appeal to me but, as I was soon to learn, the position was even worse than I had anticipated.

After the long and rather exciting journey, I slept soundly that night and dreamed about the good days that were gone. Next morning we were assigned to our new barracks, Kealy and I going on to the one at Listowel and Raftery being sent to the one at Causeway, a nice little village near the Kerry coast. Kealy and I arrived at Listowel police barracks that same afternoon and one of the first men to welcome us was our provocative companion of the previous night. He was none other than Constable Thomas R. (Tom) Reidy, of Connelly, County Clare, who had been returning from his annual leave and had simply been amusing himself by pretending to us that he was a Sinn Féin enthusiast. Reidy was a colourful character and before we had reached Listowel he had told the story with such exaggeration that we were made to look very foolish indeed.

7

LISTOWEL:
JULY–DECEMBER 1919

Listowel police barracks lacked the homeliness to which I had been accustomed in the smaller, rural barracks of County Sligo. It was a district headquarters and carried a complement of sixteen to eighteen constables, a head constable, a district inspector and, later, an acting-county inspector. In County Kerry at that time political agitation was working up to its inevitable physical-force climax, and yet the tension I had noticed on the part of the police in Tralee was not apparent in Listowel where, for instance, it was still possible for unarmed police patrols to move about by day. Those on night patrols, however, were obliged to carry carbines or revolvers.

The countryside around Listowel, unlike most other parts of Kerry, is fairly level and fertile and the town, consequently, is an important dairying centre. In the early mornings lines of carts with their loads of milk churns stretched along the streets on their way to the local creamery. The drivers were mainly young women or girls, some of whom were very beautiful. They wore dark-coloured shawls, which gave them a nun-like appearance. They also seemed to be taller than the women I had met in the west of Ireland.

LAND AGITATION: RATTOO HOUSE

As usual local political agitation was given an agrarian emphasis. There was a dispute in progress in the estate of the knight of Kerry, which was situated at Ballinruddery about a mile from the town.[1]

Another 'agitation' was being conducted at Rattoo, near Ballyduff and some eight miles on the other side of Listowel.[2] Here Michael O'Brien, the land steward who was employed by Miss Ella Frances Browne of Rattoo House,[3] had been fired on and wounded and so, two days after my arrival in Listowel, I was transferred with three other policemen for a four-month period to Rattoo House to guard Miss Browne, her land-steward and her possessions.[4]

The house itself stood well back from the road and was approached by a long, winding avenue through heavily timbered woodland. Our accommodation in the house was more than satisfactory. Together with O'Brien, we spent our waking hours in a large, comfortable, ground-floor sitting room where we were waited on by a staff of servants, and at night we retired to separate bedrooms upstairs.

Our duty was to keep close to O'Brien day and night. Thus two of us had to accompany him wherever he went. Whether he went out on the land to superintend the farm workers or went to a distant fair or local tavern he always had to have an armed escort. When attending fairs, even in neighbouring counties, two of us in civilian clothes, each armed with a revolver, had to keep watch over him. Guarding O'Brien was not an easy or agreeable task, as he was neither a teetotaller nor a man of tact. Night after night he insisted on going to the local pub at Ballyduff where he loudly voiced his unpopular political views, and one of his favourite gambits was to stand drinks all round and then start a provocative and dangerous argument. With the coming of winter and the long hours of darkness our duty became more dangerous. Moreover, with lordly disregard for his own safety and ours, our ward always chose the way through the wood from the village where both we and himself could be most conveniently shot at. However, although police had been ambushed at Ballylongford a few miles off, and the local members of the IRA must have regarded us as an easy target, we were not attacked.[5]

THE 'ATTACK'

I had been in residence at Rattoo House scarcely a month when the midnight air was rent with rifle fire. Somebody shouted 'the house is surrounded by armed men'. We readied our carbines and prepared to defend the house. After some time the servants, the steward and Miss Browne herself crouched near us and pointed into the surrounding shrubberies where they insisted that they had seen men moving. It would have taken half a battalion to protect such a rambling mansion and we hesitated to draw fire but, as was to be expected from the conquering stock from which she stemmed, Miss Browne gave the order to fire and shamed us into shattering the midnight silence with burst after burst from our carbines. When we stopped firing the night air was filled with the screeching of the hundreds of crows which populated Miss Browne's woods. Whether imaginary or otherwise the attack had been beaten off and we all felt a sense of elation. Our hostess produced her best bottle of wine and the steward drank a toast to the 'four greatest warriors in Ireland' in which the 'heroes' themselves somewhat dubiously joined. Two factors, however, detracted from the victory. There had been no answering gunfire to our resounding volleys and the aged invalid, Mrs Browne, who was bedridden upstairs and had been forgotten in the height of the fray, had nearly died of fright. This last we did not discover until next day, and dawn found us sitting round a big fire tired but happy after our night's good work. After daybreak the only two casualties we collected were a hawk with a broken wing and Miss Browne's pet cat which had been killed by a carbine bullet. Neither were there any footprints of raiders, but old Mrs Browne was thoroughly alarmed and insisted on applying for military protection.

MILITARY PROTECTION

In due course the county inspector of the RIC arrived, perfunctorily questioned the senior constable about the incident and sent for military reinforcements.[6] At twilight that same evening an officer and a detachment of thirty soldiers in full war kit marched up the avenue and halted on the drive in front of Rattoo House where they grounded arms and some of them began to assemble a few machine guns.

After Miss Browne had introduced us to the officer commanding this outfit he got down to business in a most impressive way and immediately insisted on 'inspecting the defences'. While his men 'stood at ease' in the gathering gloom, this 'live wire', armed with a large Webley revolver and an even larger torch and accompanied by me, lit his way through the shrubberies, muttering 'Yes, this is a likely place for the Shinners to get through. I shall post one man here and two men over there. When my men intercept the Shinners here, they will attempt to break through over there. I shall have a few men posted here and we shall have them like rats in a trap.'

Having strategically posted his men at the various vantage points in orthodox Sandhurst fashion, the officer adjourned with us to our big sitting room where we discussed tactics over tea and tobacco. Every hour, to the minute, he made a tour of inspection of his outposts and the midnight shrubberies rang with the martial challenge of 'Halt. Who goes there?' This bedlam continued for three nights. The invalid, Mrs Browne, was frightened out of her wits; the land steward O'Brien 'nearly died of thirst' because at the risk of his life he could not dare a visit to the local pub. Nobody in the 'Big House' got a wink of sleep while under military protection and eventually Mrs Browne decided that she might as well be shot by the IRA as die of the shock and annoyance caused by 'the manoeuvres of the British army', and begged the authorities to have the soldiers withdrawn. It was, therefore, with a sigh of relief that we heard the command, 'About turn. Quick march', and saw the officer commanding and his men march away and leave us once more 'at the mercy of the Sinn Féiners'.

With the departure of the military, everybody visibly relaxed and the land steward drank a toast to our newfound freedom. Winter closed in upon the 'Big House' and around Miss Browne's blazing fire we played cards, read books and discussed the darkening political horizon. Our senior member, Constable Patrick (Patsy) Regan, was replaced by a quiet, unassuming little sergeant named George (Georgie) Neazer, who continued in charge of the 'Protection Post' when I returned to Listowel, after my four months' stint, on Christmas Eve 1919.

SHOOTING OF SERGEANT NEAZER

Just over two months after I parted company with the little garrison, the inoffensive sergeant was shot dead and Constable Garret Doyle, another member of the garrison, wounded while escorting O'Brien, the land steward, at a fair in Rathkeale, County Limerick. Both Neazer and Doyle were on plain-clothes escort duty and carried revolvers, as was customary in such circumstances. The actual shooting took place in the dining room of a hotel at Rathkeale, where the steward and his escort were having a meal. That the shooting was intended for the two RIC men was borne out by the fact that the steward escaped uninjured and that the two revolvers were taken from the policemen.[7]

The shooting of these two inoffensive policemen, who were carrying out the elementary duty of protecting a man whose life was in danger, horrified the police at Listowel. RIC men who had hitherto been indifferent or even ambivalent with regard to the political situation now hardened their hearts against Sinn Féin and the IRA. The shooting of Sergeant Neazer and Constable Doyle brought home to me for the first time the sinister aspect of the developing struggle between Sinn Féin and the British government. Moreover, the thought that Irishmen were being shot down simply because they were policemen was alarming, especially as I knew from my association with Doyle for two months at Rattoo House that this grand Wicklow man would not have harmed a child, and I knew that the same could be said about Sergeant Neazer.

DEVELOPMENT OF CONFLICT BETWEEN SINN FÉIN AND THE SECURITY FORCES

At the beginning of 1920 the political situation had become very dangerous. Things had really started to go wrong the previous January when two RIC constables, James McDonnell and Patrick O'Connell, were ambushed and shot dead while escorting a farm cart conveying gelignite to a quarry at Soloheadbeg, three miles from Tipperary. Like the protection of individuals, the escorting of gelignite to quarries for blasting purposes was a matter of police routine and had nothing whatsoever to do with politics. After the ambush Dan Breen, Seán

Hogan, Séamus Robinson and Seán Treacy of the Third Tipperary Brigade, IRA, were much wanted men and the British government offered a reward of £1,000 for information leading to their capture. A photograph of Dan Breen showing the amount of the reward was posted up outside every police barracks in Ireland, while the descriptions of the four wanted men were given week by week in the police *Hue-and-Cry*.

The RIC had already become very unpopular largely because of the worsening political situation, and their hunt after Dan Breen and others like him only served to further estrange them from many of the people. Seán Hogan, one of the four 'wanted men', was arrested in May 1919. He was sent under police escort to Cork jail to await trial and sentence which would almost certainly have ended in his death. His comrades, Breen, Robinson and Treacy, decided to rescue Hogan. At Knocklong railway station they attacked Hogan's escort of four armed policemen. Sergeant Peter Wallace and Constable Michael Enright were shot dead and two of the attacking party, Breen and Treacy, were seriously wounded. Hogan, however, was freed.

The hue and cry set afoot after the incident at Soloheadbeg was now trebled in intensity, and police and military co-operated in a hunt for the 'wanted men' which extended through Counties Clare, Cork, Limerick and Tipperary.[8] Manhunts of this kind did not commend the police to the people, especially those living in the countryside, and from this time on the police began to be effectively ostracised. Nor were these manhunts effective in ending outrages. Thus, a mere month after the rescue of Seán Hogan, District Inspector Michael Hunt of the RIC was shot dead in Thurles.[9]

Until the end of 1919 Kerry, to a large extent, escaped the growing storm; Listowel, in particular, was comparatively quiet.[10] Our new district inspector and our new head constable were partially responsible for this latter situation. The district inspector, Thomas Flanagan, had risen from the ranks, was an experienced officer and was capable of handling the most delicate situation.[11] Head Constable Plover, who was appointed to Listowel at about the same time, was a young man who possessed a great deal of common sense and neither he nor the district inspector was in any way aggressive towards the people.[12] After the arrival of these two officers extraordinary police duty was confined to the protection of a land steward who was acting for the knight of Kerry, on whose estate an agrarian dispute was continuing.[13] The ordinary town patrols were continued as a matter of routine, and police duties did not extend beyond these two exercises. For the time being the district was peaceful. How long it would remain so was a question that we could not answer. We realised that we were on the edge of a 'war zone' and that that 'zone' was daily extending and at any time might engulf us. The peace we were enjoying was an uneasy peace, for even while we slept we might be called upon to defend our barracks, indeed our very lives, as the IRA did not announce its arrival. The fact that we sought only peace was no guarantee that we would be immune from attack. We could only watch and wait.

DISMISSAL OF INSPECTOR-GENERAL OF THE RIC
Early in January 1920 many members of the RIC received a shock from a quarter from which they least expected it. On 9 January 1920 the press announced the dismissal from the RIC of Sir Joseph A. Byrne, the inspector-general.[14] No explanation for the dismissal was given.[15] The fact that he was the first and only Catholic ever to hold the post made the announcement all the more serious for most of the rank and file of the RIC, almost 90 per cent of whom were Catholic. The dismissal of the inspector-general created a sensation both in Britain and in Ireland, and we had the sorry spectacle of some Irish daily newspapers who had consistently remained indifferent to, if not actually condoned, the shooting down of Catholic policemen, lamenting in their leaders the removal of a Catholic inspector-general from the police force. It seemed that some of the same people who did not want the RIC, in a rather curious way felt entitled to demand that the inspector-general of the force should be a Catholic. It was, of course, well known that General Byrne was opposed to the enforcement of conscription in Ireland and that he was, above all, in favour of moderation in the then current crisis.

THE POLICE UNION

A further reason for his being removed from office was hinted at in a report in the *Daily News* of 13 January 1920, which stated:

> Lord French is said to have complained bitterly of the spread of Republican sympathies among the men of the R.I.C. and the failure of the police administration either to prevent the introduction of the virus or to stamp out the disease when established.

The mention of 'Republican sympathies' within the force was an allusion to the Police Union which, although suppressed from the outset, even at that time was still showing signs of life as was evidenced by the fact that the Leinster police, at the risk of dismissal, on 11 January attended a meeting at the Dublin depot to protest against the summary dismissal of their chief. Perhaps, too, the British authorities were mindful of the misgivings which many police at that time were having about the semi-military character of the force and the role which the force would have in the impending conflict. These misgivings had been well articulated and publicised by Thomas J. McElligott ('Pro Patria'), chairman of the Police Union, who, when tendering his resignation from the force in May 1919, wrote:

> The efficiency of a police force is dependent on national goodwill which, if secured, would create what is wanted in Ireland, the same feeling between the police and people as in Great Britain. The experience of a century proves that under the present system we cannot bring about a reasonable understanding whilst we have a semi-military force, maintained not as peace officers, but as a garrison for the 'firm' government of Ireland. I am leaving the force with no regret after eleven years service. I am leaving, rather with pride, to serve the union (of which you say I am a member), the force, the men, whose interests and whose welfare I have at heart, and the country I love.[16]

Such sentiments and statements bordered on the treasonable and one of the reasons for the change at the top of the RIC was to put a stop to these trends. In any case there was no doubt as to the attitude of Byrne's successor, Thomas J. Smith, to the spread of these trends. From what the ordinary RIC constable knew of him he would regard it as his duty to stamp them out.[17]

TEMPER OF THE RIC AT THIS TIME

With the Republican army striking at our front and a 'loyal' northerner at our back we now found ourselves in a most unenviable position. The Police Union after a promising beginning was now dead, or at least dying, with its leaders dismissed, and there was no hope of continuing its organisation either inside or outside the force. Had Sinn Féin at that critical time devoted a tenth of the energy to canvassing support from within the RIC as they did to the attacking of police barracks, a happier chapter could be written about that period. Although the Police Union was dead, the spirit of the union was still alive within the force and only required some positive encouragement from outside to make very many of the RIC react against the impossible situation in which they then found themselves placed. I am certain that this reaction would have been particularly significant in counties outside the storm centre of the south, because the RIC even then was not yet seriously committed to involvement in the violent struggle which was developing. Some indication of what could have been was given some months after this particular time when, after an approach had been made by some Sinn Féin representatives, the Dublin Metropolitan Police laid aside their arms, refused to do military work and reverted to ordinary police duties.[18]

Then and later some of the Sinn Féin leaders realised that their handling of the RIC was ill considered and showed a great lack of understanding. For instance, Henry (Harry) Boland[19] not long afterwards stated on a public platform in New York that the biggest mistake Sinn Féin made was in their handling of the RIC,[20] while Michael Collins, when discussing the matter, was reported to have said that 'we should have known that the RIC were Irishmen'.[21]

At that time very many members of the RIC were as resentful against the British authorities for placing them in a position in which they were murdered and shot at as they were against the Sinn Féin organisation which executed these outrages. They viewed the attitude of the British government vis-à-vis the RIC as being analogous to that of the absentee landlord to his agent. In the well-known story the agent pointed out to the landlord that he could only collect rent from the Irish tenants at the risk of being shot dead. 'They may shoot you,' replied the landlord, 'but that is not going to terrorise me.'[22]

8

LISTOWEL: JANUARY–JUNE 1920

CHANGES IN THE RIC

The removal of Sir Joseph A. Byrne from the top position in the RIC in January 1920 was but the start of a general purge in the police hierarchy. Immediately after the inspector-general's dismissal, six county inspectors were called upon to retire on 'economic grounds' and their places were filled by more active men who had the 'right outlook' on the political situation. Then on 10 April 1920 the press announced the 'retirement' from the RIC of Messrs Ronald G. C. Flower, Edward H. Pearson and Henry D. Tyacke, assistant inspectors-general. All these high officials were known to be opposed to a policy of oppression in Ireland. They were replaced by Messrs Edward M. Clayton, Albert A. Roberts and Charles A. Walsh, men, it was stated, who had already proved their thoroughness as police officers.[1]

These changes caused considerable disquiet among many members of the force. This disquiet arose largely from the realisation that in future policemen who showed a disinclination to be associated with the uncompromising policy of the British government in Ireland would not receive much sympathy from the new administration in Dublin Castle.

Also from January 1920 onwards British ex-servicemen were filtering into the RIC as 'policemen', and as early as March two of these new 'policemen'[2] were assigned to Listowel.[3] They came in full khaki uniform but were soon afterwards supplied with police uniforms. They had no police training whatsoever and showed no inclination to settle down to routine police work. They were the advance guard of the

Black and Tans, a force that made unpleasant history in Ireland before many months had passed. The two that we got at Listowel were rather thoughtless and completely ignored police discipline until some of the men in the barracks made them toe the line.

The infusion of new blood into the higher ranks and of new British ex-servicemen into the rank and file soon had the seemingly desired effect in the RIC, as was evidenced by the shooting of the lord mayor of Cork on 20 March 1920.[4] The news of this shooting was tragic enough, but the subsequent verdict of the coroner's court incriminating members of the police force caused dismay among decent-minded men in the RIC, who by then were helplessly watching the drift from law and order to sheer anarchy. Initially, we had not accepted that members of the force were involved and had ascribed the allegation that they were responsible for the killing to Sinn Féin propaganda. Following the shooting of the lord mayor of Cork, the police and military in Counties Cork, Limerick and Tipperary seemed to set out on a systematic reign of destruction and terror. In March and April Cork city, Limerick, Thurles and many smaller towns were partially destroyed, and methodical raiding of private houses took place nightly. These developments caused a growing disenchantment on the part of many members of the RIC with the British government and its policy.[5] In Listowel we began to feel that we were living in an unreal world. In spite of the fact that Irish towns were being burned and Irish men and women were being terrorised, the 'important duty' of protecting a Mr Carson, the land steward on the estate of the knight of Kerry, had to go on. Night and day we had to traverse the dangerous, wooded road from Listowel to Ballinruddery right through the winter and spring to ensure the safety of the land steward. We grumbled a lot about the futility of this duty and also resented the fact that the danger to which it exposed us was probably considered by the new police authorities the least important aspect of the exercise.

HEROIC DEFENCE OF KILMALLOCK POLICE BARRACKS

Early in May 1920 a company of British soldiers under the command of a Captain Chadwick arrived at Listowel and camped at Ballinruddery, within hailing distance of where the land steward resided. The arrival of the military caused little diversion in the town. With things beginning to look ominous, we were pleased to have the military within a comparatively short distance of our barracks in case of attack. We were especially glad about it after Kilmallock RIC barracks was attacked towards the end of the same month. An account of this attack, given by an eyewitness, reads as follows:

On 27 May 1920 seventy men of the Republican Army, having cut off all telephone communication and barricaded the roads for a radius of fifteen miles from Kilmallock, set about taking Kilmallock RIC barracks by force. Having taken up commanding positions where the attackers had the advantage of high buildings facing the barracks the attack was launched. When the attack opened from the front, heavy weights were thrown on to the roof of the barracks from an adjoining building. The heavy weights tore open the roof into which the attackers flung bottles of petrol followed by explosives including a Mills bomb setting fire to the barracks which soon became a roaring inferno. The attack continued for over two hours while the defenders within the burning building gave back shot for shot and bomb for bomb. At this stage the attack was called off while the leader called on the police to surrender. Back came the reply from the burning building 'no surrender'. The attack was again resumed and continued until the blazing roof came tumbling down on the gallant defenders who by this time had two dead and six wounded out of the small garrison of twelve to eighteen men (exact number not known but attackers estimated a maximum of eighteen men). Sergeant O'Sullivan, leader of the defenders, still refused to surrender and retreated with his survivors to a small building at the rear of the barracks from which he still continued to fight. After a battle lasting six hours the attackers, fearing the arrival of reinforcements, withdrew, leaving the gallant sergeant and his wounded comrades in possession of the little outhouse, and the charred bodies of two of his men in the burnt-out barracks.[6]

The official police report of the attack on Kilmallock barracks indicated that the RIC defenders offered to surrender on condition that their lives be spared and that this request was denied by the attackers. This was emphasised again and again by the police authorities and had the desired effect – that of furthering the alienation of the vast majority of the RIC from Sinn Féin. The defence of Kilmallock was also held up to the RIC as an example of bravery and dedication to duty which they were encouraged to follow. As a result of the attack on Kilmallock police barracks we put up metal shutters on the barracks windows at night, a precaution not previously considered necessary.[7] Towards the end of May 1920 the status of our barracks was raised and in addition to our district inspector we got an acting county inspector.[8]

NEWTOWNSANDES POLICE HUT

The new acting county inspector, a Mr Dobbyn, came to us from Sligo and was the same gentleman who had been responsible for my own transfer from that nice, peaceful district the previous autumn.[9] It soon became evident that Listowel was too small for Mr Dobbyn and myself, so I was not surprised when, some days after his arrival, I was transferred to a police hut in a field at Newtownsandes (Moyvane) about seven miles from Listowel.[10] Why that hut had ever been put there I do not know, but there it was and there it was evidently intended to remain. There were six such huts in the district of Listowel and apart from the fact that they were most uncomfortable to live in they were an eyesore on the landscape.[11] They each consisted of a three-foot-high concrete platform with a wooden superstructure. A large, untilled field surrounded the Newtownsandes hut which stood about fifty yards from the village. In summer with a coal stove in the centre of the hut it was suffocating, while in winter, with draughts coming up through the floor, it was very cold. I was anything but impressed with my new home but settled down to make the best of it.

Sergeant William Watson, who was in charge, was one of those inoffensive men who spend their lives trying to keep out of trouble and generally succeed in getting into the most difficult situations. He certainly had problems to cope with when I arrived. The two Black and Tans who had been posted to Listowel in March had soon afterwards been sent out to Newtownsandes and, with the little sergeant and a young lad named James McNieve, were 'holding the fort'. The Black and Tans refused to get out of bed in the mornings or to go to bed at night. When not sleeping, they were drinking and there was nothing the sergeant could do about it, as they had been sent to him precisely to keep them out of harm's way in Listowel. On my arrival the sergeant confided to me that 'these two boys are capable of attacking the hut at night, as they never return until after midnight and then are generally very drunk'. He certainly had his hands full and I had genuine sympathy for him and promised my co-operation in the event of trouble. This came in the most unexpected way.

A few days after my arrival at Newtownsandes, the sergeant one evening returned from Listowel to find that his office-cum-bedroom had been almost wrecked by carbine fire from the two Black and Tans. The jamb of the door was almost completely blown away; about six feet square of the wainscoting was torn down and lying on his bed; while six zinc buckets, one within the other, which happened to be in the room, were riddled with bullets.

It all happened very simply and in broad daylight. The two Black and Tans had arrived back from the local pub and we were sitting round the fire when I began to regale them with the exploits of Dan Breen and his men. The question of defending our hut arose and one of the Black and Tans, named Thompson, said: 'A good soldier always tests his own defences first.' Taking down their carbines the two worthies went out, accompanied by young McNieve and myself. Marking a spot on one of the uprights of the hut the two Black and Tans went to the end of the garden and fired six rounds each at the mark on the upright. We then examined the mark and found that, apart from a slight impression, the bullets did not appear to have penetrated the timber upright. The carbines were again loaded and again six rounds each were fired and there was no doubt about the marksmanship of the two Black and Tans. Still the upright did not appear to have been pierced. 'Impregnable' was the unanimous decision and we went in to inspect the sergeant's office-cum-bedroom which was inside the upright used as a target. The destruction inside was complete, and even the Black and Tans were slightly shocked when they saw it. It was not the state of the hut, however, that annoyed them, but the fact that the hut was not 'impregnable'. What the people of the district thought of the RIC shooting at their own barracks I do not know, but I have no doubt that it caused some alarm among those law-abiding citizens. As senior man in the absence of the sergeant, I was not too happy about the situation and went for a walk through the fields while the two Tans went back to the pub.

I was digging in the garden behind the hut when the sergeant arrived and I believe he almost collapsed when he went into his room and saw what had happened. After a while he called me in and I explained everything to him exactly as it happened. I suggested that he report the matter and ask that we all be transferred to a decent barracks that we could defend. The poor man had visions of his three stripes coming off over the affair and he said that he would get a carpenter to repair the damage and try to keep the matter quiet. I pointed out the folly of such a course since the whole countryside must have heard the shooting and, in any case, the Black and Tans had made up their minds not to stay in the hut. Reluctantly he rang up the district inspector at Listowel and attempted to explain the situation. He evidently did not make himself too clear, for within half an hour a lorry-load of military with three officers arrived, fully armed and with a machine gun ready for action. They took it that we had been attacked by the IRA and had rushed out to our assistance. They were certainly quick off the mark and meant to put up a fight.

While the officers were examining the damage to the sergeant's bedroom, the two drunken Black and Tans came in and started to complain at having been sent to such a death trap of a barracks. The officers pointed out to them that the hut was a fortress compared with the positions they had to defend in France and accused the two Black and Tans of cowardice. This nettled the latter very much but they were far too drunk to even argue the point. The officers withdrew with their men after they informed us that the hut would be put into a better state of defence next day.

So early next morning a military lorry pulled up at the hut with about a ton of barbed wire which some soldiers set about fixing all round the hut. When they had finished a whole sea of barbed-wire entanglements surrounded the hut. Many bottles and tin cans were affixed to the wire. The soldiers told us that these would prevent the 'Shinners' from slipping noiselessly through the wire. In fact what they had succeeded in doing was to make the hut a death trap, since there was now no means of escape either front or rear in the event of the hut being set on fire as happened to Kilmallock police barracks. The two Black and Tans immediately realised this and made it the excuse for staying out all that night, returning only in the small hours of the morning.

Finding myself in a 'wire cage' with the two Black and Tans, I did some hard thinking, as a result of which some days later I mounted my bicycle and went into the Workhouse Hospital, Listowel, where I asked for the doctor who was in attendance.[12] He took me into a private room where we discussed the situation and I gave him the full details of my predicament. He was most sympathetic and after an interview lasting over half an hour agreed to give me a medical certificate for a sprained ankle. Not only that but he also agreed to give a certificate to young McNieve who was also stationed at the Newtownsandes hut, showing that he was suffering from a pain in the back, and it was arranged that we both go into hospital immediately.

When I presented the medical certificate to McNieve, at first he refused to 'go sick', but after some persuasion he agreed to accompany me to hospital. That same evening I returned from a walk limping and reported to the sergeant that I had an accident which resulted in a sprained ankle. Soon afterwards McNieve and myself set off on our bicycles for the Workhouse Hospital. We were received by the Reverend Mother in charge of the hospital, and she gave us such special attention that it was evident that she had been well posted by the doctor.[13] We were both put to bed and my ankle was carefully wrapped up in cotton wool and bandaged by the Reverend Mother herself. Every day for a week she personally changed the bandages on my ankle and was very sympathetic and attentive to both McNieve and myself.

My friend Kealy, who had accompanied me from Sligo the previous autumn, was a patient in a bed beside us. We told him what had been happening at Newtownsandes and settled down to await developments. We had not long to wait.

When I assured Sergeant Watson of my co-operation I little realised that within one week I would have him and the two Black and Tans out of Newtownsandes hut, but that is exactly what happened. On the night of my arrival in hospital four of the men from Listowel barracks called to see us and excitedly told us about the latest developments. It seems that immediately after we left Newtownsandes for hospital the sergeant rang up Listowel barracks and asked for reinforcements. Constables Michael Fitzgerald and Patrick O'Neill were told to replace us and simply refused to do so. They were immediately suspended for refusing to obey orders. All the constables in the police barracks were then assembled by the acting county inspector and each in turn refused to go to Newtownsandes. About nightfall that same evening (4 June) two military lorries went out to Newtownsandes to convey the sergeant and his two Black and Tans with all their equipment to Listowel barracks and the hut was abandoned for the first time in fifty years.

The vacation of Newtownsandes hut nearly had fatal consequences. After the police left it, a number of local people entered it. Later the military, expecting the IRA to destroy the hut, rushed out to Newtownsandes when darkness set in and seeing a light in the hut assumed that the IRA were already in possession and surrounded it. Getting no response to a call for surrender, they blazed away at the hut which was then riddled with rifle fire. Fortunately two men who were inside took shelter in the 'lockup', which was in the very centre of the hut, and in this way escaped certain death. The military forced open the hut door and found the two men whom they arrested. They threw them and a youth into the lorries and took them back to Listowel. In Listowel the two men and the youth were recognised by the RIC. The military and the RIC then conveyed them back to Newtownsandes.[14] The hut was never re-occupied by the police, as it was burned down by the IRA on the following night.

The two constables, Fitzgerald and O'Neill, who were suspended from duty heard no more about their suspensions and were on duty as usual next day. This little incident had far-reaching effects, as it proved to the RIC at Listowel that their strength lay in unity. The manner in which they had stood together in a small crisis made them loyal comrades and this was to prove useful in the greater crisis which lay ahead.

Returning to Listowel barracks after my week in hospital, I found that Sergeant Watson, instead of showing gratitude for what I had done for him, regarded me with suspicion. He feared that the developments at Newtownsandes would tell against him and that he might even lose his rank. Even at that time he did not realise that the political situation was such that, as a policeman, he could not avoid trouble no matter where he might be stationed.

MILITARY REINFORCEMENTS

Towards the end of May and early in June 1920, British troopships began to land troops all round the south coast of Ireland, from Wexford to Limerick.[15] These troops began to move inland and take up strategic positions convenient to all the important centres of population. Buildings were commandeered to accommodate the troops as military barracks were already full. Cork, Clonmel, Limerick, Tipperary, Tralee and Waterford were heavily garrisoned. Indeed, the country south of a line from Limerick to Waterford was, in effect, in a ring of British steel. Listowel, unfortunately, was within that ring.

In those days movements of British troops were taken as part of the daily routine so that this new development did not get more than passing comment. The people read the news, forgot about it and went on with the tilling of their fields and being in attendance in their shops.[16] Elsewhere, clashes were taking place between the IRA and British troops with alarming regularity, but Listowel still remained relatively calm. As the days lengthened we took our daily walks along the banks of the River Feale and endlessly discussed the worsening situation.

We were particularly concerned about our own unenviable position in the developing conflict.[17] The question of leaving the force was often discussed but always ended with Asquith's famous phrase 'wait and see'. We had not long to wait.

9

LISTOWEL POLICE MUTINY: JUNE 1920

UNUSUAL TRANSFERS

On the morning of 16 June 1920 the county inspector,[1] who was in Tralee, telephoned the district inspector at Listowel police barracks to send a constable to the railway station for an important despatch which would be arriving in a half an hour on the Tralee–Limerick train. All police despatches in those days were described as important so this particular message did not at first cause any stir and a constable was sent to the station to collect it. It was only when the district inspector came into the dayroom and read the despatch that its importance became clear to us. It was a bulky despatch and contained the transfer of fourteen men from the barracks, leaving only one constable and two sergeants at Listowel. The transfers were to take place at once and all the transferred men were to be out of the barracks by 12 noon on the following day, that is, 17 June. The British military under Captain Chadwick were to be in possession of the barracks not later than 12 noon on the same date.

A few hours after the receipt of the despatch, the military dumped four tons of coal in the yard behind the police barracks in anticipation of their taking over. That appeared to settle the matter and there seemed to be nothing to do but to accept the new situation. A good many of the men were absent on duty when the transfers arrived and it was interesting to watch their reactions as they returned off duty and heard the news.

Captain Chadwick, who was to take over our barracks, was a fine type of British officer.[2] He was the officer in charge of the company of soldiers which was camped at Ballinruddery since the previous month. He kept his men under perfect control and we were on intimate terms with him. The fourteen men transferred were being sent to various outposts in County Kerry and some were going to very remote stations. Judging by the station I was getting, it was evident that I was still far from being a favourite with the authorities. My transfer was to a little place called Cloghane, in the Dingle mountains, at the foot of Mount Brandon which rises to 3,000 feet above sea level. In peaceful times it would be a healthy spot but, with the IRA becoming more and more active, one had doubts about its advantages and I was far from impressed with my new destination.

REFUSAL TO HAND OVER POLICE BARRACKS TO MILITARY

After tea on the evening of 16 June when all the men were together in the barracks, we held a meeting in the dining room to discuss the situation. It soon became evident that all present were hostile to the transfers. As the discussion developed some of the men expressed the view that all of us should resign rather than go on the transfers, while others suggested that an appeal should be made to the authorities to reconsider their action. One reason suggested for our refusing to go on transfer was that otherwise we would be leaving our comrades, especially the head constable who was very popular with his men, and their families behind with the military. I was much impressed by the determination of the men and the calm way in which they were attempting to cope with the difficult problem which had arisen.

Being a newcomer to the station, I was slow in giving my views and was prepared to abide by whatever decision was reached. When asked to speak, however, I pointed out that it was evident from these latest transfers that big developments were afoot and that we had to ask ourselves how we stood in the matter. Supposing, I said, that an all-out war is contemplated, we shall have to select whether we are going to be on the British side or the Irish side, since neutrality will be out of the question. Assuming that, with the assistance of the British army, we succeeded in beating Sinn Féin, what then? The British soldiers would return to their own country leaving us with our own people whom we had succeeded in pacifying with the assistance of a foreign power. That might even be the most favourable outcome as far as we were concerned. What would happen if we and the rest of the crown forces were ultimately defeated by Sinn Féin? I pointed out that it was a case of win or lose, we personally would come out of the conflict badly, and that if we intended making a stand against being involved in the conflict it was better to make it now than later.

At this point somebody shouted: 'We should refuse to hand over to the military and refuse to go on transfer.' This got a rousing cheer and brought my short speech to a close. 'Hands up all who are in favour of holding on to our barracks,' came from somebody else. All hands went up, followed by another rousing cheer which left no doubt as to what the men felt and thought. The cheering also brought the head constable on the scene but, when he saw what was happening, he, like the gentleman he was, quietly walked away and left us to our deliberations. The vote was unanimous for holding the barracks and by the same unanimous vote I was selected to represent the fourteen men who were scheduled for transfer. Constable Michael Lillis[3] was selected to represent the head constable, the three sergeants and himself, he being the only constable not transferred.[4] When a final decision had been reached on what we should do, everybody seemed to breathe more freely and all seemed happy.

With the consent of the men I then telephoned the county inspector at Tralee and informed him of our decision. I was highly elated after the excitement of our meeting and was determined to have a straight chat with him. He gave me a patient hearing and when I was finished he cut me off without as much as a single comment. This had the effect of damping our spirits somewhat. However, there was now no turning back and, indeed, there was no evidence whatsoever of a change of heart on the part of any of my comrades. We then informed the district inspector and head constable of what we had done and, like the county inspector, they seemed dumbfounded and offered no comment. At least they did not show any hostility and it was evident that, if they were not with us, at least they were not against us, and this we appreciated very much.

For my own part, it was a moment I shall never forget. Men who for a lifetime had been accustomed to discipline and to giving allegiance to their superior officers were now calmly handing over that allegiance to a junior man selected by themselves and they did not count the consequences. They were good, clean-living men who realised that a crisis was upon them and their families, and they were taking the only steps they knew to meet it. I, one of the most junior men in the barracks, realised only too well the responsibility thrown upon my inexperienced shoulders. For nine years I had taken without complaint every indignity, insult and transfer. I was prepared to continue doing so, until this great moment had come when I was placed in a position to speak to the authorities on a new footing.

Although the county inspector had not expressed any views on the telephone when I informed him of our decision, we knew that the matter was not going to rest there and that steps would very soon be taken to cope with our stand. Before going to bed, we again debated the situation and decided to stick to the position we had taken. We fully realised how exposed that position was. We had no organisation which would lend us support, indeed we had no backing from any quarter. We could only await the next move and hope for the best.

VISIT OF COUNTY INSPECTOR: FOURTEEN CONSTABLES RESIGN

A telephone message came through that night at about ten o'clock from the county inspector at Tralee. It was a simple instruction to our district inspector to have all the men in the barracks on parade at ten o'clock next morning, that is, 17 June. Beyond telling him that the men were to wear side arms (belt and sword-bayonet) no other details were given.

County Inspector Poer O'Shee believed in punctuality, and at ten o'clock sharp he arrived at Listowel on the morning of 17 June. Addressing those assembled, which included the acting county inspector, district inspector and head constable, he pointed out the seriousness of the attitude we were taking regarding his recent order, which, he said, was an instruction from the divisional commissioner. This was the first time we heard that we had a divisional commissioner, as this was an entirely new kind of appointment, and we did not even realise the significance of the rank.[5]

When the county inspector had finished speaking, I stepped forward and informed him that I represented the men who had been transferred. He cut me short and said, 'Do you refuse to obey an order of the divisional commissioner, an order that applies to all Munster, and bring discredit on the police force?'

'Yes,' I said. 'I refuse to obey his order.'

'Then you had better resign,' was his short retort.

'Accept my resignation now,' I replied.

The county inspector seemed to be taken aback by this reply, as he paused for some time before he said, 'Any other man wish to resign?'

Like one man thirteen constables took a step forward and with one voice shouted, 'I resign.'[6]

The county inspector, who had been surprised at my reply, was clearly upset when he now found the resignations of all the transferred constables in his hands. He had never been faced with a situation like this before and was bewildered. Adopting a completely new attitude, he started to reason with us and went so far as to admit that he himself did not like the idea of working with the military. He asked us to put on paper the reasons for our dissatisfaction, and he undertook to submit them to the proper authorities. We agreed to do so, and he left the room and went into the district inspector's office, which was just across the hall from the dayroom.

We drafted a short document and gave our reasons for refusing to work with the British military under four headings. I can recall only two of these, which were:

(a) The crime register in the barracks would prove that Listowel district was entirely free from crime, apart from minor offences, and that the force there at present was quite sufficient to deal with the district which was entirely peaceful;

(b) As policemen we joined the force with characters second to none and as such we refuse to work with, or co-operate with men of low moral character, and that we could not leave our comrades and their families in the same barracks with the British military without endangering the morals of innocent children.

We gave some other reasons which were of minor importance and which I cannot recall. The document was sent in to the county inspector who came out almost immediately with it in his hand. Flinging it down on the table he said, 'Do you wish me to submit a filthy document like that to the authorities? Remove paragraph (b) and I shall submit it.' We informed the county inspector that our case was based on both paragraphs (a) and (b), and, consequently, that we were not prepared to omit paragraph (b) or to alter it by one iota.

'You shall hear more about this,' he said, as he gathered up his papers and left the barracks in a towering rage, without even a word to our district inspector who was present during the interview.

With the departure of the county inspector, zero hour – 12 noon – had passed and the British military had not taken over the barracks as planned. We had won the first round by our united stand, but we did not underestimate the strength of the forces against which we had pitted ourselves. We fully realised that we stood alone in the fight, but we had youth and determination on our side. Even the district inspector, head constable and sergeants could not hide the fact that, although remaining uninvolved in the dispute, they were proud of the stand we had taken. We awaited the next move with calm determination.

The coming of the county inspector had created a rather peculiar situation. Fourteen of us had tendered our resignations and when the county inspector left we did not know whether or not we were under suspension. It was at this point that District Inspector Flanagan showed what a fine gentleman he was. Instead of resenting our action, he came in to the dayroom and, sitting on the table, talked to us as a father might have spoken to his own children. He made no attempt whatsoever to use his authority or to find fault with the action we had taken. He just discussed the whole situation with us openly and frankly and advised all of us to stand together no matter what happened. The acting county inspector, Mr Dobbyn, kept out of the way and we saw little of him during the crisis.

SHOW OF FORCE

The 18 June was a long day. We were in a state of passive mutiny and no news came from the authorities until ten o'clock that night when a telephone message came from the county inspector's office at Tralee. Again our district inspector was instructed to have all the men on parade at ten o'clock on the following morning, that is, 19 June. No further details were given but we assumed that the county inspector had received some definite instructions from Dublin Castle and that he was coming to issue some kind of ultimatum or to dismiss us. We sat up late discussing the pros and cons of our case. I had often seen men spending a whole week preparing for a county inspector's ordinary inspection, and worrying a great deal about it. In this instance I saw men treating with indifference the arrival of a county inspector who, with the full backing of Dublin Castle, would have the power to end their official careers.

The morning of 19 June 1920 was one of those bright, sunny mornings when one thought only of green fields, high mountains and sea-washed strands. It was not the kind of morning that one would select for being cooped up in a stuffy police barracks dayroom waiting for the word that could result in one's joining the ranks of the unemployed. This thought struck me as I stood with the others lined up in the dayroom of Listowel barracks on that morning watching, and listening to, the large clock on the mantelpiece ticking away the slow minutes until the hands showed the fateful hour of ten o'clock.

The county inspector was not as punctual as usual and the mantelpiece clock continued to tick away the minutes, five, ten, fifteen and even twenty minutes past ten, and still the county inspector had not arrived. Anxiety was clearly visible on the faces of the men assembled in the dayroom and none more so than that of the acting county inspector who was showing great nervous strain. Constable Lillis, who was to have represented the men not transferred, was absent on duty and this left me without his moral support. I felt, however, that I had sufficient moral support from my comrades and I had no hesitation in taking responsibility for them. I cast my mind back again and again to the plan which had been decided on the previous night, as my only worry was that I might fail those splendid men who had placed their future in my hands. The worst that could happen was that all would be dismissed, but, having tendered our resignations two days earlier, that did not unduly worry any of us.

As the hands of the clock were nearing 10.30 a.m. we heard the familiar hum of a Crossley tender as it approached the police barracks. The dayroom to the right of the main entrance where we were assembled was facing the street and, as the tender braked at the front gate, we had a full view of its occupants and were somewhat taken aback when we saw not the county inspector and some assistants, but fifteen fully armed and helmeted policemen. We received a further unpleasant surprise when three police officers in the full dress of their high rank stepped down from the Crossley tender. One of the officers attracted our special attention, as he wore a large, white ostrich feather on his helmet and several medals across his breast. We did not know who they were until the acting county inspector recognised the officer with the feather as General Tudor, police adviser to the viceroy of Ireland.[7] One of the other officers, we were to learn subsequently, was a Colonel Leatham, a newly appointed divisional commissioner for Dublin.[8] The third officer was County Inspector George B. Heard, who also wore a medal on his breast.[9]

The armed police escort got off the Crossley tender and remained outside the police barracks gate while the officers came in to the little lawn in front of our dayroom window where our acting county inspector joined them. They made no move to come into the barracks. From what we saw we were convinced that we were all for dismissal and that the fifteen men on the tender had come to take over the police barracks.

Before we had time to get over our first surprise a second Crossley tender halted at the police barracks gate. It seemed to be packed tight with British soldiers, fully armed, and with at least three officers, including Captain Chadwick who was stationed near the town. Almost at the same time, a third tender drew up. This was full of armed and helmeted police. County Inspector Poer O'Shee was in this third tender. The county inspector and the military officers joined the other officers on the lawn, where they chatted and smoked, and all appeared to be in very good humour. By this time there were at least eight military and police officers on the lawn and yet no move had been made to come into the barracks. We could not for the life of us know what it was all about. That they were trying to overawe our little garrison we had no doubt and one could almost feel the tension in the dayroom growing. The plan we had thrashed out on the previous night practically evaporated from my mind, and in any case seemed to be futile against this display of power.

But the greatest shock of all was to come. When our patience had been almost exhausted, we heard the hum of yet another Crossley tender and in a matter of seconds it too drew up beside the other lorries in front of the police barracks gate. This last tender was packed with British troops. Two military officers stepped smartly down from the tender and, turning their backs on the barracks, stood smartly to attention facing the driver's seat on the tender. Then out stepped a one-armed man wearing the full dress of a military officer of high rank. He appeared to be about forty years of age, tall and straight, and he wore at least half-a-dozen medals across the breast of his heavily braided tunic. Nobody in the barracks had the least idea as to whom this person was, but it was evident from the attention which he received from General Tudor and the other officers that he was an officer of high rank. By this time we were dumbfounded. We suspected that this display of force could mean only one thing – a military court-martial which could result in some of us being shot. There was nothing we could do, however, but stand and wait.

After what seemed like several hours, the officers, numbering about twelve, moved into the dayroom where we were assembled. They lined themselves along the fireplace and faced us, with the table between the officers and ourselves. The gentleman with the one arm looked hard at us, placed his right foot on the form, his right elbow on his knee and gripped the armless sleeve of his tunic with his right hand. He was a man of stern and determined appearance and looked the type who would not be likely to stand for any nonsense. He introduced himself as Colonel Smyth, divisional commissioner of the military and police of Munster.[10] He stated that he had been appointed by the prime minister of England to whom alone he was responsible. He made no reference whatsoever to our previous insubordination and began to address us. When he was about to commence his speech, I saluted the colonel and pointed out that we understood that this was to be a conference between the RIC and their superiors and that we objected to the presence of military officers. The military officers looked at each other, smiled and left the room. Strange though it may seem, Colonel Smyth made no comment on my unusual conduct. We were then left with Colonel Smyth, General Tudor, Colonel Leatham and County Inspector George Heard, as well as the county inspector and acting county inspector, and our own district inspector and head constable. Outside the street was full of the black and khaki uniforms of the police and military, while passers-by wondered what the cause of all the activity was.

COLONEL SMYTH'S ADDRESS AND ITS SEQUEL

Commencing again his speech, which I had interrupted, Colonel Smyth addressed us as follows:

> Well, men, I have something of interest to tell you, something that I am sure you would not wish your wives to hear. I am going to lay all my cards on the table, but I must reserve one card for myself. Now, men, Sinn Féin has had all the sport up to this; we are going to have the sport now. The police have done splendid work, considering the odds against them. They are not sufficiently strong to do anything but

hold their barracks. This is not enough, for as long as we remain on the defensive so long will Sinn Féin have the whip-hand. We must take the offensive and beat Sinn Féin with their own tactics. Martial Law, applying to all Ireland, is coming into operation shortly, and our scheme of amalgamation must be complete by 21 June. I am promised as many troops as I require from England. Thousands are coming daily. I am getting 7,000 police from England.

Now, men, what I wish to explain to you is that you are to strengthen your comrades in the out-stations. The military are to take possession of the large centres where they will have control of the railways and lines of communication, and be able to move rapidly from place to place. Unlike police who can act as individuals and on their own initiative, military must act in large numbers, and under a good officer – he must be a good officer or I shall have him removed. If a police barracks is burned, or if the barracks, already occupied, is not suitable, then the best house in the locality is to be commandeered and the occupants thrown out in the gutter. Let them die there, the more the merrier.

You must go out at least six nights a week, and get out of the barracks by the back door or skylight so that you will not be seen. Police patrols in uniform will go out the front door as a decoy. The military and police will patrol the country roads at least five nights a week. They are not to confine themselves to the main roads but to go across the country, lie in ambush, take cover behind fences, near the roads, and when civilians are seen approaching, shout, 'Hands up.' Should the order be not obeyed immediately, shoot, and shoot with effect. If the persons approaching carry their hands in their pockets or are in any way suspicious looking, shoot them down. You may make mistakes occasionally and innocent persons may be shot, but this cannot be helped and you are bound to get the right persons sometimes. The more you shoot the better I will like you, and I assure you that no policeman will get into trouble for shooting any man. In the past, policemen have got into trouble for giving evidence at coroners' inquests. As a matter of fact coroners' inquests are to be made illegal so that in future no policeman will be asked to give evidence at inquests.

Hunger strikers will be allowed to die in jail; the more the merrier. Some of them have died already, and a damn bad job they were not all allowed to die. As a matter of fact, some of them have been dealt with in a manner that their friends will never hear about. A ship will be leaving an Irish port in the near future with lots of Sinn Féiners on board. I assure you, men, it will never land.

That now is all I have to say to you. We want your assistance in carrying out this scheme in wiping out Sinn Féin. Any man who is not prepared to co-operate is a hindrance rather than a help and he had better leave the force at once.

Colonel Smyth then, pointing to the first constable in the line, asked: 'Are you prepared to co-operate?' The man, an Englishman, who happened to be one of the two Black and Tans who had fired into Newtownsandes hut, replied: 'Constable Mee speaks for us'.[11] Smyth then proceeded to go along the line, asking each man in turn the same question and getting the same reply.

Constable Thomas Hughes was next to the Black and Tan and, as I was about the seventh or eighth in the half-circle facing Smyth and the other police officers, I was partly facing Hughes.[12] I had been watching Hughes' pale face grow paler, his brows knit, his hands clench and his eyes stare at Colonel Smyth. As he referred Smyth to me I managed to catch his eye, and, in that split second, I read his message which clearly conveyed the words 'Now or never'.

By this time our plans of the previous night had completely left my mind. The time for thought had passed, the moment for action was at hand. When Smyth pointed his finger towards me I stepped forward and, with a calmness that surprised me, said:

By your accent I take it you are an Englishman. You seem to forget that you are addressing Irishmen.

He checked me at this point and said he was an Irishman, being from Banbridge, County Down. 'I am an Irishman,' I continued, 'and proud of being so, too.'

Taking off my cap I laid it on the table in front of Colonel Smyth and said: 'This is English; you may have it as a present from me.' Having done this I completely lost my temper and taking off my belt and bayonet clapped them down on the table, saying: 'These too are English. You may have them, and to hell with you, you murderer.'

Colonel Smyth quietly said to District Inspector Flanagan: 'Place that man under arrest.'

District Inspector Flanagan and Head Constable Plover came forward and linked me out of the room down to the kitchen, which was at the far end of the corridor, and remained there with me. About three minutes after being escorted into the kitchen by the district inspector and the head constable I heard a wild stampede in the corridor and in rushed most of my comrades. They were highly excited and half dragged and half pushed me back towards the dayroom.[13] When we entered the dayroom, it was empty. Colonel Smyth, General Tudor and the other police officers were in the district inspector's office and the door was closed. Colonel Smyth's cap was still on the dayroom table.

The front door was locked and only a few British soldiers were in the road near the lorries, the others had gone to various pubs for refreshments. None of them was aware of what was happening in the police barracks. District Inspector Flanagan and Head Constable Plover joined the other officers in the room across the hall. In the dayroom, the men were in an angry mood and some of them suggested that Smyth deserved to be shot.[14] My own position was unique, as I had been arrested by order of the divisional commissioner and released without his permission and at the instigation of my comrades by the district inspector and head constable. In the midst of the confusion I found myself acting as a peacemaker and trying to get order restored.

In the meantime, inside in the district inspector's office, Smyth attempted to put through a telephone call and discovered that the telephone had been disconnected. As he threw down the speaker he muttered: 'They are all Shinners out there. They have disconnected the wires.'[15] This development probably gave Smyth the impression that now it could be he himself and not Constable Mee who was the real prisoner in Listowel police barracks. Consequently he agreed to a number of placatory moves.

First, District Inspector Flanagan, whom all of us held in the highest esteem, came into the dayroom and his presence helped to restore order. He told us that General Tudor wished to speak to us as a friend. We refused to meet Tudor and asked the district inspector to get the officers out of the barracks to avoid bloodshed. Flanagan left the dayroom and again joined the officers, but came back and made a very strong appeal to us to give General Tudor a hearing. We eventually agreed to do so.

Although General Tudor came to the police barracks in full dress uniform with medals and white ostrich feather, he now appeared dressed in a nice brown tweed suit. He tried to appear calm, but it was evident that he was excited. He started off by saying:

> Well, men, I would like to say just a few words to you as a friend. Just to show that I am a friend I will shake hands with each one of you.

He then started with the first man and went right along the line and shook hands with each one of us. His opening remarks were:

> Although I am an Englishman and was born in Kent, my ancestors came from Ireland. I like Irishmen.

He then explained that Dominion Home Rule, applying to all Ireland, was to come into operation in the near future and that the RIC would come out well under the new arrangement; that, for instance, they would get twelve years added to their service for the purpose of pensions. At that stage one of our comrades, Constable Francis J. (Tommy) Byrnes, spoke up and said: 'We have heard this kind of thing in the past and know that it means nothing.[16] If you are serious about those promises why do you wish to leave us out in police huts where we can be shot like rats?'

Tudor asked him how many huts there were in the district and Byrnes replied: 'There are six huts in this district.'[17]

Tudor said: 'Consider these huts broken up as from this date.'

Realising the danger of promises and concessions, I intervened and gave the men the command to dismiss. They immediately broke ranks, and, as we left the dayroom, in defiance we commenced to sing: 'A Nation Once Again' which we followed with 'Wrap the green flag round me, boys'. We then held a quick meeting in the yard behind the police barracks after which we returned in a body to the dayroom.

When we returned to the dayroom Colonel Smyth, General Tudor and the whole party of military and police had left, Colonel Smyth leaving without his cap which had to be sent after him later in the day.[18]

At this point I went into District Inspector Flanagan's office and informed him on behalf of the men that, while we appreciated the fact that he was with us in spirit, we did not wish nor expect him to ruin his own future by backing us openly. I shall never forget his reply. With tears in his eyes he stood up, thrust his hands into his trouser pockets and walked towards the window in front of which half a dozen of our men were chatting on the lawn. 'Mee,' said he, 'when I look out there and see those fine lads who have shown such courage and bravery within the last few days, I feel that I am the happiest man in Ireland. It has been my great privilege and honour to have been placed in charge of such men and as an Irishman I would be unfit to live were I to desert them. That I shall never do, and may God bless you all.'[19]

We then telephoned the police barracks at Killarney and Tralee, both of which were important police centres.[20] We told the police in these barracks what had happened and, over the telephone, they applauded our stand and promised to stand by us. Smyth and his party went on to Tralee where Smyth's address to the police was received with sullen contempt. At Killarney he and his escort were met by the police with shouts of 'Up Listowel'. He tried to address them but could not even get a hearing.[21] At this stage, believing that the whole force was organised against him, Smyth cancelled his tour and no attempt was made by the British military to occupy Listowel police barracks.[22]

WE COMMUNICATE WITH THE IRA

After ensuring support from the other important police barracks for our stand, we next set about getting our version of the incident to the outside world. So I went up to the bedroom, which incidentally was the only private room in the building, and, while Colonel Smyth's words were still burning in my brain, I committed them to paper. After some time my comrades, Thomas Hughes, John Donovan[23] and Michael Fitzgerald, joined me.[24] They read over my statement and agreed that it was a verbatim report of Smyth's speech. With a full sense of their responsibility and in the knowledge that in so doing they were possibly signing their own death warrants, those three, who had already taken part in what, in effect, was a mutiny, now joined me in appending their signatures to the statement.

To place the signed statement in the hands of the press was our next aim. Accordingly, that night the four of us who signed the statement secretly visited the parochial house, Listowel, and placed the statement, together with other relevant facts, before Father Charles O'Sullivan, CC.[25] He immediately perceived the importance of the document and suggested that the most effective way to have it published would be to send it direct to IRA headquarters. This he promised to do. We agreed with his suggestion. So the following morning our document was on its way to Dublin.[26]

Apart from acknowledging its receipt and almost immediately afterwards returning the document for further signatures, the intelligence section of the IRA headquarters staff took no further action. We explained to Father O'Sullivan, through whom we communicated with the IRA, that until the contents of our statement were published and the measure of protection which such publicity might afford had been attained, we had no intention, at this stage, of exposing more than the four of us to the danger of signing what might well prove to be our death warrants. Father O'Sullivan saw our point of view and again forwarded our original statement, together with our explanation, to IRA headquarters.

As the days passed the position became more and more unreal. The British military forces did not move into the police barracks and the IRA, fearing a trap, made no move even temporarily to take over the building either.[27] We were in a 'no man's land'. We felt as completely isolated[28] as the Connaught Rangers must have felt when, just over a week later, they mutinied at Jullundur and Solon in the Himalayas and were told by their commanding officer that their action was futile because 'they were many thousands of miles from home'.[29]

10

AFTERMATH OF THE LISTOWEL POLICE MUTINY: 19 JUNE–AUGUST 1920

For some three weeks after 19 June, no official contact was made with us and we began to feel as isolated as lepers in a leper colony. Soon we realised that isolating us in this way was the means which the authorities decided to take in order to break down our resistance.[1] In the meantime the RIC received a substantial increase (14/- per week) in pay, and the rate of promotion in the force was dramatically accelerated.[2] These last developments had an immediate effect. Men who heretofore had become disenchanted with their police service now began to see a good future for themselves in the force. We noticed this change even among those who manned the various barracks near us. Some of the very men who three weeks previously would have wholeheartedly supported us in our confrontation with the authorities now could not be counted upon.

At this stage it was evident that, where the threat of force had failed, bribery in the form of increased pay and prospects of promotion was having the desired effect. We had given a courageous lead in protesting against the kind of position in which members of the RIC now found themselves, but we gradually realised that our stand was not going to receive any open support from members of the force elsewhere. Consequently a number of us considered that no further purpose could be served by our remaining in the force any longer. So on the night of 6 July 1920, at a meeting held in the barracks, five of us – Constables

Donovan, Fitzgerald, Hughes, Sheeran and myself – announced our intention of leaving the force next day without going through the formality of resigning.[3] That same night, as a matter of courtesy, we informed District Inspector Flanagan and Head Constable Plover of our intention. We also called on our friend, Father Charles O'Sullivan, CC. After a short conversation, Father O'Sullivan handed each of us a personal letter which read:

> I most earnestly bear witness that Mr … has just retired from his employment in the Irish police in circumstances which do high honour to his character as a sterling, steadfast Catholic and Irishman. At a very recent date, in a matter of national racial moment, involving the lives of the people, he has acted in a manner that could be dictated only by the very highest and purest degree of most conscientious and patriotic duty.
>
> From the facts known to me I solemnly declare that his conduct entitles him in supreme measure to the esteem, patronage and protection of his fellow countrymen everywhere.
>
> *Signed: Charles O'Sullivan, C.C.*
> *Listowel*
> *July 7, 1920*

When the county inspector had called me into the district inspector's office a week after the Smyth speech and I refused the promotion and transfer which he offered to me, he suggested that I resign or I would have to be dismissed. He informed me that if I resigned I would get a 'character' while if I was dismissed from the force I would leave without one. When I said to him that I considered a 'British character' would be a hindrance rather than a help he terminated the interview and ordered me out of the office. Now five of us were leaving the force without a 'character' and for that reason we appreciated very much the reference from Father O'Sullivan, a good Irish priest who had shared our risks and was later to suffer the indignity of having his presbytery raided by British troops.[4]

The night before the five of us left Listowel a concert was arranged in the barracks, at which we sang and caroused into the small hours of the morning. Although we were leaving next day, we had no clear idea of what we would do in the future. We arranged to keep in contact with the little garrison which we were leaving behind. We did not divulge the fact that the Smyth speech had been sent to IRA headquarters, and, at our request, Father O'Sullivan promised to keep this a secret. We felt that it would not serve any useful purpose to disclose this information at that stage and that our action might even be construed as treachery.

I RETURN HOME

On the morning of 7 July we were out of bed early as we still had some packing to do. We had slept but little as, even though the concert in the barracks on the previous night lasted into the small hours of the morning, we had afterwards continued talking for some time before retiring. Having washed and shaved and packed away the last of our things we came down to breakfast. It was a glorious morning with the sun shining brightly and the promise of a very warm day. A number of our comrades had assembled in the dining room having done the usual morning parade without us. There was little said during that last breakfast in the barracks, except for an occasional attempt at humour which fell rather flat as all were tired after the previous night.

After breakfast we went into the dayroom, collected our regulation boxes and carried them out to the police van, known as the 'Black Maria', which was parked outside the barracks waiting to take us to the railway station. Outside, creamery carts were trundling along the street and shopkeepers were removing shutters from shop windows. The people of the town were completely oblivious to what was taking place in the police barracks. In the barracks, nobody seemed to have a thought for the usual routine patrols and nobody even thought of checking our equipment, which would be ordinary procedure had we resigned in the usual way or even if we were going on an ordinary transfer. On one thing all seemed to be agreed and that was that so far as the RIC was concerned it was the end of an era. Even the two Black and Tans, Connors and Thompson, who were present, seemed to regret our departure since they had learned to look on us as the leaders of a trade union. It never dawned on them that one of the reasons why we were leaving was their presence in the force. Having bidden goodbye to our comrades we slipped quietly out of the barracks.

Sheeran made his way to his wife's home at Brosna on the Kerry–Limerick border, while Donovan, Fitzgerald, Hughes and I planned to travel by train from Listowel to Limerick and from Limerick to Tuam by hired car. A rather amusing incident took place at Listowel station. When the train pulled in, both the driver and guard got out and refused to continue the journey because they saw our regulation boxes on the platform. At that time the railwaymen were refusing to carry police, soldiers or military equipment.[5] After someone had explained to them who we were, they shook our hands warmly and actually helped with the loading of our luggage, and we were off on the first stage of our exciting journey. We had no illusions as to the risk we were taking. We were, in effect, deserters from the British forces and we had not made friendly contact with the IRA, so we could expect trouble from either of these sources. As a rather foolish precaution, Donovan, Fitzgerald and I took our Webley revolvers and a supply of ammunition with us.

At Limerick we received an enthusiastic reception from the railwaymen when the driver and guard told them who we were. As a matter of fact the reception was somewhat embarrassing since there were half-a-dozen policemen in uniform at the station and we did not wish to attract their attention. Having hired a car to take us to Tuam, we set off from Limerick and immediately ran into trouble. On the outskirts of the city we were held up by the military at a post where the road was barricaded with barbed wire and sandbags, and where an armoured car and tank were standing by. With the rifles of the sentries pointing at us, an officer walked over to our car to question us. He opened the door of the car, looked in, and seeing the police haversacks, smiled, saluted and told us to carry on. He had assumed that we were police on 'plain-clothes' duty.

Having passed the officer so successfully we were then up against a new problem. The driver of our car now realising that his passengers were members of the RIC refused to risk his life by driving us to Tuam. However, we succeeded in convincing him of who we were, and then, like the railwaymen, he went to the other extreme. He would make the flimsiest excuse to pull up at every village we came to, where, after some minutes, he would have a crowd gathered round congratulating us and insisting on treating us to drink. After some time we managed to restrain our driver from bringing us under any further notice and losing valuable time. Time meant everything to us, as we were anxious to get out of the martial law area of the south-west as quickly as possible.[6] We reached Tuam without a further hold-up and there we halted for a meal and refreshments. The excitement of leaving Listowel and our dangerous journey through the martial law area had kept our minds occupied. Now, with that all over, we realised for the first time that we were no longer policemen and that we were starting life all over again. I confess without shame that I wept as Donovan, Fitzgerald, Hughes and I bade farewell and then parted for our various destinations, Donovan and I going on to my home at Glenamaddy, County Galway, and Fitzgerald and Hughes to their homes at Ahascragh, County Galway, and Hollymount, County Mayo, respectively. It was the last time that I ever saw Fitzgerald, who almost immediately joined the IRA and, afterwards, held the rank of captain in the National Army. It was nineteen years later when I met Thomas Hughes. He was then a Catholic bishop in Nigeria.[7]

By a curious coincidence, the British military authorities put extraordinary measures into effect almost immediately after we left Listowel police barracks. Thus *The New York Times* of Saturday 10 July reported:

> For the first time since Easter week Dublin is practically surrounded by military pickets who are operating behind barricades, searching all inbound and outbound traffic.[8] These special measures, for what specific purpose is unknown, were initiated Wednesday night and have been intensified until now most of the principal roads to the city have

cordons drawn across them. Wherever the adjacent buildings have not been commandeered for the housing of soldiers, bivouacs have been hastily prepared for their accommodation. Each vehicle is stopped and inspected, carts piled high with agricultural produce exciting particular attention from the soldiers ...

Reports of 'extraordinary' and 'remarkable' military activity in many parts of the country, and particularly in and around Dublin, also appeared in the *Irish Independent* and *The Freeman's Journal* of 9 July, the former beginning its account with the headlines: 'Roads held by troops, Mysterious activities'. While the Dublin newspapers did not even guess the reasons for the unusual military activity, since no arrests were made, the special correspondent of the *New York World*, writing from London on 9 July, may have been near the truth when he wrote:

A grave revolt in the Irish constabulary is now in progress in County Kerry, where the rank and file absolutely defied their superiors and the military authorities, and this revolt is even said to spread to the head constabulary depot, at Phoenix Park, Dublin, causing the authorities in the last few days to close the park wholly to the public. This also accounts for the extraordinary military activity in and around Dublin, the closing of all roads leading to the city with barbed wire entanglements and the day and night patrolling of the roads. In Kerry's three principal towns, Listowel, Tralee and Killarney, the police openly repudiated the authorities several days ago, but no disciplinary action has yet been attempted ...

Both Viceroy French and Sir Hamar Greenwood rushed to consult Lloyd George here after this incident, French subsequently returning via Queenstown in a warship where he was furiously hooted on landing. Here evidently grave events are pending when the Castle attempts to discipline the refractory policemen. They plan first to surround the places where the police are revolting by large bodies of military with machine guns and artillery.

It seems that a partial explanation, at least, for the extraordinary military activity of those days was the fact that the British authorities credited Sinn Féin with causing the police revolt at Listowel. Moreover, it appears that they suspected that the five of us leaving the force suddenly might be a signal for Sinn Féin to attempt a second 'Easter week'.[9] In any case the intensive military activity continued in and around Dublin for some ten days after which the various barricades were again lifted.

When the four signatories to the Smyth statement had left the force, IRA headquarters, being only now convinced that the police mutiny was not an elaborate trap, made contact with the RIC at Listowel. As a result nine of the ten RIC constables who had taken part in the mutiny, and Constable Michael Lillis, all of whom we had left behind at Listowel, appended their signatures, at the request of the IRA, to our original statement, so that the truth of it was now attested by fourteen men, thirteen of whom had taken part in the incident.[10] This, seemingly, cleared the way for the document to be published. At any rate on the morning of 10 July, while I was still in bed, my sister brought me a copy of *The Freeman's Journal* and across the front page in heavy type I read:

Sensational Police Developments in Kerry

Refusals to Obey Orders

Fourteen Listowel Constables Stand Against Divisional Commissioner

Mr Smyth's Startling Speech

Police Threat of Bloody Resistance if Arrest Attempted

Statement by Disaffected Constables

Then followed word for word the speech as supplied by us to IRA headquarters through Father O'Sullivan. I actually jumped out of bed with excitement. Donovan and myself were almost too excited to read the news. In addition to the Smyth speech there was a splendid article on the incident by Robert Lynd, that fearless correspondent of the *Daily News*. The same edition also gave a full report of the British–Irish Labour Conference, then sitting in Belfast, at which the chairman, James H. Thomas, MP, severely criticised the British cabinet over the Smyth speech.[11]

BACK TO KESH

This exciting news left Donovan and myself completely bewildered and we took a walk through the fields so as to think the matter over clearly and plan our next move. We debated the question from every angle and found ourselves guilty of the following serious charges:

(1) Guilty, while servants of the crown, of disclosing and making public some of the secret plans of the security forces;

(2) Leaving the police force without giving notice, for which we left ourselves liable to severe penalties;

(3) Being in unlawful possession of firearms, namely, two Webley revolvers, same having been stolen from the British government;

(4) Spreading or attempting to spread sedition among His Majesty's forces and to cause disaffection therein, an offence punishable under the Defence of the Realm Act.

It should be mentioned, however, that the British government owed us over £7 each in pay and allowances which we did not wait to collect. We felt that this more or less balanced out the account against us for the two revolvers and we dismissed this particular charge against ourselves.

Realising that we could expect little mercy if we were picked up by the British security forces and that the people most adept at avoiding their clutches were the IRA, we decided to join the latter organisation.[12] We also decided to leave Glenamaddy at once, as word reached us that it was known to the RIC at Williamstown, a mile away, that we were at my father's home. Where to go, however, was a difficult question. For a radius of a dozen miles from my father's home the country was as flat as a tabletop. The fences were sod ditches and stone walls and there was neither hedge nor hillock which might be used for defence, attack or retreat. This may account for the fact that there was no active unit of the IRA in the area to which we might offer our services. Indeed, during the whole course of the Anglo-Irish War, no shot was fired in that peaceful district. It was obvious that there was no point in our remaining in the district. Eventually we made up our minds to go to Kesh, County Sligo, where we both started our careers in the RIC.[13] The main reason for our decision was that the hills and mountains in that region were well known to us and seemed to offer better prospects of concealment from the British security forces than the low, sod fences and stone walls of north-east Galway.

With all the roads, railways and bridges under British surveillance, we knew that it was not going to be easy to reach the Curlew mountains, sixty miles away. Initially we considered travelling cross country but finally decided to go openly by train. So that evening we bade goodbye to my parents and two young sisters, and set off on our journey. Fully armed police patrolled all the railway stations on the route, but we knew from experience that this was simply part of their routine duty. We knew that they themselves were passing through a period of confusion and that a crisis was upon them which was not of their making nor to their liking. I actually felt sorry for them and would have loved to tell them to come and join us. We passed station after station without incident, but we still had to face the ordeal of getting off the train at Ballymote which was the station nearest Kesh, our destination. We knew all the police at Ballymote and wondered what would happen when we got off there. At Boyle there were military as well as police and the train was delayed, while a good deal of questioning of passengers took place. This alarmed us somewhat and we intended getting off at the next little station, Kilfree, but here again there were military with the police, so we decided to continue on to Ballymote.

At last the great moment came when the train steamed into Ballymote station, and there on the platform were six armed policemen, all of whom we knew at a glance – Constables Ansboro, Beirne, Kelly, King, Madden and Sergeant Thomas Cunningham. There seemed to be no escape for us. We could not even think of a reasonable excuse for our presence there, above all places. And then an extraordinary thing happened. Sergeant Cunningham and his five men turned away and walked to the far end of the platform and showed not the least sign of having recognised us. We could hardly believe our eyes and we walked away and went down the town and called in for refreshments to Begley's public house at one corner of Main Street. There we were welcomed with open arms, and soon found ourselves in the centre of half-a-dozen members of the IRA who were delighted when we intimated to them our intention of joining the movement. We were taken by car to Kesh and spent the night in the home of Alexander (Alec) McCabe, TD,[14] where his mother and sister treated us like princes.[15]

The following night a social was held in the local hall at the foot of Keshcorran Hill and we were the guests of honour. Sentries were posted at the approaches to the hall and saluted smartly as we passed. As we entered the hall, a passage down the centre was cleared and a guard of honour brought smartly to attention as we walked towards the stage. When we reached the stage a cheer went up that echoed to the caves of Keshcorran Hill. For us it was a thrilling moment and one that we shall never forget. The band played the 'Soldiers Song' and all joined in the chorus.

It was seven years since I had left Kesh district, and some of the strapping young members of the IRA then present were only small boys when I left. Within the next twelve months many of those lads had distinguished themselves in various units of the Sligo Brigade under their courageous leader, William (Billy) Pilkington who later became a priest.[16] As I watched those young men dancing and making merry or taking turns at outpost duty, I could not help contrasting the crown forces I had just left and the group of men I saw before me. Backed by the world's largest empire the British forces at that moment held every stronghold and every outpost in the country. Moreover, the British army was fresh from a decisive victory in a great European war. Standing between the Irish people and this army were some 2,000 young men, many of them mere boys in their teens. Never in the history of the world, it seemed, were two armies so unequally matched. Yet, it was this nondescript army which forced the British to admit, in the words of Colonel Smyth, that 'up to this … Sinn Féin has had … the whip-hand'.

A rather amusing thing happened in connection with our visit to Kesh and Ballymote. I afterwards learned from Constable Madden of

Ballymote (one of the men who was at the station when we arrived and a man who did splendid work for the IRA during this period) that the RIC had instructions not to arrest us but to keep our movements under observation and to report all our activities. This simply bore out what we, in fact, discovered a few days after our visit to Kesh when the IRA stopped the mail train at Kilfree Junction in South Sligo. Among the mails captured was a file of correspondence dealing with our activities while in the district. I had the great pleasure of reading the file. The district inspector at Ballymote had written to all the sergeants in the Ballymote district asking for details of our activities. The replies were amusing and typical of the RIC of those days. Faked reports were sent in by sergeants whose districts we did not visit at all such as: 'Made discreet enquiries from a reliable source and ascertained that ex-Constables Mee and Donovan passed through here at about 6 p.m. on … but did not stop. They were travelling by car and were accompanied by two other men whose names my informant could not give. They were travelling in the direction of Boyle …' The head constable at Ballymote in a summary of the various reports wrote: 'I am satisfied that these men, finding themselves out of employment, are making contact with Sinn Féin with no other purpose than that of trying to secure employment. While in my district they conducted themselves very well, apart from making contacts with undesirable sources for the reasons stated.'

By this time the Listowel affair was attracting considerable public attention and, as there was a prospect of a full inquiry being held, we felt that we should go to Dublin where we could make personal contact with IRA headquarters. With Dublin surrounded by British troops and all passengers in and out of the city being held up and questioned, it was not easy to get there. Moreover, we knew that having got there it would be difficult to make the necessary contacts. We decided, therefore, to go on to Ballintogher, County Sligo, and contact my former teacher friends, Charlie McMorrow and Con O'Rourke, whom we suspected to be members of the IRA. With them I had often wished the downfall of the British chief secretary because he would not increase our salaries.

Now an opportunity to realise that wish by testifying at an inquiry into the Smyth address at Listowel seemed to be presenting itself. Thus the *Daily News* of 13 July reported:

Sir Hamar Greenwood, the Chief Secretary for Ireland, and Sir John Anderson, Under-Secretary at Dublin Castle, crossed over to England on Sunday, and the Police Commissioner concerned was invited to come to London to give his version of the affair. To a representative of the *Daily News*, who saw him at the Irish Office, Sir John Anderson said the Commissioner was an experienced officer with a distinguished military ... record, and, as his reputation was involved, it would be grossly unfair to form any opinion until he had given his explanation ... 'It is inconceivable that he made these statements but we will ask him what he did say,' said Sir John.

We went to Ballintogher and contacted McMorrow and O'Rourke who were very excited when we informed them of our intentions and felt that we had wasted valuable time already in not contacting IRA headquarters.[17] So the four of us got on the next train to Dublin.

It was a nerve-racking journey. The military and police seemed to be everywhere. Yet they seemed powerless to do anything other than swagger about brandishing rifles and revolvers, bullying passengers at railway stations and making thorough nuisances of themselves. At Broadstone station the confusion was indescribable. Between military and police and the passengers who got off the train there was barely standing room. All passengers were questioned and were given a 'rub down' by the military to make sure that they were not carrying arms. Personally I was 'rubbed down' at least five times before I got off the platform and twice I had to open my attaché case to show my pyjamas, comb and shaving kit, which was all that I carried. We hired a taxi and drove to the Hotel Gerard, 37–38 Harcourt Street.[18] The trip to the hotel was anything but a joyride – every minute seemed like an hour, but we got there without incident.

DUBLIN 'UNDER MARTIAL LAW'

Dublin 'under martial law' was a strange sight in those days. Even in between street ambushes, military activity was evident everywhere. At street corners people were being held up, searched and questioned by the military. Time and time again one saw groups standing with their hands elevated in the air while armed military interrogated and threatened them. Crossley tenders and armoured cars rushed through the busy parts of the city while pedestrians kept very much to the footpaths. People hugged the walls and kept off the roads where they were liable to be run down by recklessly driven military vehicles. The British army was at war with an army which they could not see, and they regarded everyone as a potential enemy. This attitude was more than justified by the situation. The ragged individual selling newspapers at a street corner might be an IRA Volunteer with a live bomb in his coat pocket. The apparently drunk passenger on a horse and sidecar might be an IRA officer on his way to join his company for an ambush on British troops, and even innocent-looking female passers-by might be carrying small arms from one place to another. It was all very unreal but very exciting. At the Hotel Gerard we met Alfred White who was an active member of the Dublin section of the IRA and was also in close touch with IRA headquarters.[19] That same evening Alec McCabe called to meet us and arranged for us to have an interview at headquarters on the following night.

In the meantime the debate in the British parliament on the 'Listowel affair' had begun on 14 July. The debate received detailed coverage in the Irish newspapers of 15 July and the British government was roundly criticised by much of the press for curtailing discussion of the affair.

I MEET MICHAEL COLLINS AND COUNTESS MARKIEVICZ

On the night of 15 July, Donovan and I, accompanied by our friends Charlie McMorrow and Con O'Rourke, went to meet members of the IRA headquarters staff. The meeting, which was held in the office of the Irish Labour Party at 32 Lower Abbey Street, was an informal one, and its object was to get from Donovan and myself first-hand information in connection with the Listowel police mutiny and, particularly, Colonel Smyth's address to the RIC on that occasion. It was a very mixed gathering and included Erskine Childers,[20] Michael Collins, Countess Markievicz, Alec McCabe, Thomas Johnson[21] and William O'Brien of the Labour Party,[22] Martin Fitzgerald and Patrick J. Hooper, managing director and editor of *The Freeman's Journal* respectively, as well as a number of others, whose names I cannot recall.

I had always imagined that the IRA leaders who were 'on the run' were in hiding in cellars or in some out of the way place far removed from the scene of hostilities. I was somewhat surprised, then, as I sat with some of these same leaders and calmly discussed the current situation, while military lorries were speeding through the street under the very windows of the room where our conference was taking place. As a matter of fact there seemed to be nothing to prevent anybody walking into that room and finding Michael Collins and Countess Markievicz cross-questioning two ex-policemen who were largely responsible for the aspect of the situation which was causing the British most anxiety at that time, and which probably led to the barricades then being erected around the city. The countess evidently enjoyed the little drama as she often afterwards referred to it as one of her unusual experiences.

During the course of the meeting we learned that a libel action was pending against *The Freeman's Journal* for, among other things, the publication of Colonel Smyth's speech. It also transpired that as a result of the publication of the Smyth speech the managing director and the editor of *The Freeman's Journal* had been arrested and some of the newspaper's printing presses had been smashed by British forces.[23] Fitzgerald, the managing director, was very naturally anxious to have all the details in connection with the Smyth speech and having questioned us in great detail suggested that we attend to give evidence on his behalf at the forthcoming court proceedings. We could only give evidence at the risk of our lives and told him so, and with this he seemed anything but pleased.

Collins and Countess Markievicz wanted a watertight case for the forthcoming British inquiry which the British government, through Sir John Anderson, the under-secretary, had promised. Colonel Smyth and the highest British authorities at Dublin Castle were consulting Lloyd George at the same time that we were conferring with Michael Collins and the leaders of the Labour Party. The Irish Labour Party had already got things moving. Every member of the British government had been supplied with a copy of Colonel Smyth's speech and the British Labour Party, backed by sections of the British press, were forcing the government to hold a public inquiry.[24] By this time our original statement of Smyth's speech bore fourteen signatures, ten of the signatories still serving in the force and prepared to back their signatures on oath before any tribunal. There was not a loophole in the damning evidence which we had against the British cabinet, evidence that would surely discredit Lloyd George and possibly bring down his government. Personally I was looking forward to travelling to London under armed escort as one of the principal witnesses against the British crown. What headlines we would get in the world press!

For at least three hours we sat there under a crossfire of examination. Although I fully understood and appreciated how important it was to have all the details for the inquiry, I will confess that at times I felt terribly annoyed and got the impression that too much importance was being attached to Smyth and too little to the fact that he was only the agent of his masters, the British cabinet. The question as to whether his name was spelled Smyth or Smith was discussed at length until Martin Fitzgerald, tiring of it, closed that part of the debate with a rude remark which forced Countess Markievicz to hold down her head and smile. All were agreed that Colonel Smyth was a scoundrel and I was again annoyed when it was suggested that his speech was the usual British military bluff. The 'sinking of a ship with lots of Sinn Féiners on board' was discussed, but again nobody was prepared to believe that the British government would be capable of committing such an atrocious outrage. Thomas Johnson alone believed that the British government was capable of doing this and he reminded the conference of what the British government did in South Africa during the Boer War. Johnson seemed to me to have the keenest grasp of the terrible situation then confronting the country. While the conference was fully convinced that Colonel Smyth did actually make the speech, as published, there was some doubt as to whether he had the sanction of the British cabinet and it was on that vital question that the whole case hinged. If the speech was of his own making the matter was simple enough, he would be removed from office and replaced by a more diplomatic but, perhaps, greater scoundrel. If, on the other hand, he was the spokesman of the British cabinet then the matter could not be got over so simply and the public inquiry would greatly discredit the British cabinet. That was the issue and it was on that note that the conference closed. All was now set for the big event and Donovan and I were instructed to hold ourselves in readiness for eventualities.

Looking back at my first meeting with Michael Collins I cannot say that I was impressed. As a matter of fact I was a good deal disappointed, as I had not heard of Collins before that night and I considered that the occasion demanded that we meet some of the leaders of the Irish Republican movement. Although Collins was minister for finance at that time, he was so youthful-looking that I had taken him to be a mere official from headquarters rather than an important figure. Even my schoolteacher friends knew nothing about him at that time and told me later that they were as unimpressed as I was. The way in which he asked questions and the manner in which he took notes were more characteristic of a civil servant than a military leader. And yet it was this civil service aptitude for collecting and correlating information that made him Ireland's greatest organiser of guerrilla warfare.

As I was to learn later, Collins had many qualities that made him the ideal Irish rebel leader. He was a young man of powerful, yet charming personality; he had almost unlimited energy; he was considerate towards those who shared his risks and was generous, almost to a fault. He was, by nature, an adventurer and was not afraid to face what to lesser minds appeared to be insurmountable obstacles. In a time of crisis a young leader with these qualities will always get an enthusiastic following and so it was with Michael Collins. Added to all this was his ability to get the very best out of those who came within the range of his magnetic personality. Although never actually minister for defence, it was to Collins and not to the minister for defence that the army in the field looked for inspiration, and that inspiration was always forthcoming. His motto was 'get the work done and never mind the details'. At that particular period there was, in effect, no unified command in the IRA, there being only a nominal link between headquarters and the units in the field. In districts such as Cork, Tipperary, Mayo and Longford there was a Barry,[25] a Breen, a Maguire[26] and a McKeon[27] who took command and carried on the struggle wherever and whenever possible. Whether things went well or ill, Collins saw to it that the Sinn Féin government accepted full responsibility for the actions of such local commanders.[28]

COUNTESS MARKIEVICZ

It was also the first time that I met Countess Markievicz. Although past middle age, she was still beautiful and every inch a lady. I had learned much about her background while stationed at Grange, which is convenient to Lissadell, the home of the Gore-Booths, at the foot of Benbulben where she was born and spent her youth. I had often visited Lissadell and saw her beautiful home, the pleasant gardens and the lovely silver strand on the Atlantic coast with the remains of an old pier, from which hundreds of Sligo men and women were sent into exile by the Gore-Booths in the bad old days. It was there that the countess was born in the lap of luxury and it was there that she became one of Ireland's best-known horsewomen. It was from Lissadell that she went to London to be presented at court and was then one of the most beautiful women in Europe. It was at Lissadell that she learned to love the poor and made her resolution to spend the rest of her life making reparation for the misdeeds of her forefathers by working for Ireland's poor and downtrodden.[29] For her part in the 1916 insurrection she was sentenced to death. She accepted the verdict and did not ask for mercy. Even the prospect of facing a firing squad could not force from her the one word that would have meant her freedom. Her sentence was later commuted to penal servitude for life.[30]

PROSPECT OF PUBLIC INQUIRY

On 14 July Thomas P. O'Connor, MP, raised the question of Colonel Smyth's speech in the House of Commons. He asked the chief secretary for Ireland what information he could give to the House with regard to a certain incident in Listowel police barracks and with regard to a speech alleged to have been delivered on that occasion by Divisional Commissioner Smyth. Sir Hamar Greenwood replied that he had 'seen Colonel Smyth' and had been assured by him 'that the instructions given by him to the police in Listowel, and throughout the division, were those mentioned in a debate in the House on 22 June last by the attorney-general for Ireland, and he did not exceed these instructions'. Mr O'Connor was not satisfied with this reply and asked, unsuccessfully, for leave to move the adjournment of the House to discuss 'the incident at Listowel police barracks and the remarks attributed to Divisional Commissioner Smyth as being calculated to produce serious bloodshed in Ireland'.[31]

Sir Hamar Greenwood's statement, however, placed the British government in a difficult position from which, it seemed, it could only extricate itself by permitting a public inquiry into the whole affair. So at this point, with all the evidence carefully compiled by IRA headquarters, and, no doubt, even more painstakingly collected by the British authorities, the stage seemed to be set for a full inquiry.

I had just received news from the Listowel garrison which was very heartening. It seemed that hundreds of messages of congratulation had been received in the barracks from all over Ireland, and from numerous Irish organisations in America and Australia. This was not surprising, as the world press had carried the story of the Listowel police mutiny. For instance prominence was given to Colonel Smyth's speech in most of the American newspapers, including the *New York American* (9 July 1920), *New York Evening Journal* (9 July 1920), *The New York Times* (10 July 1920), *New York Tribune* (10 July 1920), *New York World* (10 July

1920), *Gaelic American* (17 July 1920) and *The Irish World, and American Industrial Liberator* (31 July 1920). Some of these newspapers dealt with the case editorially, and in doing so left no doubt as to what they thought of the British administration in Ireland. The reaction of the Irish-American press was predictable, the editorial of *The Irish World, and American Industrial Liberator* of 31 July 1920 being fairly typical:

Plans for an Irish Amritsar Missed Fire [Misfire]

Frequently has the *Irish World* sounded a warning against a possible, nay, a probable, Irish Amritsar in Ireland in the near future. The publication of the address delivered by Chief Inspector of Constabulary Smyth, before a body of constables at Listowel on June [19], fully justifies our note of warning. Smyth, voicing the sentiments of his English employers, bade the members of the constabulary shoot down their fellow countrymen and women indiscriminately. At the same time he assured his listeners that they would not pay the legal penalty for the commission of these murders. It was a cold-blooded incitement to slaughter men and women of Irish blood guilty of loving their native land.

The Englishman, who urged the commission of atrocious crimes, had just come from London, where he had been in consultation with his English masters. He knew what they expected of him. He knew that he had a free hand. He knew that, if he employed the bloody tactics resorted to by the wholesale-murderer Dyer at Amritsar to terrorise the natives of India, he would not be held to any accountability by the British government. Emboldened by this assurance, Smyth used the plainest sort of language in his address to the members of the constabulary assembled in the Listowel barrack yard. In letting himself loose by revealing the policy he had been commissioned to carry out in Ireland, he forgot that he was speaking to the sons of Irish mothers. When he got through, Constable McNamee [Mee], [who was] one of them, reminded him of that fact in this manner 'I gather, sir, from your name and your accent, that you are an Englishman. You forget that we are Irish.'

We have before us a report of Smyth's speech written by Jeremiah

Mee, one of the constables for whom Sergeant McNamee acted as spokesman [*sic*]. The veracity of the report is attested by the writer's comrades in the constabulary squad assembled in the Listowel barrack yard to receive instructions as to how to massacre their fellow countrymen and women.

Most of Colonel Smyth's speech followed and the piece then continued:

Then followed some details as to how the constables should act in the event of a police barrack being burned or captured. Whenever that happened, they were to commandeer the best house in the neighbourhood. As to the inmates of the commandeered house here is the treatment prescribed for them: 'Let them be thrown out in the gutter, let them die there, the more the merrier.' While these Irish victims of police eviction would be dying in the gutter, the police themselves were to resolve themselves into bands of midnight murderers. They were told by Chief Inspector Smyth that the more men and women of their own blood they shot to death, the more favour they would win in the eyes of him, the imported Englishman who had been commissioned by his government to help stamp out in blood the movement for freeing the Irish nation from an alien yoke that weighed so heavily upon it, paralysing its energies.

Having given more details, the editorial concluded:

The bloodthirsty Smyth, not satisfied with this proof of how little value he set upon the lives of Irishmen, went out of his way to glory in the prospect of Irish political prisoners being starved to death if they should go on a hunger strike. We quote from his address delivered in the Listowel barrack yard: 'Hunger-strikers will be allowed to die in jail. The more the merrier. Some of them have died already, and a damn bad job they were not all allowed to die. As a matter of fact, some of them have already been dealt with in a manner their friends will never hear about. An emigrant ship will be leaving an Irish port in the near future with lots of Sinn Féiners on board. I assure you, men, it will never land.'

After reading these words, one cannot remain in doubt as to what sort of person this fellow Smyth was. His blood-thirstiness undoubtedly was his chief recommendation when he was selected by the English government to carry out its policy of terrorising Irish Republicans. That policy is outlined in an article which appears in the July number of the *National Review,* a London publication of extensive circulation. What Ireland needs, as viewed by her alien enemies, is thus stated in the *National Review:* 'The only hope for Ireland is to put some man of grit and determination, such as General Dyer [the Amritsar butcher], in Dublin Castle and give him a free hand. We believe that the mere announcement of such an appointment would prevent the necessity of doing any serious shooting, provided it was known he would be properly supported by his government.'

The *National Review* undoubtedly voices the views of Lloyd George's Tory followers who have the shaping of the Irish policy of the present British cabinet. There can be no doubt that an 'Irish Amritsar' was in contemplation. The language employed by Sergeant McNamee [Constable Mee] in the Listowel barrack yard, indicating as it did the unwillingness of the police to take a hand in massacring men and women of their own blood, and the subsequent fate which overtook the bloodthirsty scoundrel who urged them to do the massacring, unquestionably have had a great deal to do with preventing a repetition on Irish soil of the inhuman crimes perpetrated in India by the infamous Dyer whom the *National Review* would like to place at the head of Dublin Castle to teach the Irish people to submit tamely to the hideous wrongs inflicted upon their country by alien rulers.

'The fair name of England', about which J. H. Thomas, MP, showed such concern at the Belfast conference some days earlier, was now badly besmirched before the tribunal of world opinion. Even Lloyd George could not close his eyes to this. A public inquiry into all the details of Colonel Smyth's speech seemed the only way that the

British government could put an end to the extraordinary volume of unfavourable comment on the whole matter which continued in the world press.

Expecting at any moment to receive word of the inquiry, we remained close to the Hotel Gerard so that there would be no hitch in the arrangements. Our teacher friends, McMorrow and O'Rourke, remained with us and were a tower of strength to us during that anxious time. McMorrow was particularly helpful, as he was a keen follower of politics and well versed in the functioning of the British government. His dreams of a lifetime were beginning to take shape as he planned the downfall of the chief secretary for Ireland. It seemed to me that he had a complete grasp of the situation. And, unlike Collins and the others, he was convinced that Colonel Smyth was but the tool of an unscrupulous British cabinet, and that Lloyd George was the chief architect of the scheme for the intimidation of the Irish people.[32] To prepare Donovan and myself for the inquiry, McMorrow appointed himself counsel for the British cabinet and, with O'Rourke pretending to be the public prosecutor on behalf of Dáil Éireann, put Donovan and myself through a most gruelling cross-examination. This went on until we began to lose our tempers when McMorrow would remark: 'That is the very thing you are not to do at a Court of Inquiry.' Even while sitting down to our tea or taking a leisurely walk a new idea would come into McMorrow's head and the cross-examination would start all over again. The cross-examination would be followed by lectures on how we were to acquit ourselves before the tribunal. 'Remember,' McMorrow would say, 'you are up against an unscrupulous government that will stop at nothing to break down your evidence and you cannot be over-conscientious on small details. Lloyd George is the ablest man in Europe. See what he did to President Wilson and his "fourteen points".' For my own part I felt quite confident. Our case was simple and straightforward and I had the details at my fingertips. I knew the character of the other RIC witnesses. They had already been through severe tests and proved their valour and would do so again when the time came.

The stage seemed now to be well set for the big event. Then, on the morning of 19 July, we read in the *Irish Independent* the large headlines:

High Police Official Shot Dead in County Cork
Tragic Death of Colonel Smyth

The report went on to show that Colonel Smyth, who had just returned from his interview with Lloyd George, was sitting with County Inspector George F. W. Craig[33] of the RIC in the lounge of the Cork County Club when armed men entered the club and, accosting Colonel Smyth, said: 'Your orders were to shoot at sight. You are in sight now, so prepare.' Revolver fire was then opened and, despite two bullets in the head, one through the heart and two through the chest, Colonel Smyth managed to reach the passage of the club where he dropped dead.[34] Apart from County Inspector Craig, who was slightly wounded by a ricochet bullet, Colonel Smyth was without an escort, and neither military nor police were in the vicinity of the club when the shooting took place, and the men who did the shooting got away. Considering the fact that the colonel was a 'marked man', the failure to provide him with a bodyguard is difficult to explain.

We were stunned at the news of the shooting. With a watertight case prepared by IRA headquarters for an inquiry which could well bring down the British government the principal witness was shot and Lloyd George was once more able to face a hostile public and say: 'Now that my principal witness has been murdered by Irish rebels no inquiry can be held.'[35] And what about the unfortunate Irish members who now had to face an angry British parliament, while Lloyd George thundered his accusations of murder against them and 'their Irish assassins'?

My friend McMorrow had stated, in the event, somewhat prophetically: 'If Colonel Smyth does not agree to become a scapegoat Lloyd George and his cabinet will have to resign. However, at almost any cost, attempts will be made to save the British cabinet.' Colonel Smyth, in fact, refused to become the scapegoat even for Lloyd George, for we have the chief secretary's word for it that Colonel Smyth informed him that he had not exceeded the instructions given to him. Lloyd George, now faced with the prospect of an inquiry or showdown, acted as only Lloyd George could act, that is, in the most callous fashion. The fact that Colonel Smyth had been maimed during the Great War and that on his breast he wore a number of medals for bravery in defence of the empire counted for little now that the British cabinet had to be saved. After his interview with Lloyd George, Smyth was peremptorily sent back to Cork to 'regulate police duties for the Cork Assizes', which was the routine duty of the local district inspector. Considering the fact that nobody except the judge and police attended the Cork Assizes in those days it was a flimsy reason for returning a gallant officer to a highly dangerous situation. Perhaps Colonel Smyth's widow had that in mind when, on hearing of her husband's death, she said: 'My husband was a splendid officer, it is a pity that he had to die in such a rotten cause.'[36]

The Freeman's Journal of 22 July gave two interesting items of news. The first was a report of the burial of Colonel Smyth with full military honours at Banbridge, County Down. The second, underneath the first, was the version of Colonel Smyth's address to the RIC at Listowel, given to the House of Commons on 21 July by the chief secretary for Ireland. The report of this read:

> In the House of Commons yesterday, Mr Charles Palmer asked whether, in view of today's Irish debate, and having regard to the grave misconception which had arisen owing to the publication of an incorrect version of the late Colonel Smyth's speech to the police, he would have included in tomorrow's vote the order issued by Colonel Smyth on June 17 [19].
>
> Sir Hamar Greenwood said that, as the House was aware, it was not usual to publish orders issued by the police authorities, but, in view of the special circumstances of the present case, he would read the order, which had been signed by Colonel Smyth. It was as follows:

I wish to make the present situation clear to all ranks. A policeman is perfectly justified in shooting any man seen with arms who does not immediately throw up his hands when ordered (Tory cheers).

A policeman is perfectly justified in shooting any man whom he has good reason to believe is carrying arms and who does not immediately throw up his hands when ordered (Tory cheers).

Every proper precaution for the protection of the police will be given at inquests, so that no information will be given to Sinn Féin as to the identity or movements of individual police. This was ably managed by counsel at a recent inquest at Limerick.

I want to make it perfectly clear to all ranks that I will not tolerate reprisals. They bring discredit on the police, and I shall deal severely with any officer or man concerned in them.

Mr Palmer asked if the order read was not intended to stiffen and strengthen the morale of the constabulary in Ireland. The Speaker said that the chief secretary could not say what the intention was.

After reading this fabrication I was shocked at the thought that a man holding the position of chief secretary for Ireland could so demean himself by concocting such a misleading version of the dead colonel's speech.[37]

In the same day's edition of *The Freeman's Journal* another item, which was side by side with the two reports already referred to, showed the futility of sending Colonel Smyth back to Cork to 'regulate police duties for the Cork Assizes'. It was given under the heading 'Cork Grand Jurors. Two ex-Lord Mayors and an ex-Sheriff fined', and read:

When the City Commission and Cork Assizes were opened yesterday by Mr Justice Moore, ten out of thirty-two grand jurors did not answer. Of these, three had not been served, and fines of fifty pounds each were imposed upon the other seven ...

His Lordship said he understood a great many of the gentlemen he had fined held the Commission of the Peace. He would direct his

Registrar to send forward to the Lord Chancellor the names of those holding commissions of the peace who absented themselves, with a report of what happened.

Having referred to the various cases to go before them His Lordship said there were, unfortunately, three instances of murder by assassination in their city. On 11 May at Glanmire Road two policemen, Sergeant Garvey and Constable Harrington, were murdered, and on Saturday night last they had the awful murder of Divisional Commissioner Smyth.

From East Cork they had a very important case, in which eight men were charged with what was known as the Fermoy incident. When the long panel was called only three out of one hundred and thirty-seven petty jurors summoned answered their names, and two in addition were already serving on the grand jury.

His Lordship then had the panel called under a penalty of ten pounds when some twenty jurors were excused, and the remainder were fined the sums stated.

Some days after the funeral of Colonel Smyth, it was announced in the press that Captain Chadwick, stationed at Listowel, had resigned his commission in the British army.[38] This was the captain who received instructions to take over Listowel police barracks on 17 June. No reasons were given for the resignation of this officer but it is possible that the authorities were not pleased with his handling of the situation and felt that he should have taken over the barracks as instructed. Captain Chadwick was a fine type of British officer and another likely reason for his resignation was that, as an officer and a gentleman, he was not prepared to implement the policy outlined in Smyth's address and thereby discredit his uniform by staining his hands with the blood of innocent people.[39]

The chief secretary for Ireland told the British House of Commons that 'he would not tolerate reprisals which would bring discredit on the police and that any officer or man concerned in them would be severely dealt with'. However, this guarantee did not seem to have much effect on the British security forces in Ireland. So I was not surprised when, obviously on my account, my father's house was destroyed on 21–22 July. The incident was only too typical. While my parents and two younger sisters were asleep in their beds the doors were burst open and British troops fully armed and with their faces masked rushed in and dragged them out of bed.[40] In their nightclothes and shivering with the cold, they were lined up against a wall outside the house and several shots were fired over their heads until my mother collapsed from terror and cold. My father was then given three minutes to give my address. As I had no address at that time the demand was an impossible one. However, this seemed to count little with assassins who had come to spill blood. Through the intervention of one of the masked men, my father's life was spared.[41] Then the forces of 'law and order' got down to work. With spraying machines, which they had brought with them, they sprayed the dwelling house and out-offices with petrol. They then set fire to the house and out-offices. My mother was assaulted by one of the armed bullies when she tried to recover some clothes from the house. While the buildings were in flames, the troops amused themselves by firing volleys from their rifles in the air. A horse, a jennet, a sow, eleven pigs and all the fowl were burned to death. Our fox terrier bravely attacked the raiders and he died with a bullet through his heart. Having destroyed the farmhouse, animals, out-offices and furniture, they then set about burning hay, oats and all the farm implements, including carts and harness. By the time they had finished their night's work my parents and sisters were found sitting among the ruins of their home, attired only in their nightclothes, and so stunned that they did not quite realise what had happened. Colonel Smyth exhorted the police at Listowel to 'throw them out in the gutter, let them die there'. My parents did not die in the gutter, thanks to good neighbours.

This was but one of many similar incidents repeated all over Ireland during the next few months and was in keeping with the general policy outlined by Colonel Smyth in the dayroom of Listowel police barracks. Colonel Smyth might have gone to his grave but other 'Colonel Smyths' quickly took his place. In the three months after Colonel Smyth's death numerous homesteads throughout the countryside were burned and no fewer than 133 Irish towns and villages were sacked, shot up or partially destroyed by the forces of the crown.

11

WORKING WITH SINN FÉIN:
AUGUST–NOVEMBER 1920

TWO IMPORTANT INTERVIEWS WITH MICHAEL COLLINS
During the first few days of August 1920 I had two interviews with
Michael Collins, each interview lasting over two hours. The position
had deteriorated considerably from the Sinn Féin point of view since
our meeting in July. The British cabinet had succeeded in backing out
of the inquiry which it had promised into Colonel Smyth's address
at Listowel. British troops had consolidated their positions all over
Ireland. By then 7–10,000 ex-British soldiers had been recruited into
the RIC and were being housed in barracks throughout the country. In
the second half of July the Dublin Metropolitan Police had been armed
for the first time in the history of that force and were accompanying
British troops on raids in the city. Those, however, who, according to
Collins, posed the most serious threat to the IRA, were 1,200 ex-
British officers who had been recruited as 'policemen' and sent to
Ireland. They were organised into 'flying columns' and were provided
with fast-moving Crossley tenders, each tender being provided with
a machine-gun. This was the force which came to be known as the
Auxiliaries.[1] They were under the command of a war veteran, General
Crozier, who later resigned his commission in the British army because
of the atrocities committed by them.[2]

Importing ex-British soldiers and calling them 'policemen' was an
astute move by the authorities. Not only did it ensure a strengthening
of the crown forces in Ireland, but it also had a great deal of propaganda
value. For most British people the term 'policeman' reminded them

of their village constable who typified all that was best in the British administration of justice, so whenever one of these imported 'policemen' was killed, this fact was headlined in the British press and nothing was more calculated than this to inflame the British people against the independence movement in Ireland. This and the fact that, with the great influx of Black and Tans and Auxiliaries, the wolves were now mixed with the sheep, so to speak, in the RIC, were some of the difficulties then facing Michael Collins. I gathered that the latter caused him considerable concern. He gave me to understand that he received invaluable help from time to time from members of the RIC and he was then worried that what he termed 'friendly RIC men' now could be shot down with Black and Tans and Auxiliaries in ambushes.[3]

I shall always remember Michael Collins as I saw him at that time when the nation was held in the iron grip of British steel and when he had no clearly defined plan to meet it. His forces were scattered, ill equipped and few in numbers, and yet he was facing up to that terrible crisis with the coolness of a general who had the situation well in hand. The great influx of military during June 1920 had taken the IRA by surprise and there is no doubt that its object was to draw members of the IRA into the open where they would have been easily disposed of. Collins and his men, however, had other ideas, and refused to be drawn into open combat.

Despite the pressures on him, Collins did not hesitate to devote two hours of his time to a full discussion on the RIC and the unfortunate position in which they were now placed. He mentioned among other things that one could not hurt a member of the RIC without hurting a great many of one's own best friends. He invited me to give my opinions openly and without reserve, which I did. After our second discussion he asked me to draw up a memorandum on the RIC question as I saw it.[4] Soon afterwards I submitted the memorandum in which I recommended that something be done to cater for the men who had already left the force on patriotic grounds in order to encourage others to resign, that the Sinn Féin boycott of the RIC be eased and that IRA agents be appointed to make and keep friendly contact with members of the police force for the purpose of establishing a 'fifth column' within the RIC even at that late hour. I also recommended that Dáil Éireann should make a formal promise that the nation would stand behind the men who left the RIC on patriotic grounds.[5]

I AGAIN MEET COUNTESS MARKIEVICZ

Countess Markievicz, as minister for labour in the First Dáil, had her offices at 14 North Frederick Street, Dublin. It was there that I met her a few days after my second interview with Michael Collins. She was seated at her table writing rapidly while she smoked a cigarette, which was held in a very long holder. Having finished the note which she was writing she handed it to the office boy who was standing before her and instructed him to bring back a reply. She then rose from her chair, offered me a cigarette, which she lit with her own lighter, and walked over to the front window and looked out. 'Are you sure you were not followed here?' was her first question. I assured her that I was not and that I had carried out the instructions which I had received on how to approach the office. 'You cannot be too careful,' she replied, as she sat down beside me and began to discuss the political situation and especially recent developments. She asked me to repeat word for word Colonel Smyth's speech and all that had happened in connection with the incident at Listowel. When she learned that I had been stationed at Grange, County Sligo, she became very interested and while we smoked cigarettes we talked about the district around Lissadell which I knew almost as well as she did. It was lunchtime before she mentioned the object of our interview and then she only informed me that I was to call back after lunch, as she wished to discuss it with me. She scribbled a note on a scrap of paper and handed it to me. The note was addressed to Mrs Mary O'Brien of O'Brien's Hotel, 80 Parnell Street, and she advised me to put up there as Mrs O'Brien was a great friend of hers.[6]

Countess Markievicz, or Madame as she was affectionately known to her friends, believed in doing things in dramatic style. When we met after lunch she handed me a book, tied with green tape, and set about administering to me the oath of allegiance to the Irish Republic.

Standing to attention I held the book in my right hand, and with my left arm raised I repeated the words of the oath after the countess who also stood to attention. Having completed the ceremony of oath-taking she sat down, handed me another cigarette and said, 'Thank God at least one RIC man has taken an oath to the Irish Republic.' I afterwards discovered that the book was a book of poems by William Butler Yeats.

'Are you prepared to take service with the Irish Republic?' was her next question, and when I replied in the affirmative she explained what she had in mind for me. She said that she was setting up a bureau to cater for resigned and dismissed members of the RIC and DMP and that she thought I would be the right person to take charge of the bureau, as I would know and understand the needs of such men. Furthermore, it would give me an opportunity of making 'useful' contacts with the force. She had discussed the matter with Michael Collins with whom I was to keep in contact. I understood what she meant and gladly accepted the post which I realised was no sinecure but was highly dangerous work, since it meant 'spreading sedition among His Majesty's forces in Ireland'.

I was then introduced to the members of her staff, all of whom were selected from the ranks of the IRA, Cumann na mBan and Fianna Éireann, even down to the messenger boy who was a Fianna Éireann scout. Not alone was I not a member of any of these organisations, but I was fresh from the enemy camp. For that reason alone I felt that Madame was paying me a high compliment in accepting my services within her exclusive circle. The secretary of the department, Richard (Dick) Cotter, was one of a number of brothers who took part in the Easter Rising and had done terms of penal servitude in Frongoch and other jails.[7] Another member of the staff, Miss Lily O'Brennan, a member of the Cumann na mBan executive, had a number of responsibilities, including the running of an employment bureau for members of the IRA, removing 'wanted men' to safe surroundings and catering for members of Cumann na mBan who had been arrested and thrown into jail.[8] One measure of the high regard in which she was held within the movement was the fact that she afterwards accompanied the Irish delegates to London during the Treaty negotiations. Miss Moira Kennedy-Byrne, whose home at 61 Highfield Road, Rathgar, was one of the covering addresses of the department, was a tireless worker, and a particular friend of the countess.[9] But, in my opinion, the outstanding member of the staff was Eilís Ryan, a captain of Cumann na mBan and member of its executive, of which the countess was president.[10] It was Miss Ryan who always paved the way for my risky encounters with those members of the RIC and DMP whom I had to interview in the course of my work. It was she who, on one occasion, was successful in placing a member of Cumann na mBan as cook with the viceroy of Ireland, thereby forming a direct link between the Cumann na mBan executive and the vice-regal lodge.

AT THE 'MINISTRY OF LABOUR'

Our offices were situated at 14 North Frederick Street. Brass plates on the door stated Miss Annie Higgins, music teacher; S. Bowe, art studio; and J. Murray.[11] The offices consisted of a large flat on the second floor of No. 14, and in each of the front windows was a large sign which read 'Flat to let'. Apart from some tables, a number of chairs and a few pianos with music permanently displayed – so that in the event of a surprise raid the female staff could masquerade as teachers and students of music – there was little else in the offices. Two planks reached up from the garden to the back window of the second storey to enable the staff to make a hasty retreat if there was a raid. I can recall only one occasion when the planks were used. On that occasion an armoured car and two lorries halted opposite our offices and when we saw the military alighting we naturally assumed that our office was about to be raided. Like clockwork the whole staff disappeared down the planks to scatter in different directions and did not return until late that evening. We then learned that there was no raid and that the lorries had pulled up because of a mechanical breakdown of the armoured car which was conveying prisoners to Mountjoy jail.

The conditions under which the cabinet of Dáil Éireann worked in 1920–21 were almost unbelievable. Those ministers who were not in jail were on the run and had their offices in various places throughout the city, and yet, through messengers and agents, were able to keep up contact with all these offices and with the other departments of Dáil Éireann. In the period from August to November 1920 we had no fewer than three ministers for labour.[12] When Countess Markievicz was arrested on 26 September she was replaced by Joseph (Joe) McGrath[13] and when he was arrested on 26 November he was replaced by Joseph (Joe) MacDonagh[14] who managed to carry on until the Truce in July 1921.[15]

The 'Flat to let' sign proved very effective, as ours was one of the few Republican offices that was never raided by the crown forces. In addition to my other work I was appointed 'caretaker' of the flat and when prospective flat hunters called I had to interview them. The rent I then demanded would put to shame the worst profiteer of the present day, so that the prospective tenant generally never even got round to asking to inspect the flat, and when he did so I told him that it was not convenient for me that he should look over it on that day.

During the first few days in my new office I had very little to do. I had a room all to myself, as mine was a one-man department. The countess gave me a good deal of her personal attention and chain-smoked as we discussed the possibility of undermining the morale of the police force. She had seen and agreed with the memorandum which I had submitted to Collins regarding the RIC.

She seemed to be very pleased at having me in her ministry. At any rate during the next couple of months she introduced me to almost every visitor to her office. In this way I met most of the IRA leaders in Dublin at that time as well as many prominent IRA members from the country who visited the city from time to time. Her usual practice was to walk into my office with her visitor and casually say, 'This is Mr ... who is wanted by the police.' 'This is an RIC man from Kerry. Have you met him before?' She would then laugh heartily at the shock the visitor would get. On one occasion Joe MacDonagh, dressed as a priest, called at her ministry. He was a rather nervous type of man. She played out her little joke on him but, she told me some years later, he never forgave her for the shock he received.

Three years later, after she had attended a meeting in Sligo, she told me how I came to be employed in her office. After the first interview which I had with the Republican leaders and others at the offices of the Labour Party, Collins and herself differed as to whether I could be trusted. To prove her point, she offered to take me into her ministry, and promised that if I proved to be a spy she herself would shoot me.[16]

I was only eight days in my new job when I took a week's leave. I travelled down to Dromahair, County Leitrim, where I stayed in Jeiter's Hotel for a few days,[17] while Miss Anne (Annie) O'Rourke and I finalised the arrangements for our marriage in Ballintogher parish church. We were married on 16 August and after a two-day honeymoon I returned to my office in Dublin.

On the evening of my return Michael Collins sent word to me to meet him that night in an upstairs room in Michael Higgins' licensed premises at 38 Upper Abbey Street. I had been sitting in the room for about ten minutes when Collins bounced into the room accompanied by Alec McCabe. Collins immediately began to ask me questions about all aspects of the RIC. He took copious notes, which he checked and rechecked as the conversation proceeded. Eventually after about two hours he seemed to be satisfied that he had received all the useful information that I could give him on the RIC, he thanked me and left as briskly as he had arrived.

Some weeks after resuming work in my office, that is, early in September, the countess and I sent out a circular which attracted the immediate attention of the British authorities. The circular was addressed to all local bodies in Ireland and those who employed large numbers of men. It was signed by the countess as minister for labour and read:

A chara,

At the present time a large number of RIC have left the force owing to their repugnance to the outrages that are taking place and in which they are required to take part. Some of these men have narrowly escaped with their lives. In one case, in which I have the details, a man was dismissed for refusing to participate in sacking a town, and was fired at on leaving the barracks.

These men, whether they were dismissed for refusing to carry out instructions or whether they resigned as a protest, are now without any means of support.

I am addressing this to you as I believe you to be one who would object on principle to the outrages on the people that are taking place, and that you would view with horror the burning of creameries and homesteads, the burning and looting of towns, and the daily terrors which the people have to suffer from the callous shootings as a result of which so many have lost their lives.

In expectation of your being willing to come to the aid of men victimised because they would not allow themselves to be used for such work, I write to ask you to co-operate with me in finding work for these men, and I would ask you, if there are any vacant jobs under your patronage for which they would be suitable, to communicate with me.

The majority of these men seek employment as clerks, stewards, agents, motor drivers, etc.

Mise do chara,

Countess de Markievicz, Minister for Labour, Dáil Éireann.

Please reply to the Secretary, General Employment Agency, 61 Highfield Road, Rathgar, Dublin.

The response to the circular was not encouraging. Although many employers indicated that they were sympathetic to our aims, in fact we were not able to place any resigned men in suitable employment.[18] Yet the circular, or at least knowledge of it, seemed to have been effective in another way, as resignations from the force so increased that by November no fewer than 1,100 men had left the RIC and DMP in protest against British atrocities in Ireland.[19] I am convinced that at least treble that number would have left had serious efforts been made some months earlier to ensure the re-employment of such men. The circular was condemned by the British authorities as 'spreading sedition', and that it was having an effect was proved by attacks made on it by the British press. The circular was also roundly and repeatedly condemned by the government propaganda newssheet, the *Weekly Summary*.[20]

AN ATTEMPT TO TRAP ME

At the outset our bureau was kept busy and applications for jobs came pouring in from resigned and dismissed members of the RIC. Each applicant was given a form on which he supplied a number of details, including the date he joined and the date he left the RIC or DMP, and his number. In this way we were able to identify men who, from time to time, came up for interview. This was a necessary safeguard, as we had no doubt that the authorities would, at some stage, set a trap for us. I acknowledged all correspondence in my own name so that the resigned men would have confidence in the efforts that were being made to cater for them. I also dealt with correspondence to local bodies and to other employers. The result was that the police authorities were soon able to link my activities with those of the countess.

Towards the end of September 1920 two men in civilian clothes called at my father's home seeking information on my whereabouts. They informed my father that they were from IRA headquarters and that they had heard that I had been captured and was being held probably by the Black and Tans. They added that they had been sent by Countess Markievicz who was worried about me as she had sent me on an important mission a week earlier and that I had not since been heard of. My father, of course, did not know my address, and he actually suspected that the two men who called were not what they pretended to be. Within a few days I received a message from him, in a roundabout way, telling me of the visit. About the same time two men, possibly the same two, called at our covering address, 61 Highfield Road, Rathgar, and said they had a very urgent message for me. They gave their names as Thomas Hughes and John Donovan, two of the men who had left Listowel with me the previous July. Next day I was able to contact Donovan, who knew nothing whatsoever about the visit, and I knew that Tom Hughes was then a student in University College,

Galway.[21] These two incidents put me on my guard and afterwards I met ex-members of the RIC and DMP only after they had been vetted by Miss Ryan, who proved to be a splendid detective.

I INTERVIEW A DEPUTATION OF DUBLIN METROPOLITAN POLICE

As already mentioned, from the middle of July 1920 the Dublin Metropolitan Police had been armed and were accompanying the military on raids throughout the city. This constituted a very serious threat to the Republican leaders as most of them were well known to the Metropolitan Police.[22] Moreover, some members of the RIC were being sent to Dublin from various parts of Ireland to co-operate with the Dublin police in tracking down the better-known members of the IRA. As a result of this development members of the DMP were being shot and that force was rapidly finding itself in the same unenviable position as the RIC.

Early in October 1920 I received a message from Michael Collins informing me that I was to meet a deputation of the Dublin Metropolitan Police. Word had come to IRA headquarters that the Dublin police were dissatisfied with the conditions under which they were then working and that they were anxious to obtain certain guarantees from Dáil Éireann. I met Collins in an upstairs room in Higgins' of 38 Upper Abbey Street, where we discussed the matter. He indicated that I was to use my own judgement as to the time and place of the interview with the deputation. At first I did not like the idea of meeting members of the DMP, especially in view of the two efforts that had already been made to trap me, but Collins assured me that this was no trap and that the necessary precautions had been taken.

Back in the office I broached the matter to Miss Ryan who immediately set about arranging the interview. A day or two later she accompanied me to a small shop in Parnell Street,[23] where we met the deputation which consisted of three members of the DMP in plain clothes. In a small room, opening off the shop, we held our discussions. A member of the deputation explained that the Dublin police were very dissatisfied with the new developments and they were anxious to obtain guarantees from Dáil Éireann that, in the event of their refusing to carry arms, the shooting of members of the DMP would cease. I pointed out to them that their carrying of arms was only part of the trouble and that the IRA took a far more serious view of their accompanying the British forces on raids in the city. Provided they did not carry arms and that they ceased their activities against the IRA, I assured them that I was in a position to give them the guarantees they sought. I gave them a full outline of the unhappy position in which the RIC now found themselves. I impressed upon them that while there might have been some excuse for the RIC, who were scattered and unorganised, to have allowed themselves to be manoeuvred into this position, there was not the same excuse for the Dublin police, who could meet and stand together as a united body. Provided they stood together as an organised body and refused to do military work, I argued, there was nothing the authorities could do about it, and the IRA would treat them strictly as policemen and the shootings of Dublin Metropolitan Policemen would cease.

Two days after the interview, the Dublin Metropolitan Police held a meeting which their commissioner attended. By a unanimous vote they refused to carry arms or do military work, and from that day onwards not a single member of that force was shot by the IRA.[24] Moreover, not alone did the Dublin Metropolitan Police refuse to carry arms and do military work, but they refused to co-operate with the 'special' members of the RIC sent up from the country districts to 'spot' IRA activists.[25] Their action greatly eased the position of the IRA in Dublin. Michael Collins naturally was highly pleased over these developments and it was he who saw to it that the IRA part of the arrangement was kept to the letter.[26]

12

I RETURN TO KERRY:
24–30 OCTOBER 1920

DEVELOPMENTS IN LISTOWEL

It is now time to give some account of my comrades whom I left in
Listowel police barracks when I and the four others took our hurried
departure on 7 July 1920. It will be remembered that, when leaving, we
promised to keep in touch with our comrades. This I had endeavoured
to do, although the contact I maintained with them was, because of the
temper of the times, rather sporadic.

Among those whom we left behind were Constables Dolan,[1] Kelly,[2]
McNamara[3] and Sinnott,[4] four young men who before and during
the mutiny, and afterwards, showed a great measure of courage and
determination. During his entire time at Listowel McNamara refused
to carry arms, even a revolver for his own protection, and, for some
weeks before the mutiny, he, Dolan, Kelly and Sinnott refused to do
any military work or, indeed, to co-operate with the military in any way.
Eventually Kelly also had refused to carry arms and, with McNamara,
presented a kind of challenge to the authorities which they chose to
ignore.

A few days after our departure three lorry-loads of Black and Tans
and police arrived at Listowel from Limerick to take possession of the
police barracks. They announced their arrival in Listowel by firing shots
at random as they drove through the town. The RIC who replaced us
were specially selected, some of them having shown their determination
in the heroic defence of Kilmallock police barracks.

Soon afterwards the remaining mutineers in the barracks, save four, were transferred to other stations.[5] Those left in Listowel were Dolan, Kelly, McNamara and Sinnott. These had the satisfaction of reading a great number of congratulatory messages which poured into the barracks from all parts of the world after the publication, on 10 July, of the events surrounding the police mutiny.[6] Kelly and McNamara, it seems, were kept in Listowel barracks in order to be given special treatment by the Black and Tans. In any case they were invariably detailed to go with the Black and Tans on midnight raids which involved the burning of farm buildings, creameries and homesteads, and the beating-up and terrorising of civilians. Also, whenever policemen were required from the barracks for duty outside the Listowel police district Kelly and McNamara were always selected. In this way they spent some days at Limerick Junction where they and their comrade, Loughlin Dolan, refused to board and search outgoing trains. By an unhappy coincidence Kelly and McNamara were assigned to Cork city on 17 July where, some hours after they arrived at Union Quay police barracks to take up duty, Divisional Commissioner Smyth was shot in the County Club.[7]

During the course of my first interview with Michael Collins I mentioned the predicament of these men and asked for instructions as to what they ought to do. His advice was that they should remain in the force, try to form an 'underground' and make available as much information as possible about the security forces. I immediately conveyed this decision to them and Kelly, McNamara and Sinnott agreed to the suggestion, and a line of communication was established between them and me which remained unbroken for the next three months.[8] Week after week they sent on valuable information regarding the movement of troops, and also confidential instructions to the force, all of which I passed on to Collins.[9] It was dangerous work and would have meant the immediate death of these men had they been caught at it.

Towards the end of October I received word that Kelly, McNamara and District Inspector Flanagan of Listowel had been suspended and that Kelly and McNamara were awaiting trial by military court-martial.[10] Some weeks earlier Paddy Landers of Listowel, an officer in the IRA, had been arrested and the police found confidential police documents in his possession, and he was sent to await trial in Limerick jail.[11] I immediately suspected a connection between the two cases.[12] In my mind's eye I saw my two comrades facing a firing squad, so I at once sent word to Michael Collins that I wished to see him. That same night, in Michael Higgins' of 38 Upper Abbey Street, Collins and I discussed the case and it was decided that I should start for Listowel next morning. Collins felt that if I succeeded in reaching Listowel, and contacting the two men and a sufficient number of their comrades, it might be possible to use the sympathy of the Kerry RIC for District Inspector Flanagan and his two men to have the threat of a mass walkout made to the authorities. In any case it should be possible, Collins felt, to arrange for a getaway for the two men. At worst, he said, I could bring to the men awaiting court-martial an assurance that in any sacrifice they might be called upon to make they would have the sympathy and support of the nation.

I had no illusion as to the dangers involved in the journey on which I was going. I knew that since the Listowel mutiny the British had been busy convincing my old comrades in the RIC that I was a traitor, and that I could expect little sympathy from most of the men who had replaced me in Listowel should I fall into their hands.

JOURNEY SOUTH

I set off for Listowel next morning by train. It was fifteen months, almost to the day, since I had travelled south to Listowel from Sligo as a policeman. Now I was travelling there again, not as a policeman, but as an outlaw. Before I had travelled many miles, I felt that my luck was in. My only companions in the railway carriage were two cattle dealers on their way to a fair at Listowel. Cattle dealers as a class are very sociable and talkative, and my companions were no exception to the rule. They left me in no doubt as to where their sympathies lay, especially after the first stop where all male passengers were searched and questioned by military and police. As the train got underway after the first halt I hinted to my companions that I did not stand well with the British forces, and they immediately suggested that I pose as a cattle dealer on the same errand as themselves. They even gave me a new name, Brett, the name of a cattle dealer of their acquaintance. With my new name and new avocation, I felt a sense of security, and one of my new colleagues jokingly remarked that I should have brought a wisp of straw to chew, as it would have helped me to look the part of a cattle dealer.

As the train swept along, the many burned and blackened gables of creameries, barracks and private houses showed that the Anglo-Irish struggle was reaching a climax. At railway stations the rough handling of passengers by Black and Tans, Auxiliaries and police was infuriating. It made me sad to see the rapid deterioration that had taken place in the 'old RIC' in the space of a few months. I could not help noting that they no longer seemed to take an interest in their personal appearance. No longer did they display the well-creased pants, waxed moustaches, shining buckles and well-polished boots. Frustration was written on their faces. While their new masters the Black and Tans and Auxiliaries searched, questioned and bullied peaceful passengers, the 'old RIC' simply looked on with little interest in the work in hand. No longer did the senior member of the party take control as in the old days of police discipline. Now it was the wilder elements who took charge. This, so far as I was concerned, was all to the good. I knew that it would be easier to convince a member of the Black and Tans than an RIC constable that I was merely a peaceful cattle dealer.

As our train travelled south through Kildare, Laois, Offaly and then the 'disturbed areas' of Tipperary and Limerick, this seeming frustration on the part of the RIC made me confident that my mission would be successful. I felt that I would have no difficulty in contacting some of my former comrades who were still stationed in Kerry. Moreover, I was confident that I could persuade them to lead a united stand by the RIC in Kerry against their present unforeseen conditions of service.

With my mind filled with such optimistic thoughts, our train pulled in at Limerick Junction and we learned to our surprise that there was no connection for Listowel that day. To me this was a great shock as the last place where I wished to spend a night was Limerick, which was then headquarters for some of the most notorious ruffians in the Black and Tan force. It was at this point that my cattle-dealer friends proved to be most helpful. They had to get to Listowel that night at all costs in order to be in time for the fair, so we decided to hire a car to take us to Newcastle West, where we would get a connection for Listowel. This trip involved a cross-country run of thirty to forty miles right through the martial law area, during which we were held up, searched and questioned no fewer then ten times by British forces.

At regular intervals, barricades with barbed-wire entanglements were erected across the road and manned by British troops. This was the real war zone in the martial law area and nothing was allowed to pass without the minutest scrutiny. On a number of occasions I regretted my foolhardiness in undertaking such a perilous road journey, but there was no turning back and nothing to be gained by futile regrets. At each barricade we had to get out of the car, while, with numerous rifles pointing at us, we were thoroughly searched and questioned.

At Rathkeale I came under the suspicion of some members of the RIC and was taken into the police barracks for questioning. Inside the dayroom my mind was a whirlwind of past memories. The rifles on the rack, the belts, batons and forage caps hung on the wall were reminders of other days. My mind also registered the fact that it was here at Rathkeale that two of my former comrades, Sergeant Neazer and Constable Doyle, had been shot by members of the IRA the previous March. At least a dozen police and Black and Tans were present during my very severe cross-examination and the least mistake on my part would have spelled disaster to my plans, not to speak of the consequences to myself. During the interrogation the two cattle dealers were brought into the dayroom and verified that I was well known to them. In addition they objected to being detained and running the risk of missing their train at Newcastle West. Eventually whatever suspicions the RIC had were allayed and we were allowed to go on our way.

This was by no means the end of our troubles. At all the roadblocks between Rathkeale and Newcastle West we had to go through the same searching and questioning procedure. We did manage, however, to reach Newcastle West an hour after dark and just in time to catch the train to Listowel. Darkness can be a greater enemy than daylight to the man on the run, especially when he is travelling by train. The person on the dark platform can have a full view of a passenger, without himself being seen. As the train trundled through the dark night I knew that at each wayside station unseen eyes would be keenly scrutinising me and the nearer I drew to my destination the greater were the chances that I would be recognised, perhaps by a former comrade.

BACK IN LISTOWEL

I felt genuine fear on that cold, dark night as the train crawled slowly into Listowel station and I saw on the platform six fully armed policemen, two of whom I knew and who would recognise me. Slowly, very slowly, the train moved past the six policemen and stopped dead when the compartment I occupied was less than ten paces beyond them. My heart practically stopped with the train. There on the platform they stood in a group scanning the passengers as they alighted from the train. Cold with fear I thought that this was the end so far as I was concerned. I was unable to think or make up my mind what to do. Again my two cattle-dealer friends came to my rescue. Realising my predicament, they practically lifted me bodily from the seat and, without a moment's hesitation, flanked me into the stationmaster's office, which was directly opposite the compartment where I sat. There I was pushed into an inner room, off the office, and cautioned not to move until called for. They departed immediately leaving me in complete darkness. Although we had been travelling together all day, they had not asked for my name nor had I asked for theirs. They left me so suddenly that I did not even have time to thank them for all they had done for me.

There I stood in the dark room afraid to draw my breath for what appeared to be a full hour, but which in reality was no more than ten minutes. Then I was visited by a porter, carrying his lantern.[13] He was evidently well-posted by my two friends, for he marched in swinging his lantern singing a little ditty of a song. He asked no questions but simply told me that the coast was clear. I felt that some explanation was due to this discreet porter and, when I revealed my identity, he became quite alarmed.

Father Charles O'Sullivan had proved a worthy confidant during the mutiny and now my first objective was to go to the parochial house, where I hoped to meet him. On the advice of the porter, I took a circuitous route through the fields, as it was too risky to proceed directly through the town. The porter in fact accompanied me to within sight of the parochial house and there he left me with a fervent prayer for my safe journey. Father O'Sullivan was not at home when I called and I was very disappointed.

I then thought of another great friend, Paddy Breen, publican, of Church Street.[14] To get to Breen's from the parochial house meant walking practically the whole length of the town. It also meant that I would have to pass the police barracks. I decided that there was no alternative but to walk straight to my friend's home. Before I had proceeded 300 yards I found myself heading directly into the police patrol, to avoid which I had gone to so much trouble at the railway station. As I drew near their attention was suddenly attracted by two young men who had been walking in front of me on the footpath. While members of the patrol questioned these men, I walked past without looking to the right or left.

When I entered Breen's public house, which was near the police barracks, I could hardly believe what I saw. The bar was crowded with Black and Tans and members of the RIC, singing and carousing and evidently in good humour. I turned left and leisurely opened the door leading into the hall from the bar. I quietly closed the door and went upstairs to the front drawing room, which was empty and in darkness. I sat there for at least ten minutes to compose myself. When I rang the bell Miss Mary (May) Breen came along and, not knowing who I was or how I got into the drawing room, was first inclined to raise her voice in protest before I could make myself known to her.[15] When she realised who I was she drew the blinds and went off to fetch her father who gave me a hearty welcome.

Soon I had the whole Breen family around me and was sitting down to a meal, my first in over twelve hours. When I had finished eating, I was joined by James Crowley, TD, and two or three local members of the IRA.[16] I intimated to the latter that I was particularly anxious to meet my former comrades, Kelly and McNamara, and also my friend, the former general secretary of the Police Union, Thomas J. McElligott, whose home was at Duagh, near Listowel. One of the IRA men disappeared and returned within twenty minutes with McElligott. Later we were joined by Kelly and McNamara who had been given notice of their dismissal.

I also sent word to District Inspector Flanagan that I would appreciate his coming to meet me and giving me an opportunity to talk to him. At that time he was suspended from police duties and was staying at Moran's Hotel in Church Street where he, also, was awaiting his dismissal. He declined my request and sent back a warning that I should leave Listowel at once because if I were arrested I would be shot like a dog and would get Kelly and McNamara shot also. I understood his reluctance to have anything more to do with me. He had already done more than one man's part and was the one and only district inspector in Ireland who had gallantly stood by his men and had thereby sacrificed his position and his future. He was dismissed a few days later.[17]

Without the district inspector, then, I opened a discussion on the possibility of establishing an 'underground' within the RIC. I was under no illusion as to the difficulties involved in such a venture. The fatal shooting of the two policemen at Soloheadbeg had opened a gulf between the Sinn Féin movement and the RIC and subsequently the gulf had grown wider. Sinn Féin itself, on the one hand, and the British government, on the other, were responsible for this development. Almost from its inception Sinn Féin had adopted a policy of hostility to the RIC. Then in April 1919 a decree was passed by Dáil Éireann advising the Irish people to ostracise members of the force. Not alone were the police themselves to be treated as outcasts, but also their wives and children. In particular no contacts were permitted between members of the IRA and the RIC. This brought its own disadvantages to Sinn Féin, for members of the IRA who might have done good intelligence work by being in contact with friendly RIC men were debarred from attempting it, lest they themselves might be branded as spies. Furthermore, by this time, some 1,100 members of the RIC, many of them with families, had left the force, and the efforts of Sinn Féin or the sympathisers of Sinn Féin to find alternative employment for them had, on the whole, been dismally unsuccessful.[18] This was in marked contrast to the case of railwaymen and other workers who had lost their employment because of national sympathies. A sum of over £100,000 had been collected to help these and their families.[19] Added to this was the fact that some members of the RIC, who were prepared to back, at least tacitly, the IRA during the previous June and July, had since received injuries, and some had died at the hands of that organisation. For instance, one of the Listowel mutineers, who had been most outspoken in his opposition to the policy of the British authorities during the mutiny, was now in hospital suffering from wounds which he had received when on patrol near the new barracks to which he had been transferred.[20]

The British authorities, on the other hand, had been quick to take advantage of these developments. Increases in pay and rapid promotion became the order of the day for the RIC. A special newssheet known as the *Weekly Summary* was issued and supplied free to every police barracks in Ireland. It had the sanction of the chief secretary for Ireland and was nicknamed 'Sir Hamar Greenwood's *Weekly Summary*'. It pictured the IRA as a band of cut-throat murderers whose main object was the murdering of policemen. Also, week by week, this paper gave a most depressing picture of resigned policemen walking about unemployed and practically hungry, and still ostracised by the people. Almost every week I came in for special attention and was alleged to have a very comfortable position with Countess Markievicz, while the dupes, whom I had betrayed, were left to starve. It was stated again and again that I was a deserter from the force and was now plotting its destruction with a woman who had murdered several policemen in Dublin during Easter week.

In these circumstances, then, it is not surprising that I was not encouraged from any quarter to attempt to establish an underground within the RIC. The general feeling was that the opportunity for doing so had been lost some months previously.

Kelly and McNamara, however, informed the meeting that there was a great deal of discontent in most police barracks, notwithstanding the best efforts of the British authorities. This arose mainly from constant disagreements between the 'old RIC' and the Black and Tans, and, although these two forces were compelled to live together, the meeting was assured that they were never likely to coalesce and work in harmony.

I was very impressed by the courage and determination of Kelly and McNamara. They had been fighting a losing rearguard action for the past three months. Although now definitely cornered, they were still full of fight and would not hear of making good their escape when I suggested this to them. They preferred to see the matter through to the last and, to quote McNamara, stated: 'If all goes to all we shall go down fighting and feel proud of it.'

It was well after curfew when the meeting broke up. Then those attending it slipped out through Breen's back door into the 'backway'. I retired almost immediately. As I lay in bed in the shadow of the RIC barracks many thoughts, pleasant and otherwise, crossed my mind until I fell asleep from sheer exhaustion.

It was far into the next day when I was awakened by the lowing of cattle at the fair of Listowel.[21] My mind turned to my two cattle-dealer friends who were out there somewhere trying to make bargains with farmers from all over North Kerry. I stayed in bed for most of the day and that evening I left Listowel to visit some of my former comrades at Tralee and Killarney.

I arrived back in Dublin after four days. I can still picture the pleasant face of Michael Collins when a week later I presented my written report and he sat there listening to my account of adventures in the not-too-sunny south of those hectic days.

When I had finished telling him of my experiences he suggested that I should go to the US and give evidence concerning the Listowel police mutiny before the American Commission of Inquiry into Conditions in Ireland.[22] He argued that having me, the spokesman of the mutineers, before the commission would be of great propaganda value. However, I declined on the grounds that if I went to the US all the valuable contacts which I had developed with serving and ex-members of the RIC could be lost. Moreover, I pointed out that I had just recently been married and my going to the US could involve my being separated from my wife for quite some time. Collins, whom I always found to be most reasonable, accepted my points. He then asked me who I considered should go and I suggested Kelly and McNamara.

FINAL CURTAIN ON LISTOWEL MUTINEERS

Constables Kelly and McNamara left Listowel police barracks on 1 November 1920. Although they had carried out valuable intelligence work for Michael Collins since June of that year, the only charge which the British authorities had been able to bring against them was gross insubordination.[23] On this charge they were tried on 15 October and were sentenced to be dismissed from the police force, the dismissal becoming effective on 1 November. Their superior, District Inspector Flanagan, was retired about the same time. The charge against him was 'lack of discipline'.

In January 1921 the parochial house (presbytery) in Listowel was raided by a party of Black and Tans. In the raid the original report of Colonel Smyth's speech, as supplied to IRA headquarters, was discovered. The report bore the signatures of the fourteen constables who had mutinied, including six who were still in the force, one of whom had actually been promoted in the meantime. These six were called to Dublin Castle and presented with the document which bore their signatures. On acknowledging their signatures, they were instantly dismissed.[24]

MICHAEL KELLY AND JOHN P. McNAMARA

In the meantime Kelly and McNamara reached the US whither they had been sent by Michael Collins.[25] On their arrival in New York they were met by Michael Kelly's brother, John, and an Irish-American millionaire, named Thomas A. Broderick,[26] and were taken directly to 156 Olive Street, New Haven, Connecticut, where John Kelly had lodgings.[27] Something of the difficult and dangerous nature of the situation of Kelly and McNamara can be gathered from the fact that some days later they were both badly beaten in these lodgings by a group of Mayomen who resented their former membership of the RIC.[28] After about three weeks they returned to New York and met Harry Boland, Sinn Féin's representative in the US. Then at Waterbury, Connecticut, on 14 February 1921 they began a speaking tour of that state[29] on behalf of the AARIR.[30] On 7 March, while back in New Haven, they signed affidavits describing conditions in the Listowel area. These were incorporated as Appendices E and F in the interim report of the American Commission of Inquiry into Conditions in Ireland which was published later that year. In their statements they verified on oath the account of Colonel Smyth's speech as given by us to IRA headquarters and later published in the press of the world. They also testified to their own personal experiences of British oppression in Ireland for the four months July to October 1920. They reported how, prior to June 1920, Listowel was one of the most peaceful towns in Ireland and was free from crime of any kind. They told how the Black and Tans announced their arrival in that peaceful town by firing shots at random through the streets.[31] They told how a seventeen-year-old chemist's apprentice from Carrueragh, Knockanure, named Timothy (Tim) Stack, was brought into the police barracks and kept there for two days during which time he was beaten and kicked, and finally released without even the shadow of a charge being preferred against him.[32]

In his submission Kelly stated that after he was suspended on 15 October he was taken out as a hostage by the Black and Tans on a midnight tour of terror and arson which he described as follows:

The Black and Tans first visited the home of Jerry Sullivan of Inch, about ten miles from Listowel. There they dragged from his bed Patrick O'Sullivan and beat him severely with clubs, rifles and fists, kicked him in the face and on the body and left him severely wounded in the yard. When his sister protested they grabbed her and cut off her hair and threatened the parents that they would be killed if they did not get back into bed and make no outcry. From there they went to the home of McElligott at Lixnaw. They dragged his two sons out of bed and beat the boys until they were nearly dead. From there they went to the home of Grady, searching for the young man of the family. While they were breaking in the front door, young Grady escaped through a back window and ran across the fields. Members of the Black and Tans ran after him but they were unable to catch him. They then returned to the house and dragged out of bed a young man who was working on the place and beat him severely. Young Grady's sister raised an outcry and they grabbed her and cut off her hair. From there they went on to the home of Lovett and pulled out the young man in his night clothes and dragged him along the road by his hair. They beat him and kicked him severely, and when his mother and sister cried out in fear, they fired two shots in the air and told them that they would be killed if they did not get back to bed and keep quiet. Then they grabbed the sister and cut off her hair. From there they went on to a co-operative creamery at Lixnaw, the largest creamery in north Kerry. They broke in the door, stole 1,000 pounds of butter, and sprinkled gasoline over the walls, floors and machinery and set fire to the place, completely destroying it. From there they returned to the barracks at Listowel, arriving at about five o'clock in the morning. No questions were ever asked of them by their superior officers, and no investigation made by the authorities.

Kelly also described how one night at the end of October ten Black and Tans went to the home of James Houlihan of Ballyduff, where members of the party dragged Houlihan's son from bed and shot him dead in the yard, after which they stabbed his body with their bayonets. On the same night, it seems, these Black and Tans burned six houses in the village of Ballyduff, and when they returned to barracks at eight o'clock next morning they were not asked any questions by their superior officers.[33]

First-hand evidence of men like Kelly and McNamara made inevitable a verdict from this important commission holding Lloyd George and the British government responsible for many of the atrocities committed in Ireland during that period. The chairman of the commission, Francis P. Walsh, devoted two full pages of his summary of evidence to Colonel Smyth's speech and closed his case against the British government with this remarkable passage:

> The history of the last three months of 1920 is one well known to the commission through the testimony of eye-witnesses and expert English investigators. It is needless, therefore, to reiterate what is already contained in the commission's records. The burning and sacking of farms, creameries, private houses and even great cities like Cork; the complete destruction of the economic and industrial life of the nation; the raids upon cathedrals, convents and institutions of learning; the murder of two priests under circumstances of the utmost brutality; and finally the murder of a woman (Mrs Ellen Quinn) with a child in her arms and another about to be born, justified by Sir Hamar Greenwood as a 'precautionary measure'; all these are matters which directly or indirectly have been brought to the attention of your Hon. Commission. *They are the circumstantial evidence which proves that Divisional Commissioner Smyth outlined to the policemen of Listowel barracks the official policy of the British government in Ireland.*[34]

I felt that this last passage was not only a tribute to the quality of the evidence submitted by people like Kelly and McNamara to the commission, but also a full justification for the action of the Listowel mutineers.

Although in giving first-hand accounts of some of the activities of the crown forces in Ireland Kelly and McNamara did a great service to their country, this was more than equalled by their campaign throughout the state of Connecticut on behalf of the movement for Irish freedom. Some concept of the value of their efforts in this regard can be gleaned from the following letter to the Committee of Inquiry into Resignations from the RIC, which was established by the Irish government on 24 January 1934:

109 Fairlawn Avenue,
Waterbury,
Connecticut,
29 March 1934.

To whom it may concern:

The following statement of facts is made so that it may be a matter of record how I feel about the services rendered to the cause of Irish liberty by two members of the Irish constabulary, Messrs. McNamara and Kelly, who mutinied at Listowel, County Kerry, during the Black and Tan regime.

Being a native of Lisselton, County Kerry, which is a suburb of Listowel, I had heard a great deal about McNamara and Kelly long before they arrived in the United States. Glowing reports came to me from my relatives, who stated that the service rendered by these men was the greatest uplift to Irish morale since 1916. It was my pleasure to meet McNamara and Kelly when they landed in New York. The delegation was led by Harry Boland, who paid a never-to-be forgotten tribute to them. I saw McNamara hand an envelope to Harry Boland which Harry told me later was a message from Mick Collins, and was of great importance. A little while later McNamara and Kelly were carried on the shoulders of men to a waiting automobile.

After a few days in New York Kelly and McNamara reported to me in Newhaven, Connecticut. I was State Secretary of the American Association for the Recognition of the Irish Republic and arranged speaking engagements for them throughout the State. In many instances the hall was so packed that we had to enter through the fire escapes. Thousands of dollars were raised for Ireland through their efforts. Their words carried great weight. Banquets were tendered them by many organisations devoted to the cause of Irish liberty.

About two months after their arrival, I had occasion to go to New York City to see Harry Boland and I heard Harry lament the fact that instead of denying the right of young men in Ireland to join the R.I.C. every effort should have been made to at first organise them, and have each and every one of the young men swear allegiance to the flag of Ireland. After this had been accomplished, they should have been allowed to enlist in the R.I.C. Of course he made it explicitly clear that he meant young men of the McNamara and Kelly calibre. He envisioned that overnight every police barracks in Ireland would be in the hands of the Irish Republican Army, with little or no bloodshed.

I have personal knowledge that after McNamara and Kelly gave evidence before the American Commission on Conditions in Ireland they volunteered to return to Ireland to further serve their country.

It was amazing the tremendous interest their presence in Connecticut created in our battle for recognition of the Irish Republic. It is a matter of record that membership in the AARIR increased by thousands and we found it difficult to obtain a hall large enough to accommodate the throngs who wanted to attend their meetings.

They were received officially by the mayors of all the large cities, and by dozens of first select men of smaller towns. I was present at all of these functions and the esteem in which they were held is difficult to describe.

My own personal observation is that McNamara and Kelly did more to promote the cause of Irish liberty in the United States, through pages of publicity and personal contact, than any mission that ever reached our shores to plead Ireland's case. I feel personally indebted to these men for the help they gave me in carrying to the people of Connecticut Ireland's message. They deserve the gratitude of every Irish man and woman of this generation and should be a beacon to future generations of Irish men and women in their battle to free our land from the slavery imposed by English tyrants.

God bless them always,
John P. Barry.

13

My Travels in Britain:
23 November–20 December 1920

As I sat with Michael Collins in an upstairs room in Michael Higgins', 38 Upper Abbey Street, Dublin, on the night of 22 November 1920, I had grim forebodings of the future. Outside the sound of rifle and machine-gun fire was mingled with the rumbling of military lorries as they were driven furiously through the streets. There were few pedestrians out that night and even in their homes people felt far from safe. On the previous day, appropriately named 'Bloody Sunday', fourteen British secret service officers were shot by the IRA. That same afternoon, while attending a football match at Croke Park, Dublin, fourteen civilians were shot and a great number wounded as a reprisal by British troops.

I recall 'Bloody Sunday' quite clearly as it was only through good fortune that I missed meeting the vengeful crown forces on two occasions on that fateful day.[1] At that time my wife was staying with me at Fleming's Hotel, 32 Gardiner Place. On our way to a late Mass on the morning of 21 November we saw a large sign outside a newsagent's shop which read: 'Fourteen British officers shot dead in Dublin'. I could scarcely conceal a feeling of tension from my wife, as I expected that pretty drastic reprisals would be taken by the crown forces to avenge their comrades. Moreover, at the request of Michael Collins, I had already agreed to travel to England with a despatch on 23 November, and I realised that security at the exit and entry points to the country would probably be tightened as a result of the latest shootings. After lunch my wife and I decided to spend the afternoon at Croke Park.

When we had walked about halfway to the park my wife expressed a wish to go to Howth rather than to the football match. We doubled back to the city centre and took the tram to Howth, thereby missing the tragic attack by the crown forces on those attending the match in Croke Park. At Howth we met some friends, who were staying at the Hotel Gerard, 37–38 Harcourt Street. They strongly advised us to transfer to their hotel from Flemings, which, they said, would very probably be raided as a result of the latest flare-up.[2] On our return from Howth my wife and I made the transfer, and only an hour later Fleming's Hotel was raided.

MAKING CONTACT IN LONDON

On 22 November I received from Michael Collins my final instructions for travelling to London on the following night with an urgent despatch for Seán McGrath,[3] general secretary of the Irish Self-Determination League of Great Britain.[4] My errand was necessitated by the fact that certain plans made by some members of the League had to be cancelled because copies of them had just been captured by the British troops in a raid in one of the IRA offices in Dublin.[5] The first national convention of the Irish Self-Determination League was due to take place at Manchester five days later, Collins told me, and it was important that the general secretary of the League be in possession of the despatch before going on to the Manchester meetings where over 1,000 delegates from England, Wales and Scotland were expected to assemble.[6]

Collins also informed me that he was sending me on this mission because I had been so successful in getting through 'martial law' areas on previous occasions, and also because of my military appearance, which he maintained was the best passport for a trip across the Irish sea, as lots of military would be crossing in the same boat. 'What happened to your little moustache?' was his very first question, when we met. I explained how the countess had insisted on my removing it because it gave me a military appearance. 'Be damn to her,' he said, 'she should know by now that a military appearance is the best disguise for our men at the present time.' He then proceeded to give me detailed instructions on how to prepare for the journey. 'Your most important requirements are a new pair of spats, a box of the best cigars, a walking stick or cane and a good crease in your pants. Hire a taxi to the boat and get there just on time so that you will not be too long waiting before the boat sails. Get into friendly chat with some of the military officers. You can do this by passing round your cigars and even if they do not smoke cigars it will at least be an introduction and will save you being questioned or searched. That is how I get across myself and you should have no difficulty if you keep your head screwed on.'[7]

He gave me an address in Dublin to which I was to communicate in case of an emergency, but not otherwise. This was a covering address for Joe McGrath, then acting minister for labour in Dáil Éireann. I memorised the address and was then given a small slip of paper on which Collins had written: 'This is to introduce bearer who will explain. Mick.' I concealed the private despatch on my person according to instructions.

On the night of 23 November 1920, disguised as a military-looking gentleman and complete with white spats, a nice cane, kid-gloves, well-creased pants and smoking an expensive cigar, I left Barry's Hotel, at Great Denmark Street, and walked to the corner of Gardiner Place where I hired a taxi and set off for the North Wall to catch the boat at eight o'clock. Armed pickets were posted at almost all street corners and did not take the slightest notice of me as I was driven past. Military lorries and swarms of British troops were at the quayside, and passengers were being searched and questioned on the boat. At the top of the gangway my eye caught a group of four officers, standing apart and chatting. I made a beeline for the four officers, made some casual remark and passed round my cigars. Only two of the four accepted, but it was a sufficient introduction and enabled me to keep up a rather disjointed conversation until the boat moved out and I was neither searched nor questioned. I offered a silent prayer for Michael Collins and marvelled at his knowledge of the British military.

The following morning in London I stayed on in the hotel, where

I had breakfast, until about ten o'clock when I set out to contact Seán McGrath and deliver my despatch. As this was my first visit to London, finding McGrath, I realised, was not going to be as easy as I had anticipated. Moreover, I did not wish to attract attention by making too many inquiries. Eventually, however, I got to the address and I knocked on the door which was opened by a small, white-haired woman who informed me that she was caretaker of the premises and that Mr McGrath had left there three months earlier. She had no idea, she told me, as to where I would find him as he had left before she became caretaker. Having some experience of the caretaking business in my own office in Frederick Street, Dublin, I felt that the good lady knew more than she was prepared to admit. Her only reaction, however, was one of alarm when I informed her that I had an urgent message for Mr McGrath from a friend of his in Dublin, and she only became more anxious to get rid of me. I was terribly disappointed, being now without a contact in London.

As my conversation with the caretaker was ending, a girl of about seventeen years of age entered the hall and, without speaking to anybody, took a letter off the letter rack and put it into her bag and walked smartly out the door. As she put the letter into her bag I got a fleeting glimpse of the name McGrath on the envelope, so bidding the caretaker good morning I walked after the girl. Having followed her for about thirty yards I overtook her and handed her the small slip of paper which read: 'This is to introduce bearer who will explain. Mick.'

I told her I wanted to see Mr McGrath urgently as I had news for him from Dublin. She recognised Collins' note immediately and invited me to accompany her. She was a person of very few words. We boarded a bus and after travelling about a mile got off and descended into the underground. After travelling some miles we ascended to street level and a short walk brought us to McGrath's office.[8] McGrath, Art O'Brien[9] and other members of the executive of the Irish Self-Determination League were making last-minute preparations for the Manchester meetings. I delivered the despatch and breathed a sigh of relief.

IRISH SELF-DETERMINATION LEAGUE CONVENTION AT SALFORD

After delivering my despatch I intended to remain in London until the afternoon of the following day and then accompany the London delegates to Manchester, where the convention was to take place on 27–28 November. There I would meet delegates from all over Britain. This I was anxious to do as Collins and Joe McGrath had suggested that, while in England, I might be able to place some of the ex-RIC men in employment and that, to this end, I should seek the assistance of members of the Irish Self-Determination League.

In the early afternoon of 25 November word reached me at the hotel that, in view of certain developments, I was to go to Manchester alone and report at 9 p.m. on that night at the Coal Exchange Hall, Market Place, where the London delegates would again contact me. When I called at this address in Manchester, where the convention was to be held, the hall was in darkness and about a dozen policemen were guarding it. One of the policemen informed me that the meetings which were to be held there over the weekend had been banned.

I was now completely lost in Manchester and had not the remotest idea how I was to make contact again with McGrath and his party. I walked aimlessly down a side street and entered a well-lit public house called 'The Old Boar'. I found that the pub was packed with Irishmen from all over Britain who were delegates to the conference and were openly discussing the banned meeting. The strangest coincidence of all was that the secretary of the Manchester branch of the League, Liam McMahon, was there.[10] McMahon put me in touch with my London friends, who, like myself, had travelled singly from London in order not to attract too much attention after the meeting had been banned.

The Manchester ban did not prevent the officers of the Irish Self-Determination League from holding their convention. Salford was only across the river and the ban did not extend to that municipality so it was decided to hold the meetings there instead.[11] This loophole in the law arose because in Britain at that time only the chief constable of a district could ban a meeting in that district. When the chief constable in Salford discovered that the convention was to be held there he also banned it. But, when a meeting is proclaimed, forty-eight hours must elapse before the proclamation takes effect. The organisers were well versed in these fine points of the law and so on 26 November over 1,000 delegates assembled in Salford Town Hall to attend the first national convention of the Irish Self-Determination League of Great Britain.[12] The delegates were, according to the rules of the organisation, Irish or of Irish descent. Notices banning the meeting were posted round the hall but the organisers had two full days to get through their agenda before the ban took effect.

As I sat there for two days watching the proceedings and listening to the inflammatory speeches of some of the delegates, I was truly amazed. Had this same meeting been held in an Irish town and the same speeches been made, that Irish town would have been put to the flames and most of the delegates consigned to penal servitude. I kept my eye on the policemen and was surprised to see that they were not even taking notes of the proceedings. They were there simply to see that no 'breach of the peace' was committed. Arthur Griffith, acting president of the Irish Republic, was billed as the main speaker, but due to his detention by the crown forces in Ireland was unable to address the convention.[13] While Seán Milroy,[14] the director of organisation of the League, acting for Griffith, was denouncing the British cabinet in most eloquent terms, I actually saw one of the policemen having a quiet sleep on his chair in a corner.[15] In the light of my experience as an Irish policeman the whole thing seemed very unreal.

Although the traditional procession through the streets of Manchester in commemoration of 'The Manchester Martyrs' had been banned by the authorities, with thousands of others I paid tribute to the dead patriots by marching to a Mass which was specially celebrated for the repose of their souls on the morning of the second day of the convention, which happened to be 'Manchester Martyrs Sunday'.[16] Even such a procession in Ireland at that time would have been attacked by the British security forces. The convention resumed after lunch. Late that afternoon Seán McGrath invited me on to the platform, where he introduced me to the delegates. He gave a general outline of Colonel Smyth's address to the RIC at Listowel and the reaction of the police there to it. This brought cheers and loud applause and I felt quite embarrassed as I stood waiting to address the meeting. The speeches which Milroy and I made seemed to be the only ones that impressed the police in the hall. Immediately after speaking I came down to the body of the hall and I was approached by a policeman who told me that I was wanted outside. So this is the end of my journey, I thought to myself, as I accompanied the policeman to a porch in the hall where about half-a-dozen policemen were waiting for us. I was mistaken, however, for instead of arresting me they escorted me to the nearest hotel where I became their guest of honour for well over an hour. To these English policemen I was a police hero and that was all that mattered. They insisted on my repeating the details of the police revolt and I was embarrassed at the respectful attention they gave me.

On the evening of 28 November the proceedings were brought to a close with the singing of the Irish national anthem. A few hours later the meeting was 'officially banned'. I was impressed at the manner in which the convention had been conducted and felt that my attendance at it had been well worthwhile, as I had made contact with many delegates from England and Wales, and I promised to visit a number of them in the course of a tour which McGrath had arranged for me.

TOUR OF ENGLAND AND WALES

On the evening of 28 November 1920, accompanied by Seán McGrath, I left Manchester for Liverpool on the first stage of my tour. We went straight from Liverpool railway station to the Socialist Club, where I was made an honorary member, and we met many Irishmen including some from Sligo whom I had known some years earlier. About twenty minutes after McGrath and I had left the Socialist Club it was raided and over thirty people were taken into custody. We were in another part of the city in Hughes's public house, a favourite place of call for Irishmen, when we received news of the raid. Almost simultaneously we heard shouts from the street: 'Policeman Shot'. We went out into the street where there was a wild stampede which reminded me of Dublin, except that there was no shooting.

This particular killing was a most unfortunate affair and did a good deal of damage to the Irish Self-Determination League, although it was in no way responsible for the tragedy. It seems that a policeman in his ordinary rounds on beat-duty noticed a man standing at the gateway of a cotton factory with his hands behind his back. The man had a heavy bolt cutter and, when accosted by the policeman, fired point blank.[17] An Irishman was arrested for the shooting and put on trial, which lasted for several days, but the case was dismissed for want of evidence. It was a good decision, for the Irishman was innocent. The man who did the shooting was later arrested and sent to jail on an entirely different charge.[18]

Seán McGrath and I had intended spending a few days in Liverpool, but this unfortunate shooting changed our plans and we went on to Leeds, where soon after arrival we parted, as McGrath received an urgent message to go on some important business.

Having said goodbye to Seán McGrath, as I had some time on my hands, I decided to walk back to my hotel. On the way I asked a policeman, who was on beat-duty, for directions. He spoke with a pronounced south-of-Ireland accent and said to me: 'You are an RIC man.' I acknowledged the fact and he asked me to wait for fifteen minutes when he would be free to have a chat with me. When he came off duty we went to where he was staying and he changed into civilian clothes. We then retired to a nearby hotel. His name was Quinlan and he was from County Tipperary. I told him that my name was Walsh and that I was stationed at Ballymote, County Sligo. For the next three hours I sat in the hotel bar room being lectured by him on the advisability of resigning from the RIC. He impressed upon me that 'the RIC was no place for an Irishman at a time when Britain was sending over policemen recruited from the slums of London'. We parted on very friendly terms after I had assured him that I would hand in my resignation when I returned to Ireland.

In Leeds I visited three centres, where Irish-language classes were being held. They were well attended by boys and girls of Irish descent and also by some boys and girls whose claim to Irish descent was doubtful. I was agreeably surprised to find that the fight for Irish independence appealed to many young people in England. The Self-Determination League, which was another name for Sinn Féin, was doing splendid work promoting the Irish cause. I was delighted to witness the pride which Irish people in England had in their national heritage.

From Leeds I went north to Middlesbrough, and from there on to Newcastle-on-Tyne, Sheffield, Birmingham, Chester, Swansea and Cardiff, where I concluded my tour about eight days before Christmas 1920. I attended meetings of the Irish Self-Determination League in these various centres, at all of which collections were made for the Irish cause. At each meeting I was called on to give first-hand information on conditions in Ireland and soon had developed into a tolerably good platform speaker.

At Cardiff I completed the report of my tour, which made a rather bulky document. To get the report safely to Dublin was my next task. I fully realised how important this was. If the document was captured it would give away much secret information concerning the Irish Self-Determination League and its members. A Mr Murphy, who was on the executive of the Cardiff branch of the League, solved the difficulty by agreeing to send his wife to Dublin with the despatch.

RETURN TO DUBLIN

I made sure that Mrs Murphy would be better equipped with alternative addresses than I had been when starting for London. I gave her four private addresses in Dublin with a personal note to each with instructions as to the disposal of the despatch. Although we travelled together, it was arranged that we treat each other as strangers and, in the event of my being arrested, she was to carry on and not show any signs of being acquainted with me. Fortunately there was no necessity for all these elaborate precautions. Long before our ship tied up at the quay in Dublin we could see the military awaiting our arrival. Mrs Murphy made her way unobtrusively through the lines of soldiers, while I returned the salute that was intended for military officers in whose company I was, as I disembarked.

I was pleased to find that our offices at 14 North Frederick Street were still intact, and Mrs Murphy and myself got a warm welcome from Dick Cotter, Lily O'Brennan, Eilís Ryan and the other members of the staff. Mrs Murphy returned to Cardiff after a few days.

14

DRUMKEERAN, DROMAHAIR: 24 DECEMBER 1920–JANUARY 1921

By Christmas week 1920 a new viciousness had crept into the prosecution of the Anglo-Irish War on the part of the British. The British authorities, still smarting under the defeat they had suffered by the 'break-up' of their spy ring on 'Bloody Sunday' and goaded by some sections of the British press, began openly to allow the crown forces to indulge in reprisals on the civilian population. Martial law was in force in Dublin and in most of the country and, under cover of curfew, which kept people indoors, savage crimes were being committed by the British forces. There was nationwide raiding of private homes. Most of the members of Dáil Éireann had been arrested and thrown into jail. British troops, in the presence of their officers, had put the centre of Cork city to the flames and property valued at over £4,000,000 was destroyed in one night. While Cork city was in flames the British troops fired on the fire brigade and cut their hoses, an act which could hardly be said to be in keeping with the rules of civilised warfare. Cork, apparently, was burned because a convoy of British troops was attacked within a mile of their headquarters in that city. When the question of the burning of Cork was raised in the British House of Commons the British prime minister and the British chief secretary for Ireland gave the extraordinary reply that the city had been destroyed by Irish rebels.[1] What happened in Cork was taking place all over Ireland, though to a lesser extent.

Sinn Féin activists, however, continued to extend the security forces. In Dublin, where there were thousands of British troops, no British soldier in uniform dared walk the streets. The only uniforms to be seen in the streets were those of the Dublin Metropolitan Police, who had refused to cooperate with the British military. During curfew armoured cars and military lorries, with wire cages as a protection against bomb attacks, patrolled the streets and were being ambushed night after night and often even in broad daylight. Dublin was a nightmare city.

The *Irish Bulletin* carried news of IRA actions and of British atrocities and it was difficult to concentrate on routine work amid so much destruction, vengeance and hate.[2] In the midst of all this I read one little item of news that cheered me up. At Tubbercurry, County Sligo, District Inspector John Russell seemingly had called out 'the old RIC' and forced the Black and Tans to hand back loot which they had taken from shops in the town.[3]

As far as I was concerned the work of placing in employment resigned members of the RIC had for all practical purposes ceased. The partial destruction of the economic life of the nation had thrown thousands out of work and made it impossible to secure jobs for anybody. Fortunately, during my tour in England, I had some success placing ex-RIC men in employment, and I would have been able to do much more were it not for the fact that those leaders of the Irish Self-Determination League who were prepared to assist me were very soon afterwards arrested and interned.

Many of the policemen who had resigned from the force came in for a bad time at the hands of the crown forces and had to flee the country. In Tuam, ex-Constable Hugh Ruddy was dragged from his home, stripped naked, flogged and compelled to leave the town.[4] In Cliffony, County Sligo, ex-Constable Bernard Conway had his home burned by the crown forces on 28 October 1920. When he and his aged mother went to live in another house, that too was burned, and Conway was dragged out to be shot. Fortunately his attackers were so drunk that he succeeded in escaping amid a hail of bullets.[5]

I TRAVEL TO SLIGO ON CHRISTMAS EVE

The very thought of spending Christmas in Dublin appalled me, so on Christmas Eve I set out for my wife's home at Drumkeeran, Dromahair,

County Leitrim. This necessitated my boarding the train to Sligo. The train which left Dublin for Sligo on that Christmas Eve 1920 was a long and crowded one, as everybody who could do so was anxious to get away from a city where at that time human life counted for little. The train was over four hours late in reaching Sligo because of hold-ups by the military at every station along the line. At each station all the male passengers were taken off the train and lined along the platform, where they were searched, questioned and sometimes assaulted by drunken Auxiliaries or Black and Tans. At Mullingar I saw a drunken Black and Tan assault a boy of about fifteen years of age by striking him across the face with his hand. A woman at a carriage window shouted 'Cowardly dog', while some other women passengers shouted 'Up the Republic' and sang rebel songs. This did not improve what was already a tense situation and I was glad when the train moved off after some arrests were made amid the jeers and cheers of the women passengers. The farther we travelled the more drunk the crown forces appeared to be, due no doubt to their long wait for the much-delayed train and their determination, come what may, to celebrate Christmas. As the train progressed towards Sligo the passengers became fewer, and, correspondingly, were subjected to a greater measure of harassment by the crown forces. At Dromod station, County Leitrim, a Black and Tan, who was obviously drunk, terrified the passengers. He wore a long, belted coat, a tasselled cap and had a revolver strapped to his leg in addition to a revolver in each hand. He staggered round the platform threatening everybody and using the most vile language. Although I had been questioned twice by the military, he began to ply me with questions which I could not answer even had I wished to. As he was about to assault me, an officer came up and ordered him away. The officer then resumed the questioning. But when I told him that I was in the British civil service and that I was going home to bury my father he became quite sympathetic.

At each railway station I gave a different name. I knew that it was police practice to have a man identified at one station and then telephone the police at a station farther on, giving particulars of the man and instructions for his arrest. This was done in order to protect 'spotters', whom the police engaged for this kind of work.

Although I had bought a ticket to take me to Sligo, I meant to get off before reaching that town where I was well known to the RIC. I had a chat with the guard of the train and told him of my difficulties. He informed me that at least twenty men had already got off the train along quiet stretches of the line, where he had arranged to slow down to let them off. He promised to let me off between Ballisodare and Sligo. This, however, was not necessary because, to our surprise, when we pulled in at Collooney there were neither military nor police at the station. It would appear that they tired of waiting and went downtown for refreshments. I got off the train, but just as it was moving away I saw the headlights of four military lorries rushing towards the station. As I was deciding in which direction to make good my escape, a railway porter came up and locked me into a cattle wagon at the end of the platform, where, he said, I would be safe. From my vantage point I could see at least a couple of dozen men in uniform. I heard them abusing the railway officials with vile language for allowing the train to continue on its journey without their checking it. They were evidently bent on more refreshments because they departed rather quickly, leaving the little station in darkness. As the sound of the lorries died away the porter set me free and sent downtown for a car to take me on the rest of my journey. It was long after midnight when I set off from Collooney station for my wife's home at Drumkeeran, Dromahair, County Leitrim, with the guard wishing me a safe journey and a happy Christmas.

15

BELFAST BOYCOTT:
JANUARY–MARCH 1921

When I returned to Dublin early in January 1921 I found very little to do in my office.[1] Resignations from the RIC had practically come to an end. The economic situation in Ireland was very bad, and with pressure being exerted on Irish organisations in Britain by means of the Defence of the Realm Act, the prospects of their finding employment for ex-RIC men were anything but bright. There was little I could do except come in to my office each day and acknowledge letters from resigned men who hoped that we could find employment for them. I was much relieved, therefore, when, early in February, I was appointed an organiser of the Belfast Boycott.[2]

The Belfast Boycott arose out of the following circumstances. From July 1920 pogroms were taking place against Catholic workmen in Belfast. Under the very eyes and, indeed, one can say almost with the collusion of the authorities, hundreds of Catholic workmen were beaten up and driven from the Belfast shipyards. About the same time many Catholic families had their homes put to the flames by mobs of Unionist supporters acting like fanatical bigots. Over 2,000 Belfast Catholic refugees who had lost everything, including their homes and belongings as well as their jobs, poured into Dublin.[3] A few of those who encouraged, and many who condoned, these outrages against the Catholic population in Belfast were at the same time sending their commercial travellers all over Ireland and were selling their goods to Catholic traders. In particular, the Northern and Ulster Banks were doing a thriving business in the South of Ireland. In the autumn of 1920

Dáil Éireann issued a directive imposing a boycott of Belfast banks and Belfast goods as an appropriate response to the pogroms and continuing bigotry in Belfast. While the majority of traders throughout the South complied with this directive by terminating their business with the northern banks and cutting off trading with Belfast merchants, there were many who were not prepared to observe the boycott for one reason or another, these generally being personal reasons.

The Belfast merchants soon realised the seriousness of the boycott and took steps to counter it by way of extended credit to traders and by cutting prices. This, the arrest on 26 November 1920 of Michael Staines, the first director of the boycott, and a certain amount of apathy prevented the boycott from being effective.[4] So in February 1921 it was decided to intensify the campaign and nine organisers including myself were sent out to various districts to administer the boycott.[5] Our main tasks were to form committees in every village and town, to encourage the withdrawal of as many accounts as possible from the Belfast banks and above all to ensure a universal observance by traders of the boycott directive. In our work we had the full backing of local units of the IRA who also carried out the more hazardous actions associated with the boycott, such as holding up trains and destroying Belfast goods in transit.

The nine of us attended a number of meetings at which we were instructed on our responsibilities and also on our mode of procedure.[6] One instruction was that we were to go through the countryside, disguised as commercial travellers. Thus, when our briefing session was over, the nine of us, including some women,[7] went down to the Irish Co-Operative Society, Middle Abbey Street, Dublin, where we were provided with samples of tweeds and serges by the manager, James Doyle, an active supporter of Sinn Féin.[8] I do not believe that a single one of the nine had any experience of the drapery business. However, that was but a mere detail in those days. Mr Doyle's terms to us were generous. If we made sales we would get 10 per cent commission and if we sold nothing at all we could return the merchandise.

Although I was looking forward to working in the country, I fully realised the risks that would be involved. In the city I was a stranger among the thousands. In the country I would be a stranger among the few. The possibility of meeting members of the RIC whom I knew and who would recognise me would be greatly increased. I did not underestimate the competence of the RIC, one of whose responsibilities was to keep an eye on strangers who entered their districts. I knew that uniformed policemen would meet every train and I knew that these uniformed policemen were but one half of the surveillance laid on at railway stations, the more dangerous half being a secret-service man in civilian clothes who would shadow me to my hotel to find out who I was.[9] It would now be my business to leave a trail of convincing evidence that would satisfy such a dangerous shadow. I considered that my new surroundings required a change of disguise so, discarding the military pose which I had adopted since being advised to do so by Collins, I now reverted to the disguise recommended to me by Countess Markievicz, that of slouching along with drooping shoulders and very long strides. The district to which I was appointed encompassed the counties of Louth, Meath, Armagh and Down. The day after I collected my samples from Mr Doyle I set out for Drogheda.

DROGHEDA AND DUNDALK

I arrived at my hotel from the railway station just in time to witness the funeral cortège of two Drogheda men who had been killed some days earlier by the crown forces.[10] Hundreds of men, women and young girls marched behind the coffins, from which British troops had torn the tricolours. The military air of the men and the firm step of the Cumann na mBan members reminded one of a victory parade rather than a funeral. There was no evidence of defeat in Drogheda, I mused, and the British troops might well be advised to add a few more sandbags to their defences, for vengeance was surely round the corner.

After the funeral I made contact with Philip (Phil) Monahan who was the mayor of Drogheda.[11] He advised me to let things cool off in the town and to call back in a week or two. I decided, therefore, to go on to Dundalk, but before doing so I received some useful advice as to my best mode of procedure from Phil Monahan, who was himself a draper. He advised me to sell my tweeds in suit lengths. He also gave me the names of three drapers in Drogheda besides his own and, on his instructions, I made an entry in my order book showing that these four Drogheda traders had purchased a number of suit-lengths at 10/6d (52½p) per yard. The object of this exercise was to be able to account for my presence in Drogheda if I were held up by the military. I overlooked, however, one very important point, namely, that drapery travellers do not take bicycles around with them. It was not until a week later that I realised the seriousness of this mistake, which landed me in a very difficult situation.

From Drogheda I went to Dundalk, where I spent about a week. I formed branches of the Belfast Boycott Committee around the district and gave detailed instructions at many meetings as to how to enforce the boycott. Then, as in Drogheda, I entered a number of orders in my book and left for Newry.

NEWRY

At Newry I checked in to the White Cross Hotel[12] where I met a very friendly commercial traveller who, after lunch, took me for a run in his car to Warrenpoint and Newcastle, where he had business to transact.

The following morning I had an important appointment in connection with the Belfast Boycott at Hilltown, which is about nine miles from Newry on a byroad off the Rathfriland road. I started before nine o'clock in the morning and this was an elementary mistake, as travellers do not usually call on their customers so early in the morning. Moreover, with my attaché case full of samples of tweeds and serges strapped to my bicycle, I did not look the part of the commercial traveller I was supposed to be. Furthermore, instead of turning right for Hilltown a short distance outside the town, I continued on the Rathfriland road by mistake. Finally, what ensured my temporary downfall in Newry was that this last mistake was observed by a member of the RIC. Just after passing the Hilltown road I met a young RIC sergeant walking smartly towards the barracks evidently making for the nine o'clock parade, as it was then only a few minutes to nine o'clock. We bade each other good morning and continued our different ways. When I found that I was on the wrong road I turned back and overtook the sergeant as I came to the Hilltown road. This confirmed his suspicion that I was a stranger in the district.

About two or three miles outside Newry, at a little place called Mayobridge, I was overtaken by a Crossley tender which pulled up beside me as I dismounted to walk the hill. In the tender were eight RIC constables, two sergeants (including the youngish-looking one I passed on the road) and a head constable. All were armed with carbines, except the head constable who carried a revolver only. They got off the tender and formed a circle around me, while the sergeant, who had spotted me earlier, searched me and began to question me.

For the next half hour the young sergeant put me through a bout of questioning that would have staggered anybody not trained in the same school as I had been. He first opened my attaché case and took out my samples of tweeds and serges as well as my order book. He then opened the order book which he scrutinised very carefully and drew a pencil line under the last entry. 'You are nine days on the road,' he said, 'and you have sold only five at 10/6 [52½p].' Then holding in one hand my few samples he said: 'Do you mean to tell me that you are a commercial traveller and that in nine days you have sold goods only to the value of £2.12.6d [£2.62½]?'

'You are not a commercial traveller,' I replied, 'or you would know how to read an order book.'

'What does "one only at 10/6" [52½] mean?' was his next question.

'It means,' I replied, 'one length of cloth one hundred yards long and it also means that in the nine days I have sold goods to the value of £262.10.0 [£262.50] and not £2.12.6 [£2.62½] as you state. Seeing that I am opening up this district for the first time you will admit, I think, that I am not doing as badly as you thought.' He immediately shifted to safer ground.

I felt greatly relieved as I realised that I had won the first round. I had given my name as William Walsh and my home address as Kilkerrin, County Galway, which is only a few miles from my home at Glenamaddy. It was fortunate for me that I did this for otherwise I could not have answered the questions which then followed in rapid succession. 'Give the names of three people of standing in Kilkerrin.'

'In my absence,' I replied, 'the three most important people in Kilkerrin are the parish priest and the local sergeant,' whose names I gave, 'and Martin O'Grady the publican.' Some of the constables were amused at my reply, but a stern look from the head constable caused them to look serious again. 'Where did you serve your time to the drapery business?' 'How long are you employed with your present employers?' 'Where and by whom were you employed before you took up your present employment?' 'What RIC men do you know in your home district?' 'Give the names of any RIC men who joined the police force from your home district.' I replied that I served my time with Fitzgibbons of Castlerea and that I was employed with that firm until I took up my present employment three years ago. To the last question I gave the name Brady, which was that of a man from Glenamaddy who had joined the RIC. 'That's right,' spoke up one of the constables, 'John Brady of Warrenpoint is a native of Glenamaddy, County Galway.' I succeeded in pretending to be unconcerned when I heard this. I afterward learned that not only was Brady then stationed at Warrenpoint, but that Patrick Keaveney, a neighbour of mine, was stationed at Newcastle, the two places I had visited the previous evening.

The young sergeant, who was doing all the questioning, then read a letter which I had received from my wife that morning. Fortunately I was addressed in it as William, and it was signed Annie.

At this stage the two sergeants and the head constable went off some distance for a private conference, while one of my guard devoted his time to examining and admiring the nice Dripsey tweeds which were lying on the saddle of my bicycle which one of the constables held. The constable asked me what a costume length would cost. I told him that we sold only wholesale, that the wholesale price was 10/6 (52½p) a yard, but that the retail price was £1 per yard. I will confess that necessity had, by this time, made me an easy liar since my very existence depended on my ability to live up to a lie.

After the two sergeants and the head constable returned the young sergeant resumed cross-questioning me. 'This is a very guarded letter,' he said.

'All letters have to be guarded nowadays,' I replied, 'seeing that they may be publicly read by the police.'

'Are you married?'

'No.'

'Who is this letter from?'

'My sweetheart.' He then read a particular paragraph of my letter which he asked me to explain. 'I am answering and will continue to answer all your reasonable questions,' I replied, 'but when you ask me to explain in public my love affairs I must draw the line. As a gentleman and an officer of the law,' I added, 'I am sure you will agree that I am not unreasonable when I insist on this privilege.'

The sergeants and the head constable withdrew again for a further conference. Although I could not catch the conversation, I noticed that on this occasion the head constable had taken charge and was doing most of the talking. After my initial shock at being arrested I was slowly regaining my confidence. I was certain by now that the police did not quite know what to make of me and I expected a fair deal from the fine-looking head constable.

When the sergeant and the head constable returned the latter spoke to me for the first time. He told me to get into the lorry. My bicycle was put in after me by one of the constables, watched by a group of curious people who, by this time, had assembled on the road. The lorry was reversed and I was taken to Newry barracks.

I was not put into the lockup but was allowed to sit at the dayroom fire. I was given a good dinner and was very well treated. At that time there were no Black and Tans or Auxiliaries in the north. Except in the case of riots, the administration of law and order was still in the hands of the RIC who acted on the principle that a man was innocent until they were able to prove him guilty.

For four hours I sat in the dayroom. The belts, batons and swords, hanging on the walls, and the white deal table and forms made the surroundings seem very familiar. As I conversed with the constables, I had to keep a constant check on myself lest I might give myself away by even a word or phrase. I was quite familiar with every object in the dayroom; the patrol book, the diary, the duty slip on the wall, the acts of parliament on the shelf, and even with the slang used by the constables. Yet to have shown myself to be familiar with any of these things would have been disastrous. In addition to this strain I expected that eventually I would be confronted with Constable Brady of Warrenpoint, who could not but immediately recognise me and would not be able to do anything to save me, since he would not know that I was going under the name William Walsh.

After four hours, which seemed like four years, the head constable came in to the dayroom. After asking me a few casual questions, such as how long I intended to remain in Newry and where I intended going from there, he told me I was free to return to my hotel. I told him that I would be spending two days in Newry and that from there I would go to Portadown where I would be staying at Grew's Hotel.[13] He told me to drop in and see him at ten o'clock next morning.

When I got back to my hotel I found that my bedroom had been searched by the police and that the proprietor had been questioned about me. Two Belfast travellers were staying in the hotel and one of them was anxious to get the full details regarding my arrest. I cut him rather short by dismissing the matter and saying that it was a case of mistaken identity, and that the police were real gentlemen who were trying to do their duty in a courteous way in rather difficult times.

About nine o'clock that night James V. McFadden, the constable who had been admiring my samples, called and asked if he could borrow them so that his wife might select a costume-length of tweed. I was only too glad to oblige and in less than twenty minutes McFadden returned and gave me an order for a costume-length of a very nice piece of Dripsey tweed. I took out my pen and wrote in a prominent place in my order book, 'Constable J. McFadden, The Island, Newry. One costume-length at 10/6 [52½] per yard.' This was the first genuine order in my order book. During the subsequent few months I received a number of such orders from members of the RIC. Constable McFadden and myself had some refreshments at the hotel bar. I deliberately avoided mentioning my arrest until he broached the subject. When he did so I treated the matter lightly and told him that I was used to that kind of thing, and that most travellers had the same kind of experience, and that we often 'got a laugh out of it' when discussing our various experiences, when we met in hotels afterwards. He assured me that I would hear no more about it and that, as I suspected, the whole trouble arose through my taking the wrong turn that morning.

Next day I called at the barracks, as requested, and met the head constable who offered a nice apology for the inconvenience caused me and wished me good luck as we shook hands and parted. I was not surprised at this incident. I knew that when the RIC checked up on a stranger they did it thoroughly. The story I had given them evidently sounded reasonable. Obviously the young sergeant was not completely convinced, but he deferred to the head constable who represented all that was good in a police force that was rapidly nearing its end.

Lest there should be any misunderstanding concerning my spending an afternoon in the police barracks at Newry, after my release I posted a letter through a third party to the Irish Co-Operative Society in Dublin, informing them that I had been arrested and to alert all concerned. I knew that the news would be passed on to headquarters by Mr Doyle, the manager. Although I had intended spending only two days in Newry, I now decided to spend three days around the district so as to throw off all suspicion. I confined myself entirely to the commercial side of my business and received friendly salutes from members of the RIC as I went on my rounds as a drapery traveller.

PORTADOWN

From Newry I went on to Portadown. I decided to travel first class, as befitted a commercial traveller. As I sat in a first-class carriage on my way to Portadown I reviewed my brush with the RIC. I concluded that the incident had been positively advantageous to me, as it had enabled me to make a genuine sale to a member of the RIC, Constable

McFadden, whose name in my order book would be as useful as a passport if I got into a tight corner again; also the questions put to me by the young sergeant alerted me to the type of questions I might, if arrested again, be called upon to answer.

The first thing I did on reaching Portadown was to get rid of my bicycle by railing it back to Dublin. I did not wish to repeat my mistake at Newry, where I literally cycled into the hands of the RIC. Then I gave my cases to the hotel boots at the railway station and set off for Grew's Hotel with the air of a seasoned commercial traveller.

At Grew's I booked my room, had lunch and then opened the large parcel of drapery samples which, on my instructions, had been forwarded by post. With a well-filled sample case I then started out to open up new business in Portadown. I might as well have tried to sell heather on the Hill of Howth as to sell Dublin goods to Protestant merchants in Portadown. The very sight of my business card was enough to make them bristle with hate. This and the lack of sales did not upset me in the least. I was simply intent on leaving behind a trail that would satisfy the police shadow whom I had noticed at the hotel that I was a genuine commercial traveller trying to break new ground. From this time on I never made contacts with the local members of the IRA during my first days in a town, but would concentrate only on pushing sales. At Portadown I met a few Catholic drapers who were willing to support a Dublin firm. This they did not only out of sympathy with Dublin but in order to strike a blow, even if a small one, at Belfast.

That night, having posted my orders, I went to the cinema (the pictures) in order to avoid commercial travellers who tend to discuss business all the time. They seemed to know every traveller in Ireland and the firm for whom he travelled. I now dreaded them more than the RIC, for their knowledge of fellow commercial travellers was much more extensive. I knew that my best way to avoid awkward questions was to keep my meetings with them to a minimum.

Next day I contacted a businessman who, I had been told in Newry, would put me in contact with the IRA. He agreed to do so and promised to send me word at the hotel at eight o'clock that night. At eight o'clock to the minute a boy of about sixteen years of age called and together we went downtown. After walking for about ten minutes we came to a disused house, which was shuttered and in complete darkness. The boy knocked and we were admitted to a room which was in semi-darkness, the only light being a candle standing in a saucer on a small table in the middle of the room. There were about a dozen men sitting around. Immediately I sensed a coldness in their attitude towards me. Soon I realised that I was actually under arrest.

A man who appeared to be in charge lifted the candle in order to give more light and he asked me if I knew any of the people present. I told him that I had not the remotest idea as to who they were. A small man was then asked if he recognised me. He replied that he did not. He then went on to explain his presence in Portadown. It seems that he had received instructions from Dublin to replace William Walsh who was arrested in Newry, and that was all he knew. I realised then that there had been a complete misunderstanding and I pointed out that I was the William Walsh who had been arrested at Newry and I gave all the details of that incident. I learned also the circumstance which had led to the confrontation. It seems that soon after I had my interview with the friendly draper, who promised to arrange a meeting with local members of the IRA, the small man from Belfast, who called himself Smith, came along and introduced himself as the Belfast Boycott organiser without making any comment on why he was there.[14] This naturally made the merchant suspicious of both Smith and myself, and when he got in touch with the OC of the local unit of the IRA it was decided to have both of us picked up and questioned. I now saw that the position was rather amusing and I was beginning to enjoy it. I complimented the 'boys' on their efficiency and suggested that Smith and myself be kept under open arrest until they received some verification from headquarters on our standing in the movement. They were satisfied, however, with the explanations given by Smith and myself and the matter ended there. Next day Smith returned to Belfast.

Railway officials at Richhill, some three miles from Portadown, were relabelling Belfast goods and reconsigning them to the West and South of Ireland. This was part of an elaborate attempt which was being made to break the Belfast Boycott. Traders receiving these goods were able to say and to prove that the goods came not from Belfast but from County Armagh, which was not on the boycott list. The railway officials at Richhill had been cautioned about the practice and had ignored all warnings. It was in connection with this situation that I had called to Portadown. I consulted with the OC of the local unit of the IRA on the matter and it was decided that drastic action required to be taken.

The IRA burned Richhill railway station to the ground a week or two later.[15] This had a very definite effect in preventing similar efforts to break the Belfast Boycott elsewhere.

I visited many towns and villages in County Armagh and, in addition to organising the boycott, I was becoming more competent as a drapery traveller. There were few towns or villages where I did not open up new business, as most Catholic traders in the North were only too glad to buy from Dublin and strike a blow at bigots in Belfast, who still looked for Catholic trade while they condoned or even incited men to hound Catholics from their homes and from their places of employment.

I MEET AN ORANGEMAN

I had an extraordinary experience in a town in County Armagh. I called on a wholesale draper, an Orangeman, who had an extensive trade with Catholic convents and Catholic institutions all over Ireland. The proprietor was standing in the centre of his shop when I called, presented my card and canvassed him for business. Having read my card carefully and slowly, he crumpled it into a little ball, dropped it on the floor and crushed it with the sole of his shoe. Then he walked away without even speaking to me. That night at a meeting in the town I mentioned the incident and I got the names and addresses of several Catholic institutions which this firm supplied with goods. I also gave a full report of the incident to the general secretary when I returned to Dublin a week later. The result was that this gentleman lost all his Catholic contracts all over Ireland. It was hoped that this would prove to him that bigotry did not pay, even in Northern Ireland.

16

BELFAST BOYCOTT: MARCH 1921–JANUARY 1922

Towards the end of March I was transferred to a district, which encompassed Counties Derry, Donegal, Fermanagh and Tyrone, with Derry as its centre.[1] I was pleased with the transfer, as I knew Derry fairly well and I looked forward to travelling through Donegal with its lovely mountains and lakes.

My first day in Derry was a day of surprises. When I got off the train one of the first men I saw was a plain-clothes policeman whom I knew. His name was Michael Barlow and we had spent six months together in the depot in Dublin. He recognised me at once but turned and walked away. His special duty was to watch the trains at Derry station and to keep an eye out for strangers. For the next few months we met several times but never spoke or pretended to recognise one another. I met many of these silent policemen whose British uniforms covered Irish hearts and whose services, during a trying period in Irish history, will never be known or recognised.[2]

Soon after my arrival I called on a Derry draper who was friendly to the cause, for the purpose of introducing myself. The shop was crowded so I merely presented my business card, intending to disclose my identity later. To my surprise the draper was keenly interested in my tweeds and serges and gave me an order for £90 worth of goods. Having done so well on the business side I made up my mind to let it go at that and not to disclose my real business, which it was not necessary to do, as I had other contacts in Derry. The following night the same draper was chairman of the meeting which I was addressing. After the meeting he smilingly said: 'That was a good one you put over on me yesterday.' I explained why I did not disclose my real identity and added that he could cancel the order if he wished. He declined to do so. In fact he informed me that my tweeds and serges were extra-good value and complimented me on the way I 'stood over my goods'. I asked him what 'standing over goods' meant and he replied: 'It means transferring the traveller's confidence to the buyer. You,' he said, 'appeared to have complete confidence in your goods and I was impressed by that, apart from the fact that you were offering good value.' This draper paid me the compliment of asking me to travel for him some four months later, after the Truce, and I often regretted not having done so, as the life of a commercial traveller can be very pleasant and interesting.

It is a common complaint in the north-east corner of Ireland that southern politicians do not understand the northern people or their problems. Indeed, I can well believe this to be true. What is, perhaps, most difficult to understand about northern people is their attitude to religion. It is impossible, of course, to write about the North without referring to the religious question. The southerner crossing the border for the first time will be amazed at the constant discussion of religion while he sees little of it practised. Catholics and Protestants act as if they belonged to two different factions rather than to two religious denominations. Catholics as well as Protestants are great offenders in this regard and it is not unusual to hear a phrase such as: 'He's a very decent man, although he is a Protestant.' Northern Catholics actually believe that they are better Catholics than their southern counterparts because, as they say, they have to fight for their religion.

Derry at that time was typical of other towns in the North, and even worse than most, because its population was practically 50 per cent Catholic and 50 per cent Protestant. It was also the venue for one of the more important annual Orange parades. On numerous occasions, in the line of duty, I witnessed that annual parade on August 12 in celebration of the siege of Derry.[3] On the eve of the event labourers, tradesmen and businessmen carried buckets of boiling water, soap and brushes to the Walker monument, which they scrubbed and cleaned from top to bottom. On the following day thousands of Orangemen, regaled with orange sashes from shoulder to waist, marched round the city walls. At least a hundred drummers from Belfast and Derry, with sleeves folded and necks bare, beat their great lambeg drums until the knuckles of many of them were red with blood. The drummers, seemingly, were expected to bleed for the cause. At any rate I observed that after the procession some drummers marched up to the Walker monument and rubbed their bleeding hands on the statue so recently scrubbed clean.[4] The most deplorable aspect of the celebration was that the object of the procession was not only to do honour to a dead hero but to strike terror into the hearts of their Catholic neighbours and thereby to stir up sectarian strife. And, lest there should be any doubt as to how the Orangemen felt about Catholicism, the burning of an effigy of the pope constituted a part of this annual ritual. The Catholics in the Bogside, on their part, invariably took a hand in the proceedings by setting fire to their chimneys, while the procession proceeded round the historical walls. And sometimes, with the wind blowing from the Bogside towards the walls, clouds of smoke and soot darkened the heavens and made the city an inferno of roaring drums and choking smoke.

THE BOYCOTT OF DERRY

In Derry city I found a very well organised branch of the Belfast Boycott Committee. However, the problem which the branch was then facing seemed almost insurmountable. Derry itself was not on the boycott 'blacklist' and was free to trade with the rest of Ireland. Moreover, more than nine-tenths of its traders, including the wholesale houses, were challenging the organisers and were openly buying from Belfast. Thus Derry was, in effect, being used as a dumping ground for Belfast goods. The situation was serious and it was not easy to see how it could be rectified. For instance, to follow our usual procedure and include all shops in Derry city on a 'blacklist' would have seriously hurt those who were prepared to fall into line and refuse to purchase Belfast goods.

I made a general report of the position to Dublin and asked for instructions. The first reaction to my report was that the director of the Belfast Boycott Committee sanctioned the appointment of John (Johnnie) Fox, who was to act as my assistant in Derry. Fox, a Derryman, was a splendid fellow.[5] He had a thorough knowledge of the district, and he was able to supply the most detailed information on most of the traders in the area. He was middle-aged and had spent a long term in jail for his political convictions which left him somewhat embittered, and it was with great difficulty that I was able to keep him from going to extremes. Like most Catholics in the North, Fox regarded all Catholics as his friends and all others as his enemies. He had been insulted so often by Unionist traders that he had given up appealing to their common sense or sense of fair play. Besides appointing Fox to assist me, headquarters also suggested the compiling of a 'black list' for Derry city, but we found that such a list would be so cumbersome as to be almost useless. We decided, instead, to compile a 'white list', that is, a list of Derry traders who were prepared to abide by the rules of our organisation and cease buying from Belfast. Having completed the list we got thousands of copies of it printed for distribution to shopkeepers and traders, especially in County Donegal, which was the main outlet for Derry trade. And these shopkeepers and traders in Donegal were then to be encouraged to buy or trade only with Derry merchants whose names appeared on our 'white list'.

Leaving Fox in charge in Derry city I set out for County Donegal. I went first to Letterkenny, where I met Peadar O'Donnell,[6] OC of the IRA in the area, Dr Joseph P. McGinley, TD,[7] and Charles Flattery, solicitor, who was a judge in the local Sinn Féin Court and IRA intelligence officer for County Donegal.[8] My meeting with these three gave me a flying start, and within the next few weeks I must have been the hardest-worked 'commercial traveller' in Ireland. I travelled from Fanad Head to Ballyshannon and established active branches of the Belfast Boycott Committee in every town and village throughout the county. As a result our 'white list' was extensively distributed, and shopkeepers and traders in Donegal were instructed to make it clear to Derry travellers that no business could be done with them until their firms 'came into line' and ceased trading with Belfast. It was amusing to listen to travellers in the hotels at night discussing their experiences in Donegal. Dublin travellers were elated at gaining many new customers, while their northern counterparts complained of losing many old customers due to the political situation. My tweed business was going ahead in leaps and bounds and by this time I was able to 'talk shop' with the best of them.

The day I arrived at Letterkenny I had an unpleasant surprise. At the railway station I saw no evidence of a hotel boots so, in typical commercial traveller style, I left my cases at the station and walked to McCarry's Hotel. I instructed Miss Kathleen (Kate) McCarry, the proprietress, to send the boots for my cases and went upstairs to the commercial room.[9] Half an hour later sitting at the commercial room window, I saw a British officer coming towards the hotel carrying my two cases. Walking beside him was a young lady. For a full half-hour I remained sitting where I was expecting every minute to be confronted by the British officer, but nothing happened. Eventually, I went downstairs to make inquiries and there on the floor beside the bar were my two cases. Sitting on the counter was the officer talking to the barmaid, the same lady who had accompanied him from the station. It would appear that the young lady, who was barmaid and boots in the hotel, was carrying my cases from the station, when she was overtaken by the officer, who, like a real gentleman, took the cases and carried them to the hotel for her. I felt greatly relieved as I carried my cases the rest of the way to the commercial room.

Returning to Derry after an absence of three weeks I found my assistant Fox in some trouble. Some members of the local organisation took it upon themselves to smash two plate-glass windows in the shop of a merchant who refused to join in the boycott. The incident might well have led to a riot. Indeed much smaller incidents have led to riots in Derry city.

This development had certainly lowered our flag in the city and left the organisation open to the charge of rowdyism. I sent a messenger with a note to the trader and asked him to send his bill for replacement of the windows, at the same time apologising for the disorderly conduct of our members. To his credit it must be said his bill was reasonable. I sent it to the director of the Belfast Boycott Committee with a full explanation, and by return of post a cheque for the full amount was paid. This same trader stopped Fox in the street later to express his appreciation of what we had done and gave a definite undertaking that he would cease dealing with Belfast.

This incident helped us as it put the boycott on a new standing in Derry and Unionist traders thereafter often sent for Fox to discuss questions relating to the boycott, and day by day new names were being added to our 'white list'. The pressure from Donegal through the loss of trade was beginning to tell, and Unionist as well as Catholic traders fell into line. On one occasion thirty-six Italian ice-cream merchants in Derry sent us a memorandum over their thirty-six names pledging compliance with our organisation's directives.

Derry merchants were now faced with the choice to trade with Belfast or Donegal, and, with very few exceptions, they very wisely chose in favour of Donegal. As our organisation became perfected, heavy fines were imposed for non-observance of the Belfast Boycott. Many traders had to pay these fines or lose their trade, as nobody dared go into a shop which was under an IRA ban. The fines collected from offenders made the enforcement of the boycott almost, if not wholly, self-supporting.

The holding up of trains and the burning of Belfast goods in transit could have given rise to looting on the part of the raiders. It speaks well for those who were involved in such operations that in the eight counties which I organised there was only one charge of looting, and, on investigation, that was proved to be without foundation. The charge in question was made direct to de Valera by the manager of a large firm.[10] He gave a list of goods which, he alleged, had been looted, as well as the names of the firms from whom the goods had been ordered. I was sent from Derry to investigate the case. An examination of this trader's books showed that in three years he had not placed an order with one particular firm which he had mentioned in his complaint. The investigation ultimately went on to establish that the charge was groundless and that a personal spleen between the OC of the local unit of the IRA and the manager of the firm was the sole reason why the complaint had been made.

On another occasion I was sent from Derry to a town in the West of Ireland to investigate a complaint by a number of traders from whom rather heavy fines had been collected. The traders had sent a deputation to the director of the Belfast Boycott in Dublin to demand that an investigation be made into the case. I made some preliminary inquiries and when I met the traders I was able to produce an invoice, showing that the chairman of the deputation had purchased three chests of tea within that very month from a pork butcher in County Armagh who was generally known to be acting as a Belfast agent. The invoice had been forwarded to me, after I had requested their assistance, by the intelligence department of the IRA, the efficiency of which in those days was almost uncanny, as they were able to acquire information from every conceivable source including government departments, railway companies and even Dublin Castle itself.[11]

THE WOUNDING OF DISTRICT INSPECTOR WALSH

As already indicated, I was responsible at that time for the prosecution of the Belfast Boycott not only in Counties Derry and Donegal, but also in Counties Fermanagh and Tyrone. Thus early in May 1921 I was directed to go to Dungannon to meet an organiser from Belfast. He drew my attention to the fact that Belfast firms were dumping goods in Dungannon, and Belfast bakeries, in particular, were doing an extensive trade around that district. A meeting was called at Dungannon which the Belfast organiser and I attended. It was decided that as a first step a bread van be burned on the road while on its delivery rounds. This would act as a warning to others and let them see that the organisation was in earnest.

Next day two bread vans were held up and burned. Police were rushed to the scene but the drivers of the vans could give no information beyond the fact that a number of armed men held them up and burned the vans. They could not identify anybody. The local district inspector of the RIC, a young, active man named Walsh, later returned alone to the scene of the burning which was a foolhardy thing for him to do. I do not think that he was even armed. On the way to the scene of the burnings he met a young man, who was 'on the run'. Again very foolishly the district inspector held him up and said: 'I have you at last.'

'Not yet,' was the reply, as the district inspector dropped on the road with a revolver bullet lodged in his shoulder. He was taken to hospital and his condition was described as serious, but he recovered after some months.

While these things were happening my Belfast friend and myself were having a quiet chat in the hotel, never dreaming that our instructions would be put into operation so swiftly and with such serious consequences. Things looked very dangerous in Dungannon later that day and during the evening rifle and revolver shots resounded through the streets. At eight o'clock we had attended a mission at which the congregation almost stampeded as shots rang out while the priest was preaching. He appealed to the people to keep their seats and remain calm. His own calm demeanour was an inspiring example to his congregation and he preached a lovely sermon and seemed deaf to the rifle shots that could clearly be heard from outside. A few arrests were made but nothing more serious than that happened.[12] In company with two commercial travellers I left next morning for Cookstown, where a bad shooting affray had taken place the previous night. I was glad to get back to Derry on the following day.

I had an amusing experience one day going from Enniskillen to Lisnaskea, a village some ten miles from Enniskillen. At Enniskillen station I was joined by a traveller, who told me that he was a Jew. We had a very enjoyable chat on the journey and arranged to be back together by the next train to Enniskillen. When our train pulled in at Lisnaskea station I noticed four members of the RIC on the platform. As my friend and I came alongside them they grabbed the Jew and held him, while I walked away as if I had been unacquainted with him. I felt very mean at such shabby desertion of my newfound friend, but there was nothing I could do to help him and he seemed capable of looking after himself. Returning by the next train we again joined company when he told me about everything that had happened to him. For over half an hour, it seems, he was subjected to a very severe questioning in matters relating to the IRA (he spat out when mentioning the IRA). His two cases of wares were turned out on the platform and examined minutely and, according to him, his false teeth were removed and examined. He was in a violent temper and continuously railed against the RIC.

I met this Jew two or three times afterwards doing his rounds of Fermanagh, Tyrone and Donegal and he was the last man in the world one would expect to be an IRA agent. Yet, I was later to discover, that is exactly what he was, and a very good one too.[13]

17

BACK TO NORMAL:
FEBRUARY 1922–MAY 1953

1921 and 1922 were eventful years.[1] The Truce between the Sinn Féin activists and the crown forces came into effect on 11 July 1921, the Treaty between the Irish representatives and His Majesty's government was signed on 6 December 1921. Michael Collins met Sir James Craig in London at the end of February 1922 and promised to call off the Belfast Boycott and end IRA activity in the North in return for a promise that the Northern Ireland government would protect the interests of the nationalist minority.[2] Collins and de Valera signed a pre-election pact on 20 May 1922 and a clear majority of the representatives who were returned to Dáil Éireann in the general election of 16 June 1922 were in favour of acceptance of the Treaty; Republicans, however, refused to abide by the decision of the electorate and the Civil War erupted on 28 June 1922. Jeremiah Mee was relieved at the Truce, bitterly disappointed with the Treaty, somewhat heartened by the Collins–de Valera pact and dismayed by the outbreak of the Civil War.

As a result of the Collins-Craig meeting a notice was issued to all inspectors and organisers of the Belfast Boycott, intimating that the organisation was being wound up within a month.[3] Most of those thus rendered jobless, however, were offered employment in the Irish White Cross. Jeremiah Mee had already made the transfer, his appointment to the Irish White Cross having become effective on 1 February 1922. The Irish White Cross was a charitable organisation which had been established some years previously in order to alleviate the distress of victims of the Anglo-Irish War. Most of its monies were subscribed by

Irish-Americans, but a considerable amount of them were also collected throughout Ireland.[4] As an organiser, Mee's duty was to ensure that an active branch of the Irish White Cross was established in every parish throughout his area. He was also expected to report on the operation of branches, to investigate the financial circumstances of those in receipt of help and to consider new applications for grants from the fund. In this connection between February and August 1922 he travelled extensively throughout his area, which consisted of Counties Carlow, Laois, Meath, Offaly and Westmeath.

With the intensification of the Civil War in the autumn of 1922 the distribution of Irish White Cross funds petered out and eventually the whole operation ground to a halt. Mee again found himself unemployed. But worse was to come. Strongly anti-Treaty in sentiment, he had kept aloof from the Civil War, yet on 12 August 1922 he was interned at Custume Barracks, Athlone, by the Free State forces. He was released after four weeks, on 13 September 1922, and went to his wife's home at Drumkeeran, Dromahair. The next year was probably the most difficult of his life. He found it impossible to obtain suitable employment. Yet he resisted the temptation to become embittered or to emigrate.

In September 1923 he secured an appointment as a superintendent with the British Petroleum (BP) Company Ltd. His function was to oversee the distribution of petrol and oil from the company's depot in Sligo, and also to develop new outlets in the area for the company's products. Some of the working conditions associated with his new post were quite unsatisfactory. Also, he and his colleagues soon adverted to the fact that, apparently, promotion in the company above the level of superintendent was closed to Irish Catholics. Consequently, Mee and a number of his colleagues, with a view to improving their conditions of employment, decided to establish an association to this end. They informed the management of their intention and were almost immediately threatened with dismissal if they persisted in it. Nevertheless, they went ahead and at a general meeting in Barry's Hotel, Great Denmark Street, Dublin, in August 1925, the association, called the Irish BP Protective Association, was established, and soon afterwards it was affiliated to the Irish Union of Distributive Workers and Clerks. Some weeks after the establishment of the association, a number of superintendents, including Mee, received dismissal notices. There followed a bitter and protracted strike in which Mee and his colleagues were eventually worsted. Mee again found himself out of work. Fortunately, this was not for long, as in February 1926 he took up an appointment with Russian Oil Products (ROP) Ltd, a rival to his old firm. He continued with this firm until 1932.

Then with the formation of the first Fianna Fáil government in 1932 he applied for reinstatement as a civil servant on the grounds that he was a former employee of the First Dáil. He received an appointment as an employment-insurance inspector in the Department of Local Government and Public Health, and was stationed in Longford. In 1936 he was transferred to Mullingar.

Later, in 1948, he was transferred to Dublin and in that same year he and his family, who had been residing in Mullingar, settled in the city. In 1949 Jeremiah Mee began a close friendship with the late Philip Rooney, who is best known as the author of the successful novel, *Captain Boycott*. Rooney encouraged Mee to record his fascinating reminiscences and helped him to have a series of seven articles on the Listowel police mutiny published between 25 November 1951 and 6 January 1952 in the Irish edition of *Reynolds News*, a former British Sunday newspaper, and later between 15 March and 26 April 1952 in the *Leitrim Leader*.

Throughout 1951 and 1952 Mee busied himself with his memoirs with a view to having them published. One feature of these memoirs was Mee's absolute reticence about his private life. He had a far more successful private life than most people. From 16 August 1920 until his death he was happily married to the former Miss Annie O'Rourke of Drumkeeran, Dromahair, County Leitrim, by whom he had two sons and four daughters, all of whom became eminently useful citizens. Another feature of his memoirs was that he did not have the pleasure of seeing them completed and published.

A good correspondent, he kept in touch with many of his former comrades, particularly Thomas Hughes who subsequently became bishop of Ondo-Ilorin in Nigeria. He made numerous representations to various Irish governments on behalf of some of his comrades who received inadequate or no pensions. For instance, it was typical of the man that, during the weeks before his death, he was taking great pains to ensure that his former comrade and fellow mutineer, John P. McNamara, would receive a pension. After a brief illness, Jeremiah Mee died on 8 May 1953. He was buried in Glasnevin Cemetery, Dublin, beside his wife who pre-deceased him in 1948.

APPENDIX 1

THE ROYAL IRISH CONSTABULARY

An attempt to establish an effective police force in Ireland was made in 1787 when the Irish parliament passed an act which set up a body of constables for the purpose of enforcing order in the country. This force proved to be altogether inadequate for the task required of it and a further act was passed in 1792 which was designed to make the force more efficient. In the period immediately after the Act of Union, the force became ineffectual. Then in 1814 an act was passed at Westminster which empowered the lord lieutenant to appoint a chief magistrate, a chief constable and fifty constables for each county. These appointments were known as the Peace Preservation Force, which remained in existence until the Constabulary Act of 1836.

In the meantime, in 1822, Sir Robert Peel, who was largely responsible for the 1814 Act, had founded the Irish Constabulary, consisting of an inspector-general for each province, controlling between them a force of 5,000 or 6,000 officers and men. These men were dressed in a dark-green uniform, were armed with flintlock carbines, and were soon popularly known as 'Peelers'.

Entitled 'An Act to consolidate the Laws relating to the Constabulary Force in Ireland', the Act of 1836, which was inspired by Thomas Drummond, under-secretary for Ireland from 1835 to 1840, completed the work of Sir Robert Peel. Popularly known as 'Drummond's Act', it formed the basis of the constitution of the Irish police force as it was to remain for the next eighty-six years. Apart from the police in the city of Dublin with which it did not concern itself, it placed nearly all the police in the country, both those belonging to the Peace Preservation Force and to the Irish Constabulary, under a central control.[1]

A reading of the 1836 act is essential for an understanding of the RIC. The act repeals certain previous acts of the reigns of George III and George IV which gave powers to appoint constables 'in certain cases'. Constables previously appointed were to be merged in the new force now created. Power was given to the lord lieutenant to appoint an 'Inspector-General of Police throughout Ireland, who shall reside in Dublin and shall be charged and invested with the general Direction and Superintendence of the Force to be established under this Act'; also 'One of two fit and proper persons to be Deputies to the said Inspector-General':

> And in order to provide for one uniform System of Rules and Regulations throughout the whole Establishment of Police in Ireland, be it enacted. That it shall and may be lawful for such Inspector-General from time to time to frame Rules, Orders, and Regulations for the general Government of the several Persons to be appointed under this Act.

Power was also given for the appointment of county inspectors and sub-inspectors. Finally, power was given for the appointment of the actual rank and file of the force:

> And be it enacted, That it shall be lawful for the Lord Lieutenant or other Chief Governor or Governors of Ireland to appoint from time to time at his Will and Pleasure, in and for each County of a City and County of a Town, except the said County of the City of Dublin, One Chief Constable, Two Head Constables, and any such Number of Constables and Sub-Constables, not exceeding One hundred, as may be deemed by him or them to be necessary and sufficient for the Preservation of the Peace therein, and in and for each Barony, Half Barony, or other division of Barony in each County at large, One Chief Constable, Two Head Constables, and any Number of Constables and Sub-Constables, not exceeding Sixteen.

And be it enacted, That no Person shall be appointed to be a Chief or other Constable or Sub-Constable under this Act unless he shall be of a sound Constitution, able-bodied, and under the Age of Forty Years, able to read and write, of a good Character for Honesty, Fidelity, and Activity; and that no person shall be appointed to be such Chief or other Constable or Sub-Constable who shall be a Game-keeper, Wood-ranger, Tithe Proctor, Viewer of Tithes, Bailiff, Sheriff's Bailiff, or Parish Clerk, or who shall be a hired Servant in the Employment of any Person whomsoever, or who shall keep any House for the Sale of Beer, Wines, or Spirituous Liquors by Retail.

And be it enacted, That no Person appointed under this Act ... shall be capable of holding the said Office or of acting in any way therein, until he shall take and subscribe the Oath here following; (that is to say)

I, A.B., do swear, That I will well and truly serve our Sovereign Lord the King in the Office of (Inspector, Constable. etc.) without Favour or Affection, Malice or Ill-Will; that I will see and cause His Majesty's Peace to be kept and preserved, and that I will prevent to the best of my Power all Offences against the same; And that while I shall continue to hold the said Office I will, to the best of my Skill and Knowledge, discharge all the Duties thereof, in the execution of Warrants and otherwise, faithfully according to Law; and that I do not now belong, and that I will not, while I shall hold the said Office, join, subscribe, or belong to any political Society whatsoever, or to any secret Society whatsoever, unless to the Society of Freemasons, So help me GOD.

And be it enacted, That it shall be lawful for the Lord Lieutenant ... to fix and appoint such annual Salaries as to him may from Time to Time seem proper, not exceeding the several Sums herein-after specified (that is to say) to the Inspector-General of Police an annual Salary not exceeding One thousand five hundred Pounds, to each Deputy Inspector an annual Salary not exceeding Eight hundred Pounds ... to each County Inspector an annual Salary not exceeding Five hundred Pounds, to each Sub-Inspector an annual Salary not exceeding Two hundred and Fifty Pounds, to each Chief Constable an annual Salary not exceeding One hundred and fifty Pounds, to each Head Constable an annual Salary not exceeding Seventy Pounds, to each Constable an annual Salary not exceeding Thirty-five Pounds, to each Sub-Constable an annual Salary not exceeding Twenty-five Pounds.[2]

In 1839 the reserve force was created and from 1842 on it was the practice to appoint cadets to be trained for the position of sub-inspector.

From 1814 the general expenditure on the police, including the salaries of its members, was defrayed partly by Grand Jury presentments, and partly out of the Consolidated Fund. Then in 1846 an act was passed which provided that the whole expense of the police should be borne by the Consolidated Fund, except a moiety of the cost of additional constabulary force applied for by the magistrates of any county or district, or of the reserve force stationed there by the lord lieutenant.

The Irish police force, as structured by Thomas Drummond, for a long time realised one of its main aims, namely, that of ensuring the continuation of British rule in Ireland. Its semi-military character, which arose from the way in which it was armed (with carbines and swords), officered (most of its supervisory staff spent some time in the regular army), and housed (its barracks were described with some justification as 'the blockhouses of Imperial rule in Ireland'),[3] grew, in a sense, out of the kind of work which it was expected to do. Thus the Irish Constabulary bore the brunt of the Tithe War, the Young Ireland threat, the Fenian Rising and the Land War. The force acquired the designation 'Royal' from Queen Victoria in 1867 in recognition of its services in the suppression of the Fenian Rising.

A cadet scheme whereby members of the Anglo-Irish ascendancy (sons of the gentry) were given commands at the rank of district inspector applied throughout the force's entire history. However, it was modified somewhat in 1895, from which date half the commissioned ranks in the force were filled by men who had risen from the ranks (rankers).

Thom's Directory for 1912 gives the RIC establishment for the year ending on 30 September 1910 as:

An Inspector-General, 1 Deputy Inspector-General, 2 Assistant Inspectors-General, 1 Commandant, 1 Surgeon, Veterinary Surgeon, 1 Barrack Master and Storekeeper, Police Instructor and Schoolmaster, 1 Town Inspector (Belfast), 36 County Inspectors, 196 District Inspectors, 233 Head-Constables, 1,681 Sergeants, 370 Acting-Sergeants, and 8,171 Constables – total 10,697.

And the expenditure on the force for the year ending 31 March 1911 was as follows:

Superintending officers' salaries and allowances	£15,003
Pay, allowances and travelling expenses	871,043
Clothing	37,700
Arms, ammunition, accoutrements and saddlery	2,441
Horses and forage	15,610
Rent of barracks, furniture, fuel, light and water	51,948
Pensions and gratuities[4]	411,348
Miscellaneous	13,480
	£1,418,573

During the early years of this century until the Easter Rising of 1916 the duties of the RIC were, on the whole, less exacting than usual. Much of their non-routine duty concerned isolated agrarian disputes.

A significant number of the younger members of the RIC joined the British army in 1914, many of them not returning to the force and some being killed in action during World War One.[5]

From 1917 on some members of the RIC were demanding the right to belong to a union. These members opened a branch office of the British-based National Union of Police and Prison Officers (NUP&PO) at 8 D'Olier Street, Dublin, in December 1918, after the home secretary had indicated on 12 September 1918 that there was no official objection to British police joining that union. In the meantime the question as to whether to allow the RIC to join this union was being deliberated by the Irish administration. Eventually the RIC was informed on 4 February 1919 that the lord lieutenant 'could not see his way to permitting them to join the NUP&PO'. However, by that time about a third of the membership of the RIC had joined the Irish branch of the NUP&PO. For more on the 'Police Union' see Appendix 3.

Between 1918 and 1920 conditions of service in the RIC were radically improved. A rise in pay was given to all members of the force in the second half of 1918 to compensate for the rise in the cost of living during the last part of the war. Then as a result of the Commission of Inquiry into the conditions of police service, which was presided over by Lord Desborough in 1919, dramatic improvements in pay and other conditions of service were granted to members of the force early in 1920.[6] Further improvements in their conditions of employment were granted to the men in June 1920 (see pp. 103, 352 n.2 and 391–2 n.13).

The force was caught up in the turmoil of the Anglo-Irish War from 1919 to July 1921 and during this period its character was changed radically.[7] It was disbanded on 31 August 1922, its place being taken by the Garda Síochána and the Royal Ulster Constabulary (RUC).[8]

The RIC exerted a major influence upon the development of the colonial police forces of the British Empire, serving as a model for many of these forces of the last century, being a major source of recruitment for their officers and even training some of their personnel at the depot in the Phoenix Park.

For more on the RIC, see H. L. Adam, *The Police Encyclopaedia, etc.* 1– (London 1920–); S. Breathnach, *The Irish Police from Earliest Times to the Present Day* (Dublin 1974); G. Broeker, *Rural Disorder and Police Reform in Ireland 1812–36* (London 1970); R. Curtis, *The History of the Royal Irish Constabulary* (Dublin 1871); G. Dillon, 'Legal and political position in pre-1916 Ireland', *University Review* 3 (1962), pp. 50–1; G. C. Duggan, 'The Royal Irish Constabulary', in *1916: The Easter Rising* (ed. O. D. Edwards and F. Pyle, London 1968), pp. 91–9; G. G. Green, *In the Royal Irish Constabulary* (London 1905); J. Herlihy, *The Royal*

Irish Constabulary 1816–1922 (Dublin 1999); I. O. [C. J. C. Street], *The Administration of Ireland, 1920* (London 1921); C. Jeffries, *The Colonial Police* (London 1952); H. R. Jones, *The Policeman's Manual of Sir Andrew Reed, K.C.B., C.V.O.* (7th ed., Dublin 1908); C. W. Leatham, *Sketch and stories of the Royal Irish Constabulary* (Dublin 1909); T. W. Williams (ed.) *The Irish Struggle 1916–1926* (London 1966), pp. 167–81; file in Garda archives called 'Notes for a history of police in Ireland' by Patrick J. Carroll (which is a sequel to a series on the beginning of the DMP).

There is an important and interesting eulogy of the rank and file of the RIC on pp. 393–5 of T. O'Rorke, *The History of Sligo: town and county* I (Dublin 1890).

Appendix 2

Inismurray Island

Inismurray Island is situated in Donegal Bay some seven miles due west of the village of Cliffony. It is a little more than a mile long and slightly more than half a mile wide. It consists of some 350 statute acres, 130 of these being shallow soil and cutaway bog.

In the *Irish Monthly* of August 1877 (pp. 433–9) there is an interesting piece on the island by Father John Healy, CC, Grange, who visited it on 21 September of the previous year.[1] At that time ninety-six people, besides four policemen, resided on the island. The islanders' livestock consisted of a number of small cows and sheep, as well as a few donkeys. Some thirty-five acres of the island were under crops of barley, potatoes and rye. Some time previously, it seems, much more barley had been grown and used in poteen-making which had been carried on extensively on the island, the islanders finding a ready market for their product on the mainland. However, this activity was brought to an end, at least temporarily, in the early 1870s when four members of the RIC were permanently stationed on the island.[2]

With the ending of poteen-making the resourceful islanders concentrated on their two other traditional activities, kelp-making and fishing. They produced the kelp from drift seaweed and delivered it by boat to Mullaghmore where it was sold to an agent of a Glasgow firm at £4 per ton. There was excellent fishing around the island, the most common kinds of fish being mackerel, pollock, ballan wrasse (bollen), and lobster. However, due to the rough seas in the area and also to the very rocky shoreline, they were able to fish only during the summer months.

Father Healy commented thus on the clothes of the islanders:

> The dress of the men consists generally of a coarse woollen vest and
> trousers, the women have somewhat differently shaped garments of the
> same material, while the gender of most of the juveniles, as far as their
> dress gave indication thereof, was decidedly epicene.

On the educational facilities on the island at that time, he observed:

> A national school was opened a few years ago. Most of the children can
> now read and write and are well instructed in the Christian doctrine.
> A short time ago Irish was exclusively the language of the people, but
> English is now commonly spoken. The schoolhouse at present is a
> cold and dreary timber-roofed shed, with only too much ventilation,
> and an earthen floor, where the poorly clad children put in a shivering
> and reluctant attendance in winter. The annual visit to this school for
> the results-examination is a source of terror to most of the Board's
> inspectors.

The island was and is part of the Catholic parish of Cliffony, in the
diocese of Elphin.[3] Mass was celebrated on the island only occasionally.
So each Sunday the islanders gathered in the tiny chapel of St Molaise,
which is part of the ruins of a sixth-century monastery, founded by
Saints Molaise and Columcille, and there they recited the Rosary. When
the weather was inclement they recited the Rosary in a few specified
homes. The people of the island had a strong personal devotion to St
Molaise, their patron, whom they referred to as 'Father Molosh'.

A few jottings on the island and its inhabitants which have been left by
Constable Jeremiah Mee further chart the history of that interesting little
place. Between 1918 and 1919 Mee made a number of visits to the island
in search of poteen and poteen-making equipment. It seems that after the
evacuation of the police barracks from the island in 1893 poteen-making
had again become an important occupation of the islanders, supplementing
considerably their income from fishing and the production of kelp. The

population had halved since 1877, there being only about fifty people on the island in 1918. The population was then made up of twelve families: of these four were named Heraughty, three Brady and one each with the names, Harte, McGowan, Mannion, O'Doyle and Watters. The local national school continued with only a handful of pupils. Moreover, by this time, the supply of turf, the island's only fuel, was practically exhausted. The people still gathered on Sundays in the chapel of St Molaise to recite the Rosary. Occasionally the priest came out from Cliffony to hear the islanders' confessions and to celebrate Mass.

As a result of his numerous trips to the island Mee became familiar with a number of the traditions and superstitions of the islanders. One interesting feature of the island was that it had its own king. He was the direct descendant of a man who was appointed king about 1830. It seems that the circumstances surrounding the latter's appointment were as follows. One day some members of the Gore-Booth family were out in their yacht off Inismurray Island when a sudden storm arose. The yacht was damaged and all on board were in danger of being drowned. Patrick Heraughty and his three sons rowed out from the island to the yacht and took the party on board, except the skipper, back to safety. The skipper had refused to leave his craft and set out for Mullaghmore, which, however, he never reached. In the meantime the Gore-Booths stayed for a few days on the island until the storm abated. In appreciation of his heroism and hospitality, the Gore-Booth family appointed Patrick Heraughty king of the island, a title which was held by his direct descendant, Michael Watters, in 1918. The king's function included settling disputes which arose among the islanders, 'giving out' the Rosary at St Molaise's little chapel on Sundays and officially welcoming visitors to the island.

The islanders, it seems, were exceedingly superstitious. This gave rise, for instance, to their having two burial grounds, one for men and one for women, as there was a strong tradition that if a man were buried in the women's plot he would be over the ground next morning and vice versa. The most interesting superstition referred to by Father Healy concerned some 'Cursing Stones' about which he wrote:

The islanders assert that if these stones are 'turned against anyone', that is, turned against a person with evil intent, some signal chastisement or untimely death will overtake that person within twelve months, if he deserves it, otherwise, the penalty will fall on the head of him who unjustly invoked the divine wrath.

In October 1948 the eleven families which still resided on the island – some fifty persons in all – settled on the mainland nearby.[4]

Appendix 3

A. Thomas J. McElligott ('Pro Patria') and the Police Union

Thomas J. McElligott, the second eldest in a family of sixteen, was born in a small hill-farm at Lacca, Duagh, County Kerry, on 2 April 1888. From 1891 to 1900 he attended the local national school at Derrindaffe. Except for a very brief period, during which he was apprenticed to a draper in Listowel, he spent the next seven years helping his father on the family farm.

In the spring of 1907 he applied for membership of the RIC, and on 25 October of that year he was called to train in the depot at Phoenix Park. On 5 May 1908 he received his first appointment. It was to Watergrasshill, ten miles north-east of Cork city. Two years later he was transferred to Crosshaven, County Cork. He was a keen and efficient policeman, and, after passing the 'P' examination he was promoted acting sergeant on 1 November 1914.[1] On 6 March 1915 he was transferred to the Reserve at the depot and soon afterwards he was appointed an inspector of weights and measures. He was transferred to Trim, County Meath, on 9 January 1917 and was promoted sergeant on 1 February 1918.

The Rising of 1916 and particularly its immediate aftermath had a considerable effect on him. Sooner than most of his comrades, he foresaw the dilemma in which members of the paramilitary RIC would be placed in the event of a serious conflict between Irish separatists and the crown forces. In the latter half of 1916 and throughout 1917 he discussed this aspect of service in the RIC with many of his comrades and discovered that most of them shared his distaste for being a member of an armed police force. During the course of his discussions a number of minor grievances, some of a local, others of a national character, were brought to his attention.

He became the articulate spokesman of a group within the RIC who felt that members of the force should be representatively organised in order that their grievances be presented effectively. About this time (1917–18), in spite of much government opposition, some of the British police had succeeded in reorganising the National Union of Police and Prison Officers, which had been founded in 1913 and was soon afterwards officially suppressed.[2] McElligott and his comrades, particularly William Hetherton,[3] Patrick J. McGuire and Edward Tarpey,[4] personally canvassed support throughout the DMP and RIC for an organisation which would concern itself with the interests of members of these forces, and would, at the same time, be affiliated to the National Union of Police and Prison Officers. Concurrently with these efforts there was a good deal of discussion not only in the *Constabulary Gazette* but also in the daily press on conditions in the RIC and the need for increased pay and pensions for members of the force.[5] McElligott and his comrades were agreeably surprised at the good response to their efforts to establish an organisation, whose aim would be the protection of the interests of the non-officer members of the DMP and RIC, and, accordingly, an Irish branch of the NUP&PO was founded with Thomas J. McElligott as its general secretary. This enabled McElligott, a few of his closest supporters and representatives of the DMP to assure the delegates to the conference which was held in the Mansion House on 18 April 1918 to organise national opposition to conscription, that, in the event of conscription being imposed by the British authorities, many members of the DMP[6] and RIC would, if called upon, join in a general strike.[7] McElligott also submitted a 'plan of resistance to conscription' to the Mansion House Conference, which was warmly endorsed.

Just as the conscription crisis of 1918 swelled the ranks of the Volunteers, so it also gave an impetus to the efforts being made by McElligott and his comrades to establish a union for members of the RIC. On 12 September 1918, after an agitation lasting almost a year and a strike by the police which began on 31 August 1918, the NUP&PO received official recognition from the British government. McElligott, as general secretary, immediately applied to the Dublin authorities for official recognition of the Irish Police and Prison Officers Union on the grounds that it was an affiliated branch of the now officially recognised NUP&PO. After waiting in vain for some months for a response to his application, McElligott opened an office for the union at 8 D'Olier Street, Dublin, in December 1918. Eventually, on 4 February 1919, McElligott received an official reply to the effect that after much deliberation the lord lieutenant 'could not see his way to permit the RIC to join the NUP&PO'. And, during the week ending 8 February, members of the force throughout Ireland were informed by the authorities that they were not to join the NUP&PO, as they belonged to a semi-military force under direct control of the crown and subject in many respects to the discipline and general conditions of employment of the army and navy.[8] This made a confrontation between the authorities and the union inevitable as, according to a report in the *Irish Independent* of 8 February, 'practically all the DMP had joined [the union], including the Harbour police. The majority of prison officials were also members, and so far about 3,500 of the RIC.'[9]

In the meantime the authorities in Dublin Castle were only too well aware of the growing impatience of many members of the RIC with the fact that their more serious grievances were not being dealt with.[10] Some administrative reforms were carried out. Further reforms were promised, and the inspector-general of the force went on an extensive fact-finding tour during February with a view to recommending what shape they should take. The authorities hoped, obviously, that these initiatives would dissipate somewhat the growing enthusiasm in the force for a strong, representative union. However, the rank and file membership, it seems, was not very impressed, as is clear from the following piece, which was inspired by McElligott and appeared in the *Irish Independent* of 6 March 1919:

Reform in the RIC

The Inspector-General of the Royal Irish Constabulary, it is understood, is now going through the country investigating the causes of the present discontent in the force. His object, apparently, is to ascertain the facts by personal interviews with the men. While giving General Byrne every credit for his good intentions it is necessary to point out that this method of investigation cannot be satisfactory. The members of the force are scarcely likely in personal interviews with the head of the Constabulary to state their grievances frankly and fully from the quite natural fear of being 'marked men' in the future. But, indeed, there is no necessity for this tour by the Inspector-General. He has the case of the men before him, with clear statements of their complaints and their hopes. What is wanted is a complete reform of the constitution of the force, beginning with the abolition of the cadet system, then throwing open promotion up to and including the rank of county inspector to the men and giving fair play to the Catholic members of the force. Already reform of a sort has begun by the permanent closing of 22 district stations. This may be a useful measure of economy, but it does not touch the grievances of the men. Rather it accentuates them, for a mere reduction in the number of district inspectors means less chance of promotion from the ranks, while it increases the disparity with the county inspectors by leaving their number intact. The men have asked for a special Irish Committee to investigate their case, and a proof of their reasonableness and confidence in the justice of their claims is the proposal that Mr Headlam, the Treasury Remembrancer, the Bishop of Ross and Sir Horace Plunkett should comprise the committee. A fairer proposal could not be made, yet it was turned down. The Home Office has appointed a committee, with Lord Desborough as chairman, to investigate the grievances of the police forces in Great Britain. Ireland, of course, is left out, but this would be an opportune time for the Government to set up an independent Irish Committee to go into the case of the RIC.

The Irish Union of Police and Prison Officers was invited, as an affiliated branch, to attend the annual conference of the NUP&PO in London on 24–27 March 1919. William Hetherton of Dublin, Thomas J. McElligott of Trim and John Brennan of Sligo led the DMP, RIC and prison officer delegates respectively. At the conference McElligott, in a trenchant speech, put forward the demands of the police members of the union. These were the amelioration of the financial and other material conditions of their service, a reform of promotion procedures, the disarming of the force and ensuring that they were employed as peace officers for the benefit of all sections of the community. Hetherton, who was elected to the executive committee of the NUP&PO, also spoke. Brennan spoke on behalf of the Irish prison officers. He followed up a previous resolution, which demanded that the increases of pay and pensions, and improvement in service conditions recently recommended by a parliamentary committee for the British police and prison officers, should be applied to their Irish counterparts, with a proposal which stressed that, in addition, all concessions of a general nature, including increases in pay and pensions, granted in future should be applied immediately to Ireland without further agitation. The addresses of the Irish delegates were very well received and the conference pledged support for their Irish comrades.

A report on the conference which appeared in the *Irish Independent* of 28 March 1919 caused much embarrassment to the Irish delegates. The report stated, among other things, that:

> The delegates listened attentively to the statements as to the position of Irish police officers and warders, as affected by the large number of political prisoners, and to the details of what constituted political offences in Ireland. The Irish delegates expressed their repugnance in having to deal officially with men with whom they were politically in agreement, and their sentiments were generally endorsed by the council.

There was a considerable unfavourable correspondence in the newspapers on the report, especially that part of it which is given above. Typical of the contributions was the following, which appeared in the

Belfast Telegraph of 31 March 1919. It gave most of the report which appeared in the *Irish Independent* and added:

> It is not clear whether the statement re the political agreement with Sinn Féin prisoners was made by a police officer or a prison officer. Two of the latter attended the delegate meeting as representing the Irish Prisons Service, and if the statement contained in above extract was made by either of them a majority of the Irish Prisons Service would condemn and repudiate both them and their statement. We as Irish prison officers are bound by oaths to perform our duties as loyal subjects of his Majesty the King, and whatever our opinions may be we should have no politics in matters of duty, or allow none to interfere with our duties. If, as these delegates state, they are politically in agreement with the Sinn Féiners, surely in honesty they ought to resign and join these men instead of wearing the King's uniform, for no one holding such opinions could be trusted either as a police or prison officer.

The sentence which caused the controversy, and which when taken out of context was quite misleading, had come from Brennan's address and he published a note and a letter repudiating the original report in the *Irish Independent* of 1 and 11 April respectively. McElligott, signing himself RIC delegate, also repudiated the *Irish Independent* report of 28 March in letters to the same newspaper on 2 and 12 April. In the former, he explained that at the conference:

> The Irish prison officers claimed to be put on the same basis and receive the same concessions as all other prison officers in the UK. In support of this it was urged (1) that if they were civil servants no distinction would be made between men serving in Ireland and in Great Britain; and (2) that they had more difficult and disagreeable duties to perform in Ireland in connection with the political prisoners. Without expressing either approval or condemnation, we explained how we were affected by political crimes and political prisoners, and it is correct to say 'the delegates listened attentively'.

In the letter he drew attention to the repudiations of the libellous report in the *Irish Independent* by Mr Brennan and the RIC delegate.

During March and April attempts were made to discredit McElligott and, thereby, the Irish Police and Prison Officers Union, by the publication of a number of misleading letters in the *Constabulary Gazette* under McElligott's by then well-known *nom de plume*, 'Pro Patria'. However, he quickly exposed these efforts in a letter which he had published in the *Irish Independent* of 12 May. The number of letters which he was having published in the newspapers at this time under his *nom de plume* was remarkable. Thus between 25 January and 26 April he had fourteen published: eleven in the *Irish Independent* and three in other newspapers.[11]

In mid-April, at the invitation of officials of the NUP&PO, he went, with two English policemen, on a speaking tour in England to encourage policemen to join the union.

The first and last general meeting of the RIC members of the Irish Police and Prison Officers Union was held in Dublin on 29 and 30 April and was a personal triumph for McElligott. The delegates elected him chairman and the conference adopted the various points of policy placed before it by the executive, most of which McElligott had been proposing publicly and privately for some two years. McElligott wrote the following report on the conference for the special conference number of the 'Police Union' newssheet:

RIC All-Ireland (Union) Conference

The first meeting – a Conference – of RIC representatives was held in Dublin (in the Branch Office), on the 29th and 30th April, for the purpose of setting up a uniform system of organisation throughout Ireland.

Bro. McElligott was unanimously elected Chairman.

As a policy three things had to be considered (1) the Union, (2) reform, and (3) better conditions of service. We had to devise a scheme to serve the first, to secure the second, and to safeguard the third.

It was unanimously decided to form an Organisation Committee in each County, and the following constitution of such Committee was agreed upon:

(1) That a Committee be appointed in each County, consisting, if possible, of a Chairman, Treasurer, and Secretary, and two members from each district. The Secretary to be registered at Headquarters in 6 D'Olier Street, and all County correspondence to be conducted through him. The Committee can be formed into a County Branch of the NUP&PO in accordance with rule xiii.

The members of the Committee in each District are to undertake the organisation of the Union by interviewing non-members and requesting them to join, keeping a list of members, supply of application forms, and sending cards, etc., to Organising Secretary.

To facilitate the work of organisation, the delegates attending the Conference will take back a list giving names and addresses of all members in County, and a supply of application forms.

(2) Two thousand copies of the Magazine will be got in D'Olier Street. The RIC requiring 1,400. The Branch Secretary to order a supply for each County, at least one or two copies for each station. The Committee to undertake sale and distribution of same, and return cash to Head Offices in D'Olier Street. This is only a temporary arrangement. Copies of special Conference number to be procured if possible.

(3) Rule Books. The Branch Secretary to order a supply of Rule Books for every member of the Union in County. Price 3d [1p].

(4) The Branch Secretary also to order a supply of Badges for each member. Price 1/– [5p].

Proposed by Bro. —— (Limerick), seconded by Bro. —— (Waterford), and carried unanimously: 'That this conference, representing the whole of Ireland, do pledge ourselves to stand by our British comrades, and give them the assurance of our sympathy and support in their fight for full rights and recognition of the National Union of Police and Prison Officers, and extend to them our warmest thanks for the support given to us in our fight for emancipation, and, further, pass a vote of thanks for the kindly and enthusiastic reception given to our delegates who attended conference at Memorial Hall, London.'

Proposed by Bro. —— (Wicklow), seconded by Bro. —— (Dublin), and carried unanimously: 'That we endorse the resolution passed by the Council of Delegates to immediately disarm the Royal Irish Constabulary, and do further urge that the rifles are responsible for all attacks on the police raids on barracks, and loss of life; that they are not required by the DMP, and that they are useless and unnecessary for the RIC except for drill and ceremonial purposes; that men are withdrawn from practical police duties, and, like soldiers confined to barracks, which are now being converted into magazines and stores for arms, ammunition, and in some cases explosives and that failing immediate disarmament, means be adopted for giving effect to the resolution.'

Proposed by Bro. —— (Kilkenny), seconded by Bro. —— (Westmeath), and carried unanimously: 'That the cadet system of officering the force be abolished, and that all promotions be made from the ranks, as in every other police force; that rankers be immediately admitted into the higher ranks, which must be no longer reserved for a particular class, and that the proposed appointments of military cadets be cancelled.'

Proposed by Bro. —— (Cork), seconded by Bro. —— (Armagh), and carried unanimously: 'That we endorse the resolution passed by the Council of Delegates, demanding that the projected increases and revisions of the pay, pensions, and conditions of service of the Parliamentary Police Committee shall apply equally to the Irish Police, and we further urge that a Bill based on the Report be introduced for all ranks in the Irish Police at the same time as the Bills for the Police in Great Britain.'

Proposed by Bro. —— (Derry), seconded by Bro. —— (Depot, ex-Army), and passed unanimously: 'That this Conference respectfully ask our Authorities to give sympathetic consideration to the claims already put forward by our comrades who have rejoined the Force from the Army.'

Proposed by Bro. —— (Down), seconded by Bro. —— (Waterford): 'That this conference, representing the whole of Ireland, express disapproval at the action of any County Force in petitioning our Authorities for a rise in pay etc., pending the findings of Lord Desborough's Commission, when a national memorial will be sent forward. We call upon our comrades throughout Ireland to avoid any County or sectional action, as such is inopportune and detrimental to our interests, and also to cancel or withdraw all current circulars on the subject.'

An addendum to this resolution was proposed by Bro. —— (Cork), and seconded by Bro. —— (Belfast) 'That, in accordance with the Cork circular, application be made on the 6th May, through the I.G., to the Chief Secretary to appoint a day to receive a deputation, with the object of having recommendations of Parliamentary Police Committee applied equally to the Irish Police, and that in the event of application being granted, permission be also granted to hold a meeting in each County for the purpose of electing a delegate, and allowing the delegates to meet in Dublin to select the deputation.'

After a long discussion, the addendum was adopted, the 'wee county' dissenting.

The addendum created a difficult situation by approving what was condemned – 'sectional action'. Under the circumstances sectional action had to be taken somewhere to bring about organisation. The Cork City Committee, NUP&PO, circularised all Ireland on the 18th April, stating that they would make (and requesting every district to make) on 3rd May an application, through I.G., to the Chief Secretary to receive a deputation. At the Conference it was stated that all replies were in favour of the circular, therefore it could not be prevented (in two days), and should be supported. In order to facilitate 'slack' Counties, that date was changed to 6th, and after the Conference, as a result of further representations, it was postponed to the 12th, with the result that applications were made on three different dates.

A vote of thanks to the Chairman concluded a memorable, and, I think I can say, a historic Conference.

I wish it to be clearly understood that sectional action must be avoided everywhere in future, and that the decisions of a Conference will not be altered by subsequent representations.

The delegates have felt the spirit of trade unionism, they have seen the dawn of freedom, and every man left the Conference determined to fight for and stand by, his Union and his comrades in Great Britain.

The movement is spreading like a prairie fire, fanned by every passing breeze, and wisely left unchecked, unnoticed, and unopposed.

Organisation started at once. The office staff had everything in readiness, so that one Delegate reported 'Organisation Committee appointed' next day.

Now every Delegate, every member, should ask himself: 'What have I done, what am I doing, and what will I do to make the Union a success?'

Things to remember: Through the Union – the London Police strike – the R.I.C. got an increase of eleven shillings per week instead of one. Because they have a Union they will be treated like men, not like slaves, and in future they will get what they never got, fair play and a living wage. We realise now that we are all brothers, members of one family; that we have a common cause, and that we must have a common platform. The object of the Union is to 'maintain', not to 'subvert', discipline. United we wish to see tried 'the restrictive arts of Government' – a recognition that Ireland is in the United Kingdom, and that unity 'will serve to sinew the State in times of danger'.

Sir J. M. Barrie, a Scotsman, in one of his plays, said the English so dearly loved the Irish they would never consent to separate from them. Little did he dream that a time would come when the Irish would so love the English that they would fear separation, and cry out 'Save the Union'.

We will succeed, and of course we know that we cannot be seriously opposed in maintaining a real Union (the Union of Crown Forces) between Great Britain and Ireland.

T. J. McElligott, Chairman,
Member of Executive Committee.

Copies of the resolutions, which were passed at the conference, were sent by the general secretary to the chief secretary for Ireland, the inspector-general of the RIC, the chief commissioner of the DMP, the home secretary and the press.

The fact that the names of those who participated in the various discussions at the conference were not disclosed indicates that the members of the union expected the authorities to make some discriminatory moves against the union membership. These moves began almost immediately after the conference. County and district inspectors let it be known that they strongly disapproved of men joining the Police Union. In many places self-confessed members of the union found themselves the objects of special attention at monthly and quarterly inspections, and some were transferred to less desirable stations ('bog-stations'). Also a policy, which had begun in 1918 and which was referred to in the House of Lords on 20 June 1918 by Lord Wimborne, as removing 'from the Irish government nearly all those who sympathised with the cause of Irish nationality, or those who professed the Catholic faith' and which 'was not confined to the office of the lord lieutenant or to the chief secretary but extended to the lord chief justice, and to the commander of the forces in Ireland – and extended even to simple colonels' (see *Irish Independent*, 21 June 1918), was intensified. According to Thomas J. McElligott (cf. p. 232–3 and his papers), the implementation of this policy prompted a letter from Timothy M. (Tim) Healy to the *Sunday Express* in June 1918 in which he asked '… what statute enacts that thirty out of thirty-two county inspectors in Ireland must be "Tories"?'[12] In spite of such protests this trend continued. Thus in the *Irish Independent* of 1 January 1919 one finds: 'At present there are only three Catholic county inspectors as against thirty-four Protestants.' And, a month later, in the *Weekly Freeman* of 1 February 1919 it was stated: '… of the thirty-seven county inspectors, thirty-four are Protestants and three are Catholics.'

Pressure was maintained on those who were known to be officials of the union. McElligott, who was still stationed at Trim, County Meath, was forced to resign on 22 May 1919.[13] In his letter of resignation,

which he published in the Police Union newssheet, he pledged that
he would continue his work for the union and its members.[14] On 4
June McElligott wrote a letter to Tim Healy which, in effect, appealed
for a public indication of the latter's support of the Police Union, but
Healy declined to give such an indication of support on the grounds
that at that time he had 'no way of giving effect to my views'. Early
in August, together with Sergeant Lakey of London, a member of the
executive of the NUP&PO, McElligott attended a private session of the
annual Trade Union Congress, then being held at Drogheda, at which
he put forward the policy of his union and was assured of the support
of Congress.[15] From this time on he was a lifelong friend of Thomas
(Tom) Johnson, leader of the Irish Labour Party.

By now McElligott was finding it well-nigh impossible to publicise
his views. This he had always managed to do in letters to the newspapers.
However, on 12 September 1919 he received a letter from Timothy R.
Harrington, editor of the *Irish Independent*, which stated:

> My experience for several weeks past was that the Press Censor
> invariably prohibited the publication of your letters, the reason being, I
> believe, that they apprehended there was much more underneath what
> you wrote than what appeared on the surface. The same reason applies
> to the enclosed communication.
>
> Since the Press Censorship ceased we have been definitely and
> specifically cautioned and warned that we incur grave risk to our
> publications if we publish any of your letters, and under the circumstances
> I regret I am unable to publish enclosed.

About the middle of December McElligott had a number of meetings
with Austin Stack, minister of home affairs in the First Dáil, at
which he discussed at length the worsening plight of the RIC in the
developing hostilities between the forces of Sinn Féin and the forces
of the crown.[16] Earlier in October he was back home in Lacca, Duagh,
County Kerry. He continued his work for the Police Union which, in
spite of official discouragement, remained in existence. He was now, in

effect, a full-time organiser of the union, and acted also as its chairman, secretary and treasurer.

A new level of intensity in the official campaign against the union and all it stood for was reached in January 1920 when the inspector-general himself, Sir Joseph A. Byrne, a Catholic and a moderate, was dismissed without any official explanation being given for this action. It seems that one of the reasons for his dismissal was a lack of ruthlessness in his efforts to stamp out the Police Union and the nationalist feeling which characterised many of its members. It was generally known that another, and, perhaps, the decisive reason for his dismissal was that he stated in his annual report for 1919: 'If we had no rifles we should be quite safe; we do not need rifles for the discharge of our ordinary duties.'[17] The rank and file of the RIC were shocked by the dismissal of General Byrne who was popular and known to be concerned for the welfare of his men. The Police Union organised a protest meeting of the police of Leinster in the depot at Dublin against the dismissal of their chief. And, in spite of the threat that those who attended it would be dismissed, the meeting was a wonderful success. However, at the request of General Byrne, no further protest meetings were sponsored by the union.

Changes continued to be made up to the first week in April in the leadership of the RIC at all levels. In a number of cases moderate men were replaced by policemen who were more 'in line with government policy', that is, who were more committed to an all-out confrontation between the RIC and Sinn Féin.

On 20 March 1920 Tomás MacCurtain, Sinn Féin lord mayor of Cork, was shot dead in his home. On 17 April the inquest on the killing concluded with a unanimous verdict of wilful murder against some unknown members of the RIC. Not only the verdict but the conduct of the police during the inquest, which had opened on 20 March, disturbed even those who supported the Irish government. Thus a letter from Dr Daniel Cohalan, bishop of Cork, was published in *The Freeman's Journal* of 29 March 1920 in which he gravely censured the police. Towards the end of the letter Cohalan wrote:

There is a question which I, as an individual bishop, do not undertake to answer, but I respectfully submit that it might be a question, a moral question, for the general body of the bishops.

The question is this: Should the bishops tell the police that they are not bound in conscience to perform the many acts of coercion which are goading the people beyond restraint; that there can be lawfulness and unlawfulness in executive government; that when that mode of government has no sanction in the moral law its execution has no sanction in the moral law?

About the middle of April after conferring with Michael Collins on the significance of the bishop's question and the way in which it was posed, McElligott, at Collins' request, travelled to Cork to meet Terence MacSwiney, lord mayor of the city and OC Cork Brigade No. 1, IRA. McElligott wished to discover from MacSwiney if it would be worthwhile to approach the bishop with a view to asking him to state explicitly the duty of members of the RIC to refuse to carry out immoral orders. Collins, presumably, hoped that any pronouncement from the bishop along these lines could be used to damage further the morale of the force. McElligott met MacSwiney and Florence O'Donoghue, adjutant and intelligence officer of Cork Brigade No. 1, IRA, at the City Hall and was advised that an interview with the bishop on the matter in question would be futile. However, this was not the end of the affair. In accordance with McElligott's suggestion, Collins, it seems, subsequently had delivered to some members of the Catholic hierarchy, one of whom was Dr John M. Harty, archbishop of Cashel and Emly, copies of secret orders issued to the RIC which were difficult to justify on moral grounds and which had been intercepted by his intelligence network (information taken from letter, dated 23 March 1952, from Thomas J. McElligott to Maurice (Moss) Twomey).

From January 1920 McElligott and a committee had been supervising a national collection which he organised on behalf of Patrick J. McGuire and Edward Tarpey, two men who were closely identified with the union and who, like himself, had been dismissed the previous May.

(Their dismissals came on 28 May, a week after McElligott's.) Eventually, in spite of his explicit wishes to the contrary, McElligott was also included in the testimonial to which a substantial part (almost half) of the membership of the RIC – members, former members and friends of the Police Union – contributed.[18] About the middle of June McElligott and the committee began to wind up the collection which realised £5,281.10 (£5,281 2s), this sum being later divided equally between McElligott, McGuire and Tarpey.

Then on 19 June came the Listowel police mutiny. Six of the fourteen constables involved in this incident had been members of the Police Union and, in fact, had given McElligott generous contributions to the McElligott, McGuire, Tarpey Testimonial the previous month. In a circular which he issued to members of the RIC on 20 August 1920, McElligott claimed, in effect, that the Police Union was flourishing, stating, among other things, 'In Leinster, Munster and Connacht – excepting Kildare, King's, Queen's and Mayo – the overwhelming majority are in the Union ... Ulster is backward, but every county is represented ... I cannot forget a strong "three-figure minority" in Belfast and a workable "two-figure majority" in Derry city.' However, it is most likely that his sole evidence for this assertion was the subscription list of the testimonial. At any rate there is a significant correspondence between the areas mentioned above, where the union was, according to McElligott, strongly represented, and those areas from which there was a good response to the testimonial. In fact, it seems that at this time the Police Union had more or less petered out. In spite of this, when Michael Collins sent Jeremiah Mee, principal in the Listowel police mutiny, to Listowel, in particular, and Kerry, in general, in October 1920 to explore the possibility of a mass walkout by members of the RIC in that county, one of the first people Mee met in connection to this was Thomas J. McElligott, who, besides his connection with the Police Union, was one of the architects of a new policy by Sinn Féin towards the RIC (cf. Appendix 10).[19] In the meantime a thinly veiled pro-Sinn Féin propagandist piece by McElligott on the question of the police in Ireland was published in the *American Weekly News Bulletin*, 22 March 1920 (see pp. 231–4). This was followed by a lengthy letter which appeared in *The Freeman's Journal* of 25 May 1920 in which McElligott, writing again on the question of police reform, urged (1) abolition of the cadet system, (2) all promotion from the ranks, (3) Catholic emancipation overhead, (4) abolition of county system by amalgamation of counties, and (5) disarmament of the force.[20]

During 1921 he placed his knowledge of the RIC at the service of the Sinn Féin propaganda department of Dáil Éireann. He also made an occasional contribution on police matters to Irish-Ireland publications. Thus in the 3 December 1921 issue of *Young Ireland* there is a piece by him which treats with the greatest cynicism the claims that arms had been stolen from the police barracks in the Unionist village of Kesh, County Fermanagh.

On 20 October 1921 he was appointed an inspector in the Irish White Cross. This involved his visiting parish branches of the organisation and reporting on their operations. It also entailed investigating the material circumstances of the various individuals who were in receipt of help from the Irish White Cross and also considering further applications for financial assistance. In this connection between 27 October 1921 and 7 January 1922 he travelled extensively in West Cork, Clare, all the counties of Connacht and Donegal.

Meanwhile, in August and September 1921, McElligott had written a number of letters to Michael Collins suggesting that an organisation be established for resigned and dismissed members of the RIC. Collins was sympathetic to the suggestion (see p. 283), and, accordingly, McElligott, on behalf of a small, ad-hoc committee, issued a circular on 11 October 1921 to the resigned and dismissed members of the RIC and DMP setting out the aims and desirability of such an organisation and inviting them to join it. There was a good response to McElligott's letter. Later, county committees were established and delegates selected to attend a national conference of the organisation. This was held at the Mansion House, Dublin, on 24 January 1922, McElligott being both the organising secretary of, and principal speaker at, the conference. At the conference McElligott was elected to the executive committee of the

Constable Jeremiah Mee (1889–1953) in his RIC uniform.

Members of the RIC in Cork *c.* 1920. *Courtesy of Mercier Archives*

Constable Daniel B. O'Connell (1887–1975).

Sergeant Patrick Flynn (1866–1936).

Constable John Donovan (1891–1964).

Bishop Thomas Hughes (1891–1957) in 1944.

Constable James Gormley (1891–1916).

John Cotter (1897–1977).

General (Sir) Hugh H. Tudor (1871–1965), police adviser to the viceroy, with members of the RIC and Auxiliaries at the Depot, Phoenix Park, in 1921.

General (Sir) Joseph Aloysius Byrne (1874–1942), inspector-general of the RIC.

Lieutenant Gerald B. F. Smyth, RE (1885–1920), in 1912.

District Inspector Thomas Flanagan, RIC (1872–1932).

Constable Patrick J. Sheeran (1892–1969).

Constable Michael Fitzgerald, Free State army (1898–1945).

Constable Bernard Conway (1893–1979).

Constable Thomas W. Hargaden (1895–1976). His whistle chain, belt, handcuff case and baton case appear clearly in the picture.

Ruins of the home of Bernard Conway some nine months after its destruction by members of the crown forces on the night of 28 October 1920. Also included are Conway's mother, Mrs Bridget Conway and niece, Miss Bridget Conway.

Constable Michael Lillis (1886–1959) in the backyard of Listowel police barracks, Christmas Day 1911.

Listowel police barracks in August 1922 after it had been burnt by members of the anti-Treaty forces.

Constable Francis J. Byrnes (1886–1965) with carbine and sword-bayonet.

Constable John P. McNamara (1899–1969) with black cane stick.

Countess Markievicz (1868–1927), first minister for labour in the First Dáil.
Courtesy of Mercier Archives

Constable Michael Kelly (1893–1979).

Eilís bean Uí Chonaill (*née* Ryan) (1897–1979), staff member of the ministry of labour in the First Dáil.

Joseph M. MacDonagh (1883–1922), third minister of labour in the First Dáil and acting director of the Belfast Boycott.

Lily O'Brennan (1878–1948), staff member of the ministry of labour in the First Dáil.

Richard Cotter (1891–1929), secretary of the ministry of labour in the First Dáil.

Patrick J. McGuire (1893–1959).

Thomas J. McElligott ('Pro Patria') (1888–1961).

resigned and dismissed members of the RIC and DMP (1916–21), and was appointed to a delegation which was instructed by the conference to meet Arthur Griffith and also Éamon de Valera.[21] During the course of his address to the conference, McElligott commended all members, including those present, of the RIC and DMP who had resigned or were dismissed because of their unwillingness to co-operate with the British forces in their campaign of repression in Ireland. He also stated that members of the RIC who served until disbandment were 'a disgrace to their country' – this blanket condemnation, which was echoed in more moderate terms on the same occasion by Jeremiah Mee, provoked a lively correspondence in the newspapers at that time.[22]

McElligott was most disappointed with the terms of the Treaty and adopted an anti-Treaty stance in the subsequent acrimonious debate. Nevertheless, in June 1922 he was nominated by Michael Collins and Arthur Griffith to a commission which had been set up to advise on the shape of the new Irish police force then coming into being. Not least as a result of his strong representations, it was decided that the new force should be unarmed and that promotion should be from the ranks, two principles which he had been advocating for quite some time.

Next, he was nominated by some of his former comrades to a five-man commission established to investigate the plight of those members of the RIC and DMP who had resigned or been dismissed between 1916 and 1921. Before the commission began its deliberations, however, he received a letter from the Department of Justice questioning his credentials to sit on the commission. While this issue was being discussed by McElligott and the department, he was arrested and interned. This occurred at the beginning of November 1922, apparently because his strong anti-Treaty views were generally known, as was his friendship and association with Austin Stack, one of the principals in the tragic struggle between the Free State and Republican forces then in progress.

McElligott was interned in Hut 24, Hare Park, the Curragh. During the next three months he threw himself into the life of the camp, organising and attending Irish- and French-language classes, physical training sessions and courses of political indoctrination. After his release in early February 1923 he returned to his home at Lacca, Duagh, County Kerry.

In May of that same year he was caught in a big round-up of Republicans and imprisoned in Mountjoy jail, Dublin, where for the next three months he shared a cell with Count George N. Plunkett. At the end of this period he was interned under the Emergency Powers Act of 9 August 1923 at the Curragh in Tintown No. 3 internment camp, where he shared Hut 19 for the next four months with some forty-five others, among whom were such subsequently well-known Republicans as Neil Blaney, Michael Hilliard, Brian Ó h-Uigín and Dr James (Jim) Ryan. Although he doubted its usefulness, he joined in the general hunger strike of Republican prisoners, which was begun in mid October, and among his papers he has left an interesting account of his thirty-five-day ordeal. The strike was called off on 22 November and he was released on 1 December. After spending a week in the Mater Hospital, Dublin, he returned to his home at Lacca, Duagh.

In the autumn of 1924 he married Miss Honora Mangan and settled in the Mangan family farm at Bedford, a mile north of Listowel. He continued to take a keen interest in politics and to be an enthusiastic follower of de Valera. Although unhappy at the manner in which it caused a further division in the Republican movement, McElligott supported de Valera when in March 1927 he broke away from Sinn Féin to found the Fianna Fáil party and five months later took his seat in Dáil Éireann. After the Fianna Fáil party formed a government in 1932 McElligott was appointed to a National Grain Council. Earlier McElligott had been the subject of some controversy when de Valera, first on 16 November 1927 and, later, on 17 July 1928, questioned Earnán de Blaghd, the minister for finance, in the Dáil on an unsuccessful application which McElligott had made for a pension.[23] McElligott continued to be prominently associated with the Organisation of Resigned and Dismissed RIC and DMP (1916–1921), which had been founded on 24 January 1922, in order to press the government for a just treatment of their claims. And, since he had led a deputation to discuss the organisation's claims with de Valera and Austin Stack in the spring of 1922, it was not surprising that he played a major role in the negotiations which took place in 1934 between this organisation and the first Fianna Fáil government.

In 1938 he bought a property, Easton House, at Leixlip, County Kildare, where he ran a family farm. From about that time on he was greatly influenced by Walter Nash, a minister for finance in the Labour government in New Zealand.[24] He considered that the socialist policies proposed and, to a large extent, implemented by Nash and his colleagues would be as beneficial to Ireland as they were to New Zealand because of significant similarities between the two countries. This, in turn, led to his becoming intensely interested in financial reform, and, in 1943, he published pamphlets entitled *National Monetary Policy (No. 15)* and *National Agricultural Policy* (No. 17) in the series 'Towards a New Ireland', issued during World War Two by The Irish People Cooperative Society.

He gradually became disillusioned with the policies of the Fianna Fáil party and government, not least because of its failure to make any progress towards eliminating the partition of Ireland, and, although not joining it, he supported Seán MacBride's party, Clann na Poblachta, which was founded in 1948. He was appointed to the national executive of the Trees for Ireland Committee in 1949. After the IRA border campaign of the 1950s, he was associated with organisations working for the welfare of the resultant political prisoners. He continued to write to the newspapers on the various topics in which he was interested. He constantly underlined the growing imbalance between the nation's urban and rural populations, and he was a tireless advocate of decentralisation. He died on 24 June 1961.[25]

B. Dublin Metropolitan Police Catholic Society

At a specially summoned meeting of representatives from each barrack, held on Tuesday evening, the following resolution was unanimously agreed to, and directions given to have same conveyed to the Conference of the Leaders of the Irish Parties to be held in the Mansion House, on Thursday 18th inst:

> That we the members of the above Society, representing three-fourths of the Dublin Metropolitan Police Force,[26] desire to inform the Conference that, in the event of the Conscription Act being enforced in this country, we will whole-heartedly give our support to whatever line of action may be agreed upon by your Conference, and are prepared to take our stand with our fellow-countrymen in resisting its application.
> JAMES MURRAY,
> 17th April 1918.
> Secretary

Thousands of the RIC throughout the length and breadth of Ireland have signed this pledge to resist conscription, and joined with their co-religionists and fellow-countrymen in declaring their intention to resist the scourge. Now is the time for you to assert your manhood; you owe your allegiance to your Faith and Fatherland, not to an ascendancy in Dublin Castle or Downing Street. Don't be idle! Don't resign now, but be ready when called upon! Friends will visit you, give them your assistance.[27]

C. TRIBUTE TO THOMAS J. MCELLIGOTT'S CONTRIBUTION TO THE DEFEAT OF CONSCRIPTION[28]

Immediately before the anti-conscription campaign in this country, Mr McElligott was in touch with the people concerned, and that is on record. The President can ascertain that, and the Minister for Finance, I am sure, is well aware that he submitted to that conference in the Mansion House a memorandum dealing with the best means of fighting conscription and that memorandum was adopted. Amongst the people who have already stated that in the Press is Mr Thomas Johnson. Mr Johnson wrote a letter to the Press setting out all these facts and stating that the memorandum was furnished at that time and set out all the circumstances in connection with it. I have also a letter from Mr Nugent of the AOH setting out some of the facts and stating that when he was in the British House of Commons information was conveyed to him through Mr McElligott. I shall read a portion of that letter which was written to Mr McElligott and dated the 30th July 1928:

As soon as the Ancient Order of Hibernians learned early in 1917 that it was the intention of the British Government to enforce Conscription in Ireland we proceeded to organise all the available forces to resist so gross a tyranny. Amongst these forces were the two great police organisations, the Royal Irish Constabulary and the Dublin Metropolitan Police. You were one of the first to respond and your action was wholly spontaneous. You immediately sent me an intimation that you were prepared and anxious to assist the Anti-Conscription Movement, your attitude being that you looked upon the threat of compulsory enlistment as an outrage on the Irish Nation so long as the majority of the Irish representatives were opposed to it.

Inquiries made at the time satisfied me that there was no ulterior motive behind your action – that you were acting solely from the impulse of patriotism. In the first place, you were popular with your colleagues. Secondly, you had been successful in obtaining promotion as a sergeant, not through any services rendered to the enemies of Ireland, but because you had passed with flying colours in the examination for what was known as the 'P' list. You not only assisted in the organisation of the police force in Meath, but you furnished me with valuable introductions, some of them even to members of the force who held positions on the Headquarters' Staff. I was then, and I am still, convinced that the organisation of the police force – both the RIC and the DMP – had a mighty influence in altering the decision of the Government, or rather the Ascendancy, who were behind the Government and had been egging it on, and the Military junta in the control of the Army.

Largely through your influence and by means of the wonderfully effective system of communications you had already established I was able to obtain copies at the very earliest moment of all the circulars and secret documents that were being sent to the County and District Inspectors of the Constabulary. So effective indeed was your action, and so completely did it on many occasions defeat the purposes of the Government, that the then Chief Secretary, Mr Shortt, declared in the British House of Commons that I had obtained circulars and utilised the information contained in them before there had been time for them to be communicated to the rank and file of the police force.

The services rendered by Irishmen to their country and the sacrifices made by them for the national cause in the past often not only went unrewarded but were actually forgotten, or slurred over as of no account; but I can at least bear testimony to what you did, and pay tribute to the patriotic motives by which you and other members of the RIC were inspired at a great crisis in the National movement when vital issues were at stake.

After Mr Johnson's letter was published, there was a leading article in the *Irish Independent* which set out that the editor of the *Independent* himself could vouch, of his own personal knowledge, as to Mr Mc-Elligott's activities at the time. This is the extract:

As Mr Thomas Johnson and others have testified, he gave valuable assistance to the National cause during the anti-conscription campaign. Through all that crisis he conveyed useful information to the leaders of the resistance movement; for several years he was in constant communication with the editor of the *Irish Independent*; and we have no hesitation in asserting that the movement inaugurated by him was one of the driving forces behind the subsequent resignations.

D. THE IRISH POLICE QUESTION[29]

In order to understand Ireland we must see how it is governed, and to understand the police we must see how they are employed. The world knows how Ireland is governed but few will realise that, in the words of Sir Horace Plunkett, 'this monstrous substitute for statesmanship is superimposed upon the largest police force in proportion to population in the world'. Yet this police force, supported by a huge army of occupation, has not only failed in maintaining law and order but it has succeeded in making the government of Ireland impossible.

The police are not to blame; they are the best disciplined and, in one sense, the most efficient police force in the world. But the system – a nationalised, armed and political force, employed in maintaining a brutal and indefensible system of police government – is wholly responsible for the outrages and murders of today.

Ireland has long enjoyed the privilege of a nationalised police force, i.e., a semi-military organisation officered by a class ascendancy and controlled, not by local authorities, but by the crown, as a substitute for peace officers. Unlike all other policemen, the RIC are equipped in military fashion with rifles, bayonets and bombs, and their barracks (not stations) are now converted into fortresses. They are political inasmuch as they are employed to maintain 'the party in power', to persecute, prosecute and coerce all who do not hold views in agreement with Dublin Castle, to prohibit and suppress the rights and opinions of the majority and to encourage offences by the minority. Hence the RIC have earned the title 'enemies of their country' and unfortunately they are socially ostracised. Such is the situation as seen from without.

Seen from within it is much more serious. The inner system of police government is notoriously political and, as Sir Horace Plunkett said at the National Liberal Club, 'Ulster applies the moral coercion to the British Government who pass it on in the shape of physical coercion to the rest of Ireland.' The moral coercion is applied in secret but it is an open secret. The physical coercion is applied openly and secretly by Dublin Castle. It is applied openly where force is wrongfully and unreasonably used in order to create ill-feeling between the people and the police. It is applied secretly by many secret orders which goad and drive the people into violence, retaliation and rebellion. This statement is founded on facts which can be proved if necessary.

Dublin Castle says:

(a) Smash disloyal bands and this will have a salutary effect.

(b) In cases of cattle driving, etc., call in the military on all sides, remember that 'it is essential that the people should be roughly handled'.[30]

(c) Shoot your prisoner if the escort is attacked, as a district inspector publicly admitted in cross examination at a court-martial.[31]

How many bands in Ireland would be considered 'loyal'? Who will believe that smashing them will have a salutary effect? Why is it essential that the people should be roughly handled? How would armed police and military give effect to such an order? If the district inspector shot his prisoner what would be the result?

With over eleven years experience in the RIC (half that time a sergeant) I say that the inner system is based on this principle that it is necessary to perpetuate and maintain ill-feeling between police and people – whilst waiting for an 'atmosphere' favourable for a settlement. This is both easy and simple under the same military system where the police are not under the control of local authorities or even chief magistrate of a city. In Ireland a policeman cannot be stationed in his native county, or in any county where either himself or his wife have any relations. Familiarity with the public is an offence against police regulations punishable with transfer. Hence it is ordained that the police must be alienated from the people from top to bottom.

County inspectors invariably belong to the religious ascendancy; but, though this cannot be excused, justified or defended on religious grounds, still it arises more from a political than a religious motivation. The county inspector is in the county where Dublin Castle is in Ireland and hence it is easy to understand Mr T. M. Healy asking in the

Sunday Express what statute enacts that thirty out of thirty-two county inspectors in Ireland must be 'Tories'.[32]

The proportion of police to population cannot be justified even on military grounds. Scotland, with roughly the same area and population as Ireland, has less than 6,000 police. Ireland has a fixed quota of over 12,000. As the country is over-policed and the police over-officered, there is an authority for every 3.1 men and a sergeant for every 3.88 constables.

Even under the Act of Union the police system in Ireland is brutal, obsolete, uneconomical and indefensible. The present condition of our unhappy country, and, above all, the spectacle of a fine police force murdered and ground down without mercy or consideration between those who are determined by all means and at all costs to maintain law and order and those who by any means and at any cost are determined to make the present government of Ireland impossible is to be deplored. Both sides to the present conflict have decided that force against force is the remedy, and damn the consequences. As a result of this policy the police force has broken down, barracks have been closed all over the country and the people left without any police protection. Even so, the police are powerless to protect others by force, powerless to protect themselves. The Army of Occupation is for the protection of semi-military police and to help them in maintaining law and order. It has failed. Outrages and murders will continue, few will be brought to justice, and no one will be found to play the role of informer now. Increase the army by 500,000 men, put a guard or garrison in every city, town or village, or scatter them like sheep on the mountains, and it will make no difference. Take them all away and a state of war still exists. In other words, force will not prevent the Irish people from demanding self-determination and unfortunately the Government is employing the police to suppress this demand in the most provocative manner possible.

The deficiency is in moral force and the police themselves are convinced that moral force will succeed where military and semi-military force have been tried and failed. By immediately disarming the RIC raids on barracks will be prevented and all police stations throughout

Ireland will be safe from attack as the DMP stations are at present. In the outskirts of the city there are two police stations within 100 yards of each other – one RIC and one DMP. The former is locked, barred and bolted and the men confined within a fortress of sandbags and wire, armed with rifles, bombs and rockets. The latter is even more open than Bishopsgate Police Station in London and less likely to be raided.

The police question then goes to the root of the Irish question itself. One cannot be settled without the other.

E. Letter from Most Revd Daniel Cohalan, DD, Bishop of Cork, to the Editor of *The Times*[33]

Sir,

The decision of the Cabinet to allow the Lord Mayor of Cork to die in prison is greatly to be deplored. This decision and the whole Government administration in Ireland are vividly reminiscent of the Balfourian administration in the days of the land agitation. Now, as then, the orders of the day are 'Don't hesitate to shoot', 'put them under lock and key', 'humiliate your political opponents when you have them in gaol by equating them with common criminals', 'let the fellows die in gaol'. These formulas expressed the haughty and disdainful policy of the Salisbury-Balfour Government towards the land serfs and workers in Ireland in the days of the land struggle. The world is supposed to have been made safe for democracy, but the Government of Ireland is now infinitely more lawless than it was during the land agitation; and unfortunately there is no Gladstone to awaken England to a sense of the enormities committed in her name in Ireland.

The Balfourian policy was resumed when Sir Edward Carson was sent to Belfast to preach a crusade against Home Rule. Let there be no mistake about it: Sir Edward Carson, in his Ulster campaign, was merely the tool of the Unionist Party. All the leaders of Unionism endorsed his policy. It was a villainous policy, and it is only now that the fruits are ripening. In the last analysis the Carson campaign was an appeal to religious hatred and fanaticism. It was said in effect to the Protestants of Ulster: Your political and religious liberties will be lost under Home Rule; you will be governed by Home Rule; you would, perhaps, have nothing to fear from your Catholic neighbours if they were left alone, but under Home Rule you will be dominated by an intolerant foreign potentate, the Pope of Rome. And with the single and honourable exception of the late Sir Mark Sykes, there was not to be found a single British Unionist, Protestant or Catholic, to protest against this campaign of evil. It destroyed the Liberal Government; and its fruits can be seen in the attacks on the persons and property of Catholics in Belfast, Derry and Lisburn. These attacks on the person and property of Catholics, where Protestants are in a notable majority, are bad in themselves, but they are particularly evil in a country like Ireland, where the unlawful actions of one party tend to become in time a principle of action by another party; and it would be deplorable if the rule of life in Ireland became attacks on the person and property of Catholics by Protestants in the north, and in the south attacks by Catholics on the person and property of Protestants.

The Prime Minister, in a reply to Miss MacSwiney, which by its terms has deeply wounded the wife and sisters of the Lord Mayor of Cork, said 'that it is the first duty of the Government to afford every protection to those brave men who are discharging their difficult duty in the face of grave peril'. Allow me then, Sir, to state the facts about the police question, as these facts absolutely demonstrate the revival of the old Balfourian reign of oppression, only more intensified, and at the same time the absolute chaos and bankruptcy of government in Ireland.

1. There have been many murders of policemen in Ireland. These have been condemned by the Catholic hierarchy; and on a recent occasion when a policeman was murdered in the porch of a church I myself inflicted the canonical punishment of 'interdict from the Church' on the criminals.

2. Several innocent people have been murdered by the police in the way of reprisals. The government of Ireland has come to this –

that when a policeman is murdered no attempt is made to discover the murderer, but the police in retaliation murdered somebody else. When a policeman is murdered in the South the Crown lawyers say the murderer cannot be discovered because the people sympathise with the murderer; but if a civilian is murdered by the police or soldiers, or if a Catholic is murdered in the North of Ireland, the murderer goes free without any Government imputation against the general Protestant public.

3. The late Lord Mayor of Cork was murdered by the police on the morning of 20 March 1920. Up to the present day the Government has done nothing to discover the murderers of Lord Mayor MacCurtain. The reason is obvious. I now say to the Prime Minister: Establish a judicial tribunal of inquiry which can be trusted, and you will get positive convincing proof that the murder was committed by the police; you will get positive convincing proof that District Inspector Swanzy, recently murdered at Lisburn, was himself deeply implicated in the murder of the Lord Mayor in Cork, where he was at the time Inspector of the Police. And let this contrast be noticed; Mr Swanzy was a Protestant and Unionist, and, though he was known to have taken part in organising the murder of Lord Mayor MacCurtain, there was no retaliation on his fellow-Protestants and Unionists in Cork; but when Mr Swanzy himself was murdered, in turn, in Lisburn, the houses of several Catholics were burned in retaliation. Mr Swanzy should have been removed from office after the murder in Cork; and then most probably he himself would not have been murdered.

4. Colonel Smyth, Divisional Commissioner of Police, was shot on account of the programme of police action which he propounded to the police at Listowel; and undoubtedly the Irish Government is responsible for his murder by retaining him in his office after that deplorable speech. Again I say to the Prime Minister: Set up a trustworthy judicial tribunal and, despite Sir Hamar Greenwood's denial, you will get convincing proof that Colonel Smyth did deliver the speech imputed to him; and you will also get information which may astonish you as to what organisation the murderers belonged.

5. Mr Lloyd George speaks of the police as brave men, discharging a difficult duty. The police are brave men; but the police are not now discharging any of the real police duties in Ireland. The fundamental trouble in regard to the police is that they have been converted into a military force, that they have been drawn off from their real police duty, that they are being employed solely in watching and tracking political opponents of the Coercionist Government. It is now a familiar (and true) expression, that the government of Ireland is government by imprisonment, by deportation, by arson, by murder. Fortunately there is very little of ordinary crime in Ireland; but if a non-political murder were committed the police would be helpless to make investigations. If a theft or a robbery takes place there is no use in reporting it to the constabulary. Street traffic, offences on the streets, drunken brawls or quarrels, violation of licensing laws – these are no longer a care to the R.I. Constabulary; the only persons to maintain order and to protect property are the Sinn Féin voluntary police, and the people of every creed and class invoke their assistance. But when a policeman is shot or fired at then 'law and order' are vindicated by murder or arson, some innocent person is shot by way of reprisal, and houses and property are burned.

It is this state of things which has at last alarmed moderate people of all classes throughout Ireland, and which is bringing them together to try to agree on a system of self-government which may be generally acceptable in Ireland. Already great progress has been made in this direction. And everyone who sincerely loves Ireland must hope and pray for the success of this movement, for the establishment of a system of self-government which will restore public order in Ireland. The establishment of an acceptable system of self-government would restore public order as speedily as the enactment of good land laws restored order after the days of the land war.

Nothing should be done that would render the work of pacification difficult. The Lord Mayor of Cork should be instantly released. What is his crime? Was there any charge of an antecedent crime imputed to him on the night of his arrest? There was none. His pockets and his desk were searched and a charge was founded on papers found on his person. What were the charges? The first was a copy of the speech he made last March at his inauguration, and which was published in the newspapers. But how is it that the speech delivered in March, and published in the papers, becomes a danger to the realm only in August? The second charge was a copy of a resolution of loyalty to Dáil Éireann. And, again, how does this become a danger to the realm? The third charge was that the military found, not on his person, but in his desk, a recent police code. But why should the possession of a police code by the Lord Mayor of a city be considered a danger to the realm? The charge against the Lord Mayor is a proof that in Ireland the police are diverted from their natural work and made the instrument of a partisan oppressive Government. Why should the police have a code which could not be entrusted to the Lord Mayor of a city?

The Lord Mayor of Cork should be liberated at once. It offends the sense of justice to learn that a man was sentenced to two years' imprisonment on such charge. The Prime Minister says that 'if the Lord Mayor were released every hunger striker, whatever his offence, would have to be let off'. Obviously that is not true. No one who loves social order would support a demand which would make imprisonment impossible, no matter what the offence. But the offences imputed to the Lord Mayor, as stated, have no substance. The tribunal was a military tribunal. The sentence of two years' imprisonment has no moral sanction; it is a manifest injustice. And as the sentence has no moral sanction the Lord Mayor should not be left to die in gaol; the Lord Mayor should be released at once.

To add a personal touch, let me add I have visited the Lord Mayor of Cork in prison. To put it mildly, I was scrupulously careful against saying anything that would confirm him in his resolution to continue the hunger strike. He said to me: 'Your lordship, my conscience is quite at ease about the course I am taking; I made a general confession this morning; I receive Holy Communion every morning; I might never again be so well prepared for death; I gladly make the sacrifice; they are trying to break the spirit of our people; my death will be an example and an appeal to our young men to make every sacrifice for Ireland.'

May I ask you, sir, is it just to prolong the suffering of such a noble specimen of our humanity? I hope you will continue to use your powerful influence for the immediate release of the Lord Mayor of Cork.

Yours faithfully.

+ DANIEL COHALAN, Bishop of Cork.

Corpus Christi Church, Maiden-lane.

August 27.

APPENDIX 4

INCIDENT AT COOKSTOWN POLICE BARRACKS ON 17 JUNE 1920

This incident was reported as follows in the *Irish Independent* of 18 June:

Another Barracks attacked
Two hours fight at Cookstown
Young man's death
Policemen on guard disarmed
Carsonite Volunteers wait for orders

A determined attack was made on Cookstown police barracks yesterday morning by armed men who gained an entrance to the building but were forced to retire. Police reinforcements who left Dungannon when the attack was reported met a motor car, in which they found Patrick Loughran, Dungannon, who was suffering from gunshot wounds. He was arrested and taken to Belfast, where he succumbed. It is stated that three raiders were seriously wounded, while Constable Henderson, one of the garrison of ten, was slightly wounded on the forehead by a bullet or flying missile. Forty Ulster Volunteers, armed with revolvers, assembled a quarter of a mile from the barracks, but did not assist the garrison as they were 'waiting for orders'.

Guards overpowered
Raiders in bare feet

The attack opened at 2.30 a.m. and lasted over an hour, the official report reckoning the number of attackers at thirty, while other accounts state there were a hundred. The raiders arrived in motor cars and, crossing a garden to the rear of the barracks, they entered through a back window, there being no defensive works in the rear. All the raiders were masked.

Constables Hargaden and Henderson who were on guard were at once overpowered, disarmed and tied up. The raiders, who had taken off their boots, then went upstairs, according to the *Belfast Telegraph* [of June 17], to the room where the eleven-year-old daughter of Head Constable [Henry] O'Neill was sleeping. They carried her down to the guardroom and, in answer to her pathetic appeals not to shoot her father or mother, they assured her that no harm would come to her or to her parents.

Meanwhile other raiders knocked at the head constable's bedroom door and, in answer to his enquiry as to who was there, the reply came, 'officer', in tones which were an almost perfect imitation of District Inspector [George] Hall's voice. Two shots were then fired through the door, one bullet passing within a few inches of the head constable's head. He immediately returned the fire with his revolver and the raiders retired from the barracks.

The other members of the garrison were then aroused, their comrades released, and the defence began. Bullets rained on the back of the barracks, on which side the greater portion of the attacking force was concentrated. Bombs and hand grenades were freely used on both sides …

After the raiders had withdrawn the police found blood-stained handkerchiefs and traces of blood in the vicinity. They also found several pairs of boots and stockings. It was found that the wires to Dungannon had been cut while it is stated an attempt had been made to deplete the Cookstown garrison by rumours of a contemplated attack on Coagh police barracks the same night, as a result of which a sergeant and two constables were sent to Coagh that same evening.

Waiting for Orders

Forty members of the Ulster Volunteer Force, armed with revolvers, took up a position at Oldtown [hill], a quarter of a mile from the barracks, as soon as they were aroused by the firing but, according to the *Belfast Telegraph*, they took no part in helping the defenders as they waited on instructions from the police.

District Inspector Hall, who does not reside in the barracks, was awakened by the firing and made his way to assist the garrison.

When word of the attack reached Dungannon early yesterday morning, police at once set out in motor cars for Cookstown. On nearing Newmills they met a motor car, which they stopped, and found it contained Patrick Loughran, Quinn's Lane, Dungannon, who was in a state of collapse. The police took charge of him and conveyed him to Dungannon Hospital, where it was found that he was suffering from serious gunshot wounds in the abdomen and thigh, and had apparently been already medically attended to. Dr F. C. Mann recommended that an operation should be at once performed and the man was conveyed by police escort to the Mater Hospital, Belfast, where he died yesterday. Michael McIlhogue [McIlhone] the driver of the motor-car, was also detained by the police.

In 1951 at the request of his friend Jeremiah Mee, ex-Constable Thomas W. (Liam) Hargaden recorded the inside story of this incident at Cookstown RIC Barracks.[1] It seems that Hargaden and three other constables, Bernard Conway, Denis A. Leonard, and John O'Boyle, all from the west of Ireland and all with latent Sinn Féin sympathies, were stationed in Cookstown police barracks in early 1920. Most of their comrades were northern Protestants and loyalists. As a result of numerous heated discussions in the barracks mess room on the political situation at that time a serious antagonism developed between these four men and the rest of the garrison, an antagonism which stimulated the former's latent Sinn Féin sympathies. Eventually, because of some vicious baiting of Constable Denis A. Leonard – whose Sinn Féin sympathies were notorious and for which he had been reduced in rank from sergeant to constable in 1915 – the four decided at the end of March 1920 to facilitate an IRA raid on Cookstown police barracks. They realised that such a raid, if successful, would be of great propaganda value to the IRA at that time, because Cookstown was an important barracks, as well as being situated in the heart of loyalist Ulster.

Leonard immediately made contact with a prominent Sinn Féin sympathiser in Cookstown and within a week the four constables met an IRA officer from Dungannon in Peter Mulgrew's public house in Molesworth Street. They placed their proposal before him. He was extremely cautious and simply promised to keep in touch with them. Some seven weeks later Conway and Leonard, in the company of two IRA officers from Dungannon, named William J. (Willie John) Kelly and Thomas (Tom) Leonard, attended a meeting in Keady, County Armagh, which was presided over by Charles (Charlie) Daly, then OC of the IRA in that area. At the meeting it was decided to raid the barracks at 2 a.m. on 4 June. According to a general plan, which was worked out, the door at the rear of the barracks was to be left unlocked between 1.30 and 2.30 on that particular morning.

On 1 June an IRA scout arrived at Cookstown barracks and, under the guise of being a tradesman inspecting what repairs had to be done inside the barracks, he was shown over it by Conway. On the morning of 4 June the four constables prepared for the raid. Conway was barracks orderly on that night and morning and another ensured that the door at the rear of the police barracks was left unlocked at the agreed time. And, to ensure that, in the event of a hitch, none of the raiders would be shot, Constable Liam Hargaden had rendered temporarily useless thirty rifles and twenty revolvers which were in the barracks, by filing down their strikers. However, the raid did not materialise. It seems that the scout reported unfavourably on the project, asserting that the military had taken over the barracks. The real reason, perhaps, why the IRA did not move was that they feared that, if they went ahead with the raid, they might walk into a carefully prepared trap.

The intrepid four in Cookstown again made contact with the IRA, and succeeded in dispelling their doubts. The new time which was fixed for the raid was 2 a.m. on 17 June. In the meantime Constables Conway and O'Boyle were sent on temporary duty to Coagh and Rock respectively, both places being some seven miles from Cookstown. The IRA were informed of these transfers but intimated that they would go ahead with the proposed raid as long as even one pro-Sinn Féin constable remained in Cookstown police barracks.

Accordingly Hargaden ensured that he was barracks orderly on the night of 17 June. About 1 a.m. Leonard came downstairs in a shirt, trousers and pair of stockings and unlocked the door at the rear of the police barracks. Exactly at 2.15 a.m. units of the IRA from Dungannon and Keady walked quietly into the barracks dayroom. They exchanged a password with Hargaden and proceeded to tie him up, together with a Constable Henderson who was sleeping in the dayroom. The two were then placed under guard in the coalhouse. At this stage also the raiders forced open one of the windows at the rear of the barracks in order to give the impression that this was how they had gained admission. The raiders next set about taking possession of the arms, ammunition and bombs, which were stored in the barracks. In order to do this they had to go upstairs. The head constable (and his wife and family) slept on the first floor, and the other policemen on the top floor, which contained four bedrooms with four single beds in each. Some of the raiders went to the top floor and, helped by Leonard, proceeded to collect all the firearms and ammunition which they could find. In the meantime two of them tried to enter the head constable's bedroom but found it locked. A few shots were then exchanged between those and the head constable. This awakened the sleeping policemen. A great deal of shooting followed, as the raiders made a quick exit, but not before one of them was seriously wounded. He was later discovered in a car which was held up outside Newmills. He was taken to Dungannon Hospital and later transferred to the Mater Hospital, Belfast, where he died.

As a result of the raid Constable Leonard was dismissed and warned to leave the country at once. Constables Conway, Hargaden and O'Boyle resigned within the following three months.[2]

Appendix 5

Orders Issued by Colonel Smyth

A: Orders and Notes Issued from Divisional Commissioner Smyth's Office in Cork on 10, 11, 17 June 1920

Order No. 1
by Lieut. Colonel G. F. Smyth, D.C.
10.6.1920

1. Every effort will be made to bring the garrisons of all stations up to 15 men.

2. The police will occupy the same building as the Military wherever there is a Military post except at County and District Headquarters. At Headquarters Stations they will also occupy the same building unless there are excellent reasons to the contrary. These reasons will be forwarded to this Office by return of post.

3. The number of police at combined Military and Police stations will be reduced to a minimum. At out stations three will be sufficient. The men left at these stations will be the men with the best local knowledge and will act as guides to the Military. At least one must be a Sergeant or Head Constable. The other police will be used to strengthen weak stations.

4. When the police vacate a barrack to occupy the same house as the Military, the Sinn Féiners may burn the old barrack. I do not much mind if they do, but as a preventative the following procedure will be adopted:

(a) Before vacating the barracks select the house of a leading Sinn Féiner and send me the particulars of it. I will then send you an order to requisition it and you will be ready to act.

(b) Warn the occupier that if the barracks are burnt, his house will be seized in lieu in 24 hours.

(c) If the barracks are burned give the occupier 24 hours to clear out and then evict him. Leave the house empty in case we need it.

(d) Consider this house as the barracks, select another, send me particulars, and warn the occupier as before.

5. Report when paragraphs 2, 3 and 4 of order have been fully complied with.

(Signed) G. F. SMYTH,
Lieut. Colonel,
D.C.

Order No. 2
by Lieut. Colonel G. F. Smyth, D.C.
(a copy of this order is to be posted in every barrack)

1. In every station where the Police or combined Police and Military are over 14 strong patrols will be sent out at night on at least five nights a week and preferably every night. Patrols to be at least eight strong.
2. Stereotyped patrols are useless. We are up against a cunning enemy and will only defeat him if every man uses his brains.
3. The following are some obvious hints:

(a) Never go out before dark.

(b) Never go out through the front door if you can get over the back wall or through a side window.

(c) Never go out twice at the same time or follow the same route twice.

(d) Never go along the road if you can avoid it. Go across country.

(e) Wear shoes if you have them.

(f) Make sure that you are not followed. Let one man drop in a ditch whilst the rest of the patrol moves on a couple of hundred yards. He will soon see if anyone is following.

4. The main object of patrolling is to stop illegal movement by night. Therefore get across country to a road, lie up behind the hedge, and hold up everyone who comes along. Put out a man a hundred yards on either side of the main group. He will shout 'Halt in the King's name' to all motors. Other traffic he will let pass and the main group will halt and search them, whilst the single man will hold up anyone who tries to escape.

5. Patrols should not as a rule move outside a three-mile radius from their barracks. If the barracks are attacked in their absence so much the better. The patrol can then take the attackers in the rear by surprise. Remember that even seasoned regular troops will not stand if surprised by night from the rear. So as long as patrols are intelligently led and surprise the enemy they have nothing to fear and everything to gain.

6. If a patrol finds roads blocked they can soon tell if their own barracks is threatened or not. If it is not, the leader must decide which is the most likely barracks in the neighbourhood to be attacked and move in that direction. He may be wrong but there is a chance that he may be right and may be able to take the attackers in the rear. If he does nothing he can expect no results and I will have him reduced to the ranks for inefficiency.

(Signed) G. F. SMYTH,
10.6.1920 Lieut. Colonel,
D.C.

Order No. 3
by Lieut. Colonel G. F. Smyth, D.C.

In future all letters relating to discipline, rewards, promotions etc. will be sent through this office.

Promotion throughout the force during the present emergency will be by selection and not by seniority. In recommendations for promotion I will be guided largely by results. I quite realise that, as far as operations go, results are purely a matter of luck.

The most energetic and capable officers may, in spite of all their efforts, have no success. But the results of their energy and capacity will be clear in their arrangements for the defence of their barracks and the comfort of their men.

(Signed) G. F. SMYTH,

Lieut. Colonel,

D.C.

10.6.1920

Order No. 4

By Lieut. Colonel G. F. Smyth, D.C.

1. In every barrack each man must have a definite position to occupy in case of alarm.

2. Each man's name will be written on the wall above his position, also a list of the bombs etc., which he requires.

3. There must be a reserve in each barracks to meet any unforeseen occurrence, even if it only consists of the Sergeant and one man. The best position for this reserve should be carefully thought out.

(Signed) G. F. SMYTH,

Lieut. Colonel,

D.C.

10.6.1920

Notes on Defences of Barracks

1. The only forms of attacks to be expected are:

(a) An explosive charge placed against or outside a wall to blow it down.

(b) An attack on the roof from an adjoining house.

(c) An explosive charge in a neighbouring house.

2. Petrol and oil will probably be used in both forms of attack.

3. For 'A' we want barbed wire. The easiest way to put up barbed wire is

to drive nails, spikes or staples into the wall about 6 feet up and pickets into the ground about 5 feet from the wall. Run the wire criss cross from the pickets to the nails and pull it as tight as possible. Then throw in loose wire to fill up. Leave gaps opposite the doors and make knife rests to close them at night.

Remember that wire which cannot be fired into is not much use and that wire which cannot be either fired into or bombed is useless as the attackers can cut it up at their leisure.

4. The existing bombing holes are far too small. We want a hole big enough to allow a man to put his head and shoulders through and listen for attackers. We want a hole big enough for a man to put out his arm and shoulder and aim and throw a bomb instead of poking it out. We want to protect the man whilst he is doing this from rifle fire.

Try this method. Take two stout pieces of wood about 4 feet long and 3 or 4 inches in diameter. Near one end of each cut a deep groove across the piece of wood into which the steel plate will fit tightly.

Then nail the piece of wood into the bottom corners of the bombing hole so that they are horizontal and the grooves are 9 inches beyond the outside face of the wall.

Take a small steel plate from one of the windows and fix it in the grooves. Drive in nails to steady it, and, if necessary, fix two pieces of wood similarly in the top corners of the hole. The plate will then sit 9 inches clear of the wall and will cover a man who is firing or bombing from the hole.

5. Remember that if you have no barbed wire you must be particularly careful that no one can work against the wall without you being able to firstly hear him and secondly bomb and shoot him.

6. Remember that it must be possible from some loophole in the barrack to fire on every possible position which an attacker may occupy.

7. To defeat 'B' which is now the Sinn Féiners main method adopt the following expedients.

(a) The Sinn Féiner has to break a hole in the neighbouring roof to get at ours. If we hear him and are ready we can shoot him as soon as he pokes his head out. To do this we must have a fire position all ready. So at the head of the barrack furthest from the adjoining house cut a good big hole in the ceiling and rig up a rough ladder so that a man can get up into the ceiling joists in a minute. If the rafters are far enough apart to let his shoulders through he will then only have to knock off the slates to fire. If they are not cut a piece out of one at once. The roof will still stand.

(b) When the Sinn Féiner has got on to the next roof he then drops bombs and weights on to the roof, firstly to break in the roof and 2nd to break in the ceiling.

We cannot stop him breaking in the roof except by shooting him, but, if we nail meshed rabbit wire to the undersides of the roof and rafters for a distance of 6 feet from the neighbouring house it will catch the first of his bombs and give us some time. With luck the bombs will roll down the wire and burst on top of the side wall.

(c) Then the Sinn Féiner next pours in oil and petrol. We have found by experiment that if the top of the ceiling is covered with a layer of earth a quarter to half an inch thick the petrol burns away and sets fire to nothing. So cover your ceiling with earth for a distance of six feet from the adjoining house. Do not put in a thick layer or you will break the ceiling.

8. To defeat 'C' if the Sinn Féiners blow in the party wall between the barracks and the neighbouring house we are still alright if we have the opposite wall of the room loopholed.

If they try to come through the breach we can shoot them. So get your loopholes made now.

Order No. 5
by Lieut. Colonel G. F. Smyth, D.S.O.
Divisional Commissioner R.I.C., Munster No. 2
Cork, 17th June 1920

1. I wish to make the present situation clear to all ranks.

2. A policeman is perfectly justified in shooting any man who is seen

with arms and who does not immediately throw up his hands when ordered.

A policeman is perfectly justified in shooting any man who he has good reason to believe is carrying arms and who does not immediately throw up his hands when ordered.

3. Every proper precaution for protection will be given to police at inquests, so that no information will be given to Sinn Féin as to identity of individuals and movements of police. This was ably managed by Counsel at a recent inquest at Limerick.

4. I wish to make it perfectly clear to all ranks that I will not tolerate any 'reprisals'. They bring discredit on the police. I will deal most severely with any Officer or man concerned in them.

(Signed) G. F. SMYTH, Lieut. Colonel,

Divisional Commissioner, R.I.C.

Order No. 6
by Lieut. Colonel G. F. Smyth, D.S.O.

1. The Police are warned that on no account are they to make use of ammunition seized from Sinn Féiners.

2. Only such ammunition as is officially issued is to be used.

3. All seized ammunition is to be buried at least 3 feet deep where it cannot be found.

17.6.1920.

(Signed) G. F. SMYTH, Lieut.-Colonel, D.S.O.

These documents were discovered on 6 March 1922 by the intelligence officer of the 4th Battalion of Waterford No. 1 Brigade, IRA, in the RIC barracks at Lady Lane, Waterford city.[1]

The following covering note was with the Order Nos. 1, 2 and 3:

Divisional Commissioner's Office

Cork, June 10th 1920

Herewith	5	Copies of	Instruction	No. 1	
	27	"	do	No. 2	For C.I. and D.I.
	27	"	Order	No. 1	Do
	27	"	do	No. 2	& for each
	27	"	do	No. 3	Station

Instruction No. 1 is only intended for District Inspr's and Head Constables. Instruction No. 2 and Orders should be distributed to each Barrack as soon as possible. Please acknowledge.

    W. D. KING

    Captain.

    By order of D.C.

Copy to C.I. Listowel

    "   Tralee

    "   Bandon

    "   Cork

    "   Mallow

    "   Waterford

    "   Wexford

[Handwritten acknowledgement reads: 'Ackd. supply for County on 12/6/20']

Instructions Nos 1 & 2 do not seem to have survived.

The following covering note was with Order No. 4, and Notes on defence of barracks:

Divisional Commissioner's Office

    Cork. 11.6.20

    Herewith 27 Copies of Instruction No. 3

           30   "   Order No. 4

           30   "   Notes on Defence of Barracks.

    Please have them distributed to the stations in your County as soon as possible.

W. D. KING

Captain.

By order of D.C.

Copy to C.I. Listowel
  "   Tralee
  "   Bandon
  "   Cork
  "   Mallow
  "   Waterford
  "   Wexford

[Handwritten acknowledgement reads: 'Ack. 13/6/20']

Again the instruction does not seem to have survived.

The flurry of orders and notes issuing from Divisional Commissioner Smyth's office at Cork indicate how seriously he took his new appointment.

In the light of Jeremiah Mee's statement, that until Colonel Smyth came to Listowel barracks on 19 June and announced who he was the garrison were unaware that a divisional commissioner had been appointed, there seems to have been a serious breakdown in communication between the divisional commissioner's office and the rank and file in the various barracks under his command. Moreover, it is probable that the situation in Listowel police barracks on 19 June would have been less explosive if the police had been made aware of the written orders which had been issued from Smyth's office in Cork, and of which much of Smyth's address in Listowel was but a paraphrase.

In the subsequent inquiry into the circumstances surrounding the 'Listowel incident' this fact, obviously, was adverted to. Thus Smyth in his written report concerning the new 'shooting regulations' which he was issuing stated: 'I knew I was treading on difficult ground, and told the men that they would get written orders on the subject … I attach a copy of these orders dated June 17, 1920. These orders were not received at Listowel for some days afterwards, as they had to be duplicated for issue' (cf. p. 259). However, this did not explain the seeming ignorance of the constables of orders issued by Smyth on 10 June. Presumably this breakdown in communications, among other things, was attributed to District Inspector Flanagan who was made the scapegoat for the affair (cf. pp. 149, 372 n.17).

B: Colonel Smyth's Version of his Address to the Police at Listowel on 19 June 1920, as Given in *The Freeman's Journal* of 26 July 1920

Mistakes Might Occur
The Official Version of Col. Smyth's Speech
Police Not to be Tied Down
By Regulations as to Firing
The References to Men 'Gone to America'

We publish below an alleged official version of the late Colonel Smyth's Listowel speech which has appeared in the English Press.

It will be seen that the version now published confirms in practically every point the fact that something was said about every issue raised.

There were references to Sinn Féiners who disappeared and never reached America, to increased latitude to fire – beyond that provided by the regulations; to the fact that 'mistakes might occur'.

It is said that the police were justified in shooting men, likely to carry arms, if they did not answer challenges.

It is admitted that the police to whom the speech was made challenged it at once, and some of them resigned on the spot. Col. Smyth's version was apparently written long after the speech was delivered.

Alleged Official Version

I pointed out that it was useless to send out stereotyped police patrols along the roads: that such patrols were regularly ambushed and shot down by the militant Sinn Féiner who kept off the roads; that the policemen must copy the Sinn Féiner and keep clear of the roads, and try to catch the Sinn Féiner who was lying up behind the ditch to ambush the policeman as he came along the road. This has been twisted by *The Freeman's Journal* to incitement to murder.

I told the police that it was the policy to hold on to every station for which we could possibly find a garrison: that if the Sinn Féiners succeeded in burning a station we would seize the most suitable house in the neighbourhood, preferably the house of a Sinn Féiner, and fit it up as a police station; that no notice must be given that we intended to seize this house or it would be burnt; that the inhabitants must be turned out of the house on to the street and the police put in as quickly as possible.

Two Denials

I did not say 'Let them die there – the more the merrier'. (A man does not die because he is turned out of his house.)

I did not say that martial law was coming into operation.

This reorganisation would be carried out by enlisting more police (I think that I mentioned 7,000) both in England and in Ireland and by drafting some police from stations where there were troops to reinforce out stations.

I pointed out that barracks garrisoned by five or six policemen were useless, as the police were too weak to come out without being attacked, that such tactics handed over the country to Sinn Féin. To meet this difficulty we proposed to bring all police barracks where there were no troops up to a strength of at least fourteen men, and each barracks would then be in a position to send out strong patrols through the country.

No Longer Tied Down

I told the police that they would no longer be tied down by the regulations in the police code as to firing on assailants; that a policeman was justified in challenging a man who was carrying arms or who he had good ground to believe was carrying arms; that mistakes might occur, but they should not as the police knew the men in each locality who were likely to carry arms for murderous purposes; that if such men did not put their hands up when challenged and ordered to do so, the police were justified in shooting; that the name of a policeman who shot a man in the course of his duty would not be revealed at the inquest by the evidence of the witnesses called by the Crown; that therefore he would not be exposed to victimisation and be murdered by the Sinn Féiners, as had occurred in the past.

More Denials

I said that no more convicted men would be released if they went on hunger strike. I did not say that 'some had died already'. I did not say that 'some of them have already been dealt with in a manner that their friends will never hear about'.

I then went on to point out to the police that the Sinn Féiners were suffering heavy casualties in attacks on barracks which the police and public knew nothing about: that the dead Sinn Féiners were buried secretly; that, if enquiries were made, it was stated that they had gone to America; that a number of men had 'gone to America' recently who would never arrive there.

This has been perverted by the *Freeman* to attacks on emigrant ships. Unfortunately the militant Sinn Féiners do not emigrate and I never made any such foolish statement.

Constable Mee's Answer

Constable Mee then stepped forward and said that I was an Englishman and did not understand Ireland or Irishmen. I assured him that I was Irish. He was in a most excited state and took off his cap and belt and threw them on the table. As far as I recollect he said, 'That is my answer'. He certainly did not say anything like the alleged statement in the *Freeman*.

I ordered him to be suspended. He went out of the room followed by the District Inspector. The remainder of the men were respectful, but obstinate. Their only grievance was the order to leave Listowel.

There was no suggestion then that I was endeavouring to incite them to a policy of reprisals. This has been invented since by some disaffected men to cover their disobedience of orders and conduct which they know will be condemned by the Royal Irish Constabulary generally.

C: COLONEL SMYTH'S VERSION OF HIS ADDRESS, AS GIVEN IN *THE IRISH TIMES* OF 30 JULY 1920[2]

The Late Colonel Smyth's Alleged Speech
His Report on the Listowel Case
Statement in Commons

In reply to Mr Charles Palmer, who, in the House of Commons yesterday, asked the Prime Minister whether, in view of the character of the alleged reports of the late Colonel Smyth's speech to the constables at Listowel, and to the fact that this officer's murder was directly attributed to the incitement due to these garbled versions of his speech, he would, in justice to the memory of Colonel Smyth and in the interests of the Royal Irish Constabulary, cause to be printed the report which Colonel Smyth made to the Government after his conduct had been impugned in the Press both here and in Ireland, and in which he gave his version of what he said and of what subsequently happened, Sir Hamar Greenwood said that it was contrary to precedent to publish the private reports of police officers but he felt that an exception should be made in this case. The following was the report on the Listowel case by Lieutenant-Colonel G. F. Smyth, Divisional Commissioner, Munster No. 2:

(1) I was informed by the Chief Inspector, Kerry, on June 18th, that several constables at Listowel had refused to go to out-stations in

the district. I went down on the 19th and, accompanied by the Chief Inspector, saw the men in the dayroom of Listowel Barracks.

(2) I told the men that I was going to be very frank with them; that I would tell them everything that I possibly could about the situation; that there were probably some things which I did not know and which I could not tell them. I did not use the expression 'I may reserve one card for myself'.

New Methods

(3) I then said that I would tell them what had happened in the past, and the methods which we proposed to adopt in the future. I pointed out that barracks garrisoned by five or six policemen were useless, as the police were too weak to come out without being attacked; that such tactics handed over the country to Sinn Féin. To meet this difficulty we proposed to bring all police barracks where there were no troops up to a strength of at least 14 men and each barrack would then be in a position to send out strong patrols through the county. This reorganisation would be carried out by enlisting more police (I think I mentioned 7,000) both in England and in Ireland and by drafting some police from stations, where there were troops, to reinforce out-stations. I pointed out that it was useless to send out stereotyped police patrols along the roads: that such patrols were regularly ambushed and shot down by the militant Sinn Féiner who kept off the roads: that the policemen must copy the Sinn Féiner and keep clear of the roads and try to catch the Sinn Féiner who was lying up behind the ditch to ambush the policeman as he came along the road. This has been twisted by *The Freeman's Journal* into incitement to murder.

(4) I did not say that martial law was coming into operation. I may have said that the re-distribution of the police had to be completed by June 21st as I had to report the strength of all stations to the Inspector-General.

(5) I did say that more troops were coming, not that 'thousands are coming daily'. The reasons that I gave for the posting of the military

are fairly given in the *Freeman*, except that I did not claim the power to break officers.

Possible Seizure of Houses

(6) I told the police that it was the policy to hold on to every station for which we could possibly find a garrison: that if the Sinn Féiners succeeded in burning a station we would seize the most suitable house in the neighbourhood, preferably the house of a Sinn Féiner and fit it up as a police station; that no notice must be given that we intended to seize this house or it would be burnt; that the inhabitants must be turned out of the house on to the streets, and the police put in as quickly as possible. I did not say 'Let them die there – the more the merrier'. (A man does not die because he is turned out of his house.)

The Shooting Regulations

(7) I told the police that they would no longer be tied down by the regulations in the police code as to firing on assailants; that a policeman was justified in challenging a man who was carrying arms, or who he had good reason to believe was carrying arms; that mistakes might occur but they should not as the police knew the men in each locality who were likely to carry arms for murderous purposes; that if such men did not put up their hands when challenged and ordered to do so, the police were justified in shooting; that the name of a policeman who shot a man in the course of his duty would not be revealed at the inquest by the evidence of the witnesses called by the Crown; that, therefore, he would not be exposed to victimisation and be murdered by the Sinn Féiners as had occurred in the past. I knew I was treading on difficult ground and told the men that they would get written orders on the subject, so that there could be no mistake. I attach a copy of these orders dated June 17th 1920. These orders were not received at Listowel for some days afterwards, as they had to be duplicated for issue.

Hunger Strike

(8) I said that no more convicted men would be released if they went on

hunger strike. I quoted a specific instance of two men in Maryborough [Portlaoise] Jail who had gone on hunger strike and who, when informed that they would not be released, had promptly desisted. I did not say that 'some had died already'. I did not then recollect any case of a man dying on hunger strike. I have since been told of one – Thomas Ashe – and recollect his case now, but I did not remember it previously. I did not say that 'some of them have already been dealt with in a manner that their friends will never hear about'.

'Gone to America'

(9) I then went on to point out to the police that the Sinn Féiners were suffering heavy casualties in attacks on barracks which the police and public knew nothing about; that the dead Sinn Féiners were buried secretly: that if inquiries were made it was stated that they had gone to America; that a number of men had 'gone to America' recently who would never arrive there. This has been perverted by the *Freeman* to attacks on emigrant ships. Unfortunately, the militant Sinn Féiners do not emigrate and I never made any such foolish statement.

(10) I wound up by telling the police that they, and they alone, could put down militant Sinn Féin: that to do so would entail danger; that they were already inured to danger; that it would entail some hardship and discomfort; that many of the police stations were too small to hold adequate garrisons without overcrowding. I asked them to put up with these hardships, knowing that by so doing they were helping to crush out murder. I then asked them if they were willing to do so, if they were willing to go to out-stations.

Constable Mee's Action

(11) Constable Mee then stepped forward and said that I was an Englishman, and did not understand Ireland or Irishmen. I assured him that I was Irish. He was in a most excited state, and took off his cap and belt and threw them on the table. As far as I can recollect he said: 'That is my answer'. He certainly did not say anything like the alleged statement in the *Freeman*. I ordered him to be suspended. He went

out of the room, followed by the District Inspector. The remainder of the men were respectful but obstinate. They felt that they were being moved out of a quiet spot and a good barracks to make way for the soldiers. They felt that the soldiers should take over the bad stations and leave the police who had already suffered in the good ones. I told them I would leave them to talk over the situation.

(12) Mr Leatham and General Tudor afterwards spoke to the men.

Cause of Disaffection

(13) I went round three country stations where I addressed the men in practically the same words as I had used at Listowel. All the men in these stations were in good spirits. I returned to Listowel and again saw the men. They were still most unwilling to go to country stations, and some of them refused to do so. Several of the men spoke to me. Their only grievance was the order to leave Listowel. There was no suggestion then that I was endeavouring to incite them to a policy of reprisals. This has been invented since by some disaffected men to cover their disobedience of orders and conduct which they know will be condemned by the Royal Irish Constabulary generally. The fact that the men refused to leave Listowel when seen by the No. 2 Chief Inspector, Kerry, on the previous day, and before they had ever seen me, confirms this.

(Signed) G. F. SMYTH, Lieut. Col.,
Divisional Commissioner, Munster No. 2
13th July, 1920.

Then follows the text of Colonel Smyth's statement as given in a previous answer in Parliament (see pp. 126–7), already printed in *The Irish Times*.

APPENDIX 6

LIST OF THOSE PRESENT IN LISTOWEL POLICE BARRACKS ON 19 JUNE 1920[1]

A: POLICE

OFFICERS

Dobbyn, Acting County Inspector Alexander M. R. (Dublin).

Flanagan, District Inspector Thomas (Roscommon).

Heard, Commandant of the RIC depot and Former County Inspector George B. (Kerry).

Leatham, Divisional Commissioner W. S. B. (Dublin).

Poer O'Shee, County Inspector John M. (Waterford).

Plover, Head Constable Patrick A. (Galway).

Smyth, Divisional Commissioner and Lieut. Colonel Gerald Bryce Ferguson (Down).

Tudor, Police Advisor to the viceroy and General Henry Hugh (Kent, England).

SERGEANTS AND CONSTABLES

The names of thirteen of the fourteen constables who signed the account of the incident of 19 June 1920 which was sent to the press are marked with an asterisk.[2]

Byrne, Sergeant Michael (Roscommon).

*Byrnes, Constable Francis J., clerk (Clare).

Connolly, Sergeant John (Clare).

Connors, Constable John J., Black and Tan (Stockport, Cheshire, England).

*Dolan, Constable Loughlin (Offaly).

*Donovan, Constable John (Limerick).

*Downey, Constable Joseph, transport driver (Kildare).

*Fitzgerald, Constable Michael (Galway).

*Hughes, Constable Thomas, clerk to district inspector (Mayo).

*Kelly, Constable Michael (Mayo).

*McNamara, Constable John P. (Clare).

*Mee, Constable Jeremiah (Galway).

*O'Neill, Constable Patrick (Wicklow).

Regan, Constable Patrick (Mayo).

*Reidy, Constable Thomas R. (Clare).

*Robinson, Constable Andrew, transport driver (Kerry).

*Sinnott, Constable John (Kilkenny).

Thompson, Constable Archibald, Black and Tan (London, England).

Watson, Sergeant William (Roscommon).

B: MILITARY

Captain Chadwick and some other officers.

APPENDIX 7

INCIDENT AT MILLTOWN POLICE BARRACKS ON 20 JUNE 1920

Having been rebuffed in his efforts to rally the garrisons at Listowel, Tralee and Killarney police barracks to his new militaristic policy, Divisional Commissioner Smyth spent the night of 19 June at Tralee. On the following day he continued his tour of the police barracks in County Kerry. An eyewitness account of what occurred when he visited Milltown barracks has been recorded on p. 128 of *Kerry's Fighting Story* as follows:

> On a Sunday evening in June 1920, Colonel Smyth, a tall man of impressive appearance, wearing full military uniform and staff cap, his breast ablaze with medal ribbons, arrived at the Milltown (County Kerry) barracks of the Royal Irish Constabulary, and summoned the sergeant and six men to the dayroom. Having taken an automatic from his pocket and placed it on the table, he directed the men to sit down. He prefaced his remarks by stating that he was responsible to no man in Ireland, that he was directly responsible to the Prime Minister. The Royal Irish Constabulary, he said, had been on the defensive too long and were now going to take the offensive. Blockhouses would be erected and barracks fortified. The houses of leading Sinn Féiners would be taken over. The police were to go out and not hesitate to shoot and, if mistakes were made, he would break no man for doing so. Rubber shoes would be provided for patrols so that they could move along the roads noiselessly. He outlined a scheme under which Royal

Irish Constabulary men dressed in khaki would accompany military raiding parties to identify Sinn Féiners. British recruits for the Royal Irish Constabulary and military reinforcements would be brought over from England. He said that the scheme which he had outlined would be issued as an order in the course of a week or ten days. The Royal Irish Constabulary men, three of whom were middle-aged, did not quickly realise what Colonel Smyth was about, and were inclined to look on his visit as one of the 'comings and goings' of highly placed officers. The Barrack Orderly, one of the younger men, said that when he joined the force he did not anticipate having to shoot anybody. Colonel Smyth said that times had changed and tactics had to be changed with them, and from that out things would be different. He made little of the arguments advanced by the young policeman, and suggested that cowardice was at the bottom of them. Dominion Home Rule, he said, was coming, and after a few years Royal Irish Constabulary men who continued to serve would be awarded big pensions. After a stay of about an hour in the barracks Colonel Smyth departed.

The sequel to this confrontation was that:

In a few days the Barrack Orderly received notification to transfer to Rathmore. He refused to accept the transfer. On the twenty-ninth of June County Inspector Poer O'Shee came to Milltown, accompanied by two lorries of Royal Irish Constabulary men armed with rifles and bombs. He spoke to the young policeman in a fatherly way and asked him why he would not take his transfer. 'Well, if you want to know,' came the reply, 'I did not join the police to lead around Black and Tans and the scum of England which have been brought into the force.' The officer tried to soften his subordinate and drew a picture of his bright prospects in the force, at the same time pointing out that such an attitude as he (the policeman) was taking would create disaffection among the other men. Seeing that the young man was adamant, the County Inspector, after an interview lasting two hours, declared he would have to suspend him. 'Take that and that,' said the policeman, throwing his revolver, belt and jacket on the table in front of the County Inspector. After spending a few days around Milltown the suspended constable went to Killarney, where he was well known, having previously served in Beaufort. There the District Inspector reasoned with him and pointed out that he was going out into a hostile people who would treat him as a spy. 'I understand well what I am doing and I'll take what is coming,' was the spirited reply.

The 'sergeant and six men' (in fact there were seven 'men') referred to above were Sergeant James Collery and Constables Patrick Brannock, John Curtin, James Lynch, Cornelius McCarthy, Peter O'Toole, John Quirke and Edward Reilly. All, except Collery, were members of the Police Union, and on 9 February 1920 had contributed to the Thomas J. McElligott, Patrick J. McGuire, Edward Tarpey Testimonial (see pp. 222–3). The man who defied Divisional Commissioner Smyth and County Inspector Poer O'Shee was Constable Peter O'Toole.

On 20 June Smyth also visited Glenbeigh police barracks, where, it seems, he spoke in much the same manner as at Listowel (eyewitness account from ex-Constable James Mulcahy).

APPENDIX 8

THE LAST DAYS SPENT BY CONSTABLES MICHAEL KELLY AND JOHN P. MCNAMARA IN LISTOWEL

The journey of Constables Michael Kelly and John P. McNamara from Listowel to New York seems to have been eventful. In a letter to Jeremiah Mee, dated 12 January 1952, McNamara described how he and Kelly became, in effect, hunted men on 1 November 1920, when their dismissals from the RIC became effective. He wrote:

> Now let me return to 1 November 1920, the day that our dismissal became effective. You know how, following the trial, I was restored to duty, and transferred to Ballylongford temporarily. Although being only a few weeks in Ballylongford, I became pretty well known among the people of the village, and I felt free to call on them whenever I wanted a favour. So on the night of 1 November 1920 transportation was provided without my even asking for it. I do not know who it was that picked me up, but I was in Listowel in no time at all. The first place I headed for was the barracks to pick up some of my belongings. It was there that I saw young Constable Morgan laid out in the dayroom. He was shot and killed in an ambush on the previous night in the village of Ballyduff.[1]
>
> I spoke for a few minutes with Constable John Sinnott, who came and warned me to get out of town the fastest way I knew how. Said Sinnott: 'Everybody around here is up in arms over the killing of young Morgan, and, furthermore, they all know that both you and Kelly were

in Cork City on the night that Smyth was shot and killed, and that you were mysteriously missing from the detail to which you were assigned [see pp. 143, 371 n.7]. I am afraid you boys will have a hard job trying to convince them of your innocence. It is the topic of conversation in the barracks here, and they have come to a definite conclusion that you men put the finger on Smyth on the night that he met his death in the Cork County Club. So to be forewarned is to be forearmed.'

I bade goodbye to Sinnott and left immediately, and headed for a certain saloon located in the Small Square in Listowel.[2] It was there I met Kelly, whose dismissal also became effective on 1 November 1920. This was our first meeting since 15 October 1920, when we both stood trial on practically the very same charges [see p. 152]. I repeated to Kelly the conversation that I had with Sinnott just a short time before. We talked the matter over for a short while, and finally decided that the best place for us to hide out would be upstairs over another saloon which was only a short distance away. Contact was made with the proprietor, who happened to live upstairs, and arrangements for our accommodation were completed in short order.

Now this particular saloon where we both remained in hiding for three days and three nights was, I had discovered, known to the IRA as 'the listening post', as it was here in this very saloon that the big majority of the military, the Auxiliaries, and the Black and Tans hung out.[3] They somehow or other liked the hospitality accorded them, and did not for a moment suspect that the proprietor was a Republican. He was an ex-British Army man himself, and naturally knew just how to play his cards, every once in a while displaying to members of the British forces the decorations he received during the First World War, but at the same time keeping his ears open to catch any information dropped by the Britishers, who, incidentally, and while in a drunken stupor, often disclosed secrets most helpful to the local Volunteers.[4]

In this way the information given to me by Constable Sinnott in the Listowel RIC barracks, regarding the link made between us and Smyth's death, was confirmed. The same night that we moved into this hide-out, the proprietor came to us, all excited, and said: 'Listen, fellows, were you both in Cork City on the night that Smyth was killed?' We both answered his question at the same time by saying that we were. 'My God,' said the proprietor, 'you two fellows are going to be shot like dogs. Do you men realise that they (meaning the British forces) have already made several raids in the town, and that their orders are to bring you men in, either dead or alive, and to shoot to kill in case that you fellows make any attempt to escape.' The proprietor was so excited by the time that he finished telling us all about what he had heard down at the bar that the cold sweat was actually rolling down his cheeks. He finished up his story by exclaiming: 'My God, if they ever find you men here, they will burn this place to the ground.'

We took his hint and departed from Listowel a few days later.[5]

APPENDIX 9

LETTERS FROM MEE AND COLGAN

A: SUBMISSION OF JEREMIAH MEE TO COUNTESS MARKIEVICZ ON THE POLICE QUESTION[1]

General Employment Agency, Dublin 27.7[9]. 20[2]

Dear Madam,

Knowing how you appreciate Irishmen who have and are making sacrifices for Ireland, I would like to put before you some interesting facts concerning ex-policemen whose interests you have at heart, and for whose welfare you have already worked hard. Needless to remind you that these are good Irishmen who would make still greater sacrifices for the Motherland.

Nothing less than genuine patriotism would induce a man to give up the only source of livelihood of himself, wife and family, and place himself at the mercy of his fellow countrymen. By doing so it cannot be said that his motive was selfishness prompted by cowardice. Recent events would go to show that a man does not make his life more secure by resigning the police force. I say, therefore, the man who resigns in such circumstances is deserving of much consideration by his country and his action should not be the means of reducing his wife and family to the borderline of hunger and want.

Now, how have those men been treated who have resigned and thrown in their lot with the Irish people, and what will the moral effect be upon those who would follow their good example?

In the first place those men do not, unfortunately, belong to any trade union that could tide them over a temporary difficulty, while their absence from home for a number of years makes them strangers more or less even in their own locality. Lots of them including married men are out of employment since last May and June and have not up to the present been offered any work.

I have at present something like sixty names on my books, and I am sorry to say that not one single suitable opening offers notwithstanding your recent appeal to the nation on behalf of these men. Of course one or two employers came along and tried to profit by these men's misfortunes, and added insult to injury by offering them *two pounds per week*, a sum not sufficient to sustain the body in nourishment, not to mention the practical needs of life.

Since my leaving the force early in July, my comrades and myself have interviewed police in such widely scattered places as Listowel, Killarney, Tralee, Limerick, Sligo, Ballymote, Mohill, Elphin, Claremorris and Dunmore, not to mention several smaller stations, so I think I might be pardoned for giving what I consider the true feelings of the great bulk of the police – I mean the Irishmen. They are nearly all willing to come out, but, having in their mind's eye some comrade or acquaintance who has done so and is yet unemployed, they point to him as an example of what they themselves would expect to get from Sinn Féin.

I would therefore, and with the best possible intentions for all concerned, suggest that if the Irish people are really serious about breaking up the present police force in Ireland, the first step is to safeguard the interests of those who have already come out and are now willing to assist us in our fight against oppression. I repeat, that in justice to these men and in justice to every Irishman who is trying to free us from the stranglehold of England, that it is up to every big employer of labour, even at the risk of some small financial sacrifice, to give employment to men like these if only temporary.

If this were done all over Ireland, in my humble opinion, police would resign by the hundred, the Volunteer ranks would be greatly strengthened with good fighting material, and English Rule in Ireland if not completely broken would at least be seriously shaken.

With apologies for trespassing on your valuable time, I am, Madam, Your obt. servant,

JERH. MEE,

Secretary.

I beg to add that the placing of men who have left the police is of the utmost National importance for the following reasons:

1. I was present at Listowel when General Tudor (head of the Police and military forces in Ireland) stated that unless the police were prepared to co-operate with the military the British Government were powerless to cope with Sinn Féin.

2. If the men who resigned were placed in decent employment immediately, and a fair guarantee given that themselves and their families would not suffer by their patriotic action, I would be prepared, on my own initiative, to guarantee at least two hundred resignations within a week or two.

3. Time means everything. Unless the Irish police are taken out at once it will be useless bringing them out later on, as the 'Black and Tans' will have a thorough knowledge of the country and will be able to do police work without the assistance of the Irish police.

It must be quite evident to the most unobservant that the police force is the one great stumbling block between Ireland and Freedom; and in my opinion there is but one way to demoralise that force, and that is by liberal treatment, in the form of decent employment to the men who come out.

Every resignation, followed by fair treatment, means at least a dozen other resignations. Further, unless something on the above lines can be shown, any attempts at organisation will be absolutely futile.

J.M.

B: Letter from William Colgan, Resigned RIC Constable, to Michael Collins[3]

Rahan,
Tullamore
Offaly
31.8.21

Sir,

I wish to bring under your notice the following facts:

Over 12 months ago, my two brothers, my brother-in-law and I (four) resigned the R.I.C. for the cause which is so dear to all of us, and, with the exception of my brother-in-law, are still unemployed.

One is a married man, (11 years service on resigning), and has been since living with his wife and 3 children in Co. Galway, his wife being his sole support.

My brother-in-law is a van-driver, residing in 18 Albert Place, Grand Canal Street, Dublin, with comparatively small earnings, and occupies a small room with his wife and one child (he had 10 years service on resigning).

My other brother and I, with 9 and 15 years service (on resigning) respectively, have been living ever since with my father who is our sole support, he being an R.I.C. pensioner with small pension, and Grand Canal Company's agent here, with very small pay. We have no land or nothing by which we could make a living since resigning.

Any of the following can bear testimony to the accuracy of my statement: Mrs Teresa Weir, Church Street, Tullamore; Rev. Fr. Tompkins, S.J., St. Stanislaus College, Rahan, Tullamore, and Rev. Jas. Flynn, P.P., Rahan, Tullamore.

Apologizing for troubling you, I am, Sir,
Yours respectfully,
William Colgan.

APPENDIX 10

SINN FÉIN POLICY (1919–21) TOWARDS MEMBERS OF THE RIC

Recognising that the RIC was the keystone of Britain's continuing rule in Ireland, Sinn Féin, by virtue of a decree which was passed in Dáil Éireann, inaugurated a boycott of the force. Within a week of this decision the secretaries of every Sinn Féin club in the country had received from the organisation's headquarters in Dublin the following document:

> Dáil decree dated 10th April, 1919, states that the police forces maintained by the English Government in Ireland be ostracised socially by the people of Ireland. You are requested to bring the following to the notice of all members of your Cumann:
>
> 1. Avoid all intercourse with such persons unless purely business matters made it absolutely necessary.
>
> 2. Do not salute them or reply to their salutations.
>
> 3. Do not take part in any social entertainment where they are expected to be present as guests.
>
> 4. Should they be allowed to attend any social entertainment such as dances, etc. our members are advised to leave immediately.
>
> 5. Carefully avoid all places they are known to visit and more particularly, public houses which they frequent.

By the end of April the boycott was being vigorously supervised by some 1,500 Sinn Féin clubs throughout the country. In many places merchants refused to sell goods to policemen, and in some places this boycott was extended even to members of policemen's families.

The boycott of the RIC became more extensive and pronounced as the Anglo-Irish War intensified. As this boycott was but, relatively speaking, a minor irritant to the RIC at that time – from 1 January 1919 to 3 December 1921, as a result of the IRA campaign, 406 policemen were killed and 690 wounded, almost all of whom were members of the pre-1920 RIC – it was seldom publicly adverted to. But from time to time this aspect of 'the war on the police' was given prominence in the press. Thus *The Irish Times* of 18 June 1920 reported a discussion in the House of Commons during which it was disclosed that the boycott of the police in Carrick-on-Shannon was so complete that supplies had to be delivered to the police there by military transport. And the following headlines, 'The Irish Pariah, Dark Days for the R.I.C., Women show him Contempt, Life in Danger, Is Boycotted', appeared over a piece on the plight of the RIC in the London *Daily Express* of 2 August 1920.[1]

Within a year of the sanctioning of the boycott campaign by Dáil Éireann, due to the suppression of the Irish branch of the National Union of Police and Prison Officers, the representations of Thomas J. McElligott, and a dramatic increase in the number of resignations from the RIC, there was a growing awareness by the leaders of Sinn Féin of nationalist feeling among a sizeable proportion of the force, and a realisation that further steps could be taken in order to destroy the RIC. Consequently, at this time, some tentative steps were taken to try to cripple the force by persuading a substantial number of its members to resign. It was fully realised that the success of this policy depended on the ability of Sinn Féin to offer and provide alternative employment for those members of the RIC who resigned. One of the architects of this new policy towards members of the RIC was Thomas J. McElligott. As a result of a discussion on 'the police question' which took place in the Munster Hotel, 22 Ellis Quay, Dublin, during the first days of June 1920 between McElligott, on the one hand, and Harry Boland and Michael Collins, on the other, McElligott submitted the following memorandum on the subject:

Resignations and Retirements from Irish Police Forces

The President and prominent Irish Americans regard the police question in Ireland as an economic one which can be settled by providing the men with an alternative – other employment and compensation. His special interview (mainly for Irish police) to *Westminster Gazette* has not been published and an envoy has come to set the scheme in motion.

Whilst the winding up of the whole of the Irish Police is under consideration it has been decided to bring about immediately the:

(a) resignation of all single men under 10 or 12 years service.

(b) retirement of all men rank and file over 30 years service.

Class (a) and all men not in receipt of a pension will be organised in a Free Men's Association – Headquarters in Dublin and a Branch in each County – for the purpose of safeguarding their interests and forwarding the National movement.

To secure (a) Resignations the following method must be adopted: – In each parish representative and respectable deputations must be selected to visit openly the homes of all parents who have sons in the police. They can discuss situation, employment and real nature of the policemen's work – not only in maintaining but, with all the weapons of war, actually enforcing the present Prussianism of Ireland. Parents can be given to understand clearly that an alternative – employment and compensation – is being provided and that as it is going to be 'a fight to a finish' it is to be hoped we shall not witness the 'danger' and disgrace of Irish policemen fighting not for but against their own country. The parents should be instructed there and then to WRITE to policeman concerned and get him if class (a) to resign forthwith. Whilst all resignations are desirable the necessary machinery has not been set up yet to deal effectively with more than young single men – the prop of the police system.

Class (b) these men can be told to go. They are entitled to full pension, ⅔ (two-third) pay, and being provided for they present no difficulty by way of compensation or employment.

USE OF FORMS F.A.: All men after being paid off on resignation, must correctly and legibly fill up form F.A. in duplicate – one copy to be retained for County Councils later, the other to be forwarded to Head-Quarters. These forms must be carefully guarded and if a form is spoiled in filling it must be destroyed. Nearly 200 men have resigned during past month. These men should be looked up and enrolled at once.

It is essential that Moral Support and national appreciation should be given to all who have 'thrown off the jacket' and public bodies can locally pass resolutions of appreciation and support. Clergymen speaking to congregations at Mass, etc. can make the work of deputations visiting parents very light, and impress the local police more seriously than the 'letter from home'.

Whilst a very large sum of money is available in America to take all these men to U.S.A. and give them very good employment now, it is, for obvious reasons, highly desirable to keep them in Ireland. Through the County Councils and American Co-operation it is possible to raise in America a Special Fund for an Industrial revival giving these men employment and shares in Irish enterprise – giving them a personal and national interest in going and serving their country.

In view of existing circumstances and the likelihood of government agents trying to discredit and prejudice the men resigning the utmost caution must be exercised and pending further instructions these men are to be assisted in becoming useful citizens. The matter is urgent and in the South and West of Ireland – especially in Galway, Mayo, Clare, Cork and Kerry – the Free Men's Association will be a powerful organisation.

P.S. The police can be given to understand that their interests are being well looked after by P.P. ['Pro Patria']

Form F.A.
The Free Men's Association

MEMBERSHIP: Open to all members of the Irish Police who have resigned as a protest against present form of Government in Ireland.

OBJECTS: To ensure that their actions will not be misrepresented, that public opinion will be instructed, to safeguard their interests and to enable them as Irishmen to find a living in their own land.

1. Name in full
2. Police force and Registered Number
3. Where last stationed
4. Date of joining Police
5.   " of Resignation
6. Single or married (if married give no. of family)
7. Age
8. Trade or Occupation
9. Any special qualifications
10. Present employment (or any prospects)
11. Native county
12. Present Postal address
13. If in receipt of any pension, income or gratuity
14. Give (a) your reasons for resigning, (b) views of police on present situation, (c) any suggestions to help the Association and the Country generally.

> Dated at ....
> Signature ....

To: The Secretary
        of F.M.A.
in duplicate.

Soon afterwards formal steps were taken to implement the policy adumbrated in McElligott's memorandum. First, in early June a statement was issued by Sinn Féin that it would provide employment for members of the police who resigned, provided they had joined before 21 January 1919. Next, at a meeting of the cabinet of Dáil Éireann on 10 June it was decided to ask the Sinn Féin organisation to arrange for influential deputations to visit the parents of policemen with a view to getting the parents to write to their sons advising them to resign. This directive was brought to the attention of Sinn Féin Cumainn (i.e., Sinn Féin constituency associations) throughout the country by the following letter and enclosure, which were sent out by Sinn Féin headquarters about the middle of July:[2]

A Chara,

Enclosed you will find a letter for each Cumann in your Comhairle Ceanntair area, outlining the policy of the Sinn Féin Organisation towards ex-members of the RIC, who have resigned owing to the circumstances of the present day.

Each Club should appoint a Deputation to wait upon the parents or other near relatives of police who are natives of your Club district and read letter No.1 to them. This letter, No. 2, should not be read, but is intended for the guidance of the Clubs.

Every effort should be made to get employment for RIC men who have already resigned. In cases where emigration is unavoidable Irish Organisations in the United States have already expressed their desire to help ex-policemen from Ireland and to secure them employment as soon as they land in America.

Sinn Féin is also in favour of Local Government Bodies passing Resolutions commending the action of police who resign.

Do chara,
Signed   Pádraig Ó Caoimh.
         Runaidhe

To:

The Secretary,

Each Comhairle Ceanntair.

No. 1. Sinn Féin

6 Harcourt Street,

Dublin.

July 1920.

A Chara,

Now that the English Controlled Police Forces in Ireland are breaking up, the country should take cognisance of the position of individual ex-members of these forces under the new regime.

Every man of Irish Birth should get a chance of becoming a loyal citizen of the Irish Republic, and of earning an honest living in Ireland. This is true even of those Irishmen who are so unfortunate as to be at present engaged in doing the work of the enemy in Ireland as members of the RIC. Many of these men joined without any clear understanding of what they were doing. They were young; they had no knowledge of Irish History. The national tradition may have been weak in their own family and in their native district. It should be made clear that those who now resign will not be regarded as enemies of Ireland, but will be granted every opportunity to make up for the past. Men who resign should get credit for an honest intention. They should be welcomed back to their native place. The local Sinn Féin club should try to help them in the same way as it helps another person in need of employment. In case nothing can be done locally, a communication should be sent to Headquarters. A Fund is being provided to assist in cases of special hardship. This communication should be fully discussed at the Sinn Féin clubs. Any men in the district who have already resigned should be helped, if necessary, at once. A Deputation consisting of influential men such as County and District Councillors should be appointed to call upon the nearest relatives of the English Controlled Police in their native place and explain to them the terms of this letter, and the relatives should be requested to communicate with them urging them to resign their membership of the English Controlled Police and return home where they will be welcomed to live and act as good Irish Citizens.

Mise,

Pádraig Ó Caoimh,

Runaidhe

It is safe to presume that the importance of providing employment for resigned members of the RIC was one of the subjects uppermost in the minds of Michael Collins and Countess Markievicz when, with others, they interviewed John Donovan and Jeremiah Mee about the 'Listowel incident' on 15 July. It is probable that this question was raised during the course of that meeting. In any case, just under three weeks after the meeting, Donovan, through the intervention of Countess Markievicz, was given employment in the Court Laundry, Harcourt Street, Dublin, and Mee was taken on as a staff member in the ministry of labour, where he was appointed to the General Employment Agency, with a special brief to find employment for ex-policemen. Early in September Mee and the countess sent out a circular to employers and trade-union officials appealing to them to help resigned members of the RIC find employment. Although not an entire failure (see p. 138), the appeal was not a success with regard to its primary aim, namely that of providing jobs for ex-policemen. This fact and the crucial importance of finding alternative employment for resigned members of the RIC were raised in a submission which Mee made to his superiors on 27 September (see Appendix 9.) Mee's submission prompted Risteárd Mac Coitir (Dick Cotter), secretary of the ministry of labour, to write on 28 September to Diarmuid Ó h-Éigeartaigh of the General Secretariat of Dáil Éireann stating that he considered that 'a fresh drive might be made through advertisements – on a pretty large scale – in the press, and by authorising Miss O'Brennan or Mr Mee to travel outside of Dublin to interview those people of importance in industrial concerns throughout the country to whom influential introductions might be secured'. In the course of the letter Cotter admitted that Mee did not consider that even this new approach would be very rewarding. Cotter also stated that he 'was writing to the Irish Transport and General Workers Union, asking them to put us in touch immediately with the proper people where there is a dearth of agricultural workers for the harvest' and that he was 'also drafting a special circular for issue to the Asylum boards throughout the country'. Although authorised by Dáil Éireann on 1 October to travel outside Dublin and canvas jobs for ex-policemen, Mee, in fact, did not do so. It seems, however, that his colleague, Miss Lily O'Brennan, did canvas a number of firms in the Dublin area for jobs for ex-policemen as well as for injured and other members of the IRA.

Total failure to provide employment for resigned and dismissed members of the RIC is admitted by Mee in a report which he submitted to Dick Cotter on 7 October. In his submission Mee stated that from 9 September when his office, the Police Employment Bureau, had been established, to the time of writing, sixty-two members of the RIC, including eleven still serving in the force, had applied to his office for employment. During the same period six employers had applied to him for staff. However, it seems that when suitable men had been sent by Mee to these employers the prospective employees were offered only inordinately low wages (£2 per week). Mee concluded his report by stating that, although twelve or fourteen of his clients were in touch with employers, he was not in a position to say that any of those who applied to his office had been employed.[3]

This report, in effect, marked the end of Sinn Féin's effort at that time to help resigned and dismissed members of the RIC to find employment and thereafter Mee acted more as an aide to Michael Collins (cf. pp. 140, 144, 159–60) than as a staff member of the ministry of labour. Mee's report must have been all the more disappointing in that it appeared a bare three weeks after Dáil Éireann had voted £350 for the Police Employment Bureau. The formal attempt by Sinn Féin to help resigned and dismissed members of the RIC find employment was abandoned when, early in January 1921, Mee was appointed an organiser of the Belfast Boycott.

The question was reopened when, in August and September 1921,

Thomas J. McElligott wrote a number of letters to Michael Collins stressing the importance of establishing an organisation for resigned and dismissed members of the RIC, the main aim of which would be to ensure that its members received suitable employment, and reminding him that a decision to found such an organisation had been taken a year previously. Collins was sympathetic, seeing the establishment of such an organisation as an encouragement to members of the then 5,000-strong old RIC to resign. McElligott then asked for an interview with Collins to discuss the matter more fully. Due to pressure of work, however, Collins was unable to meet McElligott or even to give the matter further attention. In the meantime McElligott, with the general approval of Collins, in September and October 1921, laid the foundations for what eventually became the Organisation of Resigned and Dismissed RIC and DMP (1916–21).[4]

APPENDIX 11

UNJUST TREATMENT OF RESIGNED AND DISMISSED RIC AND DMP (1916–1921) BY SUCCESSIVE IRISH GOVERNMENTS

About 1,200[1] members of the RIC, who resigned or were dismissed between Easter 1916 and the signing of the Anglo-Irish Treaty on 6 December 1921, were subsequently to claim that they had left the force or had been dismissed from it due to their being unwilling, because of nationalist sympathies, to become actively involved in the struggle between Sinn Féin and the crown forces, and some 680 of them received pensions from the Irish Free State government.[2]

The majority of these men resigned or were dismissed between February and November 1920. The efforts which were made at that time by Sinn Féin to help such men to secure alternative employment were dismally unsuccessful.

During the first half of January 1922 the Garda Síochána (Civic Guards) was established as an unarmed police force for the then emerging Irish Free State. Some officers and instructors were recruited from the RIC and DMP into the new police force. At a general meeting of the resigned and dismissed members of the RIC and DMP, which was held at the Mansion House, in Dublin, on 24 January 1922, a resolution was passed indicating that the resigned and dismissed policemen wished to be admitted to the new force. This resolution, plus the fact that they were also anxious that on their being recruited account should be taken of their previous experience and service as policemen, was brought to the attention of Michael Collins, head of the Provisional Government, and Arthur Griffith, who was then presiding over the Dáil cabinet. It seems that both leaders, in acknowledging the respective communications, guaranteed in writing that those policemen, who resigned or were dismissed because of nationalist sympathies, would be treated at least as generously as their comrades who continued to serve in the RIC and DMP until these forces were disbanded.[3]

On further representations being made, the Provisional Government set up a commission, known from its chairman as 'the Batt O'Connor Commission', to consider the claims of all policemen who resigned or were dismissed between the Rising of 1916 and the signing of the Anglo-Irish Treaty in 1921.[4] Some of the resigned and dismissed policemen nominated Thomas J. McElligott to the commission but, after his arrest in November 1922, they were represented on it by Michael J. Lyons (of Clonmel) and Michael O'Mahony (of Cork). In the meantime, after some confusion,[5] the RIC was disbanded on 31 August 1922, the members of the force being treated by the British government as generously as could be expected in the circumstances.[6]

As a result of the deliberations of the 1922–23 commission, which was extensively helped by local Sinn Féin clubs, the Superannuation and Pensions Act 1923 and the RIC (Resigned and Dismissed) Pensions Order 1924 were passed in the Dáil. The resigned and dismissed policemen were bitterly disappointed with these measures which, in effect, left them substantially less well-off than their comrades who had continued to serve until disbandment. Their disappointment was intelligible as the measures were, in effect, an abnegation of a debt of honour. Even as late as 10 October 1922, Kevin O'Higgins, minister for home affairs, had stated in Dáil Éireann that it was the intention of the government to grant to all the men who resigned or were dismissed from the RIC because of nationalist sympathies, compensation by way of pension equivalent to that which they would have received had they continued to serve until the force was disbanded (cf. Dáil Éireann: *Diospóireachta parlaiminte, tuairisc oifigiúil: Parliamentary debates, official report*, vol. I, col. 1383, 10 October 1922). Moreover, the resigned and dismissed RIC had a further grievance, in that a policy of discrimination against former members of the RIC (disbanded, resigned or dismissed) had earlier been initiated by General Eoin O'Duffy, commissioner of the new police force. This trend emerges clearly from a comparison of paragraphs 5 and 7 of a circular concerning forthcoming examinations for promotion to various ranks, which was distributed to all members of the Gardaí on 15 March 1923. On the one hand, Paragraph 5 reads:

> All members of the Guard, irrespective of rank and period of service, are eligible to compete at the examination for cadets provided the commissioner considers them fit and proper persons to be appointed as cadets.

while, on the other hand, paragraph 7 has this to say:

> Ex-members of the R.I.C. will not be eligible to compete at the forthcoming examinations for superintendents and chief superintendents. In coming to this decision I have had in mind the fact that ex-members of the R.I.C., presently holding the rank of inspector or superintendent in the Guard, have been particularly fortunate in securing such positions at the time they did. Now and since my appointment as commissioner ex-members of the R.I.C. recommended by the most responsible officers in the State, highly qualified in all respects, and many of whom fought in the I.R.A. against the British, have been denied even admission to the Guard. A few ex-members have been appointed in offices, and as instructors in technical subjects, but these are not members of the Guard – their appointment being temporary and only for a period of six months.

In the late 1920s Patrick J. O'Grady (of Tullow) and Patrick McCormack (of Meath and later Dublin), chairman and general secretary respectively of the executive committee of the Organisation of Resigned and Dismissed RIC and DMP (1916–21), began to press both the government and the opposition for a more just treatment of the claims of the members of their organisation.[7] One result of these efforts was that the government passed the Superannuation and Pensions Act 1929. This, however, effected only a minor improvement in the situation. Another result, and perhaps a more important one, was that the representatives of the resigned and dismissed policemen received an undertaking from senior members of the Fianna Fáil party that, if returned to power, they would order a review of the whole question.

Consequently when the Fianna Fáil party came to power in February 1932 the resigned and dismissed policemen had high hopes that their various grievances would be dealt with. Discussions were soon begun between representatives of the men and the new government and at the end of June a memorandum, signed on behalf of the executive committee by Edward Tarpey, Patrick McLoughlin, Michael J. Brophy and Patrick McCormack (he was honorary general secretary of the Organisation of the Resigned and Dismissed RIC and DMP from its inception in January 1922) was presented to the government. The memorandum itemised the various grievances of the resigned and dismissed men, outlined the unsatisfactory attempts which had been made up to then to deal with their problems and concluded by requesting an inquiry into the whole question in the following terms:

> Outside the emergency relief of outstanding victims we ask for an inquiry on the 'not less generous treatment terms' basis [that is, that they be treated as generously as those members of the RIC who served until they were disbanded], that the Pensions Order be repealed; and that the new terms be embodied in statute law. Feeling that the present government is in sympathy with our claims we hope that our confidence will be justified by its appropriate and speedy action in this important matter.

The negotiations between the men's representatives and the Fianna Fáil government were interrupted by the general election which was held in January 1933, but they were resumed soon afterwards. Eventually on 24 January 1934 the long-sought-after board of inquiry was set up. In the official statement announcing the establishment of the board its terms of reference were clearly set out as follows:

> The minister for finance has appointed the following committee: District Justice [Liam] Price, chairman,[8] Mr J[ohn] E. Hanna, principal officer, Department of Finance, and Mr Liam O'Doherty [ex-IRA] to inquire into the cases of any existing persons who, having resigned from the Royal Irish Constabulary on or after the 1st day of April 1916 and before the 6th day of December 1921, claim pensions under sect. 5 of the Superannuation and Pensions Act 1923, and to report to the minister for finance those cases in which it considers that the resignation or dismissal was caused by the national sympathies of the resigned or dismissed men.
>
> The minister for finance directs the committee that no claim is to be entertained in respect of any ex-member of the R.I.C. who retired from that force with a pension or gratuity, or who having resigned or having been dismissed from that force subsequently became a member of the Garda Síochána and was dismissed from it for causes within his own control or resigned from it in circumstances not entitling him to a superannuation award.
>
> The minister for finance further directs the committee that no claim is to be entertained in respect of any ex-member of the R.I.C. who had completed less than three years of service at the date of his resignation or dismissal or who joined the R.I.C. on or after the 18th April 1918.
>
> The secretary to the committee is Miss Máire Breathnach, Department of Finance.
>
> An announcement will be made in due course as to the procedure to be adopted by applicants.

On behalf of his organisation Patrick McCormack, general secretary, wrote on 21 February 1934, to Seán McEntee, minister for finance, as follows:

A chara,

I am directed by my executive committee to inform you that according to their 'terms of reference' the Committee of Inquiry (1934) into resignations and dismissals from the R.I.C. is precluded from considering the claims of certain ex-members of the R.I.C. and D.M.P. who have outstanding national records. I particularly refer to the mutineers at Listowel R.I.C. barracks and the ex-members of the D.M.P., who were acting in the defence of the Republic, when reinstatement was offered them in 1923. I am therefore to request alteration of the terms of reference so as to permit examination of these and a small number of other cases, and your kind consideration of the following:

1. Inquiry be directed to examine also the claims of men, who resigned or were dismissed from D.M.P. for national sympathies and not reinstated in that force.

2. Deletion of the prohibitions contained in paragraphs 2 and 3 of the terms of reference for committee of inquiry.

3. That the Organisation be permitted to nominate representatives on the inquiry committee now sitting.

I am also to refer to a further explanatory statement regarding above and other grievances of the Organisation, which will reach you within the next week.

This further explanatory statement was a memorandum which was drawn up by the executive committee. It was in two parts, the first being a pretty comprehensive review of the rather squalid way in which the resigned and dismissed policemen had been treated to date and the second being a submission concerning the proposed committee of inquiry. The first part was headed: 'Memorandum regarding treatment of resigned and dismissed R.I.C. and D.M.P.' and read as follows:

How the men who resigned or were dismissed from the R.I.C. and D.M.P. on account of national sympathies have been victimised is set out hereunder. It will be remembered such men were promised by

Sinn Féin, with the approval and sanction of Dáil Éireann, that they would be treated justly and far more generously than those who (not resigning) retained and used arms against the country. [9]

Committee of Inquiry, 1922–23

A committee to investigate claims sat during 1922/23. At the request of government the men nominated two representatives thereon, one of whom, Mr Thomas J. McElligott, was arrested and interned before the committee functioned, the other was given government employment during the progress of the inquiry. Owing to the civil war many were unable to present their cases or obtain the necessary documentary evidence. Out of approximately 1,215 applications received the committee recommended 628, while the number of pensions eventually granted totalled about 574, leaving 641 cases disallowed for various reasons.

The men request representation on the committee of inquiry 1934, now sitting.

Superannuation & Pensions Act, 1923

On 8th August 1923, above received official sanction. Section 5 (1), thereof, gave power to the minister for finance to authorise, by Order, the grant of pensions and regulate the scale of same. No provision was made as to the date from which pensions are payable, although in the case of certain civil servants, teachers and others therein dealt with pensions date from 1st April 1922. It is submitted under Sec. 9 of the Act quoted that the minister had power to authorise the grant of pensions to resigned and dismissed R.I.C. as from 1st April 1922, and not as he did from the passing of the Act, thereby depriving the men of pensions for the period 1st April 1922 to 7th August 1923.

Why were the men specially singled out for this treatment?

R.I.C. (Resigned & Dismissed) Pensions Order, 1924

On 12th February 1924 the minister for finance obtained approval of above (see official report).

The Order was a distinct breach of trust with the resigned and dismissed men. Labour, Farming, and Independent groups vigorously opposed the Order and requested more generous terms.

The R.I.C. Representative Body rejected the R.I.C. Pensions Order of 1922, No. 945, upon which the abovementioned Order is based: it was more favourably incorporated in the Constabulary (Ireland) Act 1922.

Under terms of the Order no compensation is awarded for period elapsed between resignation or dismissal and 31st March 1922.

No pension for period, 1st April 1922 to 7th August 1923.

Computation of actual R.I.C. service, in many instances, one year less than in the case of disbanded R.I.C.

Calculation of pensions on a less favourable scale and on a lower rate of pay, generally, than disbanded men.

No power to commute pensions.

No pensions for widows (subsequently granted) or children.

Pensions of resigned and dismissed constables are approximately 61% per annum less than those of disbanded R.I.C., due to method of computation on inequality in pay, actual service and years added thereto.

Method of calculation penalises resigned men in such a way that, to date, they have suffered the loss, all round, of approximately 2 years pension, inclusive of the period 1/4/22 to 7/8/23 for which no pensions have been paid.

To remove such anomalies actual service should be computed to date of R.I.C. disbandment, that is, 31st August 1922, and pensions in accordance with the provisions of the Constabulary (Ireland) Act, 1922, commence on the following day.

Superannuation & Pensions Act 1929

The above was introduced in February 1929, and under the Act, as finally passed, some ten men who resigned, on gratuity, from the R.I.C. were granted pensions, provided their claims were certified by the Committee of Inquiry 1922/23. The Act authorised the minister for finance to grant pensions to widows of resigned and dismissed R.I.C.

Negotiations with Fianna Fáil party

Following the introduction of last mentioned Act Messrs. McCormack and O'Grady, representing the resigned and dismissed R.I.C., met Deputies Ruttledge and Little in Dublin and after a full discussion, regarding the grievances of the men, it was decided to table an amendment.

On the committee stage of the Superannuation and Pensions Bill 1929, after consultation and agreement between Messrs. McElligott, O'Grady and McCormack, representing the men, and Messrs. Ruttledge, McGuire and Comyn for Fianna Fáil, Deputy Ruttledge tabled the following amendments (see official list of Amendments-Committee Stage & Official Dáil Report, No.5, Vol. 28 for full text):

1. Pensions of resigned and dismissed R.I.C. to date from 1st April 1922, and be in accordance with the provisions of the Constabulary (Ireland) Act, 1922.

2. Existing pensions to be raised to amounts fixed under Constabulary (Ireland) Act, 1922, as from 1st April 1922.

3. Constitution of a Committee of Inquiry of three persons, two nominated by the minister and one by the resigned and dismissed R.I.C. Organisation, to investigate claims.

When will the government give effect to Amendments 1 & 2? Why deny the men representation on the Inquiry now sitting?

R.I.C. (Resigned & Dismissed) Pensions Order, 1929

On 3rd December 1929 the minister made an Order granting a pension of £30 per annum to widows, provided the marriage took place while the husband was serving in the R.I.C. No provision was made for payment of pensions to children.

Widows, children and dependents of disbanded men, married on or before 31st August 1922, are granted pensions.

Widows, children and dependents of resigned and dismissed men, married on or before 31st August 1922, should receive similar treatment irrespective of the fact whether such a marriage took place while the husband was serving in the force or not.

Formation of New Police Force

At a general meeting in the Mansion House, Dublin, on 24th January 1922, the resigned and dismissed men adopted the following resolution: 'That in the event of the establishment of a new police force, with national good will, we desire to co-operate [and assist in the difficult and urgent task of maintaining law and order].' This information was duly communicated to the head of the Provisional government. In the absence of satisfactory assurances and for other reasons, the resigned and dismissed men, as a body, remained aloof from the newly formed Civic Guard. Some, however, mainly through necessity and not as an alternative to other compensation, did join. After some months their further recruitment was prohibited. On acceptance the resigned and dismissed men were treated as recruits and did not receive the benefit of previous police service. Moreover, on the one hand, in 1923 the official attitude towards such men was unfriendly and they were debarred from competing at examinations for promotion to the ranks of inspector and superintendent. While, on the other hand, still serving R.I.C. and later disbanded men were appointed to the higher ranks in the new force, receiving in all cases the benefit of previous police service.

It is submitted that all resigned and dismissed men in the Civic Guard, whose claims are certified by the Committee of Inquiry, should receive the benefit of previous service same as re-instated D.M.P., civil servants, teachers, local officials, etc., and that all barriers to promotion, if now in existence, be removed.

Suspension of Pension on Re-employment

In cases where pensions granted, under the Superannuation and Pensions Act, 1923, to resigned and dismissed men in the Civic Guard or other government employment exceed, for an ex-constable plus the pay of the office held, the sum of £3.18.0 [£3.90] weekly the pension is reduced to the extent of the excess. Under similar circumstances the pensions of disbanded R.I.C. constables in government employment, Irish or British, are not reducible unless exceeding the total sum of £4.10.0 [£4.50] weekly.

This injustice should be removed.

Forfeiture of Pensions

Disbanded R.I.C. in Civic Guard or other government employment may leave same or suffer dismissal therefrom without forfeiting pensions under the Constabulary (Ireland) Act, 1922, unless for a breach of the conditions governing grant of same.

Resigned and dismissed R.I.C., who leave government employment or are dismissed therefrom, automatically forfeit pensions owing to a vexatious condition governing the grant, promulgated long after those men unconditionally entered such employment.

It is requested that all men in the Civic Guard or other government employment get the option of leaving or continuing therein under the existing conditions.

Deletion of the following clause in the Pensions Order of 1924 is required for obvious reasons:

> 4. No pension shall be payable under this Order to any person who shall have been offered an appointment in any branch of the public service of Saorstat Éireann, which in the opinion of the minister for home affairs is reasonably suitable for him, and shall have declined to accept such appointment.

No such condition is imposed on disbanded R.I.C.

The second part, under the heading 'Committee of Inquiry, 1934' stated:

> Deletion of the prohibitions contained in pars. 2 & 3 of the terms of reference of the committee now sitting is requested.
>
> When the resignation manifesto was issued it contained no conditions such as those included in the paragraphs referred to. On principle all resigned and dismissed men are entitled to consideration.
>
> Pensions have already been granted, under the Superannuation and Pensions Act 1929, to men who retired on gratuity. Why preclude a small number of men who similarly retired and were prevented from

making application to the Committee of Inquiry in 1922/23. This also applies to a small number of men in receipt of pensions who retired from the R.I.C. on the advice of Sinn Féin & I.R.A. While it does not follow that every man who joined the Garda could satisfy the committee that his resignation or dismissal from the R.I.C. was due to national sympathies, even though he subsequently left the Garda, those who can should be permitted to do so. The regulations regarding pensions were promulgated long after those men were unconditionally recruited and it is penal to impose further restrictions regarding certain antecedent factors which, of themselves, may have already qualified the applicant for a pension. As it is discretionary with the minister to forfeit a pension, wholly or in part, permanently or temporarily, it is felt that the restriction ought in justice to be removed.

Par. 3 in terms of reference wholly restricts applications from a number of men with outstanding national records, including the men who took part in the mutiny at Listowel R.I.C. barracks, when Divisional Commissioner Smyth made his infamous speech. Two of the men got to America and gave evidence before the Commission of Inquiry into Irish conditions, one of these had joined the R.I.C. subsequent to 18/4/1918. There are other cases of a similar nature – not many.

The deletion of the pars. referred to will enable any man with a national record to have his claims examined.

It is not, nor has it ever been, contended that all resignations or dismissals from the R.I.C., within the period 1/4/16 to 6/12/21, were due to national sympathies.

Representation on Committee of Inquiry (1934)

The resigned and dismissed men desire representation on the committee of Inquiry. This would inspire confidence and it is but simple justice.

Resigned and Dismissed Dublin Metropolitan Police

Resigned and dismissed members of the Dublin Metropolitan Police who were acting in defence of the Republic when reinstatement terms were offered in 1923 should be permitted to present their cases to the committee now sitting. The number is small – about six – some have outstanding national records, including Mr Andrew O'Neill, who was dismissed for refusing to disarm the Irish Volunteers at Howth Road on 26th July 1914. He was subsequently reinstated after agitation in the British parliament. He resigned during the Anglo-Irish war.

In spite of the submission, which was made on behalf of the resigned and dismissed policemen, the terms of reference of the Committee of Inquiry were not substantially altered and the committee continued as initially constituted. The legislation resulting from the committee's deliberations incorporated some of the unjust anomalies which had been anticipated in the submission made by the representatives of the resigned and dismissed policemen.

These anomalies and, indeed, the entire question of the treatment of the resigned and dismissed RIC and DMP were discussed in Dáil Éireann on 26 November and 1 December 1953. During the course of the debate on 26 November it was stated by the acting minister for finance, Francis (Frank) Aiken, that the Committee of Inquiry of 1922 dealt with 1,136 applications for pensions from resigned and dismissed policemen and granted these in 631 cases, and that the Committee of Inquiry of 1934 received 330 applications and granted 50.[10] It was also pointed out, however, that, apart from the motives which prompted their resignations, quite a number of resigned and dismissed policemen were for one reason or another precluded from receiving pensions. The debate on the question was resumed on 1 December when it was agreed that no new legislation on the matter should be enacted but that the minister for finance should review the cases of a number of ex-RIC men.[11] This seems to have been the last occasion on which the unfair way the resigned and dismissed RIC and DMP (1916–21) were treated by the Irish State was debated in the Dáil. A number of improvements were effected as a result of the debate. However, the overall injustice, whereby the resigned and dismissed RIC and DMP were not treated even as generously as their comrades who had continued to serve until disbanded, was never undone.

In a piece which he prepared on those who took part in the Listowel police mutiny for the 1964 issue of *Vexilla Regis,* Chief Superintendent Henry O'Mara wrote:

> Their bravery, their sacrifice and their steadfastness received but scanty recognition. Indeed there was and is evidence of ingratitude. The men who served to the end were and are better rewarded.

Unfortunately, in the light of their treatment by an ungrateful nation, this can be applied with a fair measure of accuracy to about half of the approximately 1,200 members of the RIC and DMP who, because of their nationalist sympathies, resigned or were dismissed between 1916 and 1921.[12]

APPENDIX 12

THE BELFAST BOYCOTT

The beginning of the Belfast Boycott campaign can be traced to Tuam, County Galway, where, early in 1920, local traders, at the prompting of Sinn Féin officials, agreed to boycott all Belfast commercial travellers and goods until sectarian attacks by Protestants on the Catholic minority in the north of Ireland ceased. From Tuam the campaign spread to Dublin, where support for it grew as these attacks continued, and, particularly, with the imposition of religious and political tests on persons applying for jobs in Belfast. In July 1920 a great deal of pressure was exerted, not least by certain Belfast Catholics who had been expelled from their native city, on some members of Dáil Éireann to have the boycott made official and effective. Towards the end of July the cabinet discussed the advisability of authorising the boycott. However, due to the strong opposition of Earnán de Blaghd (Ernest Blythe), director of trade and commerce, the cabinet postponed a decision on the matter until it had been discussed at a meeting of the Dáil.

The Dáil debate on the boycott was opened by Seán McEntee, a native of Belfast and a deputy for Monaghan South, on 6 August. He began his advocacy of the boycott by presenting the following memorial signed by representative citizens of the Catholic areas of Belfast:

We, the undersigned, members of the Belfast Corporation, and others, representing the views of Irish Republicans (and many others) in that city, beg to call the earnest attention of the Dáil to the war of extermination now being waged upon us, and we appeal to you to stand by us in the struggle.

We assume that you have read the press reports of the pogrom which started on July 21st with the violent expulsion from work of well over 5,000 people; of the murders, wrecking, looting and wholesale eviction of families. The situation for expelled workers grows worse daily and all signs go to show that the persecution is to be continued with unabated vigour. No one, not being in Belfast, can have any adequate idea of what our people are suffering now and must continue to suffer.

From the first the promoters of these outrages have been publicly declaring that they are out to fight Sinn Féin and drive it from the North-Eastern Pale. Already thousands of young men from every county in Ireland have been forced to fly, and thousands of others are idle here with destitution staring them in the face. The only condition on which they will be allowed to work is that they sign a declaration of loyalty to the British Government.

We earnestly appeal to Sinn Féin, through the Dáil, to take up this straight challenge, and fight Belfast – the spearhead of British power in Ireland. The Loyalists have repeatedly declared at public meetings and in the Town Council that this time they are not fighting Popery as such, but Sinn Féin, so that mere sectarianism does not enter in.

We suggest that Sinn Féin can strike back with powerful effect by a commercial boycott of Belfast. Drastic action of this kind has already been spontaneously taken in various places but the movement ought to be national and thorough. The chief promoters of Orange intolerance here are the heads of the distributing trade throughout Ireland.

We further suggest that the most effective action [by Sinn Féin] (to make Belfast realise that it is in Ireland and must be of Ireland) is to secure that its supporters throughout the country withdraw immediately all accounts from banks having their headquarters in Belfast, and transfer them to banks with headquarters in other parts of Ireland. This action is of vital importance. It will deprive Belfast merchants, who mostly either support or assent to this war on Irish Nationalism, of the fluid capital on which their business, through the medium of Belfast banks, is largely run. Other additional measures will doubtless suggest themselves to some of the gentlemen of the Dáil. The above will meet with the fullest approval of nearly 100,000 people in Belfast.

It should be strictly enjoined that Protestants in other parts of Ireland are not to be molested in any way on account of the actions of their co-religionists in Belfast. But, of course, those of them who are in business must be given to understand clearly that if they continue to get their goods from Belfast firms they cannot dispose of them to Sinn Féiners.

Signed – Joseph Cosgrave, T.C., Denis McCullough, T.C., A. Savage, T.C., P.L.G., Jer. Barnes, T.C., Jas. McEntee, Dr Moore, Dr John O'Doherty, Mrs A. McCullough, P.L.G., Jos. Connolly. Dated 5th August, 1920.

McEntee concluded his address by proposing the motion:

That an embargo be laid upon the manufacturers of the City of Belfast, that all trade and commerce with it by citizens of the Irish Republic be forbidden and that the government of the Republic calls on all its loyal citizens to rigorously enforce the provisions of this decree.

The motion was seconded by Paul Galligan, deputy for Cavan West. It was also supported, with some reservations, by Alexander McCabe, deputy for Sligo South.

Ernest Blythe, deputy for Monaghan North as well as a minister, led the opposition to the motion. He opposed a blockade of Belfast, firstly because such action should be taken against individuals and not against a whole community and, secondly, because 'it would destroy forever the possibility of any union'. Countess Markievicz, deputy for St Patrick's, Dublin, declared, somewhat prophetically, that the proposed blockade 'would be playing into the hands of the enemy and giving them a good excuse for partition'. Desmond Fitzgerald, deputy for Pembroke, Dublin, spoke in the same vein.

Then Arthur Griffith, deputy for Cavan East and Tyrone North West, and acting president, while admitting that the course of action proposed had grave disadvantages, nevertheless considered that action of this kind was imperative. After contributions from Terence MacSwiney, deputy for Cork Mid (for the motion), Joseph McGrath, deputy for St James', Dublin (against the motion), Michael Collins, deputy for Cork South (for the motion) and Liam de Róiste, deputy for Cork City (against the motion), Griffith proposed the following amendment which was carried:

> That the imposition of political or religious tests as a condition of industrial employment in Ireland is hereby declared illegal, and that action be taken by the ministry to prevent such tests being employed in Ireland.

Apart from passing this motion Dáil Éireann or, indeed, the cabinet did little more in the matter. At best the support of the Dáil for the boycott was half-hearted. Fully one-third of its members agreed with deputies Blythe, Fitzgerald, Markievicz, McGrath and de Róiste in opposing it. Responsibility for administering the boycott was not given to Ernest Blythe, who, as director of trade and commerce, would normally be expected to handle the matter, because of his well-known lack of enthusiasm for the measure. This lack of widespread support and the opposition to it of Desmond Fitzgerald, the substitute director of propaganda, and of Erskine Childers, one of the editors of the *Irish Bulletin* (he and seven others submitted a memorandum to Dáil Éireann at the beginning of September arguing for a selective rather than a total boycott of Belfast), may explain why the motion on the boycott which was passed by Dáil Éireann on 6 August did not appear in the *Irish Bulletin*, the mouthpiece of Sinn Féin, until 18 September.

The boycott was enthusiastically backed by a number of county councils, and locally enforced by members of the IRA and Republican police. Support for it grew as the attacks on the Catholic minority in the north continued. By the end of August the boycott was gathering its own momentum. Thus the general council of county councils decreed on 31 August:

> As the imposition of religious and political tests as a condition of industrial employment in any part of Ireland has been declared illegal, this council calls on all public bodies to cease trading with the city in which such an illegal test is now attempted to be enforced.

Also by the end of August a boycott committee had been set up in Belfast and in early September this committee and others in Belfast who were promoting the boycott began to exert pressure in order to ensure its more effective implementation. A conference was held between members of the Dáil, and Labour and Republican representatives from Belfast, at which a general plan of action was agreed. As a result of the conference a committee was formed at a meeting of the Dublin Corporation on 14 September to put the boycott into effect in the city, and at a meeting of the Dáil on 17 September a somewhat unwilling Michael Staines, deputy for St Michan's, Dublin, was officially appointed director of the Belfast Boycott.

The appointment of a director, it seems, was nothing more than a gesture by the Dáil and even this was negatived on 26 November with the arrest and imprisonment of Staines. Thus when the director of trade and commerce read a report on the Belfast Boycott at the session held on 25 January 1921, a lively discussion ensued. Joseph MacDonagh, deputy for Tipperary North, said: 'he had spent some time in Belfast and went into the question of the boycott. He had sent a suggestion to the minister for finance about the feasibility of selecting eight or ten organisers for Ireland for four or five months. (For the exchange of correspondence [8–21 January 1921] on the Belfast Boycott between MacDonagh and Collins, see State Paper Office, Dáil Éireann Papers, 2/261.) He agreed that a very effective boycott could be carried out for three or four months for £1,000 or £1,500. These organisers should be placed at strategic points such as Clones, Dundalk, Derry and similar places in the south … He suggested that a sum be voted for this purpose.'

Seán McEntee considered that more propaganda on the matter was necessary.

Michael Collins said, 'he was not quite clear whether the member for North Tipperary had made an application to vote money ... Until they got up a real atmosphere they would not make the boycott a success. The results depended upon a really good man being in charge. He thought the Belfast Boycott Committee was to blame for not really being alive. For some reason or another everyone would agree that sufficient vigour and force had not been put into this business. He now proposed that £1,500 be passed for the organisation of the boycott and £1,000 for propaganda in connection with it. This boycott would have far-reaching effects. It would make a Vienna of Belfast if it remained outside Ireland.'

Arthur Griffith said 'he had an opportunity of consulting the ministry about appointing a minister for labour and they had agreed upon a member who would be willing to act'. He then proposed that the member for North Tipperary be appointed substitute minister for labour and suggested that 'as he was in touch with the Belfast campaign, he might for the time being look after it'. This was approved.

Within three weeks Joe MacDonagh had selected, trained and placed in the field the proposed boycott organisers (see p. 173) and the campaign became more effective.

The more effective prosecution of the boycott was also due to the work of MacDonagh at the central office. By the middle of March he had compiled a comprehensive blacklist of firms and had forwarded it to the mayors and council chairmen of all cities and towns, and, through his organisers, to boycott committees throughout the country. The original boycott, authorised by the cabinet of Dáil Éireann, was placed on goods coming from Belfast, Banbridge, Dromore, Lisburn and Newtownards. Thus the blacklist included firms in Ireland which continued to handle goods from these places and also firms in Ireland and Britain which had been set up for the sole purpose of distributing boycotted goods. Towards the end of June MacDonagh received authorisation from the cabinet to boycott the three northern banks by advising all Dublin merchants to refuse to accept cheques and money issued by these banks. On 25 October he issued a revised blacklist of firms, to which all but a few firms in Portadown were added some days later. This last was done because Portadown had become a major centre for the distribution of goods from the boycotted areas. On 29 November, MacDonagh forwarded to his organisers another edition of the blacklist, from which some firms had been removed and to which some others had been added.

By early December it seems that even those members of the cabinet, who initially supported and were even enthusiastic about the boycott, were no longer convinced that it was a useful exercise. At any rate, in spite of MacDonagh's insistent advocacy of a boycott of the Dublin Tramway Company for blatant violations of the Belfast Boycott, and ignoring a fine of £300 which had been imposed on it by the Belfast Boycott Committee, the cabinet directed him to postpone action in the matter. Then, also in early December, MacDonagh received a memorandum from Republican representatives in Belfast itemising not only the hardships suffered by the Republican and nationalist community from Orange mobs, but also those inflicted on it by the indiscriminate boycott of Belfast. This memorandum, which appealed to the director of the Belfast Boycott to issue permits to Republican and nationalist-owned, in effect, Catholic-owned, firms in Belfast, was forwarded to Dáil Éireann by MacDonagh on 12 December. The question of these permits was discussed by the cabinet on 12 and 13 January 1922. However, no definite decision was taken on the matter as by that time the whole question of the boycott of Belfast trade had been superseded by much wider issues.

At a meeting with Sir James Craig in London in the third week of January 1922, Collins, acting for the cabinet of Dáil Éireann, promised to call off the Belfast Boycott and end IRA activity in the North in return for a promise that the Northern Ireland government would protect the interests of the Catholic minority. Accordingly, after a meeting of the cabinet of Dáil Éireann on 24 January, the following statement was issued: 'The Dáil cabinet having considered the report of the meeting of Mr Collins and Sir James Craig in London hereby direct that the Belfast Boycott be discontinued. The boycott was originally instituted on account of the imposition of religious tests. These tests are now to be withdrawn.' The retention of Michael Staines as minister of the Belfast Boycott – he was included in the list of ministerial appointments, which were made public by Arthur Griffith on 28 February – was designed to ensure that the decision of the cabinet to terminate the boycott would be carried out. The decision to end the boycott was opposed by most of the anti-Treaty members in the Dáil, including Joe MacDonagh who, on 10 January, had been replaced as director of the boycott. They maintained, with some justification, that since the boycott had been called off the position of the nationalist minority in the North had, in fact, worsened rather than improved. They also questioned the authority of the cabinet to terminate the boycott without consulting Dáil Éireann. Lively exchanges, in which Seán McEntee was prominent, on the question of the boycott occurred at the sessions of the Dáil which were held on 1, 2 March and 28 April 1922.

In the meantime, after consideration by the cabinet on 15 March of conditions in the six-county area, a deputation from the Ulster Boycott Committee (as the boycott spread beyond Belfast the committee was renamed the Ulster Boycott Committee) was received by the ministry on 21 March, when, after a lengthy discussion, a decision on the question of the reimposition of the boycott was postponed until the cabinet meeting of 24 March. At this meeting 'it was decided that no action regarding the re-imposition of the boycott be taken until after the passing of the Irish Free State bill through the British House of Lords'.

Outside Dáil Éireann those who opposed the Treaty continued the Belfast Boycott campaign. In fact the boycott was one of the flashpoints which led to the outbreak of the Civil War. General lawlessness, the commandeering of vehicles and operations associated with the Belfast Boycott caused much frustration and anger throughout the country. This, in turn, led to a great deal of pressure being brought to bear on the Provisional Government to establish law and order and to do something about the force holding the Four Courts. It is curious that a prominent person in the series of incidents which triggered off the Civil War was Leo Henderson, the Four Courts garrison's director of the Belfast Boycott.

The beginning of the Civil War effectively marked the end of the Belfast Boycott.[1]

Addendum

An examination of the conclusions of meetings of the British cabinet, which were held throughout 1920, indicates that, although various aspects of the 'Irish Situation' were discussed from time to time and a special committee appointed on 24 June 1920 'to assist the viceroy and chief secretary for Ireland in dealing with questions arising in connection with Ireland', in that year there were only two major conferences by the cabinet on the Sinn Féin rebellion in Ireland. The first was held on 23 July. A reading of the report of this conference leaves one in no doubt that the main preoccupation of practically everyone who contributed to the discussions was the impending collapse of the RIC as a police force. The conference was informed that this created a new situation which called for either more repressive measures on the one hand, or negotiations with Sinn Féin on the other. When considering this latter course, the attempt to identify a settlement which would be acceptable to the British government, Sinn Féin and the Ulster Unionists was one which was conducted intermittently, without much variation, down to the last decade of the twentieth century. The second major conference by the British cabinet on the 'Irish Situation' was held on 29–30 December. This was essentially a report by the military and police chiefs in Ireland on the military and police situation in this country at that time and, among other things, the advantages and disadvantages of arranging a Truce with the forces of Sinn Féin were discussed.

It is significant that the first major conference by the British cabinet on the situation in Ireland was held soon after the Listowel police mutiny (19 June), the mutiny of the Connaught Rangers (27–28 June), the adverse publicity given to these two events, the assassination of Divisional Commissioner Smyth (17 July) and the increasing rate of resignations from the RIC (cf. p. 352 n.2). For this reason, and also because this conference was the most important discussion throughout the 1919–1921 period by the British cabinet of the police question in Ireland, the notes of this particular conference are reproduced here.[1]

THE SITUATION IN IRELAND

Notes of a Conference with the officers of the Irish government held at 10 Downing Street, S.W. on Friday, 23 July 1920, at 11.30 a.m. and 3.30 p.m.

Present

The Prime Minister (in the Chair).

The Right Hon. A. Bonar Law, M.P., Lord Privy Seal.

The Right Hon. A. J. Balfour, O.M., M.P., Lord President of the Council.

The Right Hon. The Earl Curzon of Kedleston, K.G., G.C.S.I., G.CJ.E., Secretary of State for Foreign Affairs.

The Right Hon. Sir Hamar Greenwood, Bart., K.C., M.P., Chief Secretary for Ireland.

The Right Hon. H. A. L. Fisher, M.P., President, Board of Education.

The Right Hon. A. Chamberlain, M.P., Chancellor of the Exchequer.

The Right Hon. Lord Birkenhead, Lord Chancellor.

The Right Hon. W. S. Churchill, M.P., Secretary of State for War.

The Right Hon. W. Long, M.P., First Lord of the Admiralty.

Field-Marshal the Right Hon. Viscount French, K.P., G.C.B., O.M., G.O.Y.O., K.C.M.G., Lord Lieutenant of Ireland.

The following were also Present

The Right Hon. Denis S. Henry, K.C., Attorney-General for Ireland.

General the Right Hon. Sir Nevil Macready, G.C.M.G., K.C.B., Commanding the Forces in Ireland.

Major-General H. H. Tudor, O.B., G.C.M.G.

Mr W. E. Wylie, Law Adviser.

The Right Hon. Sir John Anderson, K.C.B., Joint Under-Secretary for Ireland.

Colonel Sir James Craig, Bart., M.P., Parliamentary and Financial Secretary, Admiralty.

The Right Hon. J. MacMahon, Joint Under-Secretary for Ireland. (For afternoon discussion only.)

Thomas Jones	Acting Secretary
Colonel L. Storr, O.B.	Assistant Secretary
Captain L. F. Burgis	Assistant Secretary
T. St Quintin Hill	Assistant Secretary

THE SITUATION IN IRELAND

Police

Mr Wylie (Law Adviser) said that in his view the present position in Ireland meant the parting of the ways, and only harm could come of patchwork legislation. With regard to the state of the Police, he had during the last three weeks seen a large number of police officers, and had formed the strong opinion that within two months the Irish Police Force as a Police Force would cease to exist. He was referring now to the whole of Ireland, with the exception of the North-East Counties. In two months' time, fifty per cent of the Police Force would have resigned through terrorism, and the remainder would have to go about in considerable force committing counter outrages. An Irish policeman either saw white or he saw red; if he saw white, he resigned from the force through terrorism, and if he saw red he committed a counter outrage. Both conditions of mind were disastrous.[2]

Civil Courts

With regard to the Civil Courts, the entire administration of the Imperial Government had ceased. In one town, out of 45 appeals down for hearing only two came on. As for the revenue, everyone was determined to pay no taxes, and it was not fair to ask the revenue officers to collect them, for, if they attempted to do so, they did it at the peril of their lives.

Local Authorities

With regard to the Local Authorities, these were prepared to function so far as their own local affairs were concerned, but they would give no assistance in carrying out the instructions of the Irish Government.

Remedies: (1) Martial Law

There were in his opinion two remedies for the present state of affairs. The first was to proclaim at once martial law of the most stringent kind. As an Irishman, this to him was abhorrent, and afforded no solution of the problem. By proclaiming martial law it would be possible to beat the people into insensibility; but when martial law was taken off – and it must end some time – the feelings of hatred and bitterness would be intensified, and there would be a return to the present state of affairs. The second remedy was a settlement with Sinn Féin. He was aware that the English might regard this as a condonation of the murderers, but he wished to emphasize that these murderers were not real criminals. Of that he felt convinced. Fanatics they might be, and probably were, but they were themselves convinced that through murder was the only path to freedom. These men were not committing outrages through blood-lust, but because they believed they had been tricked by the British Government, and the only way to focus the eyes of Europe on their cause was by the adoption of the methods they had pursued. The Sinn Féiners were of the opinion that the application of martial law would assist their cause.

(2) Negotiations with Sinn Féin

A difficulty in regard to settling with Sinn Féin was to find anyone with whom to negotiate. He felt convinced that if England took her courage in both hands and stated that she was prepared to settle with Sinn Féin on any terms short of an Irish Republic, and that if Sinn Féin did not accept the offer martial law would be introduced, Sinn Féin would come forward and negotiate. The Sinn Féiners were convinced that they were capable of governing Ireland, and he agreed with them. He himself had started life as a Unionist, but now, after seeing the marvellous organisation which Sinn Féin had built up, he was of the opinion that the Irish were capable of governing themselves. If the Government attempted to bludgeon the Irish people, no good could possibly result, and Ireland would still remain a thorn in the side of the Empire. But if the Government played straight, within two years Ireland would be one of the strongest partners within the Empire.

When the new Administration had come over to Ireland, for six weeks there had been a lull in the Sinn Féin tactics of murder and outrage. This was caused by the hope that England would come forward and say that they were prepared to meet Sinn Féin. After six weeks this hope disappeared, and during the last fortnight things had become worse than they had ever been before. He would like it to be realised that the British Government was up against a national movement, and that if anything was to be done it must be done now.

Ulster

In answer to a question as to whether he thought Sinn Féin would accept County Option, Mr Wylie replied that he was certain Sinn Féin would accept County Option for Ulster, and they might even go so far as to consent to the six counties remaining out.

Mr Wylie was also asked what powers Sinn Féin wanted that were not given them by the present Bill, and he replied that they wanted everything except defence. They were perfectly willing that defence should be under the Imperial Parliament and that the Imperial Parliament should have control of the ports.

Sinn Féin and Outrages

In reply to a further question as to whether the Sinn Féiners he had met were responsible for planning the assassinations, Mr Wylie said that they undoubtedly knew about them, but thought that they helped their cause. At the present moment the Sinn Féiners he had met held that they could not stop the outrages so long as the British Government continued its present policy. But he thought that, given a proper atmosphere, they would be able to put down the extremists.

Police

General Tudor said that he feared that the Royal Irish Constabulary could not last much longer, as they did not consider that they were being properly supported. As a Police Force, he agreed with Mr Wylie, within a few months they would cease to function; but as a military body he thought they might have great effect. He had just recruited 500 ex-officers and a number of ex-soldiers, which formed a fine body of men, and he felt that, given the proper support, it would be possible to crush the present campaign of outrage. Asked for his suggestions as to the measures to be adopted, General Tudor outlined them as follows:

(1) No tribunal to function except as a Court-martial.

(2) A Court-martial to be the tribunal for all crimes.

(3) The establishment of identity cards in all towns in Ireland, as had been done by the Army of Occupation in Germany.

(4) That passports should be necessary for entry into Ireland. (He believed this would have a great effect on the activities of the I.R.B.)

(5) Power to restrict change of domicile.

(6) The proclaiming of certain areas as military areas, so that if a murder had been committed in a certain district a fine could be imposed on that district, and, if there was a refusal to pay, this could be met by seizing the cattle and stock of the residents sufficient to make up the amount of the fine.

(7) That there should be a special penalty of flogging imposed for the cutting of girls' hair and outrages against women.

(8) That all prisoners should be sent to this country, as the hard labour imposed in England and Scotland was more severe than in Ireland, and, further, the prisoners would not be in touch with the outside world.

(9) That steps should be taken to have the Post Office purged of traitors.

(At the present moment it was difficult to administer the Police owing to the difficulty of getting orders round to them.)

(10) That Cardinal Mannix should not be allowed to land in Ireland.[3]

General Tudor was asked if the adoption of his suggestions would give the Police a feeling that they were being supported. General Tudor replied in the affirmative, and said that the two things which had given the Police a feeling of insecurity were (1) the release of the hunger-strikers, and (2) the fact that not a single criminal had been brought to justice for murder.

Archbishop Mannix

With regard to the landing of Cardinal Mannix, the Conference decided that the Secretary of State for Foreign Affairs should send a telegram to the British Ambassador at Washington requesting him to warn Cardinal Mannix before he sailed that he would not be allowed to land in Ireland.

General Tudor, continuing, said that he did not agree with Mr Wylie that all the murderers were fanatics. Some of them undoubtedly were, but there were a number of loafers and ex-soldiers who were very highly paid for committing murders.

The Prime Minister asked if, with powers of the kind he had intimated, General Tudor could control the situation.

General Tudor said that he thought he could, provided that enough men were obtainable. The whole country was intimidated, and would thank God for strong measures. If the country was handed over to Sinn Féin, he doubted whether they could control the extremists, and he was not at all sure that the Sinn Féiners could put an end to the activities of the Gunmen.

Case of Limerick

A reference was then made to the satisfactory manner in which disorders in the city of Limerick had been dealt with, and it was stated that this was owing to the adoption of different methods.

General Tudor said that this was true, and the method adopted was that the Police went out on patrol and if a street was empty they fired down it and they also held up loungers at street corners and had them roughly searched. These methods had the effect of reducing the city to quiet.

General Macready added that it was also because there was a first-rate man as District Inspector in Limerick.[4]

Police

General Tudor was asked what he meant when he said that his measures might succeed provided he got enough men; and he replied that, at the present moment, the recruitment of the Royal Irish Constabulary was only keeping pace with resignations. If it was impossible to get the men, he must develop the idea of temporary cadet officers, 500 of whom he had obtained. These officers were drafted from England to strengthen the Royal Irish Constabulary personnel in certain parts of the country and had had a great effect.

Mr Cope (Assistant Under-Secretary), asked for his views on the situation, said he had seen Cardinal Logue, who thought that a solution of the problem might be found by the granting of Dominion Home Rule. The Cardinal placed the responsibility for the murders at the door of the British Government. With regard to these murders, Mr Cope said he thought that the Sinn Féin Courts were doing more harm to the prestige of the British Government than the assassinations. The Sinn Féin Courts were working very efficiently, but it must be remembered that the amount of ordinary crime in Ireland was very small. There were only 450 prisoners in the country when they had accommodation for 6,000. Eliminating offences against the Police, there was practically no crime in Ireland at all. The Sinn Féiners were working hard at increasing the efficiency of their Courts. With regard to General Tudor's scheme for the putting down of murder, he doubted whether it would be effective, and felt that any suppression now would come back like a boomerang on the Government.

Police

Sir John Anderson (Joint Under-Secretary) said that he agreed entirely with Mr Wylie's general proposition, and with General Tudor up to a point. If a sufficient force could be obtained there was no doubt it would be possible to reduce the country to order, but he did not think that the Royal Irish Constabulary as it existed today would be a very important factor in bringing about that result. If force was resorted to, the Royal Irish Constabulary would cease to exist, and in place of it a new force would arise, containing perhaps a certain number of old Royal Irish Constabulary men, but to all intents and purposes a new force, which would not deal with the ordinary crimes of the country. He could not help thinking that General Tudor, in stating that under certain conditions he could restore order, must have been assuming the assistance of a larger military force. The case of Limerick had been cited as an example of what might be done, but in his opinion Limerick was an isolated case due to an exceptional personality and it would not be safe to assume that it was possible to restore order in the same way everywhere.

Martial Law

The measures which General Tudor advocated were those of martial law, and were not the ordinary methods of administering civil government. The Civil Administration under martial law would either be driven to seek the protection of the military, or would cease to function altogether. Under martial law there must be one military administrator who would have the whole power in his hands, and the civil authorities would be subordinate. He himself doubted whether it would be possible to restore order or maintain a sufficiently forcible policy. The Government was up against a well-organised body, and to restore order would be a very lengthy business, which he ventured to think could not be done in the time at their disposal. He agreed with what Mr Wylie had said, that when the time came to take off martial law there would be no material left with which to work for a solution of the Irish Problem.

The Prime Minister said that Mr Wylie had mentioned that a certain atmosphere was necessary before a settlement could be reached. He would like to know if such inconveniences as had been suggested by General Tudor would create the desired atmosphere.

Mr Wylie replied that such a course of action would only create a feeling of intense hostility in Ireland, and the Irish would regard it as another piece of English tyranny; the result would be that more and more of the loyalists would tend to go over to the rebel ranks. Already the complaint of loyalists against the stoppage of race trains had been very bitter.[5]

The Prime Minister then asked for an expression of opinion on the situation from those who had not been present at previous meetings, and in particular from Sir James Craig.

Sir James Craig replied that his own personal experience made him agree on the whole with what Mr Wylie had said with regard to the condition of Ireland and the feeling in that country. He did not think that there had been sufficient energy in dealing with Sinn Féin. No overhead policy from which the Government would not deviate appeared to exist. We were more or less drifting along on various lines without co-ordination. He had urged, and did his utmost to get the Irish Home Rule Bill through the House of Commons, and had persuaded some of his colleagues to drop their opposition to the Bill. It would be a very dangerous course of policy for the Government to pursue if the House of Commons were allowed to rise without anything being done, and with no declaration of a definite policy.

Irish Education Bill

It was also essential that the Government should be very straight. Pledges had undoubtedly been broken; for instance there was the case of the Irish Education Bill. He had never been able to understand why this Bill had been introduced contemporaneously with the Home Rule Bill. It was an overestimate of the possibilities of parliamentary work and the failure to proceed with it had been regarded as one more milestone on the road of broken pledges. Even the loyalists point to this Bill as a broken pledge, and ask whether it was possible now to rely on the Government carrying out any policy that it announced. This doubt drove loyalists to Sinn Féin. He had evidence of loyalists getting protection from Sinn Féin, and he instanced a case in which a member of the House of Commons had applied to Sinn Féin in order to secure the collection of debts in Cork. This fact showed that even in England there were people who had come to regard the Sinn Féin organisation as a medium for commerce. We had got beyond the time when measures for securing the running of trains and the protection of police were of any real value. The Government should map out now what they intend to do, make an announcement of it and stick to their plan. By doing this they would tide over a very dangerous period in the late summer.

The Prime Minister enquired what sort of an announcement Sir James Craig suggested should be made.

Financial Powers of Parliaments in North & South

Sir James Craig replied that the announcement should be largely a re-affirmation of policy, Ulster should be left out of account. She already has separate treatment and a separate Parliament.[6] So far as the South and West of Ireland were concerned further concessions could be made, but such concessions would affect finance at once as they would touch on questions relating to the customs and debts due, etc. When such concessions were announced, the North would no doubt want the same, and it could be possible to co-operate with the North which was keen to be carried on in the same way as the United Kingdom. Ulster could be given more elasticity in finance. Some such steps would settle the unrest in Ulster, and the Irish Bill could be proceeded with as far as Ulster was concerned. So far as the South and West were concerned, Sir James Craig said that he could not make definite proposals unless he was given a few days in which to consult with other persons. He would then be able to put forward a definite plan. He suggested that a small Committee of three or four could, with conscientious work, elaborate a good plan. The questions to be considered by the Committee would have the following objects:

(1) An extension of the scope of the Home Rule Bill;

(2) The maintenance of law and order in Ireland;

(3) The Committee would no doubt advise on the question as to how far it would inflame public opinion to stop railways and the administration of the Post Office, etc., and how far the advantages of such a policy would outweigh the disadvantages.

The Secretary of State for Foreign Affairs stated that he had gathered from Sir James Craig's statement that Sir James agreed with Mr Wylie's views, viz., that repression, however effective, must break down because it could not be maintained indefinitely, and when repression was relaxed the sore would remain unhealed. Moreover, there were difficulties with the police. It was on these grounds that Mr Wylie had advocated the policy of getting into touch with Sinn Féin and offering them Dominion Home Rule. Did Sir James Craig propose the same policy?

Sir James Craig replied that he had only agreed with Mr Wylie's description of the situation in Ireland – he did not necessarily agree with his conclusions and he again urged that a small Committee should be established in order to prepare a comprehensive plan for submission to the Prime Minister.

The Chancellor of the Exchequer pointed out that Sir James Craig's plan, so far as already expounded, would give to the South and West of Ireland Dominion finance and Dominion internal administration, but it would leave the control of the army and navy to the Imperial Government. His policy was in fact the same as that suggested by Mr Wylie, but Mr Wylie would present it as Dominion Government while Sir James Craig would present it as an amendment to the Home Rule Bill. If the policy suggested was presented as an amendment to the Home Rule Bill and not as a new and distinct offer of Dominion Government, would it be acceptable to Sinn Féin?

Mr Wylie replied in the negative. He was certain that the Government must make a new departure. It was essential to remember when dealing with Irishmen that an appeal should be made to their imagination.

Sir James Craig pointed out that to make this new departure would involve a change of the whole policy of the Government in regard to the Home Rule Bill, such a change would inevitably be regarded as another instance of inconsistency.

The Prime Minister said that Mr Wylie's view was that the vast majority of the population of the South and West of Ireland would be prepared to accept Dominion Home Rule. Would the leaders of Sinn Féin be prepared to say so and to meet someone, say in Dublin, who could go into the matter with them? Would they be prepared to state openly that they accepted the sovereignty of the British Empire over Ireland and were willing to use their influence to suppress crime?

Mr Wylie replied that the Sinn Féin leaders would not say so publicly, at any rate, before the British Government made their offer. As soon as a statement was made in the House of Commons, backed by a definite pledge of England's honour, he thought that the Sinn Féin leaders would be willing to get into touch with representatives of the British Government and would do their best to work some scheme of Dominion Home Rule.

The Lord Privy Seal remarked that he had been told that certain Unionists in the South of Ireland wished the Government to follow the policy suggested by Mr Wylie. He asked Mr Wylie whether this was so.

Mr Wylie replied that it was so, undoubtedly.

Proposed Convention

The President of the Board of Education enquired whether it would meet the views of Sinn Féin if the Prime Minister was to declare that the Home Rule Bill was going to be passed and that there was no intention of altering the arrangements made for the Six Counties, but that a Convention would be summoned, say, next year in the South or West of Ireland to frame a Constitution for that part of Ireland (with the reservation that control of the Army and Navy would be left to Great Britain[)] and that the separate arrangements for the six Counties would still stand.

Mr Wylie replied that such an offer would not be considered by Sinn

Féin. The word 'Convention' was obnoxious and the mere existence of reservations in the offer would be enough to condemn it.

The Secretary of State for War asked Sir John Anderson to explain further the situation in Ireland arising from the existing dislocation of the railways and the consequent damage to trade.

Railway Policy

Sir John Anderson replied that it certainly was the case that in the last few weeks trade had been severely hampered. The railways were not functioning normally, and in the parts where disorder had occurred trade had suffered severely. If repressive measures were taken, great distress would result. No doubt up to the present moment things had gone sufficiently far to create a desire for an early settlement, and the increasing disorganisation of trade had to that extent had a beneficial effect on public opinion. But we were now at the parting of the ways, and the Government had either to give way or to go very much further in repression. If force were to be used, success in its use was indispensable, and the civil machine would have to be scrapped. The alternatives were, in fact, the declaration of martial law or some kind of agreement with Sinn Féin.

Position of Ulster under Dominion Home Rule

The Lord Privy Seal pointed out that there was a difference of view as to what would happen if the second alternative were adopted. It had been held that Sinn Féin would make an offer on the part of the British Government simply a stepping-stone for further aggrandisement. Moreover, Mr J. H. Thomas had informed the Prime Minister that Sinn Féin would accept no proposals that involved the exclusion of the Six Counties.

Mr Wylie urged that the Six Counties should be left under British control and not be given a separate Parliament. The view of Sinn Féin was that if left to administer the South and West of Ireland, Sinn Féin would be so successful that the Six Counties would want to come in and not to remain under the British Parliament.

The First Lord of the Admiralty asked what would be the effect on opinion in Ulster.

Sir James Craig thought the effect would be disastrous. The Government had already gone too far, and their pledges were too definite.

Mr Wylie remarked that Sinn Féin pointed to the statement made by the Ulster leaders in the House of Commons to the effect that Ulster wished to be left under England.

Sir John Anderson said that some little time ago there were indications that Sinn Féin would not refuse Dominion Home Rule with a separate Parliament for Ulster. The majority, it was true, were opposed to such a separate Parliament, but he believed that a great body of feeling in Ireland would be sympathetic. In any case, some definite action would have to be taken.

Arming of Ulster

The Secretary of State for War enquired what Mr Wylie thought would happen if the Protestants in the Six Counties were given weapons and were definitely charged with the duty of maintaining law and order and of policing the country? The object of such an arrangement would be the withdrawal of the troops from Ulster, and of a considerable number, if not all, of the regular police.

Mr Wylie thought that such a policy would be disastrous. Sinn Féin would arm a more numerous and an equally efficient force. In Derry there were a large number of rifles, and every man had a revolver. There would be intense civil war, and in other parts of Ulster, while there would not perhaps be definite fighting, there would be guerilla warfare and continual assassination. In Belfast the Protestants would reduce the Catholics to a state of terror. In Tyrone there would be an unceasing and unending civil war. He could not conceive that His Majesty's Government would allow this to take place.

Sir James Craig said that in his opinion such a course would be quite practicable, if it were legalised. Special Constables would have to be sworn in and take the oath of allegiance, and they should be allowed to elect their own officers, with control through the Army authorities.

Ulster would be glad to maintain law and order in the Six Counties, and would be able to do it. Ulster would not, he was convinced, terrorise the Roman Catholics, and would not allow mob law. Ulster would be able to prevent the Protestants from running amok.

General Tudor remarked that Ulster was very anxious to maintain order in the Six Counties, but did not wish to use an irregular force for this purpose. It wanted the Special Constables to be recognised, and did not desire the Ulster Volunteers to be utilised.

The Prime Minister suggested that the proposals now put forward for the maintenance of law and order in Ulster by Ulstermen should be examined.

General Tudor thought that a policy of allowing Ulster to maintain order for herself would encourage the loyalists and would show that the Government did differentiate between rebels and loyalists.

The Prime Minister remarked that he was not thinking of such differentiation, but of releasing troops and police. If Ulster would police itself, 7 battalions and some 2,000 to 3,000 police would be released for use elsewhere.

Sir John Anderson remarked that he had discussed with many persons in Ireland a proposal to use Protestants as police or as an auxiliary force. He thought that if the policy of force were decided on it would undoubtedly be necessary to take some such action in the ordinary course of events. Military efficiency might or might not be increased thereby, but it was certain that the South of Ireland would become ablaze at once. There would be a massacre of Protestants in the South and West. To the remark that the position could not well be worse than it was now, he replied that the isolated murders of Police were not the limit of possible Sinn Féin activities.

Sir James MacMahon (Joint Under-Secretary) said that, in his opinion, any attempt at repression would fail; and not only would it fail, but it would deprive the Government of any friends amongst the Nationalists whom they might have left.[7] He was satisfied that those methods would not catch the ruffians, but, on the contrary, would drive into the opposite camp a great number of people who held moderate opinions.

With regard to the two Parliaments in Ireland, as suggested under the existing Bill, he felt certain that they would result in more trouble than at present. In the South there would be no Parliament worthy of the name. It was true they might take the oath of allegiance, but they would repudiate the oath in advance and then assume all the functions which the act of parliament did not give them. The Southern Parliament would then become an unlawful assembly and would have to be broken up. This would be used as propaganda, and it would be said that the Imperial Government only gave Southern Ireland a Parliament in order to take it away again.

His suggestion was a Bill extending to the 32 Counties in Ireland, with power to any County to vote itself out if it did not like the provisions of the Bill. Every Ulster elector had so far voted against Home Rule, but if there existed a Parliament in Dublin and it was put to the Ulster electors whether they would join or not, the issue was quite a different one, and he thought that those who were of the opinion that the majority of the Six Counties would vote themselves out were mistaken. He had discussed this matter with many of his Orange friends, and they had agreed that they would only put up a fight against a Dublin Parliament if their interests were attacked.

With regard to the assassinations, he had been talking to Cardinal Logue, whom he had found weeping over the murder of Colonel Smyth, which had shocked him beyond measure, and he had denounced the perpetrators. He had asked the Cardinal if there was no means of even temporarily stopping the present assassinations, and he had replied by asking what was the good of attempting the impossible when the Government provided the excuse for these men to commit such outrages?

In reply to a question, Sir James MacMahon stated that the Roman Catholic Church had always been opposed to a Republic. Sir James MacMahon was asked whether the priests gave absolution to murderers, and replied that if the priest knew the facts he would not give absolution, but in a confession a man did not always state that he had committed a murder, as he did not regard such an act as a crime.

Sir James MacMahon then gave a short history of the Sinn Féin movement, and stated that the real Sinn Féin movement was against these acts of violence, which were in reality carried on by a very small section of extremists who attached themselves for their own purposes to Sinn Féin.

Some discussion then followed regarding the administration of certain funds received in Ireland, which it was alleged had been used for the purpose of paying the murderers. Sir James MacMahon contended that so far no proof had been produced to show that the funds were used for the purpose of paying the murderers, or that the persons named organised the gang. Further, Sir James MacMahon contested the statement that the assassins were paid. He contended, on the other hand, that they were mostly young political fanatics, members of Secret Societies who were forced to commit these murders at the peril of their lives.

Sir James MacMahon was then asked why, if so many of the leading lights in the Sinn Féin movement were prepared to accept Dominion Home Rule, they stated they would accept nothing less than a Republic? Sir James MacMahon replied that they did this on the principle of a man who wished to sell a horse and stated that he required £100 when in reality he was prepared to accept £70.

The Prime Minister said that he would like to know:

(1) The price the Government would have to pay;
(2) What the Government would get in return;
(3) Who would guarantee that the Government would get it'?

The Government wanted peace and order in Ireland, and Sir James MacMahon had said that this could not be got by coercion.

What measure of Home Rule, then, would produce the desired results? No Sinn Féiner had ever said that he would accept Dominion Home Rule.

Sir James MacMahon said that he thought the Sinn Féiners would accept a Home Rule Bill giving them Customs and Excise, but reserving the Army and Navy to the Imperial Government. They would be willing to pay a small fixed contribution to the Imperial Exchequer, and agree to County Option. He thought this would be accepted by the majority, and the Church would accept such a scheme with glee. The following scheme, he thought, they might accept, but it would be more difficult:

> For the Government to pass a Dominion Home Rule Bill for the 26 Counties in Ireland, on the same terms as he had mentioned above, stipulating that the Six Counties should remain as they are at present, under the Imperial Government.

The Prime Minister said that this meant putting financial pressure on the Six Counties to come in.

Sir James MacMahon replied that that would mean that Ulster would be willing to sell her rights of remaining under the Imperial Parliament in order to obtain financial advantages.

A question was asked, if Dominion Home Rule was given to the South and they attempted to work the Act, would the gang of assassins dominate the situation in the South, or would the Parliament be able to put them down, when the Imperial Government with all the enormous resources at its command had failed to do so.

Sir James MacMahon replied that history proved that it would be possible for the Southern Parliament to put down the gang of assassins.

The Prime Minister asked what Ireland would get under Dominion Home Rule which it did not get under the present Bill? There was Finance (leaving the Imperial contribution to the Dominion itself), Excise, Customs, Defence.

Sir James MacMahon said that Sinn Féin would be prepared to agree that Defence should be reserved to the Imperial Parliament. As regards Finance, he could not say definitely but he had heard the basis of a contribution of £1 per head of the population mentioned.

The Chancellor of the Exchequer said that what Sir James MacMahon suggested was really complete fiscal autonomy, leaving to Ireland the power to make any Imperial contribution she thought fit.

The Prime Minister then asked, if all this was given to them and they were told that the Six Counties were excluded, having, if they wished, a Parliament of their own, would such a proposition be acceptable?

Sir James MacMahon replied in the negative. The contention of the Sinn Féiners was that if the Six Counties remained under the Imperial Parliament there was still a chance of their eventually joining with the Dublin Parliament. If, on the other hand, the Six Counties had a Parliament of their own, all hope of a union of the whole of Ireland under one Parliament must be given up.

2 Whitehall Gardens, S.W.
23rd July, 1920.

NOTES

1: BEGINNINGS: AUGUST 1909–FEBRUARY 1911

1 'Nap' or Napoleon was a popular card game in which five cards were dealt singly to each player from a full pack. The player on the dealer's left 'declared' to win what number of tricks he thought he could – two, three, four or 'Nap'/Napoleon (the whole five), or, with a poor hand, 'passed'. The next player then had the opportunity of calling higher and taking the lead in that case, unless he, in turn, was over-called. The first card played by the caller constituted trumps. Should the leader 'make' the number of tricks which he had 'declared' he received stakes as previously agreed from his opponents. Should he fail he paid out accordingly. In a 'Nap' declaration the 'pay out' for failure was generally single and for success double, but this arrangement varied. With an exceptionally poor hand 'Misere' could be called by any player and take precedence over all else (unless another had called three). Here the caller's task was to avoid winning any trick, and forfeit or gain were usually as for three tricks (see *Pears' Shilling Cyclopaedia*, under 'Cards').

2 See Appendix 1.

3 Initially Irish policemen were trained at centres in each of the provinces, but these training centres, except the one situated in the Phoenix Park, Dublin, ceased to function about 1840, and thereafter all recruits passed through the remaining depot which was greatly enlarged from that time on (information from James R. W. Goulden).

4 Mee is officially listed as having joined the RIC on 16 August 1910 (see PRO, London, Home Office Papers, 184/34, under Mee, Jeremiah – 65466).

5 The beginnings of the DMP are rather obscure. One is given an insight into its evolution from a group of nightwatchmen and various other privately hired protectors of person and property into a modern police force in an excellent series of fourteen articles by a deputy commissioner of the Garda Síochána, Padraig Ó Cearbhaill (see P. Ó Cearbhaill, 'Notes for a history of police in Ireland', *Iris an Gharda*, Eanair 1961–Feaobra 1962). The force was highly organised by 1839 when the first code of regulations of the DMP was issued. This code was issued in abridged form in 1889, and the entire code, with some additions and modifications, was again issued in 1908. Many members of the DMP joined the Irish branch of the British-based National Union of Police and Prison Officers. As in the case of the RIC its members received dramatic pay increases

in 1919 and 1920. After a short period of uncertainty the force, apart from its G-division, decided not to get involved in the Anglo-Irish War (see pp. 140–1). As a result it was not disbanded after the Treaty but remained the sole law-enforcement agency within the Greater Dublin area until 1 April 1925 when it was amalgamated with the Garda Síochána.

6   Francis (Frank) and Thomas H. (Tom) Glennon were sons of a policeman and natives of County Sligo (information from Bernard Conway). For more on Tom Glennon, see R. Kipling, *The Irish Guards in the Great War*, II, under Glennon, Sergeant.

7   A police constable's salary in 1911 went from £39 per annum for under six months' service to £70.20 (£70.4s.0d.) for twenty years' service and over (information from James R. W. Goulden).

8   Constables, however, were not permitted, under pain of dismissal, to marry until they had spent seven years in the force (information from James R. W. Goulden).

9   This place name appears thus in the Ordnance Survey Map, but locally it is written Keash and pronounced Kaysh. For his appointment, see p. 337 n.11.

2: KESH: FEBRUARY 1911–AUGUST 1913

1   Constables were promoted to the rank of sergeant either by seniority, by passing the P examination or by consistently good police work (information from James R. W. Goulden).

2   Francis Comerford. He was promoted district inspector (3rd class) from the rank of head constable on 27 April 1908 and he became district inspector 2nd class then 1st class on 13 September 1909 and 16 June 1919 respectively (information from James R. W. Goulden).

3   In circumstances such as these the police officer in charge, before taking any action, generally read a statement charging all persons to disperse 'upon the pains contained in the Act made in the 27th year of King George III to prevent tumultuous risings and assemblies'. Many officers kept a copy of this statement in the lining of their helmets (information from James R. W. Goulden).

4   No report of the incident is to be found in the March 1911 issue of the *Sligo Champion*.

5   Robert Ievers Sullivan. He joined the RIC on 8 September 1888 and was promoted to the rank of county inspector on 4 April 1908 (information from James R. W. Goulden).

6   This institute was founded by Eugene Sandow. It was advertised in the newspapers at that time as an international, physical-culture movement, which one joined by sending a subscription and following a recommended course of physical training.

7   'Patterns' originated from the practice of visiting holy wells, each of which was dedicated to its own patron saint, hence the name 'patterns', a garbled version of

'patrons'. Eventually, however, the religious aspect of the 'pattern' lapsed and it became simply an annual occasion for general festivities.

8   For more on James Larkin, see E. Larkin, *James Larkin, Irish Labour Leader 1876–1947*.

9   'On 8th March, 1913, the crew of the S.S. *Sligo*, belonging to the Sligo Steam Navigation Company, deserted on the refusal of their demand for cattle money, i.e., money for attending to cattle in transit to Liverpool. The Company thereupon employed a non-Union crew, but on the return of the vessel to Sligo the dockers there (Transport Union men) refused to work with these men. This was followed by the Company's Mill-hands going out on strike, and the dispute soon spread to carters and other labourers and developed into a trial of strength between the employers and the Transport Union. Efforts were made by an official from the Board of Trade to effect a settlement, but without success. The demand of the Transport Union was that no free labour should be employed at the quay. The strike was finally settled in May and was a complete victory for the Irish Transport Union. All the non-Union labourers except four and all the carters who worked during the strike were forced to submit to fines of £1 to £3 and had to join the Union. Larkin was represented by P. T. Daly during these labour troubles in Sligo. In consequence of some serious disorder on the quays, in which one life was lost, and of rioting throughout the town, a large force of extra police had to be drafted in for the preservation of the peace of the borough' (official document quoted in E. Larkin, *James Larkin, Irish Labour Leader, 1876–1947*, p. 114).

10   For more on Sir Edward Carson, see E. Marjoribanks and I. Colvin, *Life of Lord Carson*, I–III.

11   This was but a particular application of the general duty of members of the force to take special care to discover the identity, business and destination of all suspicious strangers who entered their sub-district. This aspect of the work of the RIC is touched on in R. Hawkins, 'Government versus secret societies: the Parnell era', in *Secret Societies in Ireland*, pp. 100–12.

12   There seems to be some exaggeration here. It may well be that some resident magistrates were appointed solely because of their influence with the government. However, at that time (1912) there were sixty-five magistrates in Ireland, of whom thirty-three were either barristers-at-law or held university degrees, while another nineteen were ex-officers of the RIC. Moreover, it was exceptional for the resident magistrate not to be on the bench (information from James R. W. Goulden).

3: COLLOONEY: AUGUST 1913–MAY 1914

1   George R. E. Foley. He was appointed district inspector, 3rd class, on 23 June 1911 and district inspector, 2nd class, on 4 February 1913. He later served in

World War One reaching the rank of major. After the war he returned to the RIC and was acting county inspector for Mayo in early 1921 (information from James R. W. Goulden).

2 James Monahan. He was appointed head constable on 1 November 1910 (information from James R. W. Goulden).

3 The main consideration leading to the siting of a police district headquarters in Collooney would not have been the size of the town's population or the incidence of crime in the district, but rather the fact that Collooney was an important rail and road junction.

4 By virtue of a general directive signed by Duncan McGregor, inspector-general, on 1 April 1845, a diary recording 'the proceedings of the [barracks'] party during each day of twenty-four hours' was kept in every barracks (information from James R. W. Goulden).

5 This ban did not arise from the code of regulations of the RIC. It was imposed by the Gaelic Athletic Association (GAA) itself. For instance rule 8 on p. 22 of the *Gaelic Athletic Association, Official Guide 1914–15* reads: 'Police, jail warders, soldiers, sailors of the Royal Navy, militiamen, or pensioners of the constabulary, army or navy, shall not be eligible for membership of clubs.' A ban was enforced by rule 21 until November 2001 which banned members of the British security forces from membership of the Association (cf. M. Cronin, M. Durken, P. Rouse, *The GAA: A People's History*, p. 174).

6 For an insight into the life and duties of a policeman in Ireland about that time, see H. R. Jones, *The Policeman's Manual of Sir Andrew Reed, K.C.B., C.V.O.*

7 The district inspector's caution was well justified, as a considerable amount of reporting of subordinates, comrades and officers to the authorities went on in the ranks of the RIC. David Neligan contrasted the RIC unfavourably with the DMP in this regard. Reminiscing on his days in the DMP, he wrote: 'The code of regulations was so stiff that an officer could easily make a man's life a hell, but I never saw that happen. In this they were supposed to differ from the RIC who often reported one another. I knew an RIC man who unhorsed an inspector and a head constable! Curiously enough, he was a mild sort of fellow to speak to, but apparently a terror with a pen! Having a sound knowledge of the code, he was able to pick holes in those fellows. Three or four men cooped up in a little cross-roads station were, I suppose, bound to get on one another's nerves eventually' (*The Spy in the Castle*, p. 52). For more on David Neligan, see *Dictionary of Irish Biography* (ed. J. McGuire and J. Quinn, Cambridge, 2001) under Neligan, David.

4: GEEVAGH: MAY 1914–AUGUST 1915

1 The *Hue-and-Cry*, whose full title was *The Police Gazette or Hue-and-Cry*, was

a two-sheet, weekly newspaper containing the descriptions of 'wanted men', which was circulated to members of the RIC.

2   The Irish Volunteer movement was founded in Dublin on 25 Nov. 1913. For more, see F. X. Martin (ed.), *The Irish Volunteers, 1913–15: recollections and documents*. For the subsequent divisions in the movement, and some useful references, see J. A. Gaughan, *Listowel and its Vicinity*, p. 364.

3   The then leader of the Irish Parliamentary Party. For more on Redmond, see D. Gwynn, *John Redmond*.

5: BALLINTOGHER: AUGUST 1915–JUNE 1918

1   The proprietor was Jeremiah (Jerry) Mulrooney. The use of rented private houses as police barracks was fairly common (information from James R. W. Goulden).

2   In view of Mee's extraordinarily active life it is interesting to note that the most vivid recollection Michael Kelly has of his former comrade is that 'he was very intense and full of nervous energy'.

3   Sergeant Patrick Flynn (1866–1936) had nine children: eight girls and one boy. A native of Glenfarne, County Leitrim, he spent his early years in the RIC in County Kerry. On being promoted, he was transferred to Ballintogher. He was transferred to Sligo in 1919, where in April 1920 he retired prematurely when some members of the Black and Tans were posted to his barracks (information from his son, Michael J. (Milo) Flynn).

4   Jeremiah Mee later married Con O'Rourke's sister, Annie (see p. 137).

5   Michael G. Glynn appointed district inspector, 3rd class, on 4 February 1913, and 2nd class on 9 December 1914 (information from James R. W. Goulden).

6   Gormley was a member of the party which was ambushed on its way to the relief of Ashbourne police barracks. For an account of the battle of Ashbourne, see S. Ó Luing, *I Die in a Good Cause*, pp. 82–6. Gormley was buried in the New Cemetery, An Uaimh (Navan), County Meath.

7   There were also signs of changing attitudes among members of the RIC. For instance the following report appeared in the *Irish Independent* of 27 November 1917:

Constable 'hands in gun'
Could not serve two masters

Constable Thomas O'Leary, Cloontumper Hut, Claremorris, a native of [Knockdooragh, Headford, County] Kerry, has been dismissed from the force after four years' service. It is alleged that recently he was irregular in his conduct in the matter of tillage returns. Inquiries were being made as to where he spent certain hours during which he was absent from barracks and before any decision was reached the district inspector, Mr. B[ernard] O'Connor, received a letter from him in which he said: 'My sympathies are with Sinn Féin, with the men who fell during Easter week, and with those who are trying to free Ireland. I cannot serve two masters, and therefore I am handing in my gun.' This letter was sent to the higher authorities, following which O'Leary was paid off. On departure he received a send-off by Bekan Sinn Féiners.

Moreover, the number of RIC constables being dismissed from and resigning from the force gradually increased and became significant during the climax of the anti-conscription campaign.

8   Griffith was the founder of Sinn Féin. For more see S. Ó Luing, *Art Ó Gríofa.*

9   This mode of procedure was, in fact, more characteristic of Fenianism than of the early Sinn Féin non-violent tradition as represented by Arthur Griffith (cf. R. Davis, *Arthur Griffith and Non-Violent Sinn Féin*).

10 The reporting of such cases in the newspapers swelled the ranks of Sinn Féin. One can readily understand why this should be by reading the following report which appeared in the *Sligo Champion* of 2 March 1918: 'A unique scene was witnessed at Sligo Courthouse [on February 27] during the hearing of a charge of unlawful assembly against eight young men from the Ballymote district. The defendants were: Alex McCabe, B. Brady, E. Killeen, B. Kenny, T. Cawley, P. Farry, P. Rogers, and T. Langan ... The magistrate [Captain Fitzpatrick, R.M.] asked the defendants to remove their caps, but they paid no attention to the request. They began smoking cigarettes and the courthouse, which was packed with local Sinn Féiners and other interested spectators, shortly had the appearance of a smoking saloon. At a later period in the evidence the defendant McCabe said to the other defendants: "I think we should have a song." All the defendants stood up on their seats and sang songs referring to Ireland and freedom. The magistrate then ordered the defendants seven days imprisonment for contempt of court ...'

The report continued that the prisoners had to be carried out one by one by four constables, and conveyed by a military lorry to jail, amid tremendous excitement; that the crowd, armed with hurleys, assumed a threatening attitude and, when a collision seemed imminent, the military came on the scene with fixed bayonets. It was also stated that when, prior to his appearance in court, Mr McCabe was arrested at Ballymote railway station, he resisted so violently that it took ten policemen to carry him to the barracks.

11 The practice of 'breaking the land' also caused Sinn Féin some serious problems, not least in County Sligo. In the early part of 1918 there was a considerable increase in such activity throughout the county (see *Sligo Champion*, 23 February, 2, 9, 30 March 1918) and a great deal of consequent bad publicity for Sinn Féin. This called forth the following restraining letter from Alexander (Alec) McCabe which appeared in the *Irish Independent* of 28 February 1918:

Dear Sir,

As the impression seems to have got abroad that the Sinn Féin Executive give unqualified licence to land commandeering and countenance all kinds of indiscriminate interference with the rights of private property, let it be known that the South-Sligo Sinn Féin [Comhairle] Ceanntair rules that no residential farm under forty acres is allowed to be entered on. Land devoted to the feeding of milch cows, or the production of other necessaries, are also exempted. So that taking everything into consideration it is evident there is little victimisation of any class in this movement.

A. McCabe,

Ballymote, 28 February 1918.

This problem – land seizures in the western counties – became most acute for Sinn Féin in the spring of 1920. For some useful references to this, see A. Mitchell, *Labour in Irish Politics 1890–1930*, p. 137.

12 This incident occurred on 16 February 1918. Agitation for the division of the farm at Toberanania – the farm of an absentee proprietor – had been going on for some years. Then Hugh Maguire, JP, bought it and this led to the symbolic division of the land. John (Seán) McGarry, who was joint secretary of the Ballintogher Sinn Féin club (see *Sligo Champion*, 6 October 1917), his brother, Timothy (Thady) McGarry and Michael Mulligan (all of Correa) each received a six-month sentence for their involvement in it (*Sligo Champion*, 30 March 1918; also information from Harold McBrien).

13 The national campaign against conscription caused a number of resignations from the RIC. For instance on 24 April 1918, John P. Lydon (1887–1974), Hugh O'Donnell (1892–1973) and William Riordan (1895–1977) tendered their resignations in protest against the attempt by the British authorities to impose conscription on Ireland. The reaction of the authorities to this development indicated how serious they regarded it to be. At 2 a.m. on the following morning the three constables were replaced at Murrisk, County Mayo, by three others, and were taken under arrest to the county headquarters at Castlebar, where they were held for three days before being released (information from William Riordan).

One of the other constables who resigned from the RIC at this time in protest against the proposal to impose conscription on Ireland was Denis Tuohy of Kenmare, County Kerry. On 1 May 1921 he was arrested by the crown forces, taken to a temporary prison in Kenmare and, while there, assassinated. On 11 May an official statement was issued to the effect that Tuohy had been shot while 'attempting to escape' (see *Irish Bulletin*, 18 May 1921). In the *Irish Independent* of 12 May 1921 to a report of this incident was appended the following significant addendum: [Note – To date 78 persons have been killed in attempting to escape or on failing to obey a call to halt, as alleged by crown forces.]

6: GRANGE: JUNE 1918–JULY 1919

1   See Appendix 2.

2   Father Michael O'Flanagan was born on 12 August 1876 at Cloontower, near Castlerea, County Roscommon. He was educated at Cloonbonive national school and Summerhill College, Sligo. In 1894 he entered St Patrick's College, Maynooth, and he was ordained for the diocese of Elphin in 1900. After his ordination he was sent by his bishop to the US on a fund-raising tour. On the completion of the tour he ministered for some seven years in various parts of the US. After his return home in 1907 he taught for five years in Summerhill College. In 1912 he was appointed curate in Roscommon, and at the end of 1914 he was transferred to Cliffony, County Sligo. In 1915 he supported his Cliffony parishioners in their dispute with the Congested Districts Board on the question of turbary rights. He was transferred to Crossna, near Boyle, County Roscommon, in 1916. His oratorical skill and dynamic energy were important factors in having Count Plunkett returned for Sinn Féin in the North Roscommon by-election of 3 February 1917. He took a prominent part in the anti-conscription campaign of 1918. An outstanding orator, from 1917 on he was in great demand as a speaker at nationalist meetings and rallies. As a result of his addressing election meetings outside his own diocese he came into conflict with the ecclesiastical authorities and he was suspended on 19 June 1918. The suspension, however, was removed in 1919 and he was again appointed as a curate in Roscommon. During the Anglo-Irish War (1920–21) he was a judge in a local Sinn Féin Court and during this period also he was vice-president of the Gaelic League. Between November 1921 and the beginning of 1926, he travelled extensively in the US and Australia promoting the cause of Sinn Féin. At an extraordinary Sinn Féin Ard Fheis, which was held on 9 March 1926, as vice-president of Sinn Féin (he was such since 25 October 1917) he successfully persuaded a majority of the delegates to reject a motion put forward by de Valera to the effect that, if the oath of allegiance was removed, entry to the Dublin and Belfast parliaments would become a matter of policy not principle for Republicans. The following day de Valera resigned his position as president of Sinn Féin and not long afterwards founded the Fianna Fáil party. Father O'Flanagan became one of de Valera's severest critics and blamed him for destroying Sinn Féin. Becoming disillusioned with politics, he himself resigned from Sinn Féin towards the end of 1927. However, he continued to be a promoter of the Sinn Féin cause in the late 1920s and early 1930s. His unqualified support for the Republican side in the Spanish Civil War (1936–38) found him allied with the Communists, who exploited

his support to good effect. Thus in 1937 he was sent on a speaking tour of the US and Canada by the Friends of the Irish Republic and the Medical Section of the North American Committee to aid Spanish Democracy. On his return from the US he settled in Sandyford, near Dublin, and in retirement interested himself in Irish history. He died on 7 August 1942. For a Marxist view of Father O'Flanagan and excerpts from some of his addresses, see C. D. Greaves, *Father Michael O'Flanagan, Republican Priest* and D. Carroll, *They Have Fooled You Again: Michael O'Flanagan (1876–1942), Priest, Republican, Social Critic.*

3   Sergeant Patrick Perry (acting sergeant, 1906; sergeant, 1909) was transferred in May 1913 from Bunnanadden to Cliffony, where he replaced Sergeant Anthony Gaughan (my grandfather), the latter taking Perry's place at Bunnanadden. Perry was killed in the ambush at Moneygold, near Grange, on 25 October 1920 (information from James R. W. Goulden, see also pp. 62, 336 n.10 on that ambush).

4   Constable Clarke was seriously wounded in the ambush at Moneygold, near Grange (see pp. 62, 336 n.10).

5   Widow of the pacifist Francis J. C. Sheehy-Skeffington, who was killed on the Wednesday of Easter week 1916. For more on Hanna Sheehy-Skeffington, see C. C. O'Brien, *States of Ireland*, under Sheehy, Hanna.

6   See Appendix 3.

7   *Ibid.*

8   With the suppression of the Police Union, the powerlessness of the ordinary constable to have a say in what his role should be in the impending conflict is well illustrated by an incident which occurred in mid-July 1920. Seemingly, on 16 July a Head Constable Clarke forwarded an application to the inspector-general, Thomas J. Smith, requesting permission to summon a meeting of the Representative Body (the body which traditionally concerned itself with the interests of members of the RIC) to discuss 'very objectionable duties and other matters'. On the application these duties were described as: 'accompanying military on patrol duty; searching any person or vehicle met while on such patrol; being under command of military irrespective of rank, service or experience; raiding for arms, etc. at any time, particularly in the night time'. The inspector-general in his reply to Clarke withheld permission for a meeting of the Representative Body, saying, among other things, that the matter was 'not very urgent'. Thereupon Constable Timothy Brennan issued a circular on 25 July describing the correspondence which had taken place between Head Constable Clarke and Inspector-General Smith and stating that as far as the constabulary were concerned the matters at issue were very urgent. He also appealed for lists of 'objectionable duties' from barracks throughout the country. Some such lists were forwarded, of which the following one from Moate, County Westmeath, was typical:

The men from this station are unanimous that the following suggestion should be put before the Representative Body:

The men should not be armed on day patrols, which we consider would leave us less liable to attack, as in the case of the DMP who are immune from attacks since they ceased to carry arms on ordinary duty.

However, due to pressure from the authorities and the growing viciousness of the Anglo-Irish War, this agitation quickly petered out. On being thus obstructed from raising grievances with the Representative Body, those involved next communicated with officials of the Police Union who sent the entire correspondence to Sinn Féin headquarters, and a piece on the matter duly appeared in the *Irish Bulletin* of 19 August 1920.

(In the spring of 1918 the Timothy Brennan mentioned above had been active in organising opposition among members of the RIC to the attempt to impose conscription on Ireland. In 1919 he was selected to represent the RIC constables of Leinster on the Representative Body. On 6 July 1920 he issued a circular to his constituents indicating, in effect, that the Representative Body was unable to press their grievances and vaguely suggesting that members of the RIC should organise a protest against the then-government's police policy. He was severely reprimanded for issuing this circular, which was the subject of a piece under the headline 'Amazing appeal to R.I.C.' in the *Daily Herald* of 20 July 1920. Then came his involvement in the unsuccessful attempt by Head Constable Clarke to have a meeting of the Representative Body called, after which he appealed to the constables of Leinster to indicate that they regarded their grievance as being urgent and thereby implicitly demand a meeting of the Representative Body to discuss them. Brennan's to-be-expected dismissal for this last act of defiance and the appearance of the above account in the *Irish Bulletin* occurred on the same day – 19 August 1920. For more on Brennan, see *Weekly Freeman*, 21 August, 4 September 1920, and *The Freeman's Journal*, 25 January 1922. A copy of the circular organising opposition to conscription which Brennan had posted to every district headquarters in 1918 is to be found in the papers of Thomas J. McElligott, as is the circular which he issued to his constituents on 6 July 1920.)

9   Henry J. Moore. He was appointed district inspector (3rd class) on 17 November 1909 (information from James R. W. Goulden).

10 This ambush occurred on 25 October 1920. Of the police patrol of nine, which was attacked, three were killed and three wounded, one critically. This last was Constable Lynch, who died that night in hospital (*The Freeman's Journal*, 26 and 27 October 1920). For a very full account of this ambush and its aftermath, see the *Sligo Champion*, 30 October 1920.

11 Mee was appointed to County Kerry as from 15 July 1919; his appointment to County Sligo was from 1 March 1911 (see PRO London, Home Office Papers, 184/34, under Mee, Jeremiah).

12 The ambushes at Soloheadbeg and Knocklong are generally regarded as having initiated the Anglo-Irish War. For more on Daniel (Dan) Breen, Seán Hogan, Seamus Robinson and Seán Treacy, who were prominent in these incidents, see D. Breen, *My Fight for Irish Freedom* and D. Ryan, *Seán Treacy and the Third Tipperary Brigade, I.R.A.*

13 Mee's never having seen a barracks orderly armed with a revolver is remarkable, as a directive was issued to the entire force in Easter week 1916 that thereafter everyone on barracks orderly duty was to wear a revolver and not a baton, and this directive was never rescinded (information from James R. W. Goulden).

7: LISTOWEL: JULY–DECEMBER 1919

1 Although this agitation probably received a modicum of respectability from the intervention in February 1918 of the North Kerry Volunteers in a dispute concerning some fields between Lord Listowel and some residents of the town (cf. J. A. Gaughan, *Listowel and its Vicinity*, pp. 313, 358–60), it arose basically because some of the tenants of the knight of Kerry wished to acquire land at their landlord's expense. After some years the residue of the Ballinruddery estate was divided and each of the agitators received some seven acres of land (information from William (Willie) Keane).

2 Again this agitation had little political significance. Michael O'Brien was given some land by his employer, Ella Frances Browne, and some local people, who considered themselves as much entitled to receive land as O'Brien, caused the agitation. O'Brien was fired on, identified his attacker, and, as a result, had to have police protection thereafter (information from Seamus O'Brien).

3 Ella Frances Browne was heiress to part of the Gunn estate of Rattoo. For more, see J. A. Gaughan, *Listowel and its Vicinity*, under Browne, Miss Ella Frances.

4 Mee's three comrades on this assignment were Constables Atkinson, McAlister and Regan (cf. entry under 19 November 1919 in RIC diary used in Listowel police barracks from 20 June 1918 to 4 June 1920).

5 Shots may have been fired at the police in the Ballylongford area at about this time but the first policeman to be injured in that area seems to have been a Constable Clarke who was seriously wounded in the village on the night of 3 January 1920 (see J. A. Gaughan, *Listowel and its Vicinity*, p. 366).

6 George B. Heard. He joined the RIC as an officer on 18 January 1892, was appointed district inspector (1st class) an 6 May 1905 and county inspector on 23 May 1916 (information from James R. W. Goulden). The announcement of

his appointment as commandant of the RIC depot appeared in *The Freeman's Journal* of 12 April 1920.

7   On p. 229 in *Limerick's Fighting Story* (ed. J. M. McCarthy, Tralee, n.d.) is the following account of this incident: 'One such action took place at the March fair of Rathkeale in 1920. Two RIC men from Tralee were in Ward's Hotel and they were escorting an enemy civilian. Commandant Seán Finn assembled a small group of Rathkeale IRA men who were then "on the run" with a view to holding up and disarming the police. There was 'to be no shooting except in self-defence. The IRA entered the hotel and, having walked into the dining-room where the police were sitting, gave the order "hands up". To their great surprise Neazer drew his gun. The IRA men fired and killed him and wounded the constable. The arms of both were then collected and the attackers withdrew.' (Apart from Finn, those who took part in this incident of 10 March were: Patrick (Paddy) O'Shaughnessy, Seán Reidy, James (Jimmy) and Patrick (Paddy) Roche; members of Rathkeale Company, 4th Battalion, West Limerick Brigade, IRA; and also Seán Hogan (information from Jimmy Roche; also see *The Freeman's Journal*, 12 and 13 March 1920).)

In spite of the above reconstruction of the incident, it is quite likely that Neazer was killed because of his former excessive zeal in the performance of his duty. He had been one of the most politically active policemen in Tralee from 1912 to 1919 (information from Daniel Nolan of Tralee; see also D. Ryan, *The Rising: the complete story of Easter Week*, p. 239, and *Sinn Féin Rebellion Handbook, Easter 1916*, p. 257, where there is a reference to his having received an award for dedication to duty). Neazer was promoted sergeant in 1918 and transferred to Listowel in 1919 (information from James R. W. Goulden). For an extraordinary tribute to his and Sergeant Michael Byrne's efficiency, see *The Kerryman*, 13 February 1915.

8   1919–1921 was but one of a number of periods during which the military were called to assist, and work in conjunction with, the police in Ireland. For an interesting piece on the employment of units of the British army in aid of the civil power in Ireland in 1881–2, see R. Hawkins, 'An army on police work, 1881–2; Ross of Bladensberg's memorandum', *The Irish Sword*, XI (1973), pp. 75–117. Hawkins points out that the Ross of Bladensberg memorandum on this experiment was forwarded on 2 March 1918 to the officer commanding the crown forces in Ireland, the inspector-general of the RIC, and the under-secretary for consideration. The last, in submitting his copy to the viceroy, wrote: 'This is an interesting report, and of present value though the circumstances of 1918 are not quite the same as in the early 1880s. The amount of crime at that time in disturbed districts was enormously greater. The arrangements which are now in force for the co-operation of soldiers and police have been made very quickly, and promise to work well.'

9 This occurred on 23 June 1919. For an account of the circumstances, see *The Freeman's Journal*, 25 June 1919.

10 Listowel police district could be described as quiet at that time only when compared to the more disturbed parts of the country. In fact a number of 'outrages' did occur in the Listowel district at that time, as is clear from entries on 10 December 1918, 9 January, 26 May, and 7 June 1919 in the RIC Diary used in Listowel police barracks from 20 June 1918 to 4 June 1920. (The dramatic increase in 'outrages' in 1920 can be gauged from entries in the same diary on 3, 11, 16, 20 January; 4, 11, 12, 17, 20 February [3 'outrages' listed on this date], 4, 31 March, 30 April, 11, 15 May 1920.) Moreover, there was considerable ill feeling towards the police in the district. This arose from the shooting of Daniel Scanlon in Ballybunion on 11 July 1917, a riot at Listowel Races on 10 October 1917 at which the police fired on the crowd, seriously wounding one person, and much police activity throughout 1918 and 1919 (see J. A. Gaughan, *Listowel and its Vicinity*, pp. 354–66; also information from Michael Kelly).

11 Thomas Flanagan was born at Elphin, Co. Roscommon, on 12 November 1872. He joined the RIC on 26 August 1889. He had considerable experience as a policeman, having served at Kill, County Waterford; Tournafulla, Strand and Kilteely, County Limerick; Kilmoon, Ashbourne, Navan and Trim, County Meath; the depot; Newcastle, County Tipperary; Moville, County Donegal; and Ennistymon, County Clare. He was promoted acting sergeant on 1 October 1898, sergeant on 1 January 1901 and head constable on 19 December 1916. On 9 July 1919 he was promoted district inspector (3rd class) and transferred from Ennistymon to Listowel. On 1 April 1920 he became a district inspector, 2nd class. He is officially listed as having retired (aged about fifty) on 21 October 1920 and he died on 8 May 1932 (PRO London, Home Office Papers. 184/28, under Flanagan, Thomas; also information from James R. W. Goulden).

12 A native of County Galway, Patrick H. Plover was promoted head constable on 1 June 1919. He had served in the Irish Guards Regiment from 1914 to 1918 (information from James R. W. Goulden).

13 He was a Scotsman, named Carson, and he resided in the knight of Kerry's house at Ballinruddery (information from Willie Keane).

14 A bemedalled veteran of the Boer War, Brigadier-General Sir Joseph A. Byrne was appointed the tenth inspector-general of the RIC on 1 August 1916. For a detailed biographical note on Byrne, see *Who was Who 1941–50*. There was a flurry of news coverage and comment on his dismissal. Cf. in particular, *Daily News*, 9, 12, 13, 15 January 1920.

15 The unofficial account of the dismissal of the inspector-general alleges that it was occasioned by a total disagreement between Byrne and the viceroy, Viscount (Field-Marshal) French, on the disposition of the police force in Ireland. On the

one hand, Byrne argued for a continuation of the RIC presence in every parish in the country on the grounds that: (a) to vacate the smaller police barracks would present the IRA with more territory in which they would be able to operate freely, (b) people who did not sympathise with the IRA felt a measure of protection in having the police at hand, (c) absence from an area involved a loss of reliable information. On the other hand, French tended to look on the members of the RIC as soldiers and considered that they could not successfully defend many of these barracks, especially the smaller ones, so he urged a withdrawal to the larger and better-fortified ones. According to the story the two men eventually had a choleric session, after which Byrne adjourned to the Kildare Street Club, where he aired his uncomplimentary view of the viceroy. French was informed, and a few days later Byrne found a letter on his desk in which he was given 'an indefinite leave of absence'. He was never officially dismissed and continued on full pay. He later filled a number of important posts in the colonial service. He was popular with the officers and men of the RIC for his fairness, and for a long time after disbandment he attended the RIC officers association annual dinner in London (information from James R. W. Goulden).

The *Daily News* of 9 January 1920 described the manner of Byrne's dismissal as follows: 'Without having asked the favour, he was given a month's leave on December 10, on the grounds that he had been overworked. He retired to Newcastle, on the Down coast, to play golf, and the full month was allowed to expire before he was requested to send in his resignation.' And the issue of 13 January 1920 stated that the reasons for his dismissal were 'the spread of Republican sympathies among the men of the R.I.C.' and the general unsatisfactory performance of the force.

16 McElligott's letter of resignation was reproduced in the Police Union newssheet. Its concluding paragraph in a fuller form than that which appears above is to be found in *Dáil Éireann: Díospóireachta parlaiminte, tuairisc oifigiúil: Parliamentary debates, official report*, vol. 27, cols. 688–689, 22 November 1928.

17 Thomas J. Smith was promoted district inspector, 3rd class, on 16 October 1882, district inspector, 2nd class, on 15 June 1885, district inspector, 1st class, on 1 May 1894 and county inspector on 8 December 1905. He served as county inspector in County Roscommon, County Galway (East Riding) and in Belfast. He was inspector-general from January 1920 until the force was disbanded on 31 August 1922 (information from James R. W. Goulden). For an unsympathetic piece on Smith, which recalled his 'considerate treatment of the Carsonite gun-runners' see *The Freeman's Journal*, 5 March 1920.

The attitude of Sinn Féin to the replacement of Byrne by Smith at that time is captured by David Neligan when he writes: 'At this time the R.I.C. was headed by an ex-British army officer, named Byrne, but he did not prove warlike enough for the administration, so they fired him and appointed an Orangeman, named Smith' (*The Spy in the Castle*, p. 75).

18 Cf. pp. 140–1.

19 Henry (Harry) Boland was born in Dublin in April 1887. He was educated at Synge Street Christian Brothers Schools and later at De La Salle College, Castletown, County Laois. Having left school he opened a tailor's shop in Henry Street, Dublin. He was prominent in GAA circles in Dublin both as a player (a hurler) and as an official, and he was chairman of the Dublin County Board from 1911 to 1916. A member of the IRB from 1904, he was responsible for encouraging his close friend, Michael Collins, to join that organisation. He was a member of the Volunteers from 1913 and took part in the Rising of 1916. For his part in the rebellion he was sentenced to ten years' penal servitude on 11 May 1916, but was released on 17 June 1917. After his release he was active in reorganising Sinn Féin and at the Ard Fheis, which was held on 25 October 1917, he was elected to the executive of Sinn Féin. He was elected as Sinn Féin representative for South Roscommon in the general election of November 1918. With Collins he engineered the escape of de Valera and others from Lincoln jail on 3 February 1919. In May 1919 he went to the US as an official representative of Dáil Éireann and from then until June 1921, except during the period of a visit home which began in May 1920, he was engaged in promoting the Sinn Féin cause throughout the US. He was a prominent opponent of the Treaty and was fatally wounded during the Civil War on 31 July 1922. He died on 2 August 1922. For more on him, see profile in *An Camán*, 15 Aibrean 1933.

20 At a meeting in the US Harry Boland, in the presence of Constables Kelly and McNamara, stated that Sinn Féin had underestimated the strength of nationalist feeling among many members of the RIC (information taken from letter to Jeremiah Mee from John P. McNamara, dated 12 January 1952).

21 There is little evidence to warrant Mee's suggestion that Collins and the Sinn Féin leadership by acting differently could have won over the RIC to the cause of Sinn Féin. Indeed, most of the evidence indicates that the RIC as a body (also the DMP) until the advantage began to swing to Sinn Féin remained remarkably loyal to the British authorities. This is borne out by the failure of the Police Union which was regarded as a serious setback by Sinn Féin. As David Neligan noted: 'So far as Collins and Sinn Féin were concerned, this Union business was a dead loss as Collins had hoped to break up the police forces in Ireland in that way. When these men got increased wages they turned their backs on McElligott and on the Union and incidentally on Sinn Féin' (*The Spy in the Castle*, p. 56).

22 This is generally attributed to Lord Clanricarde who owned extensive estates in Counties Clare and Galway.

8: LISTOWEL: JANUARY–JUNE 1920

1   More evidence than that presented in this paragraph, which corresponds practically verbatim to a paragraph in the *Irish Bulletin* of 27 Oct. 1920, would be necessary to establish that there was a purge in the police hierarchy at that time. Thus, although thirteen county inspectors retired immediately after the 'dismissal' of the inspector-general, all, except three, had reached retirement age. Moreover, Flower (he joined the RIC on 1 December 1880) had forty or almost forty years' service and so also was entitled to retire (information from James R. W. Goulden). For the press announcement, see *The Freeman's Journal*, 10 April 1920.

2   These responded to an appeal to join the RIC. They were soon known as the Black and Tans because a shortage of equipment obliged them to wear khaki uniforms with the black-green caps and belts of the police. The name was not original nor was it intended to be complimentary, being already applied to a well-known pack of hounds in County Limerick.

3   They were: John J. Connors of Stockport and Archibald Thompson. For more on Thompson, see p. 346 n.11.

4   For this and the life story of Tomás MacCurtain, see F. O'Donoghue, *Tomás MacCurtain: Soldier and Patriot* (Tralee 1971).

5   This disenchantment was not confined to serving members. Some RIC pensioners began to regret their lifelong loyalty to, and service of, the British government. Many RIC pensioners privately questioned the advisability of the developing militaristic policy of the British government. Due to their vulnerability to British displeasure, their sentiments were seldom publicly expressed. On at least one occasion, however, during the 1920–21 period, a group of RIC pensioners called on the British government to reconsider its policy towards Ireland. This occurred on 11 September 1920 and was reported as follows in the *Weekly Freeman* of 18 Sept. 1920:

Two hundred Cork RIC pensioners
Their demand for the release of the Lord Mayor

At a meeting held in Cork on Saturday night two hundred RIC pensioners passed a resolution urging the government to reconsider its position in reference to the imprisonment of the Lord Mayor, as well as of the other political prisoners on hunger strike, and order their immediate release before a catastrophe of the greatest magnitude was precipitated. The resolution further stated that unless a Truce of some sort was immediately established, the entire country would drop from the precipice on which it stood into the abyss of blood and strife, with untold suffering, which would eventually recoil on the British themselves.

Having expressed the opinion that the offences for which the Lord Mayor was tried were trivial in the extreme when compared to the punishment inflicted, the resolution concluded by condemning and expressing abhorrence of murder of all kinds and deprecating reprisals on the part of the RIC and military no matter how great the provocation.

It was decided to telegraph copies of the resolution to the government, the prime minister and the home secretary.

This development whereby the traditional loyalty of RIC pensioners was seriously undermined and, in many cases, utterly destroyed, constituted a serious setback for British intelligence in Ireland which depended a great deal on such people (see p. 387 n.4).

6   *Limerick's Fighting Story, 1916–21: told by the men who made it* (Tralee 1948), pp. 79–80. For more on Sergeant, later District Inspector, O'Sullivan, see J. A. Gaughan, *Listowel and its Vicinity*, under O'Sullivan, Tobias.

7   Other steps had already been taken to prepare the RIC at Listowel for a possible attack on their barracks. Thus on 23 February and 24 and 29 March they received lectures from a military officer on 'Bombing', 'The care of arms' and 'The defence of barracks' (see RIC diary used in Listowel police barracks, entries under 23 February and 24 and 29 March).

8   This rank was initiated in 1920. By this means the authorities gave responsibility to a number of relatively young and active officers, whilst reducing the extra expense which that entailed (information from James R. W. Goulden).

9   Alexander M. R. Dobbyn. A graduate of Dublin University, he was appointed district inspector (3rd class) on 20 October 1898, 2nd class on 29 November 1901, 1st class on 1 January 1911, and county inspector in Armagh on 27 July 1920 (information from James R. W. Goulden).

10 This was almost on the site of the present garda station, and was on the property of the Brosnan family.

11 These huts were at Duagh, Lisselton, Lixnaw, Lyracrompane, Mountcoal and Newtownsandes.

12 The doctor attached to Listowel hospital at that time, was Dr John T. Dillon. However, in his papers, Mee gives the name of the 'doctor' as O'Sullivan. The person he met could have been James O'Sullivan, a chemist, of Market Street, who, although not attached to the hospital, sometimes did duty there and was generally known as Dr O'Sullivan (information from Sister Mary Pascal Kelly).

13 Sister Mary Charles O'Keeffe was superior in St Brigid's convent at that time (information from Sister Mary Pascal Kelly).

14 The two men in question were Michael Foran and James O'Mahony (information

from Denis (Dinny) McElligott). For the official police version of this incident, see entry under 5 June 1920 in RIC diary used in Listowel police barracks.

15 The *Irish Independent* of 4 June 1920 reported these movements under the headline: 'Troops pouring into Ireland'.

16 The people were given a clear warning of what was to come in a piece in the *Irish Independent* of 15 May 1920. Under the headings: 'More Vigorous Irish Policy', 'Blockhouses Plan for Country' and 'Machine-guns for the Constabulary', it was reported that the British High Command had decided 'to undertake the re-conquest of Ireland as a serious military problem'. Plans to this end, the report continued, which were submitted to the cabinet by General Macready, included a scheme for the establishment of hundreds of blockhouses throughout the country, each of which was to be manned by thirty to fifty soldiers, armed with machine guns and bombs and with adequate motor transport. It seems that the plan envisaged a further militarising of the RIC. Each police barracks was to be supplied with a machine gun, and demobilised military officers were to be recruited and attached to many police barracks. And armour, 'consisting of steel plates hung on canvas', was to be supplied to the police.

17 The piece in the *Irish Independent* of 15 May 1920 was not the only public indication given to the police at this time about their future role. In an important address in London on 13 May 1920 Lord Birkenhead, the lord chancellor, stated: '… the RIC are now part of the armed forces of the crown' (see *The Irish Times*, 14 May 1920), and 'We [the cabinet] have taken special steps today so that at this moment not one of these men [the RIC] in their brave and heroic work will be left unattended by one or other of the members of the armed forces of the crown' (see *Irish Independent*, 15 May 1920).

9: LISTOWEL POLICE MUTINY: JUNE 1920

1 John M. Poer O'Shee. He was appointed district inspector (3rd class) on 17 January 1895, 2nd class on 29 September 1898, 1st class on 1 December 1907, and on 1 May 1920 was appointed county inspector in Kerry, where he replaced George B. Heard (see pp. 337–8 n.6). After the Listowel police mutiny he was transferred to Lisburn, County Antrim (information from James R. W. Goulden).

2 An incident which occurred early in June 1920 throws some light on the characters of Captain Chadwick and District Inspector Thomas Flanagan. It seems that military patrols were searching houses, presumably for arms, in the Listowel district, and after one such search a girl entered Listowel police barracks and complained that her wristlet-watch had been stolen. The matter was investigated by District Inspector Flanagan, who received the fullest co-operation from Captain Chadwick, and the missing watch was discovered in the possession of one of the

soldiers camped at Ballinruddery. The watch was returned and Captain Chadwick promised to have the soldier involved court-martialled (information from John Byrnes, son of the late ex-Constable Francis J. Byrnes).

3   Michael Lillis was born at Kilbaha, near Carrigaholt, County Clare, on 7 October 1886. He joined the RIC on 13 July 1908. He served at Listowel from 1909 to 1920. He died on 8 February 1959. For more, see pp. 370 n.5, 374–5 n. 24. See also G. Allen, *The Garda Síochána: policing independent Ireland 1922–82*, p. 29.

4   These were Sergeants Michael Byrne, John Connolly and William Watson.

5   Although this rank was in existence during the Land War in the 1880s, it was soon afterwards allowed to lapse, and was not reintroduced until June 1920 (information from James R. W. Goulden). Mee's statement clearly implies that a number of directives for all ranks, which had been forwarded to Listowel police barracks from Colonel and Divisional Commissioner Smyth's office in Cork (see Appendix 5), were not communicated to the constables. Such lack of co-operation was probably due as much to District Inspector Flanagan's resentment to the police force being 'taken over' by the army (two weeks previously extensive civil and military authority in Munster had been given to Smyth) as to his opposition to the new policy which he was expected to implement (see pp. 253–4).

6   The thirteen constables were Francis J. Byrnes, Loughlin Dolan, John Donovan, Joseph Downey, Michael Fitzgerald, Thomas Hughes, Michael Kelly, John P. McNamara, Patrick O'Neill, Thomas R. Reidy, Andrew Robinson, John Sinnott and Archibald Thompson.

7   Major-General Sir Henry Hugh Tudor, KCB, was born in 1871. He served with distinction in the Boer War and also in World War One, being wounded both in South Africa and in France. At the end of World War One he was a Major-General and OC of the 9th Division. (For some details of his distinguished service during World War One, see S. Gillon, *The K.O.S.B. in the Great War*, under Tudor, Major-Gen. H. H.) He was appointed police adviser to the viceroy of Ireland in May 1920 (see *The Irish Times*, 22 May 1920). In 1922 he became inspector-general of police and prisons and GOC in Palestine. He retired in 1925 and died in St John's, Newfoundland, on 25 September 1965.

Tudor's main responsibility as head of the Irish police was to co-ordinate the operations of the DMP and RIC, and to develop an effective secret service or detective branch to replace the previous one which by May 1920 had been rendered 'non-existent' by the forces of Sinn Féin (cf. PRO London, CAB 23/37, CP 2556, pp. 231 and 235).

8   William S. B. Leatham was appointed district inspector (3rd class) on 14 February 1899, 2nd class on 19 January 1902 and 1st class on 1 June 1911. He was seconded for military service during World War One, becoming a major in

the 6th Battalion of the Royal Irish Rifles. He was invalided out of the war in 1916 and given the rank of colonel (information from James R. W. Goulden).

9 See pp. 337–8 n.6, 344 n.1.

10 Lieut. Colonel Gerald Bryce Ferguson Smyth, DSO, was born at Dalhousie, Punjab, India, on 7 September 1885. He joined the British army in 1905 and served in the Royal Engineers. He was promoted captain in 1914 and went to the front with the Expeditionary Force. In October 1914 he was seriously wounded in action, losing his left arm and being awarded the DSO. On 2 December 1916 he was appointed to the command of a battalion of the King's Own Scottish Borderers. Between that time and the end of the war he was mentioned in despatches four times. (For his distinguished war-career in the KOSB, see S. Gillon, *The K.O.S.B. in the Great War*, under Smyth. DSO, Brig.-Gen. G.B.F. (R.E.) (OC 6th Battalion KOSB).)

Colonel Smyth began his career in the RIC when, on 3 June 1920, he was appointed divisional commissioner of Munster. The then head of police in Ireland, General Tudor, recommended Smyth for the post, being fully aware of the latter's sterling qualities, having had him as a subordinate officer in the 9th Division during World War One. For more on Smyth, see R. Linn, *A History of Banbridge*, pp. 136–40.

11 The Englishman in question was Archibald Thompson from London. In the *Leitrim Leader* of 22 March 1952 Mee gave the following description of Thompson: 'He was a lanky, herring-gutted man, a good three or four inches taller than any of us in the barracks, and none of us was small. His face was long, lean and melancholy-looking, the forehead narrow and like a bony knee under a thatch of rusty-coloured hair. Whatever brought Thompson to Ireland, it was not any over-developed sense of patriotism. He had an old soldier's dislike for officers and a true old soldier's love for all the beer he could buy or scrounge. Outside his love for beer he showed no interest in anything ...'

12 Thomas Hughes joined the RIC in 1911. For more on Hughes, later Bishop Hughes, see *The African Missionary*, June–July 1957, pp. 2–7.

13 In the meantime strange things occurred in the dayroom. When Mee was led from the dayroom there was a long and awkward silence and then Constable Hughes asked Smyth: 'Are we to understand that our spokesman is being placed under arrest?' To which Smyth replied: 'That is correct.' At this response Hughes rushed out of the dayroom and was promptly followed by most of his comrades.

14 Some hothead apparently shouted: 'If a hand is laid on our spokesman again this room will run red with blood' (affidavit on the 'Listowel affair' written and signed by Michael Kelly and John P. McNamara in 1950).

15 What occurred in the office was afterwards disclosed to John P. McNamara by District Inspector Thomas Flanagan. It seems that it was McNamara who

disconnected the telephone (information taken from a letter to Jeremiah Mee from John P. McNamara, dated 12 January 1952; however, Michael Kelly tended to doubt that this interlude occurred or that the telephone was disconnected, ascribing this assertion to exaggeration on McNamara's part).

16 Francis J. Byrnes was born at Tulla, County Clare, in 1886. He joined the RIC in 1907, and served at Listowel (1908–20) and Camlough, County Armagh (1920–21). Cf. also pp. 370 n.5, 374 n.24. He died on 23 January 1965 (information from John Byrnes).

17 In fact by this time there were only two police huts in the district, as those at Duagh, Lisselton, Lixnaw and Newtownsandes had already been evacuated on 18 April, 15 May, 17 May and 4 June respectively. The two remaining huts, at Lyracrompane and Mountcoal, were evacuated before the end of July (see RIC diary used in Listowel barracks, entries under 14, 17 May and 4 June, and J. A. Gaughan, *Listowel and its Vicinity*, pp. 367, 369, 374).

18 The above coincides with the account of the incident which is to be found in the Mee papers and the affidavit of Kelly and McNamara. Moreover, apart from some details, the accuracy of the above account has been confirmed by ex-Constable Thomas Grennan, who was stationed in Listowel police district from December 1918 to 1 November 1920 and in Listowel police barracks from 3 July 1920 to 1 November 1920, and by ex-Constable Michael Kelly, who was barracks orderly in Listowel police barracks on the morning of 19 June 1920.

During the course of a lengthy interview in his home in New York, on 22 October 1974, having during the previous week carefully read the foregoing account, Michael Kelly confirmed its substantial accuracy but stated that, according to his recollection, Smyth, before he addressed the assembled policemen, threw his revolver on the table before him, as if to emphasise the seriousness of the occasion; that, when Mee's arrest was ordered by Smyth, Mee was simply 'beckoned and called' from the room by Sergeant Byrne and then led to the kitchen; that Constable Thomas Hughes brushed against Smyth and knocked over a form as he rushed from the dayroom as Smyth attempted to block his way; that when the other constables left the dayroom, he, that is Kelly and Loughlin Dolan, who was also barracks orderly for that day, remained behind; that at this point Tudor led the officers into the district inspector's office; that after conferring for about thirty minutes Tudor requested an opportunity to address the constables; that this request was granted on condition that no action would be taken against anyone for what had occurred; that Tudor then shook hands with all the constables and spoke to them in a quiet and friendly manner before leaving the barracks with all the visiting officers.

19 Flanagan was true to his word. Later, fearful lest drastic measures would be taken against his men for their involvement in the mutiny, he forwarded a report of

the incident of 19 June and its antecedent of 17 June to John J. (Jack) Jones, Labour MP for West Ham, Silverton division, with a request that the matter be raised at Westminster. Constable Thomas Grennan, in mufti, delivered the report personally to Jack Jones' agent, Thomas (Tom) McHugh, in the cloakroom of Sheffield railway station (information from Thomas Grennan).

20 In Tralee police barracks there was a telephone in the county inspector's office and in Killarney it was situated in the district inspector's office (information from James R. W. Goulden).

21 In fact Smyth did get a hearing, initially at any rate, and indicated to the constables at Killarney that, as was the plan for Listowel, almost all of them would be transferred to outlying stations and would be replaced by a lieutenant and fifty soldiers. These, with the help of the few constables left in Killarney, would patrol the town and its vicinity. It transpired that the function of the remaining constables would be to point out to the military the homes of members of Sinn Féin and of those who sympathised with that organisation. Constable Daniel B. O'Connell, on behalf of his comrades, informed Smyth that they would not act as military guides, and pointed out the danger in which they and their families would find themselves if they engaged in such activity. Moreover, he asserted that he and his comrades belonged to a civil force and were answerable in matters of discipline only to the inspector-general of the RIC. After some further verbal exchanges between Smyth and O'Connell, General Tudor, who, with County Inspector Poer O'Shee, was also present, gave the order to dismiss to the men, a number of whom, as they filed out of the dayroom, shouted 'Up Listowel'.

The day after this incident Father Dominic O'Connor, OFMCap., who was staying as a guest in the Franciscan Friary in Killarney, sent word to Constable O'Connell that he wished to see him. When the latter called on Father Dominic he described to the priest what occurred in Killarney police barracks, also mentioning what he knew about the incident at Listowel. Father Dominic then asked O'Connell to write an account of the incidents at Killarney and Listowel in the form of a letter, which could thereafter be used for propaganda purposes ('to show influential people in the community that the police were not against the Sinn Féin movement'). It seems that this letter was used by the Sinn Féin publicity department (the information above has been taken from a letter to his sister, Mrs Kathleen Ryan, from Daniel B. O'Connell, dated 25 May 1974; and a letter to me from the same person, dated 7 February 1975. Cf. also J. A. Gaughan, *Listowel and its Vicinity*, p. 448; D. Neligan, *The Spy in the Castle*, p. 94; and *Irish Bulletin*, 13 July 1920, *Cork Weekly Examiner*, 17 July 1920 and *Sunday Press*, 26 August 1951 in which some further details of Smyth's confrontation with the police at Killarney are given).

Constable Daniel B. O'Connell was born at Limerick on 16 October 1887. A son of Sergeant Daniel O'Connell, who was an enthusiastic promoter of The Queen's Jubilee Fund of the Royal Irish Constabulary (Widows and Orphans' Fund) to which members of the RIC made voluntary contributions (for more on this fund, see *RIC Constabulary List, 1917*, p. 216), he joined the RIC in 1908. After he completed his training at the depot he served at Gortatlea, near Castleisland, and Killarney. Some weeks after the incident at Killarney he was transferred to Belmullet, County Mayo, where, on arrival, he was handed a telegram which informed him that he had been dismissed. He emigrated to the US immediately afterwards. He died on 14 June 1975 (information from Mrs Kathleen Ryan).

It is interesting to note that Daniel B. O'Connell was a brother of Edward M. (Billy) O'Connell, later an inspector in the Special Branch of the Garda Síochána, who, it seems, was the victim of serious injustice at the hands of the de Valera administration of 1933 (cf. C. Brady, *Guardians of the Peace*, pp. 176–7, 181–2).

For more on Fr Dominic, see *Rebel Cork's Fighting Story, from 1916 to the Truce with Britain*, pp. 203–5. Cf. also Gaire, *A Brief History of the Diocese of Baker*, pp. 343–4, and *The Freeman's Journal*, 10 January 1921.

As news of the incident which occurred in Listowel police barracks on the morning of 19 June spread throughout Listowel police district, most of the members of the RIC in the area associated themselves with the stand taken by their comrades in Listowel. This was particularly true of Sergeant Edward (Ted) Devilly and Constables Roland Markham and John Tuohy, who at that time were stationed in Ballylongford. Markham and Tuohy resigned soon afterwards, both emigrating to Canada, where they joined the Toronto police force (information from Thomas Grennan and Michael Kelly).

22 This is not quite accurate, as Smyth resumed his tour in the afternoon of the following day; see Appendix 7.

23 John Donovan was born at Clarina, near Limerick city, in 1891. He joined the RIC on 15 September 1913. Having completed his training at the depot he served at Skreen (1914–15), Kesh (1915–16), Mullaghroe (1916–17), Ballymote (1917–19) and Listowel (1919–20). He died on 19 May 1964. See also pp. 139, 368 n.21.

24 Born in September 1898 at Castlegar, Ahascragh, Ballinasloe, County Galway, Fitzgerald joined the British army in September 1915 and saw active service with the Connaught Rangers from 1916 to 1918. He was demobilised in December 1918 and returned home. In August 1919 he joined the RIC, and in December of that year, after his training at the depot, he was appointed to Listowel police barracks. From July 1920 until the Truce he threw in his lot with an IRA unit in South Roscommon. During the Civil War he fought on the Free State side

reaching the rank of captain. He was demobilised in March 1924 and worked as a clerk in the Employment Exchange, Ballinasloe, from 1925 until June 1926 when he joined the Garda Síochána. He died on 8 December 1945.

25 A native of Killarney, he was ordained in St Patrick's College, Maynooth, in 1899. From 1899 to 1906 he served in the archdiocese of Westminster. On his return to the diocese of Kerry in 1906 he was appointed curate in Lixnaw. Then from 1907 to 1912 he ministered in the archdiocese of Melbourne. Later he was a curate in Listowel (1912–22), Castleisland (1923–28) and Ballybunion (1928–29). He was parish priest of Adrigole from 1929 to 1940, of Castletownbere from 1940 to 1946, and of Kenmare from 1946 to 1953. He became first a vicar-general and, later, dean of the diocese of Kerry. He died on 24 March 1953. For more, see J. A. Gaughan, *Listowel and its Vicinity*, under O'Sullivan, Father Charles.

26 An account of the mutiny and the manner in which information about it was delivered to the newspapers is to be found on pp. 369–74 of J. A. Gaughan, *Listowel and its Vicinity*. There are a number of discrepancies with regard to details between the account given there and that which appears in the Mee papers. However, a careful reading of the two accounts enables one to make a fairly accurate reconstruction of the incident.

27 Although they made no move to take over the police barracks, local units of the IRA followed developments in the barracks with great interest. They decided not to attack the police at Listowel, while the latter continued their stand against the authorities. Moreover, there is some evidence that there was collusion between the IRA and the police in the implementation of this policy. Thus about a week after the mutiny James (Jim) Crowley (cf. p. 354 n.10) sent a message to Thomas (Tom) Shanahan, who, with other members of the 3rd Battalion, Kerry Brigade No. 1, IRA had laid an ambush at Mountcoal, some four miles from Listowel, for a party of military, to ensure that nothing untoward would happen to a car-load of police from Listowel barracks who would be passing through Mountcoal on their way to Tralee two hours later. As indicated by Crowley, the police drove through the ambush position just two hours later (information from Tom Shanahan).

28 Due to its policy of boycotting policemen and even the families of policemen, the Sinn Féin movement had very few contacts with the RIC at this time and so did not appreciate the nationalist sentiment of some members of the force. Such sentiments led not only to the mutiny at Listowel on 19 June 1920, but also facilitated the capture by the IRA of Cookstown, Newmarket-on-Fergus, Tempo and Trim police barracks on 17 June, 13 June, 25 October, and 26 September 1920, respectively. For a detailed account of the IRA raid on Cookstown police barracks, see Appendix 4. For the raids on Newmarket-on-Fergus and Tempo, see pp. 354 n.12, 381–2 n.5. An account of the raid on Trim police barracks is

to be found in *The Freeman's Journal* of 27 September 1920. Constables Jeremiah Meehan and Patrick Grey were directly involved in this incident, Meehan having arranged it with a local unit of the IRA, but being on leave when it occurred, and Grey actually leaving a door open for the raiders. After the raid Constables Cotter (who served in Listowel from the beginning of 1919 until early in 1920) and Grey deserted from the RIC, and Meehan did not return from leave (information from John Cotter).

When the new Irish police force was being recruited, Cotter was invited to join it. Having joined in March 1922 he was stationed with the rest of the first Civic Guards at the Royal Dublin Society grounds, Ballsbridge, Dublin, and was appointed a kind of aide-de-camp cum bodyguard to Colonel Patrick (Paddy) Brennan, the assistant commissioner of the new force. Cotter was a prominent member of the faction which strenuously objected to the presence of disbanded RIC men in the new force and when they were not dismissed he resigned (information from John Cotter).

29 The mutiny of the Connaught Rangers began on 27–28 June 1920. For the story of the mutiny, see T. P. Kilfeather, *The Connaught Rangers*, and S. Pollock, *Mutiny for the Cause*; cf. also PRO London, British Cabinet Memoranda, CAB 24/132, C.P. 3690; *Irish Independent*, 6 July 1920; *Irish Independent*, 30 March 1922; *Sunday Independent*, 27 November 1955 and *Sligo Champion*, 13 August 1993. For the origin of the regiment and some further useful references, see G. A. Hayes-McCoy, 'The raising of the Connaught Rangers, 1793', *Galway Archaeological and Historical Society Journal*, 21 (1944), pp. 133–9.

Before concluding on the mutiny of the police at Listowel it is interesting to note that there were two other well-publicised instances of insubordination in the ranks of the RIC. The first occurred at William Street Barracks, Limerick, on 5 August 1882. It was the culmination of a widespread agitation by the police for an improvement in their pay and travelling allowances, and also for an end to an extraordinary anomaly whereby, although men who joined the force before 9 August 1866 received pensions of £62 per annum after thirty years service, those who joined after that date and had the same service had to be content with an annual pension of only £37. The strike was probably occasioned by the Limerick police being grossly overworked by a notorious special resident magistrate named Charles Dalton Clifford Lloyd (cf. C. Lloyd, *Ireland under the Land League*). A fascinating account of the incident is to be found in the *United Ireland* of 12 August 1882. The other strike, which also concerned pay and conditions of service, occurred at Musgrave Street Barracks, Belfast, on 27 July 1907. For more on this, see *Belfast Newsletter*, 29, 30, 31 July, 2, 3, 5, 9, 10 August 1907. (I am indebted to Michael Dore for drawing my attention to the Limerick police strike.)

10: AFTERMATH OF THE LISTOWEL POLICE MUTINY: 19 JUNE–AUGUST 1920

1 This inactivity on the part of the authorities could also have been due partially to indecision. In fact, there is a curious parallel between the seeming indecision of the authorities in the face of the insubordination of the RIC at Listowel and the apparent inactivity of the officers when members of the Connaught Rangers mutinied in India (cf. S. Pollock, *Mutiny for the Cause*, pp. 42, 70). The slowness to move against the Listowel mutineers was almost certainly due, initially, to the suspicion of the authorities that Sinn Féin, like the Fenians in a previous period, had 'tampered with' members of the crown forces. This suspicion was probably strengthened when news of the mutiny at Jullundur and Solon was received.

It is safe to presume that the War Office then, seeing how grave the situation could be, urged caution on the military authorities in Ireland and India. This, in turn, was most probably the cause of the unusual military activity throughout Ireland during the second and third weeks of July 1920 (cf. pp. 107–8).

2 This extra 70p (14/-) a week was given to every constable serving in a disturbed area, and was but one of a number of extra allowances which were given to members of the force at about that time (information from James R. W. Goulden).

The growing disenchantment, in the early part of 1920, of many members of the RIC with their lot, the substantial pay increases of June and the publication in *The Freeman's Journal* on 10 July of details of the 'Listowel incident' are probably the factors accounting for the following interesting statistics (which, taken from the *Irish Bulletin*, were published in the *Irish Independent* of 5 August 1920):

1920	Resignations from the RIC	Average per week
19 May–19 June	106	23.9
20 June–6 July	45	19.6
7 July–31 July	161	46.9

3 Patrick J. (Packy) Sheeran was born at Straide, County Mayo, on 16 March 1892. He joined the RIC on 16 March 1912, and having completed his training he served at Glenbeigh (1912–14), Killorglin (1914–17) and Listowel (1917–20). When stationed in Listowel in early 1920 he married Margaret Morrissey of Brosna. Although he was later to claim that he was in Listowel police barracks when Colonel Smyth visited it on 19 June (cf. RTÉ, Sound Recording 18/70: 'Incident at Listowel', first broadcast on 13 September 1966), in fact, he was on leave and in Brosna with his wife when the mutiny occurred. When he returned

from leave, however, he associated himself with his comrades, and a few weeks later left the barracks. He died on 16 April 1969. For more, see J. A. Gaughan, *Listowel and its Vicinity*, p. 369. (The inaccuracy that Sheeran was present in Listowel police barracks on 19 June was repeated in a piece on the broadcast of 13 September 1966 which appeared in the *Evening Echo* (Cork) of 17 September 1966.)

4   Listowel presbytery was searched for arms by Black and Tans during the week ending on 27 November 1920 (see *The Kerryman*, 27 November 1920).

5   On 20 May 1920 dockers began to refuse to handle war materials and on 29 May railwaymen in various parts of the country refused to work on trains carrying the crown forces or their stores. This boycott of the crown forces by dockers and railwaymen had become fairly widespread by the beginning of July. It seriously impaired military activities during the best season of the year, as work at the docks had to be done by fatigue parties of soldiers and much of the military motor transport had to be diverted to supplying stations which had been cut off by the railway 'strike'. The boycott ended on 21 December 1920. For more on this munitions transport strike, as it has been called, see A. Mitchell, *Labour in Irish Politics 1890–1930*, pp. 120–1.

The measure of support in the Listowel area for the 'striking dockers and railwaymen' can be gauged from the extraordinarily generous response to collections which were made for them about this time. Thus during the week ending on 31 July 1920 a sum of £622.32½ (£622 6s 6d) was forwarded from North Kerry to Thomas Johnson, treasurer and acting secretary of the Irish Labour Party and Trade Union Congress, £318 of which was subscribed by the people of Listowel (see *The Kerryman*, 3, 24, 31 July 1920).

6   Martial law had not been imposed on the south-west (Counties Cork, Kerry, Limerick and Tipperary) at this time. This occurred on 10 December 1920 (see D. Macardle, *The Irish Republic*, p. 416). 'Disturbed area' would be a more accurate designation of the south-west at this time. At the urging of the military authorities in Ireland, the British cabinet on 1 December 1920, 'After some interesting details from several points of view had been given of the experience of martial law in South Africa ...' agreed to its introduction; and on 30 December 1920 the cabinet agreed to an extension of the martial law area to Counties Clare, Kilkenny, Waterford and Wexford (PRO London, CAB 23/23), news of this extension being promulgated during the first week of January 1921 (see D. Macardle, *The Irish Republic*, p. 423).

7   Curiously enough during his RIC days in Listowel Hughes was known to his comrades as 'the monsignor'.

8   Members of the DMP were also involved in these security measures. It seems that there was considerable resentment on the part of some members of the DMP at being ordered to act in conjunction with the military in this matter,

and a Constable Murphy, stationed at Clontarf, refused to do this duty and was dismissed (see *The Kerryman*, 17 July 1920).

9   In this regard it is interesting to note that in the weekly summary submitted to the British cabinet on 1 July 1920 by the directorate of intelligence was the statement: 'It is believed that the extreme section [of Sinn Féin] contemplate some action soon and that Volunteers in the Dublin area have been warned to be in readiness' (PRO London, CAB 24/108, CP 2514). For another possible reason, however, for this extraordinary military activity, see p. 352 n.1.

10   For a list of those who signed the document, see Appendix 6. The IRA contacted the RIC in Listowel police barracks through James Crowley (affidavit of Kelly and McNamara).

11   James Henry Thomas (1874–1949) became Labour MP for Derby in 1910, general secretary of the National Union of Railwaymen in 1917, chairman of the parliamentary committee of the Trade Union Congress in 1919, and in the following year presided over the Annual Congress at Portsmouth. He held office in the three administrations of Sir Ramsay MacDonald (for more, see *Dictionary of National Biography*, I–XXII (ed. Sir L. Stephens and Sir Sydney Lee, London 1908–09), supplement 1941–50).

12   Mee, in fact, never became a member of the IRA (cf. State Paper Office, Dáil Éireann Papers, 2/110, item 29), nor, it seems, did Donovan. Quite a number of ex-RIC constables, however, did join the IRA, and as a result at least two of them lost their lives. Constable Patrick (Paddy) Buckley, a native of County Kerry, facilitated the capture by a local unit of the IRA of his barracks at Newmarket-on-Fergus on 13 June 1920. Buckley was subsequently dismissed and on returning to his home district joined the IRA police. In February 1922 he was arrested by Free State soldiers and placed in Tralee jail. On 7 March 1922 he and eight other Republican prisoners were taken to Ballyseedy Cross, where, as a counter-reprisal, they were blown up by Free State soldiers. Constable Thomas (Tom) Healy, another Kerryman, who was serving in Ennis, deserted from the force in July 1920. At the beginning of June 1921 he joined the East Clare Brigade, IRA. On 15 June he and nine other members of the flying column were surprised by a British military patrol and pursued across country. Soon after the British broke off the pursuit Healy died from exhaustion (information from Colonel Austin Brennan; for the details of this last incident, see *An t-Óglach*, 29 July 1921).

13   In fact Kesh was the second barracks to which Donovan was appointed. Cf. p. 349 n.23.

14   Alexander McCabe, later more generally known as Alaisdair Mac Caba, was born on 5 June 1886. He was educated at Summerhill College, Sligo, and later qualified as a national teacher in St Patrick's Training College, Drumcondra, Dublin. In 1907 he was appointed principal of Drumnagranchy national school,

near Ballymote. Six years later, while attending a study course in Dublin, he joined the IRB, and in 1915 he was elected a member of the Supreme Council of that organisation. From 1915 to 1916 he represented Connacht on the Supreme Council. Because of his Republican activities he was dismissed from his teaching post in 1915, and later that year he was arrested and detained for six months. During the Easter Rising he organised disruptive activities in Counties Cavan, Longford and Sligo. After the Rising he went 'on the run' in County Roscommon, eventually coming out of hiding to help Count Plunkett win the 1917 North Roscommon by-election for Sinn Féin. Later in 1917 he was again arrested and jailed. While still in Lincoln jail in 1918, he was elected Sinn Féin member of parliament for Sligo. He was released from jail in 1919. For the next year he was closely associated with Michael Collins in the prosecution of the Anglo-Irish War. He was captured by the crown forces in July 1920 and detained in the Curragh until the Treaty negotiations began, when he was released to take his seat in the Dáil. During the Civil War he was on the Free State side but arising out of the controversy following the mutiny in the Curragh in 1924 he resigned his Dáil seat. In 1924 he failed to have himself nominated as the Sinn Féin candidate for Sligo and retired from politics. He returned to teaching, later became an auctioneer, and in 1935, with some others, founded the Educational Building Society, of which he became secretary and managing director. He died on 31 May 1972.

15 James (Jim) McDermott of Riverstown, Nicholas Mullen of Tubbercurry and Thomas F. (Tom) O'Carroll of Ballynacarrow were also particularly helpful to Donovan and Mee at this time (information from Dr Thomas F. O'Carroll).

16 William (Billy) Pilkington was born in Sligo on 2 June 1894. He was educated at the local convent school, the Marist Brothers school and the Day Trades Preparatory School. Later he attended the Forestry College in County Wicklow. While there he met Liam Mellows who initiated him into the IRB. On the outbreak of World War One the Forestry College was closed and Pilkington returned to Sligo, where he secured employment as an apprentice in the jeweller's shop of Wehrly Brothers Ltd. A member of the Volunteers from 1913, he was active in the Anglo-Irish War from 1919 to 1921, being in charge of the ambush at Moneygold, near Grange, on 25 October 1920, and became eventually OC of the 3rd Western Division of the IRA. He was a prominent member of the Republican forces during the Civil War. He joined the Redemptorist Order in 1924 and was ordained in 1931. A missionary in Africa for many years, on retiring he resided in the Redemptorist House in Sunderland. For accounts of two daring escapes from Sligo jail which he organised in March 1920 and 29 June 1921, see *Sworn to be Free*, pp. 108–15 and 152–60. He died on 2 April 1972. For more see *Sligo Champion*, 8 April 1977.

17 Before setting off for Ballintogher, Donovan had made a 'flying' visit, 12–13 July, to the home of his future wife, Celianna Loughrey, at Castlederg, County Tyrone (information from Edward (Ned) Loughrey, Donovan's brother-in-law).

18 These two buildings were converted into flats in 1975.

19 Alfred White resided at 9 Peter Place, Adelaide Road, convenient to the Hotel Gerard. He and Charles McMorrow were married to the sisters Nora and Mary Murray. White was attached to the headquarters staff of the IRA (information from Alfred White).

20 For more on Erskine Childers, see T. Cox, *Damned Englishman: a study of Erskine Childers (1870–1922)*.

21 Thomas (Tom) Johnson was born at Liverpool on 17 May 1872. He left school and began work when only twelve and a half years of age. In 1889 he came to Ireland. From 1901 to 1918 he resided in Belfast during which time he was associated with James Connolly in the labour movement. He supported Home Rule for Ireland. Being a pacifist he took no part in the rising of Easter 1916. He was, however, prominent in the anti-conscription campaign in 1918. In 1919 he helped draft the social and economic programme of the First Dáil. From 1922 to 1927 he was leader of the Labour Party in Dáil Éireann. Constituting the official opposition, he and his colleagues made possible the establishment of democratic institutions in the emerging Irish state. After losing his Dáil seat in the general election of September 1927 he remained in public life, being a senator from 1928 to 1936. Thereafter he became the elder statesman of the Irish Labour Party, sitting on a number of government commissions and continuing to be prominent in the trade-union movement. He died on 17 January 1963. For more, see A. Mitchell, 'Thomas Johnson, 1872–1963, a pioneer Labour leader', *Studies* 58 (1969), pp. 396–404, *Liberty*, June 1974, and A. Mitchell, *Labour in Irish Politics 1890–1930*, under Johnson, Thomas.

22 William O'Brien was born at Ballygurteen, near Clonakilty, County Cork, on 23 January 1881. He was educated at the Christian Brothers Schools at Dungarvan, County Waterford, and Carrick-on-Suir, County Tipperary. In 1898, two years after arriving in Dublin, he joined James Connolly's Irish Socialist Republican Party. From 1907 on he was associated with James Larkin in organising Irish workers. He played a prominent role in the establishment of the Irish Transport and General Workers' Union in 1909, and he was secretary of the Lock-out Committee during the Dublin strike of 1913. Prominent in the anti-conscription campaign in 1918, he was later largely responsible for the fact that organised labour supported Sinn Féin in the Anglo-Irish War. He sat as a Labour member in Dáil Éireann from 1922 to 1923, from June to August 1927 and from 1937 to 1938. He died on 20 October 1968. For more, see *Liberty*, November 1968; W. O'Brien, *Forth the Banners Go: Reminiscences of William O'Brien* (Dublin 1969);

and A. Mitchell, 'William O'Brien 1881–1968, and the Irish Labour Movement', *Studies* 60 (1971), pp. 311–31. For more on the collaboration between Labour and Sinn Féin in general, and between William O'Brien and Michael Collins in particular, see A. Mitchell, *Labour in Irish Politics 1890–1930*, pp. 114–15.

23 I have not been able to confirm the accuracy of this. It is most likely, however, that the publication of the Smyth speech, together with its attendant adverse publicity, increased the hostility with which *The Freeman's Journal* was regarded by the crown forces. The editor and two directors, one of whom was Martin Fitzgerald, found themselves in jail on 9 December 1920. Their crime was the publication of an article with a photograph showing the wound on the back of a man named Arthur J. Quirke, who had been flogged by soldiers of the Berkshire regiment while a prisoner in Portobello barracks, Dublin. The accused were tried by court-martial and sentenced to twelve months' imprisonment, with a fine of £2,000 imposed on the company, although the prisoner who had been beaten, two reputable doctors who treated his wounds, and a photograph of the wounds taken two days after the beating, established the truthfulness of the newspaper's account of the affair. Seemingly, the coercive measures then in force in Ireland made such publications punishable, even though they were wholly true, if they were 'likely to cause disaffection to His Majesty's subjects'. Because of a great deal of pressure from the British press, the editor and the two directors were released on 6 January 1921 'on health grounds'. The court-martial of the editor and the two directors was not the only way in which *The Freeman's Journal* was being harassed by the crown forces at that time. For instance, members of the crown forces attempted to destroy the premises of the newspaper on 29 November and 25 December 1920 and on 7 January 1921 (see *Weekly Freeman*, 27 November; 4, 11, 18 December 1920; and 1, 8, 15 January 1921).

24 Much of the credit for the interest which the British Labour movement was taking in the matter, as well as in the overall situation in Ireland, must be given to Thomas Johnson and William O'Brien. On 12 July 1920 they attended a special Trade Union Congress in London at which they had distributed to each delegate a pamphlet which included *The Freeman's Journal* account of Divisional Commissioner Smyth's address to the constables in Listowel police barracks, a report of the atrocities committed in Ireland by the police and military in June and early July of that year, the verdict of the Irish electorate at the general election of 1918 in favour of an Irish Republic, and an appeal to the workers of Britain not to provide munitions for the extermination of the Irish people. Due in no small measure to the efforts of Johnson and O'Brien, the special conference, which initially had been called in order to settle the munitions transport strike in Ireland (cf. p. 353 n.5) by a three-to-two vote, condemned the continued military occupation of Ireland and urged its unions to consider strike action if the government did not change its policy. At the same time the British Labour

Party demanded a full investigation into the Smyth speech (see *The Freeman's Journal*, 14 July 1920, also Mee papers).

25 Thomas (Tom) Barry was OC of the West Cork flying column, IRA. For a fascinating account of his exploits and those of the men under his command, see T. Barry, *Guerilla Days in Ireland*, and *The Reality of the Anglo-Irish War 1920–21 in West Cork* (Dublin 1974).

26 Thomas (Tom) Maguire was born at Cross, County Mayo, on 28 March 1892. He was educated at the local national school. In 1913 he joined the Volunteers. He represented South Mayo in Dáil Éireann from 1921 to 1927. He was an IRA leader in County Mayo during the Anglo-Irish War and, eventually, he became OC of the Second Western Division. He took the anti-Treaty side during the Civil War. He remained a prominent member of the Sinn Féin organisation until December 1938.

27 Seán S. MacEoin was born at Bunlahy, Ballinalee, County Longford, on 30 September 1894. He was educated at Ballinalee national school. A blacksmith by trade, he joined the Sinn Féin movement in 1914. One of the best-known heroes of the Anglo-Irish War (1919–21), he was captured by the crown forces before the Truce and was sentenced to death by a military court. He was released on 8 August 1921, after Michael Collins, backed by the Dáil cabinet, had made his release a condition for proceeding with negotiations towards an Anglo-Irish settlement. One of the key figures on the Free-State side during the Civil War, he was promoted major-general and chief of staff of the National Army in 1923. Apart from a short period (1923–29), he was a representative of various constituencies from 1918 to 1965. He was at first minister for justice and later minister for defence in the inter-party government of 1948, and he was again minister for defence in the inter-party government of 1954. He died on 7 July 1973.

28 The British cabinet was in no doubt as to the cardinal role then (1920) being played by Collins in the Anglo-Irish struggle (cf. PRO London, CAB 24/111, CP 2545, 26 August and 9 September; CAB 23/23, CP 2554, 24 and 29 December). For more on Michael Collins, see *Dictionary of Irish Biography* (ed. J. McGuire and J. Quinn, Cambridge 2009) under Collins, Michael and the sources there cited.

29 On p. 219 of T. Kilgannon, *Sligo and its surroundings* occurs the following interesting paragraph:

> In concluding a lengthy notice of the history and picturesque attractions of Lissadell, the Very Rev. Archdeacon O'Rorke gives expression to his regret that Sir Robert Gore-Booth, the grandfather of the present owner, did not content himself with the extensive stretch of land already in his

own occupation, without annexing to his demesne the thickly populated townland of Ballygilgan. He narrates the circumstances attending the wholesale clearances of the poor people of this district though he omits to mention that [c. 1834] the vessel in which they were shipped was lost, and that they were all drowned off the coast of Donegal [cf. T. O'Rorke, *The History of Sligo: town and county* II (Dublin 1890), pp. 19–20]. The succeeding owners of Lissadell were apparently much affected by the impression caused through this deplorable calamity, and the late Sir Henry was always a most indulgent and even a model landlord. The present owner, Sir Josslyn, is a practical philanthropist, having, in addition to extensive farming operations, established a number of industries of various kinds which give vast employment and circulation of money in the district. Possibly the political career of the Countess Markievicz (his sister) may have been influenced also by the tragedy.

30 For more on Countess Markievicz, see A. Marreco, *The Rebel Countess*; D. James, *The Gore-Booths of Lissadell*.

31 Sir Hamar Greenwood's full statement on this occasion, as reported in *The Freeman's Journal* of 15 July 1920, read:

> The recent event presumably refers to the resignation of five R.I.C. constables in Listowel, County Kerry. On 19 June last, Divisional Commissioner Smyth made a speech to the members of the force, eighteen in number, stationed at Listowel.
>
> I have seen the report in the press, which, on the face of it, appears to have been supplied by the five constables already mentioned. I have myself seen Colonel Smyth who repudiates the accuracy of the statements contained in the report. He informed me that the instructions given by him to the police in Listowel, and throughout the division, were those mentioned in a debate in this house on 22 June last by the attorney-general for Ireland, and he did not exceed these instructions.
>
> The reason for the resignations of the five constables was their refusal to take up duty in barracks in certain disturbed parts of Kerry. They had taken up that attitude before the visit of the Divisional Commissioner. I am satisfied that the newspaper report is a wholly distorted and misleading account of what took place.

The blocking of the debate in the House of Commons on the Listowel police mutiny prompted an interesting cartoon in *The Freeman's Journal* of 15 July 1920 (see Felix M. Larkin, 'Terror and Discord: the Shemas Cartoons' in *The Freeman's Journal, 1920–1924*, pp. 26–7).

32 A fairly convincing case is made on pp. 1056–8 of the *American Commission: Evidence on conditions in Ireland comprising the completed testimony, affidavits and exhibitions presented before the Commission* that the content of Smyth's address reflected the mood and, indeed, the policy of the British cabinet at that time. For more on this, see p. 155.

33 He joined the RIC as an officer on 1 April 1895, was appointed district inspector (2nd class) on 2 February 1899, 1st class on 1 February 1908 and county inspector on 15 June 1920 (information from James R. W. Goulden).

34 On p. 80 of *Rebel Cork's Fighting Story*, under the chapter heading 'Divisional Commissioner Smyth caused RIC to mutiny in Kerry, and was shot dead in the County Club, Cork' occurs the following account of this incident:

> The County Club, resort of the landed families and high military officers, had a staff as loyal as its frequenters who enjoyed its first-class club and residential amenities. All efforts of the IRA intelligence department to penetrate into the staff were frustrated until contact was made with a young waiter. Thereafter the names of British officers, military and police, who stayed at or visited the club, were known to the IRA. Colonel Smyth was staying there during the first fortnight of July. This information was conveyed to the IRA. It was decided to shoot him on Friday evening, 16 July. That day he packed his bags and announced his intention of going away for the weekend so that the arrangements for shooting him fell through. He returned unexpectedly the following evening, and the receipt of this information caused the IRA to mobilise hastily a squad of six armed men. They entered the County Club at 10 p.m., held up the waiter, who was expecting them, and two of them passed down the passage to the lounge, where Colonel Smyth was seated with County Inspector Craig of the RIC. Advancing into the lounge, the leader of the party confronted Smyth, saying: 'Were not your orders to shoot at sight? Well, you are in sight now, so prepare.' Fire was opened. Smyth jumped to his feet and ran towards the door. Despite two bullets in the head, one through the heart and two through the chest, he succeeded in gaining the passage, where he dropped dead. He had attempted to draw his automatic but apparently his strength failed him. The county inspector received a slight bullet wound in the leg. The armed party quickly withdrew.

For the sake of completeness and accuracy, the following details can be added to the above account. The County Club extended from 80a South Mall along Crane Lane out onto Phoenix Street. It was Seán Culhane, intelligence officer, B Company, 1st Battalion, Cork Brigade No. 1, IRA, who succeeded in establishing contact with the waiter in question, Edward (Ned) Fitzgerald, who, because he was a native of Convamore, Ballyhooly, County Cork, was known to some members of the IRA in Cork city as 'Bally'. The incident occurred at 10.30 p.m. And, in fact, leaving some 'scouts' with Fitzgerald in the vestibule of the club, six armed men, namely, Seán Culhane, A. N. Other, John J. (J.J.) O'Connell, Seán O'Donoghue, Daniel (Sandow) O'Donovan and Cornelius (Corny) O'Sullivan (members of various battalions of Cork Brigade No. 1, IRA), and not two, entered the lounge or smoking room, where, besides Smyth and Craig, two other men were seated, one of whom was a Mr Barker, secretary of the club (for the above I am indebted to an eyewitness; see also *Cork Weekly Examiner* 24 July 1920, in which by far the best newspaper report on the incident and its immediate aftermath appears). It is interesting to note that the report submitted by the British directorate of intelligence to the cabinet on 22 July about the assassination of Smyth, in effect merely reiterated what had already appeared in the press. The incident was again referred to in the weekly report of 29 July, when it was stated that the *Watchword of Labour* had 'been submitted to the government ... for its scandalous treatment of the murder of Lieut. Col. Smyth' (PRO London, CAB 24/110 – intelligence reports for 22, 29 July 1920).

For some tragic sequels, both direct and indirect, to this shooting, see J. A. Gaughan, *Listowel and its Vicinity*, pp. 373–4, and C. King, *The Orange and the Green*, pp. 98–101; cf. also D. Breen, *My Fight for Irish Freedom*, pp. 145–6, where there is an account of the ill-starred attempt of Colonel Smyth's brother to avenge the killing.

35 Independently of IRA headquarters, the assassination of Smyth was carried out on the instructions of Seán O'Hegarty, acting-commandant of Cork Brigade No. 1, IRA, and other members of the staff of that brigade. It was not, however, the disaster for Sinn Féin that Mee considered it to be. On the one hand, already a great deal of attention had been drawn to the policy of the British government towards Ireland, and the actions of the crown forces in implementing that policy, by the widespread publication of Smyth's address to the police at Listowel. Moreover, in the light of most official British inquiries in Ireland before and since that time, Mee was being rather naive when he expected an inquiry into Smyth's address to be anything other than a 'white-washing exercise'. On the other hand, the late Major Florence O'Donoghue, who was adjutant and intelligence officer of Cork Brigade No. 1, IRA, from 1920 to 1921, in a lecture entitled 'Military intelligence in the Black and Tan days' which he delivered on 23 November 1943 to officers, NCOs and men of divisional headquarters, 1st Division (Southern Command, Irish Army), of which he was then intelligence officer, stated: 'The effect on public morale of the Smyth shooting was tremendous' (information taken from the papers of Major Florence O'Donoghue, which are in the National Library). When one considers that Smyth had been specially selected

by the British authorities to lead the drive against the IRA in Munster, and the fact that he had become notorious after his address at Listowel, there can be little doubt as to the accuracy of O'Donoghue's assessment of the effect of Smyth's assassination. Conversely, the incident had an adverse effect on the morale of the crown forces, particularly the RIC. This was generally accepted at that time. For instance in a piece in the *Daily Chronicle* of 19 July 1920 on the assassination of Smyth, the incident was seen almost exclusively in terms of an attack by Sinn Féin on the morale of the RIC. One measure of the adverse effect which the incident had on the morale of the RIC was the fact that, until the RIC were disbanded, constables who had any association with the Listowel police district in the summer of 1920 were ostracised by most of their police and military comrades (information from Tom Grennan).

36 It is difficult to see how Mee's interpretation of the action of the British government in returning Smyth to his post in Cork could be sustained. Immediately after Smyth was shot Mee wrote to *The Freeman's Journal* and the *Irish Independent*, expressing regret at the death of the divisional commissioner and accusing the British government of connivance thereat. (These letters were not published. Mee was not alone at that time in believing that Smyth had been assassinated by elements in the crown forces.) Later, at a general meeting of the resigned and dismissed members of the RIC at the Mansion House, Dublin, on 24 January 1922, Mee, in the course of an address, stated that Smyth had been killed by agents of the British government. His speech, including this statement, was given considerable prominence in the press on the following day. On 28 January the press carried an unsigned statement on behalf of the British authorities in Ireland which refuted some statements which Mee had made, including his accusation that Smyth had been killed by agents of the British government. Mee's reply to this letter appeared in *The Freeman's Journal* and *Irish Independent* of 30 January. It first recalled the Listowel incident, gave an abstract of Colonel Smyth's address on that occasion, and then continued:

> After the publication of this speech Colonel Smyth was called to London to make a statement, and his alleged version was withheld until after his death.
>
> On behalf of the fourteen men who signed the statement I asked, through the press, for a sworn inquiry. My letter was not published for obvious reasons. Colonel Smyth's speech, as published, has been verified by our signatures.
>
> In the cause of truth and justice and on behalf of those for whom I acted as spokesman I again demand a public sworn inquiry into the 'incident' and all its details.
>
> I regret the death of Colonel Smyth as much as the British authorities do, because he helped to expose the hidden policy of the British government.

Mee concluded by implying once more that Smyth had been killed by British agents and by recalling that his own father's house had been burned by members of the crown forces.

This ended the correspondence (for the above, see *The Freeman's Journal*, and *Irish Independent* for 25, 28, 30 January 1922).

It was not, however, Mee's last letter to the press on the Listowel police mutiny and its aftermath. In a long letter which was published in the *Irish Press* of 18 January 1946, occasioned by the appearance a week earlier of General Macready's obituary, Mee developed the thesis that when, in an interview which he gave to two French journalists in September 1920, Macready stated that 'it might be necessary to shoot half-a-hundred individuals in Ireland' and that 'We have most of their names, and the day may come when we shall be able to make a definite clearance of them', the General was capturing the true spirit of the British government's policy on Ireland from March to September 1920. And Mee concluded by alleging once again that in his address to the police in Listowel on 19 June 1920 Colonel Smyth was but articulating that policy.

37 Although Sir Hamar Greenwood's statement was an accurate reproduction of Order No. 5, as issued to all ranks by Colonel Smyth on 17 June 1920 (cf. pp. 250–1), by itself it was a misleading version of Smyth's address. For Smyth's own version of his address in Listowel, see Appendices 5b and 5c.

38 Cf. *The Freeman's Journal*, 28 July 1920, *Irish Independent*, 29 July 1920, *Weekly Freeman*, 31 July 1920, and *The Kerryman*, 31 July 1920.

39 It was generally believed that Captain Chadwick resigned partly as a protest against the content of Colonel Smyth's address to the constables in Listowel police barracks and partly because he resented the position in which the army had been placed by the British government's policy on Ireland. In this regard it is interesting to note that in *The Cork Examiner* of 7 August 1920 there was an official statement to the effect that Captain Chadwick had made an application for permission to resign his commission but that, press reports notwithstanding, he was not present in Listowel police barracks when Divisional Commissioner Smyth addressed the police there, and that his intended resignation had nothing to do with the events at Listowel. Cf. also *The Freeman's Journal*, 12 August 1920.

40 At that time Mee's two older sisters had married, three of his brothers had emigrated to the US and his brother Luke was serving in the RIC (information from Mrs Ellen Mulvihill, sister of Jeremiah Mee).

41 It may be that this gentleman, probably the leader of the raiding party, was aware that at that very time Luke Mee was serving in the RIC at Mohill, County Leitrim. Luke Mee (1892–1959) joined the RIC in 1912. Having completed his training he served at Carrick-on-Shannon (1913–17) and Mohill (1917–22).

11: WORKING WITH SINN FÉIN: AUGUST–NOVEMBER 1920

1 These were ex-British army officers who had been recruited during the early summer of 1920 to form the 1,500-strong, so-called Auxiliary Division of the RIC.

2 For more on Brigadier-General Frank Perry Crozier and the force of which he had command for some time, see F. P. Crozier, *Ireland For Ever*.

3 On the recommendation of Collins some of these were rewarded with commissions in the new Irish police force. However, due to the opposition of the rank and file, they, with a few exceptions, had to be satisfied with remaining in the new force merely as civilian advisors and training instructors (cf. C. Brady, *Guardians of the Peace*, pp. 53–64).

4 Some two months later Mee prepared a memorandum on this subject for Countess Markievicz (cf. Appendix 9a).

5 Some of these steps had already been taken (cf. Appendix 10 for this, and Sinn Féin policy between 1919 and 1921 towards members of the RIC).

6 Mee later recalled how he got a nice room at O'Brien's Hotel and remained there for some four months under the alias of Mr Maguire. He had not too far to walk to and from his office each day with his attaché case full of papers. These papers were a constant source of anxiety to him, as they consisted mainly of correspondence with resigned and intending-to-resign members of the police force. The capture of this correspondence by the authorities could have spelled disaster for these ex-policemen and policemen who were in communication with the ministry of labour of the outlawed Dáil Éireann. Mee described how, on his return from the office, he always locked his bedroom door and placed this correspondence in the fire grate so that it could be burned quickly in the event of a raid by the military.

When Michael Kelly and John P. McNamara shared a room with Mee at O'Brien's Hotel during the first week of December 1920, Kelly noticed that Mee slept in his clothes, and, whenever military lorries halted in the vicinity, generally jumped out of bed and sat by the fire grate ready to destroy his papers, should the hotel be raided (information from Michael Kelly). It seems that the crown forces almost got their hands on these papers in early December 1920. For this, cf. statement by Áine bean Éamoinn Ceannt.

7 Richard (Dick) Cotter was born of Kerry parents in Cheddar, England, on 6 May 1891. In 1900, on the death of his father, the family returned to Ireland and settled in Cork. Here Cotter was educated at the Christian Brothers Schools at Sullivan's Quay, and later, when the family transferred to Dublin, he attended the Christian Brothers Schools at South Richmond Street. He joined the Volunteers in 1913. During the Rising of 1916 he and his brothers, Joseph and Thomas, fought in Jacob's factory under the command of Thomas MacDonagh. After the

Rising he was interned at Knutsford and later at Frongoch in Wales. After his release he took a prominent part in the reorganisation of Sinn Féin and the anti-conscription campaign of 1918. From 1918 to 1919 he was Sinn Féin organiser for the Fingal district of County Dublin. In 1919 he was appointed secretary of the ministry of labour of the First Dáil. Although a brother-in-law of Mrs Éamon de Valera, he supported the Treaty, and retained his post as secretary when the ministry of labour of the First Dáil became the Department of Labour of the Free State government. He died on 6 June 1929.

8   A sister-in-law of Éamonn Ceannt, one of the executed leaders of the 1916 rebellion, Elizabeth M. (Lily) O'Brennan was born in Dublin on 29 August 1878. She was educated at the Dominican convent, Eccles Street. In April 1914 she joined Cumann na mBan, later becoming a vice-president and secretary of that organisation. She took part in the Rising of 1916. Thereafter she was an untiring worker in the National Aid Association. One of the most dedicated members of the Sinn Féin movement during the Anglo-Irish War, she was, at different times, private secretary to Erskine Childers, a staff member of the ministry of labour and an organiser of the Belfast Boycott. On 24 January 1922 she was appointed typist to Arthur Griffith, then president of the Dáil cabinet. In 1929 and 1930 she had two books published. She died on 31 May 1948. For more, see T. Cox, *Damned Englishman*, under O'Brennan.

9   She remained a confidante of Countess Markievicz until the latter's death in 1927. After the Fianna Fáil party was returned to power in 1932 she received an appointment in the civil service. She died *c.* 1945 (information from Eilís bean Uí Chonaill). She was also known as Moira O'Byrne. For more on her, see T. Cox, *Damned Englishman*, under O'Byrne, Moira.

10 Eilís Ryan (later Mrs Seán Ó Conaill or Eilís bean Uí Chonaill) was born at Lenamore, Mostrim, Co. Longford, on 20 April 1897. Educated at Lenamore national school and Maguire's Civil Service College, Dublin, in 1915 she joined Cumann na mBan and was attached to the Ard Craobh. Throughout most of Easter week 1916 she attended wounded Volunteers in the Father Mathew Hall, Church Street. In 1920 she became a member of the executive of Cumann na mBan and from 1920 to 1921 she worked at the offices of the ministry of labour of Dáil Éireann. Among her duties at the ministry of labour were those of conducting wounded Volunteers from one safe house to another, and administering funds for the dependants of killed and imprisoned Volunteers. She supported the anti-Treaty side during the Civil War. For an account of her part in the Rising, see E. Uí Chonaill, 'A Cumann na mBan recalls Easter week', *The Capuchin Annual*, 1966, pp. 271–8.

11 Higgins took part in the Rising of 1916 (information from Eilís bean Uí Chonaill).

12 The need to replace Countess Markievicz had arisen before this time. Thus Alderman Thomas Kelly was appointed substitute minister for labour by Dáil Éireann on 19 August 1919, after the arrest, on 13 June, of the countess, and acted as such until the latter's release on 21 October 1919 (see State Paper Office, Dáil Éireann Papers, 2/382).

13 Joseph (Joe) McGrath was born in Dublin on 25 August 1888. He was educated at the Christian Brothers Schools at James Street. He left school at the age of fourteen, held various jobs and, eventually, in 1916 he found employment with Messrs Craig Gardner and Co., the firm of chartered accountants. In 1913 he joined the Volunteers and he took part in the Rising of Easter 1916. In 1917 he was active in reorganising the Volunteers and also in building up the new Sinn Féin organisation. On her arrest and detention in September 1920 he succeeded Countess Markievicz as minister for labour in the First Dáil. When he, in turn, was imprisoned with Arthur Griffith and other prominent Sinn Féin leaders on 26 Nov. 1920, he was succeeded by Joseph (Joe) MacDonagh. A much-imprisoned man, he spent four spells in prison between May 1916 and his final release in July 1921. He supported the Treaty and was, first, minister for labour, and later, minister for labour, industry, commerce and economic affairs in Dáil Éireann, and a member of the Provisional Government from January 1922 until November 1924. McGrath was in sympathy with the officers who mutinied during the course of the scaling down of the Free State army in 1924. The mutiny brought to a head a great deal of discontent which existed at that time in the army. Some officers, mainly former members of Collins' elite 'squad', considered that they were not receiving due recognition in the army, and other officers, when the scaling down of the army began, suspected that the norm being followed as to whether officers were retained or demobilised was their membership or non-membership of the IRB. Largely as a result of the mutiny and the manner in which it was handled (he considered that some of his former IRA comrades were treated unfairly), he retired from active politics in October 1924. Between then and his death he made important contributions to the economic life of the country, being largely responsible for organising the Irish Sweepstakes/Hospitals' Trust, the founding of the Waterford Glass and Donegal Carpet industries, and doing a great deal to improve Irish bloodstock. He died on 26 March 1966.

14 Joseph M. (Joe) MacDonagh was born at Cloughjordan, County Tipperary, on 28 May 1883. He was educated at the local national school and Rockwell College. After leaving school he entered the Revenue Service. Although a brother of Thomas MacDonagh, one of the 1916 leaders, he did not become an active member of Sinn Féin until 1917. He was elected to the executive of Sinn Féin on 25 October 1917. In the general election of November 1918 he was returned for North Tipperary and on 15 January 1920 he was elected as

an alderman in Dublin Corporation, remaining both TD for North Tipperary and alderman of Dublin Corporation until his death. Between the early part of 1919 and the middle of 1920 he spent three terms in jail for his political activities. In 1918, together with William T. Cosgrave, he founded the firm Cosgrave and MacDonagh Ltd (which later, with the withdrawal of Cosgrave, became the firm of MacDonagh & Boland), an insurance brokerage also doing tax consultancy work. MacDonagh voted against acceptance of the terms of the Anglo-Irish Treaty, and after the outbreak of hostilities in June 1922 came under the surveillance of the Free State authorities. He was eventually arrested and imprisoned in November 1922 and he died on 25 December of that same year.

15 In view of the circumstances of the time, the ministry of labour had extraordinary success in the area of settling trade disputes, cf. D. Macardle, *The Irish Republic*, pp. 387–8.

16 It is interesting to note that authorisation for the employment of Mee in the Department of Labour was not given by the ministry of Dáil Éireann until 10 September and even then the authorisation was for his employment for only one month. However, after an exchange of memos between the Departments of Finance and Labour about the middle of October, the ministry at its meeting on 23 October decided to continue Mee's appointment indefinitely, subject to one month's notice (cf. State Paper Office, Dáil Éireann Papers 2/21).

17 It was later known as the Abbey Hotel.

18 Mee's full report, dated 7 October 1920, of his efforts to find employment for ex-policemen is to be found in State Paper Office, Dáil Éireann Papers, 2/161. For a summary of it, cf. p. 282.

19 The following interesting report appeared in *The Freeman's Journal* of 15 March 1921:

Sir Hamar Greenwood gave the following figures on the forces in Ireland as relating to the twelve months ended with last month:

	RIC	Auxiliary
Resignations	2,193	131
Dismissals	226	33
Courtmartial cases	19	15
Courtmartialled findings against the accused	16	8

These figures are particularly significant when compared to those given by Denis Henry in the House of Commons and printed in *The Irish Times* of 25 June 1920, to the effect that from the beginning of January to the end of May 1920 there were 330 resignations and forty dismissals from the RIC. Taking the two sets of figures into account it seems that (keeping in mind the inclusion of March, April and May 1920 in both sets of figures) the rate of resignations-cum-dismissals from the RIC increased more than three times during the second half of 1920 and the early part of 1921 as compared to the rate during the first half of 1920. The figure given by Mee, which presumably includes members of the DMP (see, however, pp. 393–4 n.21) and RIC who resigned or were dismissed between Easter 1916 and the beginning of November 1920, does not seem to be an exaggeration, as, according to the figures provided by Greenwood and Henry, approximately 2,570 members of the RIC resigned or were dismissed between the beginning of January 1920 and the beginning of March 1921. (For a note on how this exodus contributed towards a radical change in the character of the RIC between 1 January 1920 and 1 October 1921, see p. 388 n.7.) Mee probably arrived at his figure as a result of information which was subsequently available concerning the number of claims which were submitted to the 1922 Committee of Inquiry into Resignations and Dismissals from the RIC (cf. pp. 397–8 ns 1 & 2).

20 Besides this newssheet two books were published about this time giving the British version of the Anglo-Irish War. These were: I.O. [C. J. C. Street], *The Administration of Ireland, 1920*, and *Tales of the R.I.C.*

21 Donovan at this time was working in the Court Laundry, Harcourt Street, where he had been taken on due to the good offices of Countess Markievicz. He eventually became manager of the laundry and retired in 1960.

22 The much-wanted Dan Breen, for instance, was known by sight to many members of the DMP, some of whom went to extraordinary lengths to indicate to him their benevolent neutrality in the struggle between Sinn Féin and the IRA (see D. Breen, *My Fight for Irish Freedom*, pp. 81–3).

23 This was a small tobacconist shop, the proprietor of which was Maurice Collins. Collins took part in the 1916 Rising and, as a consequence, was dismissed from his employment. He was well known in Dublin GAA circles and his friends organised a field and flag day for him. From the proceeds he began his business in Parnell Street (information from Eilís bean Uí Chonaill, *née* Ryan). Of Collins' wife, Batt O'Connor, close friend of Michael Collins, wrote: 'Mrs Maurice Collins of Parnell Street, was another woman whom Michael Collins held in very great esteem for her coolness and bravery. Her place was continually raided by night and by day and was therefore one which could not be used as a retreat. But she did great service in other ways and was a most patriotic Irish woman' (see B. O'Connor, *With Michael Collins in the Fight for Irish Independence*, p. 140).

24 For a number of references to this decision of the Dublin Metropolitan Police to disarm, see *American Commission: Evidence on conditions in Ireland*, under Dublin

Metropolitan Police disarm. Most members of the force had become involved only with the greatest reluctance in the conflict between Sinn Féin and the crown forces. This was well known to the authorities. For instance, the morale of the force – in effect, its readiness to take a firm line against Sinn Féin – was discussed by the British cabinet as early as 14 November 1919 (cf. PRO London, CAB 23/37, CP 2556).

25 They were recruited early in 1921 and were fanatically committed to the struggle against the IRA. This commitment in the case of some of them was reinforced by having seen comrades shot in IRA ambushes. There were over thirty of them, at least one having been recruited from each county. They were invariably young, as well as being new, and displayed courage under fire. Their main duty was to meet trains coming into Dublin and to scan and search those travelling on them. They also moved about the city in civilian clothes on the lookout for IRA leaders. They especially frequented thoroughfares such as Camden Street ('the Dardanelles') and the quays, where attacks on military patrols took place almost daily. When the shooting began they sometimes joined in the exchanges. They were attached to Ship Quay barracks and were under the command of Head Constable Davis. After some time a group of them was formed into an assassination squad under the command of Constable Igoe. After the disbandment of the RIC, Igoe, a native of Kilmaine, County Mayo, joined the Palestine police and died in that country. Igoe's group was called the 'Igoe Gang' by the IRA, who were able to trace a number of mysterious killings to them. For a picture of some of the gang see D. Breen, *My Fight for Irish Freedom*, where Igoe and another notorious member of the group, a Scotsman called Fowler, are identified (information from John P. Clarke, a member of the Davis group; James R. W. Goulden. Cf. also L. O'Doherty, 'Dublin Brigade Area', *The Capuchin Annual*, 1970, pp. 390, 392–3, 532).

26 Although remaining aloof from the conflict, few of the Dublin Metropolitan Police threw in their lot with Sinn Féin. Thus David Neligan writes: 'Of all the Dublin uniformed police, only six were working with Collins. I shall name them here: T. Neary from Roscommon; two brothers named Culhane from Limerick; Mannix and O'Sullivan, Kerrymen; and Matt Byrne from Kildare' (*The Spy in the Castle*, p. 122). There were other members in the force who were less than neutral. Batt O'Connor describes how: 'while presiding at a council [Pembroke Urban Council] meeting one evening [in January 1921] word was passed to him that a military officer had received instructions to arrest me. I slipped away quietly ... it was through a DMP sergeant that I escaped arrest on that occasion. Another time this same sergeant, a friendly Kerryman named O'Hanlon, saved my house from a midnight raid. The military called to his station to get a policeman to guide them to my house and he persuaded them that they were misinformed. I was a busy building contractor, he said, with no

time for anything outside my business' (B. O'Connor, *With Michael Collins in the Fight for Irish Independence*, pp. 122–3). See also *Capuchin Annual* 1969, p. 384.

12: I RETURN TO KERRY: 24–30 OCTOBER 1920

1   Loughlin Dolan, who was a native of County Offaly (then King's County), joined the RIC in 1918. He served in Listowel from early 1919 to November 1920, when he was transferred to Cavan town, where he resigned from the force (information from Tom Grennan).

2   Michael Kelly was born at Ballycastle, County Mayo, on 4 July 1893. He joined the RIC in October 1914 and served at Glenbeigh (1915–17) and Lisselton (1917–19) before being appointed to Listowel in January 1919. In 1917 Kelly was selected to attend a course at the depot, conducted by Scotland Yard personnel, on detective work in general and the surveillance of people travelling on trains in particular.

3   John P. McNamara was born at Crusheen, County Clare, on 8 May 1899. He joined the RIC on 1 November 1918 and was appointed to Listowel on 1 June 1919. He died on 28 January 1969.

4   John Sinnott was born at Kilmacow, County Kilkenny, in 1899. He joined the RIC on 4 June 1918. From 1919 to 1920 he served at Newtownsandes and later at Listowel. He resigned from the force while at Listowel. (He himself stated that he resigned in July, whereas Kelly and McNamara implied that it was in November, cf. Appendix 8.) Sinnott later joined the Garda Síochána. He died on 29 March 1967.

5   This is not quite accurate. Byrnes was transferred to Camlough, County Armagh, in August, Downey to the depot on 1 September. Reidy to Ballyduff in August, and Robinson to Gormanston, County Meath, on 22 July. However, it was not until 20 November 1920 that Lillis was transferred to Athlone, County Westmeath, and Patrick O'Neill was not transferred.

There is evidence that O'Neill and, to a lesser extent, Lillis regretted becoming involved in the insubordination of 19 June 1920. In fact, it seems that O'Neill co-operated enthusiastically with the Black and Tans who were sent to pacify the Listowel area. Moreover, on 31 December 1920 he and a Black and Tan beat John Lawlor, a clerical student (his sole crime being that he was the son of David Lawlor, a well-known local supporter of Sinn Féin), so badly with their rifle butts that Lawlor died on the following night (for further details, see J. A. Gaughan, *Listowel and its Vicinity*, pp. 397–8). O'Neill's newly discovered enthusiasm for his job did not save him from being dismissed from the RIC with those others of his comrades who had signed the statement concerning Smyth's address and who were still serving in the force (cf. pp. 152, 374–5 n.24).

6   One of these was from Éamon de Valera, president of Sinn Féin. It was a telegram which read: 'Gallant Listowel. All Ireland at your back' (information from Michael Kelly).

7   In this instance they probably owed their lives to the goodwill of Head Constable Patrick A. Plover and Sergeant Barnes who was in charge of their small party. On their arrival at Union Quay barracks, Plover, who had been appointed head constable there after the Listowel police mutiny, immediately cautioned them not to disclose who they were as many of those stationed at Union Quay greatly resented what had occurred at Listowel police barracks. In fact, he told them that the Black and Tans stationed in the barracks had, on one occasion, to be restrained from heading for Listowel and setting fire to the police barracks there. After news of the shooting of Divisional Commissioner Smyth had circulated, the temper of most of those in the barracks became particularly ugly. Consequently Plover placed Kelly and McNamara in his office, which he instructed them to lock from the inside and open to no one but himself. In the meantime Sergeant Barnes spent much of the night quietly searching the city for his two constables and did not dare disclose his anxiety to anyone, as, in the event of their identity being known, they would have been in serious danger (information taken from a letter to Jeremiah Mee from John P. McNamara, dated 12 January 1952). As Michael Kelly recollects this incident, it was he alone who was being searched for in Cork city that night by Sergeant Barnes. Moreover, he spent the night in Union Quay police barracks not in the office of Head Constable Plover, but in the room of a friend and former classmate of his at the depot named Constable Michael Fallon.
       Not long afterwards Barnes, it seems, was largely responsible for having Constable Edward Johnston, who was stationed at Tralee, court-martialled for shooting Kerry farmer Francis (Frank) Hoffman at Farmers' Bridge on 10 December 1920 (information from Michael Kelly, cf. also *Weekly Freeman*, 8 January, 12 February 1921).

8   According to Michael Kelly, Mee conveyed this decision to Kelly and McNamara personally, travelling south and meeting them by arrangement at Listowel railway station.

9   Kelly and McNamara fed the confidential information which they received from Constable John Sinnott, who had replaced Hughes as clerk to the district inspector, to Patrick (Paddy) Breen of Church Street and James (Jim) Crowley, VS, both of whom, with the help of railway employees and friendly commercial travellers, ensured that it was forwarded to ex-Constable Mee and ultimately to Michael Collins (information taken from affidavit of Kelly and McNamara). According to Michael Kelly all information was passed by himself and McNamara to Jim Joe Buckley (see pp. 268, 397 n.3) who ensured that it got to Breen and Crowley.

10 In fact Kelly and McNamara were brought before a disciplinary court on 15 October and were dismissed from the RIC, their dismissal becoming effective on 1 November.

11 Patrick (Paddy) Landers was a prominent member of the IRA from 1916 onwards. For this and more on Paddy Landers, see J. A. Gaughan, *Listowel and its Vicinity*, under Landers, Patrick.

12 In fact there was no such connection.

13 The porter was Patrick (Paddy) Loughnane of Church Street, who was, in fact, a member of the Listowel company of the IRA (information from Dr Seamus Wilmot).

14 Patrick (Paddy) Breen was a native of Killarney. He was an avid nationalist as were his brother, Canon John Breen, president of St Michael's College, Listowel, and his sister, Miss Katherine (Kate) Breen, who kept house for Canon Breen. For more, see J. A. Gaughan, *Listowel and its Vicinity*, under Breen. For more on Kate Breen, see *Kerry's Fighting Story* (Tralee 1947), p. 195, and L. Conlon, *Cumann na mBan and the Women of Ireland 1913–1925*.

15 Later Mrs Edward Boursin.

16 From 1918 on James Crowley, VS, was an active member of Sinn Féin in Listowel. For more on him, see J. A. Gaughan, *Listowel and its Vicinity*, under Crowley, James.

17 In fact he was forced to retire and was given the pension to which he was entitled. This pension, due to the manner in which it was determined, was relatively small, and this gave rise to the generally held view that he was granted only a sergeant's pension by the British authorities. (For a note on how the resigned and dismissed members of the RIC and DMP (1916–21) fared financially, see Appendix 11.) Having left the force Flanagan went to Dublin and stayed for some time at the Sligo Hotel (information from Michael Kelly). See also p. 375 n.25.

18 For some idea of the material hardship suffered by those who resigned or were dismissed during this period, see Appendix 9b.

19 In fact £118,234 was collected between 18 June 1920 and 30 April 1921 for dockers and railwaymen who were dismissed or out of work because, in the case of the dockers, they would not handle military equipment or stores, and, in the case of the railwaymen, they refused to work on trains being used by the crown forces (for this and the history of the fund, see *Irish Labour Party and Trade Union Congress, Annual Report*, 1920, and 1921). Cf. also p. 353 n.5.

20 In August Constable Thomas R. Reidy had been transferred to Ballyduff, where, on 31 October, he was wounded when ambushed on patrol (for more on the ambush, see J. A. Gaughan, *Listowel and its Vicinity*, p. 378). Another factor which made it difficult for members of the RIC to resign was that a significant number of them came from police families, their fathers and very often their

grandfathers having served in the force. About 15 per cent of the force came from police families. This was officially encouraged. Thus sons of members of the RIC – given the usual qualifications – were eligible for entry to the depot at eighteen, whereas all others could enter only at nineteen, and sons of officers of the force could become cadets at nineteen, whereas the age for others was twenty-one (information from James R. W. Goulden).

Just as the fact that a constable's father served in the force militated against his resigning, so the fact that a constable's brother did, in fact, resign generally influenced his brother or brothers in the force to do likewise. There are, at least, two instances of three brothers resigning from the force. Thus, when Thomas Doherty (who was attached to Listowel police district), of Carrowmacbrine, Rathlee, County Sligo, resigned soon after the Listowel police mutiny, his brothers, Bartly and Patrick, who were serving at Ballina, County Mayo, and Clara, County Offaly, respectively, did likewise within ten days (information from James Doherty, son of Thomas Doherty; also PRO London, Home Office Papers, 184/33, under Doherty, Bartly). And, although their father served in the RIC, Andrew and William Colgan, of Rahan, Tullamore, County Offaly, and a brother of theirs resigned from the force about the middle of 1920 (State Paper Office, Dáil Éireann Papers, 2/258).

21 This was the annual 'big fair' of 25 October.

22 Dorothy Macardle on pp. 407–8 of *The Irish Republic* gives the following description of this commission: 'On the initiative of Dr W. J. Maloney and with the help of Frank P. Walsh and with President de Valera's approval, a committee was formed for the purpose of investigating conditions in Ireland. It was proposed to hold public hearings in Washington. Oswald Garrison Villard, editor of the *Nation*, supported the project in his paper and a committee composed of a hundred and fifty eminent American citizens was formed. By 15 September, Dr McCartan recalls, "the committee included Cardinal Gibbons, Archbishop Keane and four Catholic bishops; seven Protestant Episcopal bishops; four Methodist bishops; the governors of five States; eleven United States senators; thirteen congressmen; the mayors of five large cities; and college presidents, professors, editors and leaders of labour and industry, representative of thirty-six States, and numbering over one hundred in all" [P. MacCartan, *With de Valera in America*, p. 211].

'From this committee there was selected by ballot a list of names of members who were to act as the Court of a Commission of Inquiry into Conditions in Ireland. Five members were to constitute the court and vacancies which occurred in the court were to be filled, in rotation, from a list. The court had power to request the attendances of witnesses from Ireland representing English and Irish opinion, to pay their expenses and take their evidence at public sessions in Washington.

'As news came to America of murders, burnings and other outrages in Ireland this committee cabled its invitation to witnesses from the scene. Among those invited to attend were Lord French and Hamar Greenwood, but no British witness accepted. The committee secured promises from the British authorities that passports would not be refused to persons coming from Ireland to testify and that reprisals would not be taken against them.'

For more on the commission, see its two reports: *The American Commission on conditions in Ireland: Interim Report* and *American Commission: Evidence on conditions in Ireland comprising the completed testimony, affidavits and exhibitions presented before the Commission.*

23 In fact they were charged with assaulting Head Constable Gallagher (who had replaced Plover) and damaging police property (information from Michael Kelly).

24 This report which appeared in *The Freeman's Journal* of 4 March 1921 was not entirely accurate. At any rate the following letter was published in *The Freeman's Journal* of 10 March 1921:

> Sir,
>
> In the issue of *The Freeman's Journal* of Friday, March 4, a paragraph occurs in which, if it is not clearly stated, it is certainly implied that a document containing the names of fourteen members of the RIC, who protested against a speech – alleged to have been made in a barracks at Listowel – was found in the presbytery on the occasion of a search made there in January. I beg to say that no such document was found in this house. I had no document of the kind in my possession – neither had the curates of the parish.
>
> *Denis O'Connor, P.P.,*
> *The Presbytery, Listowel.*
> *March 7, 1921.*

According to Tom Grennan the document, which had been sent to IRA headquarters, was given to the British authorities by a secret agent. However, the rest of the report was, except for a detail, factual. The six men referred to in it were Constables Francis J. Byrnes, Joseph Downey, Patrick O'Neill, Thomas R. Reidy and Andrew Robinson and Sgt Michael Lillis. General Tudor was present at this confrontation which occurred at the end of January 1921.

Reidy was summoned from hospital to be dismissed (*The Freeman's Journal*, 4 March 1921).

Lillis had been promoted sergeant on 1 October 1920 and put back into uniform. For much of his time at Listowel, he was a plain-clothes detective, and, it was generally agreed, quite an efficient one. He was transferred to

Athlone on 20 November 1920 (PRO London, Home Office Papers, 184/33, under Lillis, Michael).

When the new Irish police force was being recruited Lillis joined up and found himself with the first batch of Civic Guards at the Royal Dublin Society grounds, Ballsbridge, Dublin, in early April 1922. However, after a week he was recognised by some recruits from North Kerry. They objected to his membership of the new police force because of his record of dedicated service in the RIC. After a tense confrontation on this issue between some members of the new force and their officers, and even a minor riot, Lillis and a number of other ex-RIC men resigned from the Guards (eyewitness account from John Cotter, also information from Gerald Stack). Lillis later became a customs official. However, Lillis' former colleague, Andrew Robinson, had no such difficulty in joining the Garda Síochána.

25 For a note on the last days spent by Kelly and McNamara in Listowel, see Appendix 8. Kelly and McNamara arrived in Dublin on 4 November. For some weeks they resided at the Sligo Hotel (this premises, then known simply as the Sligo, was at 6 Arran Quay), which at that time was popular with policemen. During this time they were interviewed on two occasions by, seemingly, the same persons as had interrogated Mee and Donovan on 15 July (see pp. 115–16). Kelly recalls Thomas Johnson, William O'Brien, Erskine Childers and Michael Collins as being present at these meetings. At the second meeting Kelly and McNamara agreed to go to the US and give evidence to the American Commission of Inquiry into conditions in Ireland, ex-District Inspector Thomas Flanagan, who was also staying at the Sligo Hotel at this time, enabling them to obtain passports. In early December Kelly and McNamara received a message from Michael Collins to transfer from the Sligo Hotel to O'Brien's Hotel, 80 Parnell Street, and to be ready to leave Dublin at twenty-four hours notice. However, it was not until 3 January 1921 that they managed to sail to Liverpool, whence on 8 January they set out on board the *Megantic* for New York, where they arrived on 21 January (information from Michael Kelly).

26 Thomas A. Broderick, a native of Abbeyfeale, County Limerick, was married to Elizabeth Galvin, of William Street, Listowel. After a number of years in the US he amassed a great personal fortune, mainly by his dealings on the stock exchange. Eventually he became a millionaire, and the proprietor of the Central and Emmet hotels, both of which were situated on West 38th Street, New York. In the summer of 1920 he visited Listowel with his wife and two daughters. One night, while drinking in Buckley's public house in the Square, he became involved in an angry argument with two Black and Tans, named Raymond and Small. Kelly and McNamara, who overheard the argument and knew the characters of Raymond and Small, disarmed the latter, as they waited in a darkened doorway to kill Broderick after the pub closed. Broderick later learned how indebted he

was to Kelly and McNamara, and so when they travelled to the US he was most generous to them. Broderick was ruined by the collapse of the stock exchange and ended up working as a barman in the Emmet Hotel, of which, before the Wall Street crash, he had been proprietor. 'Broken-hearted, he died soon afterwards' (affidavit of Kelly and McNamara, and information from Michael Kelly).

27 Affidavit of Kelly and McNamara, and information from Michael Kelly.

28 Information taken from a letter from John P. McNamara to Jeremiah Mee, dated 12 January 1952. Also information from Michael Kelly.

29 *New Haven Sunday Register*, 13 February 1921. From 1 February on they had been addressing meetings in the New Haven area. (Information taken from a letter from John P. McNamara to Jeremiah Mee, dated 12 January 1952. Also information from Michael Kelly.)

30 American Association for the Recognition of the Irish Republic. This organisation was founded by de Valera and others on 16 November 1920 and within a year had a membership of some 800,000 (D. Macardle, *The Irish Republic*, pp. 410–11, 445). In effect, it replaced a similar type of organisation, known as the Friends of Irish Freedom. For this and the background to the establishment of the AARIR, see D. Lynch, *The I.R.B. and the 1916 Insurrection*, pp. 203–14.

31 This is probably what is referred to in the *Irish Bulletin* of 8 September 1920 which has the item: 'August 27th: British troops shot up Listowel, Co. Kerry'.

32 Tim Stack, who soon afterwards emigrated to the US, had no connection with the IRA (information from Gerald Stack).

33 *The American Commission on conditions in Ireland: Interim Report*, pp. 131–51. For another account of the Lixnaw rampage, see H. Martin, *Ireland in Insurrection*, pp. 123–5. It was Seán Houlihan who was killed at Ballyduff. For more, see J. A. Gaughan, *Listowel and its Vicinity*, pp. 376–8.

34 *American Commission: Evidence on conditions in Ireland*, p. 1058. The italics are mine. It could be added that not only the crown forces by their atrocities, but also the British government which, under the terms of the 'Restoration of Order in Ireland Act' promulgated on 5 August 1920, imposed martial law on practically the whole of the southern half of Ireland and on 3 September 1920 abolished coroner's inquests and replaced them by secret military courts of inquiry (see D. Macardle, *The Irish Republic*, p. 381), proved Colonel Smyth's address to have been a remarkably accurate outline of impending British activities in Ireland.

13: MY TRAVELS IN BRITAIN: 23 NOVEMBER–20 DECEMBER 1920

1 For a comprehensive treatment of 'Bloody Sunday', see the book of the same title by J. Gleeson which was published in London in 1962.

2   Flemings Hotel was frequently raided as the proprietor, Seán O'Mahony, took part in the Rising and was a well-known Sinn Féin sympathiser.

3   Seán McGrath was born, of Tipperary parents, at Keenagh, near Ballymahon, County Longford, on 27 August 1882. In 1908 he took up a post as a clerk with the British Railway Company in London. He joined the Gaelic League in the same year. Later he became a member of the IRB and a close friend and associate of Michael Collins. At the end of 1913 he joined the Volunteers. As he stated in a letter published in the *Irish Press* on 11 July 1936 that from January 1916 until the Rising he 'was responsible on behalf of the London Volunteers for the purchase of arms and equipment and their transfer to Dublin'. He was one of the London Corps of the Volunteers who fought in the GPO during Easter week 1916. For his part in the Rising he was interned at Frongoch. He was released at the end of 1916. From almost the time of his release he was again involved in procuring and transporting arms to Ireland. In March 1918 he was imprisoned for a year at Pentonville for these activities. In July 1919 he became the general secretary of the Irish Self-Determination League of Great Britain and retained this post until the League ceased its existence in 1924. Throughout the Anglo-Irish War period he worked closely with Art O'Brien, the official spokesman in Britain for Sinn Féin. He was sorely disappointed with the terms of the Anglo-Irish Treaty but remained aloof from the subsequent Civil War. In March 1923 he and about a hundred other Irishmen and women residing in Britain were deported to Ireland. When the House of Lords declared the deportation to have been illegal he returned to Britain and, with Art O'Brien and other prominent members of the Irish Self-Determination League, was charged with conspiracy. He was convicted and was sentenced to two years imprisonment, but after a year he was released. Subsequently he identified himself with his close friend and colleague, Art O'Brien, then the centre of a great deal of controversy. He remained an active supporter of Irish and Republican causes in Britain to the end of his life. In July 1947 he and a number of others established a committee in order to pay tribute to Reginald (Reggie) Dunne and Joseph (Joe) O'Sullivan, two members of the London Battalion of the IRA, who were executed on 10 August 1922 for the assassination of Field-Marshal Sir Henry Wilson. It was typical of him that his last illness began at a meeting of the Anti-Partition of Ireland League executive in Manchester. He left the meeting, took the midnight train to London and on arrival was taken to hospital, where, a short time later, he died on 22 July 1950. (There are some useful references to the deportation episode and the subsequent trial for conspiracy in *The Freeman's Journal* of 1 January 1924.)

4   This organisation was founded in March 1919. Branches were established all over England, Wales and Scotland, there being over 300 by the summer of 1921. Patrick J. Kelly was its president, Art O'Brien was a vice-president and Seán McGrath its general secretary. Members raised funds for the relief of distress

in Ireland. The organisation established classes in the Irish language and also fostered Irish music and pastimes. Large and frequent meetings were held to demand self-determination for Ireland and members of the organisation distributed Sinn Féin literature.

5   Mee, in his papers, speculates that the message delivered by him to Seán McGrath was a countermand of a previous directive which had been issued by IRA headquarters to its units in Britain to destroy factories and warehouses as a reprisal against the British government's having sanctioned the burning and destruction of property in Ireland by its forces. See, however, footnote 17. McGrath, a close friend and fellow member of the IRB, was one of Collins' main links with the IRA in Britain. Collins' other main link was Samuel (Sam) Maguire. For instance, it seems it was through Maguire that the pre-Anglo-Irish Treaty decision by IRA headquarters staff to have Field-Marshal Sir Henry Wilson assassinated (for his indirect responsibility for the pogroms in Ulster) was conveyed by Collins to Reginald (Reggie) Dunne, OC, London Battalion, IRA (cf. commemorative brochure, entitled 'Remembrance' published by the London-based 'Dunne and O'Sullivan Memorial Committee' in March 1949; *Sunday Press*, 27 September, 4, 11,18 October 1953, and *The Irish Times*, 20 May 1961; L. O'Doherty, 'Important participators with the Leaders', *The Capuchin Annual*, 1976, pp. 114–15).

6   In fact just over 300 delegates attended on behalf of 234 branches in England and Wales. However, on the second day of the convention some 2,700 people were present at what was termed a demonstration (*Manchester Guardian*, 29 November 1920).

7   Collins travelled to England in December 1918 as a member of a small delegation, which attempted to meet President Wilson, then in London. He also crossed to England in January and February 1919 to effect the escape of de Valera and others from Lincoln jail. Collins was in the Manchester area before – in September – and after – on 2, 3 November and 25 October 1919, when, due largely to his organisational skill, Piaras Béaslaí, Austin Stack and four others made a successful escape-bid from Strangeways jail. His next trip to England seems to have been in October 1921 as a member of the Irish delegation to the Treaty negotiations in London.

8   This, it seems, was somewhere in Kentish Town. At any rate Kentish Town was given as the address for Seán McGrath, general secretary, in the attractive programme which was prepared for the First National Convention of the Irish Self-Determination League of Great Britain to be held at Manchester on 27–28 November 1920.

9   Arthur P. O'Brien (Art Ó Briain) was born in London on 25 September 1872. He was educated at St Charles College, London, and later studied civil

engineering, which profession he followed until 1919, when he was appointed envoy to Britain by Dáil Éireann. A member of the Gaelic League from 1899, he was president of the League in London from 1914 to 1935. He joined the Volunteer movement at the end of 1913. From 1916 to 1923 he was president of the Sinn Féin Council of Great Britain. In March 1919 he helped found the Irish Self-Determination League of Great Britain, and was elected a vice-president of that organisation – in 1922 he became its president, a post he held until 1924. He was Sinn Féin's spokesman in Britain during the Anglo-Irish War. He opposed acceptance of the Treaty and, with some difficulty, was dismissed from his post as envoy of Dáil Éireann to Britain by the Free State government in June 1922. However, he continued as the representative of the Irish Republic in Britain in the anti-Treaty interest. In March 1923 he and 109 other Irishmen and women, residing in Britain, were deported to Ireland. When the House of Lords declared the deportation to have been illegal, he returned to Britain and, with Seán McGrath and others, was charged with conspiracy. He was convicted and was sentenced to two years imprisonment, but after a year he was released from jail by the then Labour government. On his release in July 1924 O'Brien became a centre of great controversy in the Republican movement in Britain. There was much resentment on the part of some members of the movement at certain evidence which O'Brien gave at his trial and also at the great expenditure of Republican funds which the trial involved. An attempt was made to replace him as head of the Republican movement in Britain. However, O'Brien refused to cede his position and he became for a number of years the cause of bitter dissension in the movement in Britain. Between 1924 and 1935 he was managing editor of the Music Trades Review. On 16 July 1935 he was appointed Irish minister plenipotentiary to France and Belgium. He retired from the post on 8 October 1938. He settled in Ireland in 1939, and became a director and deputy chairman of Mineraí Teoranta. He died on 12 August 1949.

10 Liam McMahon, a member of the IRB, was born at Kildimo, County Limerick, on 24 May 1878. He was one of those who organised the escape of de Valera, Seán McGarry and Seán Milroy from Lincoln jail on 3 February 1919. Later in that year, with others, he effected the escape of Piaras Béaslaí, Austin Stack and four others from Strangeways jail. McMahon, with a number of others, founded the Anti-Partition of Ireland League in 1938. He died on 22 April 1955.

11 Notices of the change of venue of the convention were inserted in the evening newspapers of 27 November (*Manchester Guardian*, 29 November 1920).

12 Cf. p. 377–8 n.4.

13 Griffith and a number of other prominent Sinn Féin leaders were arrested in Dublin on 26 November.

14 Seán Milroy was born at Maryport in Cumberland, England, in 1877. A

journalist, he was an early supporter and close friend of Arthur Griffith. For his Sinn Féin activities he was interned in Mountjoy jail from June to August 1915. After his release he resumed his work on behalf of Sinn Féin, being in considerable demand as a lecturer – for instance, at the end of November he delivered a lecture on Wolfe Tone to the Volunteers at Tralee, County Kerry. He took part in the Rising of 1916 and was subsequently imprisoned at Reading jail. On 19 April 1917, at a general conference attended by representatives of almost every nationalist organisation, he was elected to a National Council embodying the general aims of all these organisations. He was elected to the executive of the Irish Volunteers on 19 November 1917. On 4 April 1918 he made an unsuccessful attempt, on behalf of Sinn Féin, to win a parliamentary seat in a by-election in East Tyrone. He was director of elections for Sinn Féin in the general election of December 1918. On 2 November he was arrested and later imprisoned, but, with Éamon de Valera and Seán McGarry, he escaped from Lincoln jail on 3 February 1919. Thereafter he was active in organising the Irish Self-Determination League in Britain. He was elected to Dáil Éireann for Cavan on 16 August 1921 and he voted for acceptance of the Treaty on 7 January 1922. In the meantime, on 24 May 1921, he was elected to the northern parliament for Fermanagh-Tyrone, and subsequently, as secretary of the sub-commission on Ulster which was established by the Dáil, he became for a time the official spokesman for Sinn Féin on the partition issue. In 1922 he published a propagandist pamphlet, entitled *The Case of Ulster*, in which he refuted four arguments for the partition of Ireland. He retained his Dáil Éireann seat in the general election of 1923, but in October 1924, after the army mutiny, he resigned his seat. At this time he broke with the Cumann na nGaedheal party, having become dissatisfied with its policies, particularly its attitude to the partition problem, and in March 1925 he made an unsuccessful attempt to be returned to the Dáil as an independent Republican. He became reconciled with the Cumann na nGaedheal party in 1928 and from that year until 1936 he served in the senate in that party's interest. He was a member of Dublin Corporation for many years, being first elected in 1918. He died on 30 November 1946.

15 The British cabinet and even the British Labour Party were denounced in no less eloquent terms by the Liverpool councillor, Patrick J. Kelly, president of the Irish Self-Determination League, who, it seems, delivered the main address. The convention proceedings of the first day, that is, Saturday, were held 'behind closed doors', but a full report of them, which was officially supplied, was published in *The Manchester Guardian* of 29 November 1920.

16 For more on the 'Manchester Martyrs' see P. Rose, *The Manchester Martyrs*.

17 In fact it was an innocent bystander who was shot and the incident occurred

about midnight on 27–28 November. The shooting coincided with the burning by units of the IRA of a number of warehouses in Liverpool and nearby Bootle, the action being taken as a reprisal against the destruction of property in Ireland by members of the crown forces. For more on the large-scale arson at the dock areas of Liverpool and Bootle on 27–28 November, the police version of the killing of William J. Ward at Liverpool on that same night and the subsequent charging of Matthew Fowler of Dublin with the crime, see *The Manchester Guardian*, 29, 30 November, 1 December 1920.

18 He was probably one of those who were later detained under the Defence of the Realm Act and eventually convicted of being involved in the arson at Liverpool on the night of 27–28 November (cf. *The Manchester Guardian*, 30 November 1920).

14: DRUMKEERAN, DROMAHAIR: 24 DECEMBER 1920–JANUARY 1921

1 There are a number of accounts of the systematic destruction of Cork city by the crown forces, see, for instance, F. O'Donoghue, 'The sacking of Cork city by the British, December 11/12, 1920', *Rebel Cork's Fighting Story*, pp. 117–26; A. O'Callaghan, *Cork's St Patrick's Street: a history*; B. O'Shea and G. White, *The Burning of Cork*.

2 The *Irish Bulletin* was the underground newspaper of the Sinn Féin publicity department. It was edited by Robert Brennan, Frank Gallagher and Erskine Childers.

3 After the shooting of District Inspector James J. Brady in an ambush at Chaffpool, near Tubbercurry, on 23 September 1920, some members of the crown forces terrorised the inhabitants of the town, and looted and set fire to a number of business premises. When District Inspector John Russell arrived in the town, he prevented further excesses (cf. *Sligo Champion*, 9 October 1920). Russell was promoted district inspector 3rd class from head constable on 21 September 1917, district inspector 2nd class on 23 March 1918, and district inspector 1st class on 1 March 1921 (information from James R. W. Goulden).

4 For a fully documented account of these incidents, see *American Commission: Evidence on conditions in Ireland*, comprising the completed testimony, affidavits and exhibitions presented before the commission, pp. 106–12.

5 Eyewitness account from Bernard Conway of Cliffony. Conway, who joined the RIC in February 1913 and served at Cookstown, Broughderg, Coagh and Dungannon before resigning in August 1920, deserved the ire of the crown forces. Besides being involved in the incident at Cookstown police barracks on 17 June 1920 (cf. Appendix 4), he persuaded his friend and former comrade, Constable Hugh O'Donnell, to facilitate the capture of the police barracks at Tempo, County Fermanagh, by an IRA unit on 25 October 1920 (information from Bernard Conway).

It is interesting to note that Conway had received an award for dedication to duty in connection with the 1916 Rising (see *Sinn Féin Rebellion Handbook, Easter 1916*, p. 258).

15: BELFAST BOYCOTT: JANUARY–MARCH 1921

1   Throughout 1921 Jeremiah Mee, when in Dublin, stayed at a lodging-house run by Elizabeth (Liz) Walsh at 157 North Circular Road (the house, called An Grianan, is at the junction of North Circular Road and Ellesmere Avenue), and went under the alias of Mr Cox (information from Michael McCarthy).

2   See Appendix 12.

3   Cf. D. Macardle, *The Irish Republic*, pp. 356–7, 384–6.

4   Michael Staines was born at Newport, County Mayo, on 1 May 1885. He was educated at the local national school. In 1902 he settled in Dublin. He was a member of the Volunteers from 1913, took part in the Rising of 1916, during which he was quartermaster-general of the Volunteers, and was subsequently interned at Frongoch in Wales. On being released he resumed his activities on behalf of Sinn Féin. In the general election of 1918 he was elected Sinn Féin member for St Michan's Division, Dublin. On 14 September 1920 he was placed in charge of the Belfast Boycott. However, six weeks later he was arrested and imprisoned, not being released until some days before the Anglo-Irish Truce on 11 July 1921. He was a member of the Second Dáil of 1921 and he voted for acceptance of the Treaty on 7 January 1922. On 10 January 1922 he was re-appointed director of the Belfast Boycott, the appointment being announced in the Dáil on 28 February, but the office was abolished soon afterwards. In February 1922 Staines, who had been prominently associated with the Republican police in 1920–21, became the first commissioner of the Garda Síochána, a post he held until he was replaced in August by General Eoin O'Duffy. Staines was an alderman of Dublin Corporation from 1919 to 1925, a member of the Supreme Council of the IRB in 1921–2, and a member of the Irish Senate from 1920 to 1936. He died on 25 October 1955.

5   Besides Mee there was at least one other ex-RIC constable in this group. He was Patrick MacCormack (born 1896, joined RIC on 16 July 1916, died 5 February 1941) who resigned on 10 August 1920, while serving in Loughrea, County Galway. He was later general secretary of the Organisation of Resigned and Dismissed members of the RIC and DMP (1916–21). Cf. p. 226. MacCormack and Mee, it seems, were by far the most effective organisers of the boycott (information from Mrs Margaret McEntee).

6   These were arranged by Joe MacDonagh, TD, the then acting-director of the Belfast Boycott. Others who were prominently associated with the implementation of the boycott were: Mary (May) Brady (later Mrs Henry F. MacAuley), who was

active in Belfast, and Miss Frances Brady (later Mrs Andrew Cooney), Margaret Browne (later Mrs Seán McEntee), Jane Kissane and Eileen Davitt, who were attached to the central office in Dublin (information from Mrs Frances Cooney).

7 One of these was, almost certainly, Lily O'Brennan who, with four female assistants, organised the boycott in the greater Dublin area (information taken from statement by Aine bean Éamoinn Ceannt). Another was probably a Miss Doyle who subsequently was in charge of the boycott in the area which had Cork city as its centre (cf. State Paper Office, Dáil Éireann Papers, 2/509).

8 This is not listed either at Middle Abbey Street, or Lower Abbey Street, in *Thom's Directory* for 1921. There is evidence that here and elsewhere this should read Gael Co-Operative Society, 42 Middle Abbey Street. This is corroborated as No. 42 is listed as vacant in *Thom's Directory* for 1921.

9 In the light of the lack of official information on the IRB, it seems that members of that organisation became adept at avoiding these 'spotters'. Diarmuid Lynch, head centre for Munster in 1915, recalled that at that time he never entered or departed from a town by train, but always ended or began his journey on a bicycle (D. Lynch, *The I.R.B. and the 1916 Insurrection*, p. 26).

10 Thomas Halpin and John Moran were taken from their homes and shot by members of the crown forces during the early hours of 9 February 1921. For a detailed account of this incident, see *The Freeman's Journal*, 10 February 1921. Cf. also *The Freeman's Journal*, 17 March 1921. The funerals of the dead men took place on 11 February 1921.

11 For some interesting references to Monahan, see *Weekly Freeman*, 5 May, 18 August 1923.

12 This building, which has not been used as a hotel since 1927, is in Margaret Street. Mee registered in the White Cross Hotel on 16 February as W. Walsh, Lr Abbey Street, Dublin (cf. the hotel register, which is in the possession of George Murphy). As Lower Abbey Street extended from No. 1–39 and Middle Abbey Street from No. 40 upwards, it is understandable why Mee erroneously described No. 42 as being in Lower Abbey Street.

13 The Queen's Hotel (Grew's Hotel) stood at the intersection of High Street and Thomas Street. The hotel was bought by Liptons in 1950 and, after some reconstruction, run as a large grocery-retail outlet until 1973.

14 This surname almost certainly was only an alias.

15 For a detailed account of this incident, which occurred on 17 March 1921, see *The Freeman's Journal*, 18 March 1921.

16: BELFAST BOYCOTT: MARCH 1921–JANUARY 1922

1 Although not mentioned by Mee in his memoirs, one of his first acts in his new

job, it seems, was to report unfavourably on the prosecution of the boycott in County Fermanagh. At any rate reports at the end of March and the beginning of April by Mee, under the alias W. Walsh, in which he was, by implication, critical of the performance of boycott committees in the county, and in which he sought, in effect, authorisation from 'Volunteer headquarters' to direct OCs of local units of the IRA to become involved in the more efficient organisation of the boycott, led to an exchange of letters between the Dáil Éireann Departments of Labour and Defence.

It is interesting to note that at this time Mee gave his covering address as: Miss Brittain, General Draper, Main Street, Donegal (cf. State Paper Office, Dáil Éireann Papers, 2/110).

2   There were numerous instances at this time when IRA Volunteers were saved from capture and death by the action of members of the RIC. Typical of such instances was one which occurred in February 1921 at Ballyowen, Dualla, near Cashel, County Tipperary. Volunteer Thomas (Tom) Nagle of Cashel was surrounded by a joint military-police patrol under the command of a notorious officer named Captain Lichfield. Nagle gave his name and address as 'Paddy Ryan, Ballinree, Boherlahan'. Constable Denis McCarthy, RIC, Cashel, who was guide for the patrol and who knew Nagle well, and the extent of his involvement in the IRA, corroborated the false statement and secured the suspect's freedom (see *Tipperary Star*, 1 March 1975; for some other instances, see *ibid.*, 29 March 1975).

Major Florence O'Donoghue testified to the valuable help in this regard which he, intelligence officer, Cork Brigade No. 1, IRA, received during the winter of 1920–1 from Kerry-born Sergeant William Costelloe, RIC, who was then a clerk in the county inspector's office at Union Quay police barracks, Cork (it was Michael Collins who put O'Donoghue in touch with Costelloe; information taken from the papers of Major Florence O'Donoghue). Another Kerryman, Sergeant Matt McCarthy, cousin of Fionán Lynch, TD, while in Belfast gave valuable assistance to Collins. He later joined the Garda Síochána and rose to the rank of chief superintendent.

Apart from the collaboration of Éamon Broy, Joseph Cavanagh, James C. McNamara and David Neligan in the Castle (cf. D. Neligan, *The Spy in the Castle*), probably the most valuable help received by the forces of Sinn Féin from members of the police was rendered by Sergeant Jeremiah (Jerry) Maher and Sergeant Patrick (Paddy) Casey. Both were clerks in the county inspector's office in Naas, County Kildare, and between October 1919 and the Truce in July 1921 Sergeant Maher and, after he retired in February 1921, Sergeant Casey, supplied Michael Collins with each new police code within a relatively short time of its reaching the county inspector's desk. A fascinating account of this work is given in *An t-Óglach*, Winter 1967, pp. 6–8, by Seán Kavanagh (later governor of Mountjoy jail) who was Collins' contact with the two RIC men. (The article also includes some interesting comments on the various codes used by the police during the Anglo-Irish War.) Sergeant Maher was subsequently a chief superintendent of the Garda Síochána in Naas and Sergeant Casey was a superintendent in Ennis, County Clare. Cf. p. 330 n.7 for a veiled reference to Maher.

3   For an account of this event, see C. D. Milligan, *History of the Siege of Londonderry 1689.*

4   This was a memorial pillar to Reverend George Walker, governor of the city during the siege of 1688–9. It was erected in 1828 and demolished by a unit of the Derry Brigade, Provisional IRA, on 28 August 1973.

5   Fox was a docker, and he was prominent in the Labour and Republican movements in Derry for many years (information from Earnán de Blaghd). He was also chief of the Republican police in Derry (cf. *With the IRA in the Fight for Irish Freedom: 1919 to the Truce*, p. 24).

6   For more on Peadar O'Donnell, see *Dictionary of Irish Biography* (ed. J. McGuire and J. Quinn, Cambridge 2009), under O'Donnell, Peadar.

7   Joseph P. McGinley was born at Breenagh, Letterkenny, County Donegal, on 24 April 1894. He was educated at the local national school and St Eunan's College, Letterkenny. Soon after qualifying in Queen's University, Belfast, he was appointed dispensary doctor in Letterkenny. A member of the Volunteers from 1914, he was active in the Sinn Féin movement in his native Donegal during the Anglo-Irish War. From 1921 to 1922 he was a TD for Donegal, and voted for acceptance of the Treaty on 7 January 1922. Although he did not present himself for election to the Third Dáil (1922), he remained active in politics in the Cumann na nGaedheal, later Fine Gael, interest. In 1949, on behalf of his party, he unsuccessfully contested a by-election in County Donegal. From 1923 to 1960 he was county surgeon for Donegal and he continued as the dispensary doctor in Letterkenny until 1973. McGinley was a director of Champion Publications – publishers of the *Sligo Champion* and *Donegal People's Press* from 1948 until he died on 31 January 1974.

8   Charles A. Flattery was born in Letterkenny, County Donegal, on 22 November 1884. He was educated at the local national school, St Eunan's College, and St Patrick's College, Maynooth. In 1913 he qualified as a solicitor. From about that time he became secretary of the East Donegal Comhairle Ceanntair of Sinn Féin and thereafter was prominently associated with that organisation. In 1918 he was director of elections for Sinn Féin in County Donegal. And in 1919 he became an intelligence officer in the No. 2 Brigade, 1st Northern Division, IRA. However, his main contribution to the struggle for independence was his work in

establishing Sinn Féin clubs and, later, courts throughout County Donegal. From 1923 to 1954 he was district justice for the Sligo-Leitrim district. He died on 17 June 1959.

9 For a kind reference to her, see P. O'Donnell, *The Gates Flew Open*, p. 60.

10 At that time de Valera was a member of the cabinet of Dáil Éireann and president of the Irish Republic. For more on de Valera, see the Earl of Longford and T. P. O'Neill, *Eamon de Valera*.

11 For an interesting account of IRA intelligence activities in the Castle, see D. Neligan, *The Spy in the Castle*.

12 The district inspector in question was Henry J. Walsh who was promoted district inspector (3rd class) on 1 December 1920 (information from James R. W. Goulden). The *Weekly Freeman* of 21 May 1921 described the above incidents as follows: 'District Inspector Walsh, Dungannon, was shot at by three men and seriously wounded on Tuesday night [17 May]. He went out to investigate the burning of two bread-carts, and was returning with the drivers to Dungannon to receive statements when he observed a man pulling out a revolver.

'He attacked the man but fell and received a shot in the hip. He again closed with the man. Three more shots were discharged and the assailants made off.

'Police and a hundred specials scoured the country. St Patrick's church, where devotions were in progress, was surrounded, and the worshippers were searched on leaving. Eight men were arrested.'

13 I have not been able to identify this man. It is very probable that he was neither a Jew nor a traveller but merely using this role as a cover for his real activities.

17: BACK TO NORMAL: FEBRUARY 1922–MAY 1953

1 Jeremiah Mee's memoirs do not go beyond February 1922. The following account of his life from that time until his death has been sketched in from his papers, and also with the assistance of his daughter, Mrs Eileen Mee Doyle.

2 St John Ervine's *Craigavon: Ulsterman* is the official biography of Sir James Craig.

3 They were treated generously, being given three months salary with their notices of dismissal (cf. *Minutes of Proceedings of the First Parliament of the Republic of Ireland. 1919–1921*, pp. 111, 139).

4 For more on the Irish White Cross organisation, see *Report of the Irish White Cross*.

APPENDIX I

1 Drummond's policy on law and order was remarkable for his time on two scores. He centralised the police force in order largely to eliminate the influence of local

landlords and, in Ulster, the dominance of the Orange Order in the sphere of policing. He also attempted to make the police force acceptable to the entire community by encouraging Catholics to join it both as constables and officers. Not least because of his enlightened policy, whereas before 1836 complaints about police misconduct were commonplace, between 1836 and 1847 they were quite rare.

The revenue police, the Belfast police and the Derry police were not absorbed into the Irish Constabulary until 1857, 1865 and 1870 respectively.

2   Within a few years the titles county inspector, sub-inspector and chief constable were changed to provincial inspector, county inspector and sub-inspector respectively. The office of provincial inspector was later discontinued. Then after the 1882 Police Act, which was occasioned by the Limerick police strike (cf. p. 351 n.29), sub-inspectors, constables and sub-constables were described as district-inspectors, sergeants and constables respectively.

3   The vast majority of them, however, were anything but blockhouses in the literal sense of that term. Cf. pp. 37, 43. Originally appearing in the *Morning Post* of 17 November 1920, this quotation is taken from I.O. [C. J. C. Street], *The Administration of Ireland, 1920*, p. 274.

4   This money, as far as the British government was concerned, was well spent. Due to the fact that members of the RIC were entitled to retire on pension after forty years service there was hardly a parish in Ireland wherein an ex-RIC man did not reside. Moreover, RIC pensioners generally retired to their native district where they were readily accepted as part of the community. This, together with their police training and long police experience, made them valuable sources of information for the British authorities. Furthermore, although these were under no legal obligation to act as informers, in practice they were expected to remain useful to their former employers. To cover this aspect of their retirement all RIC pensioners were obliged to present themselves each month to the local district inspector, ostensibly only to receive their pensions (information from James R. W. Goulden).

5   In fact, 'upwards of 650' members of the RIC joined the fighting forces during World War One (PRO London, Treasury Blue Notes, 1922–3, T 165/49, p. 5). Of these some 400 officers and men enlisted in the Irish Guards regiment (cf. *Irish Independent*, 3 September 1918). Some of the finest policemen in the force enlisted. Because of this and their excellent training sixty-three of the rank and file who joined up were commissioned in the field (cf. *Irish Independent*, 5 April 1919).

6   The salaries of all ranks from that of constable up to and including that of district inspector (1st class) were more than doubled, while that of county inspector was raised from £400–£500 to £700–£900 per annum (information from James R. W. Goulden).

7   Between 1 January 1920 and 1 October 1921 the composition of the RIC underwent a radical transformation. In January 1920 the strength of the force was about 9,500 (effective strength of the force on 30 September 1919 was 9,656, see *Thom's Directory* 1920). Between 1 January 1920 and 1 October 1921 some 3,500 members of the force resigned or were dismissed (cf. pp. 367–8 n.19). Also during that period the force suffered about 1,000 casualties (cf. p. 275), most of whom were members of the 'old RIC' who were invalided out of the force. This exodus of about 4,500 members from the force, however, was more than made up by the influx of about 9,000 English recruits during the same period (cf. p. 131). Thus on 1 October 1921 the strength of the force stood at about 14,000 (effective strength of the force on 30 September 1921 was 14,174, see *Thom's Directory* 1922), of which only about 5,000 had been members of the force before 1 January 1920 (cf. p. 283).

8   For an account of the beginnings of the Garda Síochána, the early tensions therein between former members of the IRA and of the RIC, and part of the subsequent history of that force, see C. Brady, *Guardians of the Peace*.

APPENDIX 2

1   He was later archbishop of Tuam, see P. J. Joyce, *John Healy, Archbishop of Tuam*.

2   This was not the first time that there was an RIC presence on the island. Some members of the force were stationed on Inismurray as early as 1836 and between then and 1893, when they finally evacuated the island. Later they returned to it on four occasions (information from Dr Patrick Heraughty).

3   It is in the civil parish of Ahamlish.

4   For more on Inismurray, see W. F. Wakeman, *Survey of the Antiquarian Remains on the Island of Inismurray* and M. Mac Cárthaigh, 'Placenames of Inismurray', *Dinnseanchas*, Meitheamh 1971, pp. 60–72.

APPENDIX 3

1   This rank was abolished on 1 March 1918, when all the then acting sergeants became sergeants. The rank, which was in existence as early as 1859 and whose appellation was changed from that of acting constable to acting sergeant in October 1883, was introduced not only from financial considerations – the acting sergeant did a sergeant's duty for less than a sergeant's pay – but also because it gave the authorities an opportunity to assess over some two to three years whether a man should be promoted sergeant or returned to the ranks (information from James R. W. Goulden).

2   This union, whose aim was to secure for its members the 'right of conference' and 'collective representation' on matters affecting their pay, service and pension, was open to all police, of either sex, below the rank of superintendent of any

'Regular or Auxiliary Constabulary in the United Kingdom'. It was also open to permanent and temporary officers, of either sex, below the rank of deputy governor of the prison service, civic guard, borstal institutes, etc. For the origin and history of this union, see T. A. Critchley, *A History of Police in England and Wales 900–1966*, pp. 184–9.

3   For an interesting reference to Hetherton (Hetherington) and also to James Murray (cf. p. 228), see D. Neligan, *The Spy in the Castle*, p. 54.

4   McGuire and Tarpey had been stationed in County Galway and, between them, in that county had recruited some 300 members into the Police Union.

McGuire was born in 1893 at Rathdowney, County Laois. He joined the RIC on 16 April 1913. Having completed his training at the depot, he served at Ballinasloe and Bookeen, County Galway, being dismissed from the latter station on 28 May 1919. He died on 1 September 1959.

For a comprehensive biographical note on Tarpey, see *An t-oibrí imdhála: the distributive worker*, November 1964, pp. 306–7.

5   Cf. for instance, *Irish Independent*, 3 October, 1, 20 November, 20, 24, 29 December 1917, 18 January, 21, 22, 28 February 1918.

The move within the force to establish a union was opposed by the editor of the *Constabulary Gazette*. This prompted the following letter, almost certainly inspired by McElligott and his associates, in the *Irish Independent* of 28 February 1918:

Dear Sir,
The chief secretary's replies to Messrs. Nugent & Byrne, M.P.s, leave us no longer in doubt. The government will not improve the pay and pensions of the force, or make any concession in allowances to single or married men, and the just demands of a loyal and efficient body of public servants are met with a blank refusal. We realise our position now; the need for 'protection' is urgent. 'Connaught's' letter in the *Constabulary Gazette* [in which he suggested that a 'protection fund' should be set up] expressed the views of the force; all were waiting to see the editor of that journal not only giving it his support, but drawing up a workable scheme on business lines. But, without consulting the men, the editor decided it was 'impracticable'
...

Our organisation is organised for every public interest but our own. Ten thousand men, without votes or influence, without a common fund or central organisation, cannot expect much public support in their fight for a living wage which cannot be got by begging petitions. The press has given us every support, especially the *Irish Independent* in its clear and pointed editorials. If the *Gazette* stands in our way, if it still regards the fund as 'impracticable' then we must cut the 'Gordian knot' and elect a treasurer of our own.

Munster.

6   The opposition within the ranks of the DMP to the enforcement of conscription was articulated by the DMP Catholic Society. The secretary of this society, James Murray, issued a statement on 17 April 1918, the eve of the anti-conscription conference at the Mansion House, to the effect that three-quarters of the members of the DMP would support whatever line of action would be approved by the conference in order to defeat the enforcement of the Conscription Act. For this statement, thousands of copies of which were distributed to members of the DMP and RIC and to the delegates to the Mansion House conference, see p. 228.

7   Following the lead given by the DMP Catholic Society which organised meetings of members of the DMP at which those present were sworn to resist conscription, McElligott had organised similar meetings for the RIC in County Meath. Thus he was in a position to guarantee that most members of the RIC in County Meath would join in a general strike against the imposition of conscription. For an extraordinary tribute to McElligott's contribution to the defeat of conscription, see pp. 228–30.

8   The following is a copy of the circular which was issued from RIC headquarters to this effect:

POLICE UNION

County Inspector: Officers and men in your county should be informed that His Excellency, the Lord Lieutenant, cannot see his way to permit members of the force to join the National Union of Police and Prison Officers, inasmuch as the RIC is a semi-military force, directly under the control of the crown, and subject, in many respects, to the same conditions of employment and discipline as the army and navy forces.

William M. Davies, Deputy Inspector-General,

RIC Office, Dublin Castle.

4/2/1919. [See *Irish Independent*, 7 February 1919.]

No such circular was sent to members of the DMP or to the Prison Officers. This is intelligible in so far as the circular was a response to what, in effect, was an attempt by members of the Cork city RIC to force the authorities to permit the police to join the NUP&PO (see *Irish Independent*, 4, 7 February 1919). Also, of course, the authorities were not as opposed to members of the DMP and the Prison Officers joining the union as they were to members of the RIC being organised in that way. However, although members of the DMP were not directed publicly to steer clear of the Police Union, they were unofficially discouraged in every possible way from belonging to it (information from David Neligan).

9   According to McElligott almost all the prison officers at Mountjoy jail were members of the union. And some of these subsequently were quite helpful to Republican prisoners (information taken from a letter, dated 8 August 1952, from Thomas J. McElligott to Major Florence O'Donoghue).

10 McElligott throughout all this period, with the collusion of the editor of the *Irish Independent*, was ensuring that these grievances would not be forgotten either by members of the RIC, the authorities or the public (cf. *Irish Independent*, 1, 25, 29 January, 1, 7, 11 February 1919).

11 Cf. *Irish Independent*, 25 January, 1, 4, 7, 8, 11, 25 February, 21 March, 5, 17, 26 April 1919; *The Freeman's Journal*, 20 March, 11 April 1919, and *Irish Catholic*, 22 February 1919. Two other letters, written by him, appeared in the *Irish Independent* of 2, 12 April 1919 (cf. p. 213). However, in the case of these he used the *nom de plume* 'R.I.C. delegate' and not 'Pro Patria'.

These contributions were welcomed by Sinn Féin. Thus Piaras Béaslaí, director of publicity on the headquarters staff of the IRA, was later to recall: 'On one occasion when I entered the back-room of Vaughan's [Hotel, 29 Parnell Square] I met a strange man who told me he was waiting for Michael Collins. Somehow I guessed at once that he was a member of the RIC and was not surprised when he told me he was "Pro Patria". This was Mr T. J. McElligott who was doing useful work for us by letters to the press calculated to create disaffection among the RIC' (see *Irish Independent*, 2 February 1953).

12 I have not been able to discover where or when this letter appeared. It could not have been in the *Sunday Express* of June 1918, as the first copy of that newspaper was not issued until 29 December 1918. Healy, it seems, was interested in police reform for quite some time. This was acknowledged by Thomas J. McElligott in a letter to the *Irish Independent* of 7 February 1919 in which he gave Healy credit for the reforms of 1895, whereby half the officer ranks of the RIC were thereafter to be open to rank and file members of the force. (This, presumably, referred to the fact that Healy raised the question of discrimination against Catholics in the RIC in the House of Commons and prompted John Morley, chief secretary for Ireland, to introduce the reforms of 1895, cf. 'One who knows', *Promotion in the Royal Irish Constabulary* (Dublin 1905), p. 20. For a characteristic contribution by Healy on this subject in the House of Commons, see *United Ireland*, 12 August 1882. In his letter, McElligott also stated that Healy was instrumental in having the rank of acting sergeant abolished cf. p. 388 n.1.

13 McElligott refused to accept a transfer to Belmullet, County Mayo, and thus had no option but to resign. In the official record which was kept of him at the Home Office, it is noted that he resigned on 22 May 1919 as a 'protest against transfer

for being a member of Police Union' (cf. PRO London, Home Office Papers, 184/33, under McElligott, Thomas J.).

About this time (March–August 1919) the NUP&PO was being outmanoeuvred and suppressed by the British government. The process began with the appointment on 1 March of a committee under the chairmanship of Lord Desborough to review the pay and conditions of service of the police. It was continued by the passing on 1 August of the Police Act 1919, which gave effect to most of the generous recommendations of the Desborough committee, outlawed the Police Union and proposed in its place an internal 'representative body for all police officers up to the rank of chief inspector' (this was to be the Police Federation which came into existence in the autumn of 1919). The process was completed by the ruthless suppression of a police strike sponsored by the NUP&PO and begun on 31 July against some of the provisions of the Police Act. For more, see T. A. Critchley, *A History of Police in England and Wales 900–1966*, pp. 184–94.

The executive of the NUP&PO were well aware that the government would use the recommendations of the Desborough committee to outmanoeuvre them and replace the Police Union with an 'association within the service' (see NLI, LO P 115, item 122 – a handbill, cf. p. 394 n.27).

The authorities in Ireland also made good use of the generous recommendations of the Desborough committee in order to deal with 'restiveness' in the police force. Moreover, in a move to offset dissatisfaction which was felt by many members of the RIC because their specific grievances had not been the subject of an inquiry (cf. p. 211), an instruction was issued from police headquarters in Dublin giving permission to the men in each county to meet and appoint a county delegate with power to represent them at a conference to be held in Dublin to consider the recommendations of the Desborough committee. It was stated that this procedure had the sanction of the inspector-general and had been adopted with a view to giving the Irish police an opportunity of expressing their views just as if the commission held an Irish sitting (see *The Freeman's Journal*, 16 May 1919).

14 Cf. p. 73.

15 Cf. Irish Labour Party and Trade Union Congress, *Annual report*, 1919, pp. 93–4, and *Irish Independent*, 4 August 1928.

16 Probably at one of these meetings he gave the information which led to the capture by the IRA of Trim police barracks. At any rate he gave to members of the IRA the name of a constable in Trim, Jeremiah Meehan, who would facilitate the capture of the police barracks (see p. 350–1 n.28) (information from David Neligan).

17 See F. O'Donoghue, *No Other Law*, p. 67.

18 There are 4,308 entries, of which 257 are anonymous in the subscription list. In view of the fact that some 3,500 members of the RIC belonged to the Police Union, it is safe to assume that the bulk of the contributors were either members or former members of the union. In a small number of instances I have been able to verify the predictable pattern whereby those who later belonged to the Organisation of Resigned and Dismissed RIC and DMP (1916–21) had been members of the Police Union and had subscribed to the Thomas J. McElligott, Patrick J. McGuire, Edward Tarpey Testimonial.

The committee organising the testimonial, it seems, were disappointed with the response to their appeal. At any rate in a letter published in the *Irish Independent* of 14 June 1920 a member of the committee, signing himself 'Wicklow', stated that, whereas they had expected almost every member of the force to contribute an average of £1 so that a total of £10,000 would be reached, in fact, only 4,200 members had subscribed. He also stated that the best response to the appeal came from the County Wicklow division, where 95 per cent of all ranks contributed £288, and the worst response was from the city of Belfast, where only 3 per cent subscribed. Moreover, he indicated that 'outside Derry and Omagh Northern Ireland is not in it'. He also stated that the fund was being closed on 20 May 1920.

19 McElligott, it seems, was still residing at this time in his home at Lacca, Duagh. However, from November 1920 until the Truce in July 1921 he spent most of his time 'on the run' in a number of farmers' houses in the Knocknagoshel area, some six miles from his home (information from Máire Breathnach).

20 These reforms, in whole or in part, were urged in an editorial in the *Irish Independent* of 1 January 1919, were suggested in letters by McElligott ('Pro Patria') in the *Irish Independent* of 25 January, 1, 7, 11 February, 5, 17 April 1919, and *The Freeman's Journal*, 11 April 1919, and were the subject of a long article in the *Weekly Freeman* of 1 February 1919. This was not the first time, however, that the reforms were publicly discussed. Thus from the beginning of the century these reforms had been suggested at one time or another by the editor of the *Constabulary Gazette* (information from James R. W. Goulden). (For an insight into his enlightened attitude to the life and work of a policeman, see Editor of *Constabulary Gazette* [J. Harding], *The Royal Irish Constabulary, a plea for reform*.) Moreover, a detailed account of how discrimination was practised against Catholics in the RIC was given in 'One who knows', *Promotion in the Royal Irish Constabulary* (Dublin 1905).

21 Although the organisation was known as the Resigned and Dismissed RIC and DMP (1916–21), only a few of its members were ex-members of the DMP, as not many members of that force resigned during the Anglo-Irish War. This last was not due to members of the DMP being any less sympathetic to Irish

nationalism than their comrades in the RIC, but the need to resign did not present itself as acutely to members of the DMP, which, as a body, opted out of the struggle between the crown forces and Sinn Féin, as to members of the RIC, whose force was caught up in that imbroglio. One such resignee and member of the organisation was Andrew O'Neill. A native of Myshall, County Carlow, he joined the DMP in 1910. On 26 July 1914 he and some of his comrades refused to carry out instructions to disarm Irish Volunteers on the Howth Road, at Clontarf, Dublin. He and two of his comrades were subsequently dismissed. After four months, due to unrest within the force and a great deal of political pressure, they were reinstated. O'Neill, however, eventually resigned in May 1918 (cf. papers of Thomas J. McElligott, and E. MacNeill, 'How the Volunteers began', in *The Irish Volunteers, 1913–15: recollections and documents* (ed. F. X. Martin), p. 75).

22 See *The Freeman's Journal* and *Irish Independent*, 25, 26 January 1922; *Irish Independent*, 27 January 1922; *The Freeman's Journal* and *Irish Independent*, 28 January 1922.

23 After some correspondence to the newspapers on the question at issue (cf. *Irish Independent*, 27 July, 4 August 1928) a remarkable tribute to McElligott appeared in the editorial of the *Irish Independent* of 28 August 1928. This did not end the public support which was given to McElligott in his efforts to obtain a pension. The *Kerry Champion* of 15 September 1928 called attention to his case by reproducing the fine tribute to him in the editorial of the *Irish Independent*. McElligott's application for a pension was discussed in the Dáil on 22 November 1928. On that occasion Patrick J. Ruttledge, TD, ably demonstrated the justice of 'Pro Patria's' case (cf. Dáil Éireann: *Díospóireachta parlaiminte, tuairisc oifigiúil: Parliamentary debates, official report*, vol. 27, cols, 686-693, 22 November 1928). And, continuing its advocacy of McElligott's case, the *Kerry Champion*, in its issue of 8 December 1928, reproduced much of Ruttledge's address in the Dáil.

24 See W. Nash, *New Zealand: a working democracy*.

25 The above information has been taken from PRO London, Home Office Papers, 184/33, under McElligott, Thomas J.; the Contribution book of the Irish branch of the National Union of Police and Prison Officers containing the subscription list of the Thomas J. McElligott, Patrick J. McGuire, Edward Tarpey Testimonial; the papers of Thomas J. McElligott, which are in the possession of his son, Gerard; from interviews with the latter person; and from the sources already cited. See *Irish Independent*, 2 Feb. 1953.

26 This is not surprising as practically all the members of the DMP were Catholics.

27 This is item 96 in the William O'Brien collection of handbills in the National Library of Ireland (NLI, LO P 114, item 96).

28 This tribute, which was paid to McElligott by Patrick J. Ruttledge, TD, in Dáil

Éireann on 22 November 1928, is to be found in Dáil Éireann: *Diospóireachta parlaiminte, tuairisc oifigiúil: Parliamentary debates*, official report, vol. 27, cols. 689-691, 22 November 1928.

29 The first draft of this letter was forwarded for publication by Thomas J. McElligott to the editor of the *Irish Independent* some time before September 1919 (see p. 220). This draft of it appeared subsequently in the *Weekly News Bulletin* of 22 March 1920.

30 The evidence for (a) and (b), it seems, was a confidential police document which was seen by McElligott (information from Gerard McElligott).

31 The evidence which McElligott, presumably, would adduce for this was a report in the *Irish Bulletin* of 11 November 1919 which quoted the *Galway Express* of 8 November 1919 as follows. 'At a "crimes" court in Galway, presided over by two stipendiary magistrates, Mr Seán Milroy, Sinn Féin Director of Organisation, was sentenced to two months' imprisonment for illegal assembly in default of finding bail. A district inspector of police admitted that he had threatened to shoot the prisoner on the way to Portumna jail if the escort was interfered with and said that his instructions were to shoot the prisoner if a rescue was attempted …' The *Galway Express* was particularly outspoken and was suppressed by the authorities as early as December 1918 (cf. *Irish Independent*, 20 December 1918).

32 Cf. p. 219.

33 This letter was published in *The Times* of 28 August 1920 and was reproduced in the *Cork Weekly Examiner* of 4 September 1920. In the edition in which it appeared in *The Times* it prompted an editorial which concluded: 'It is therefore with profound dismay that we contemplate a policy well calculated to drive Ireland to enduring and relentless hostility.' Although the letter was essentially an appeal to the editor of *The Times* to continue to use his influence in order to secure the release of the lord mayor of Cork, it throws light on the extraordinary lack of control by the then British administration over the crown forces in Ireland and the preparedness of even supporters of the government and of law and order – Dr Cohalan was one of the most trenchant critics of the IRA – to believe that the assassination of Colonel Smyth was carried out by elements in the crown forces. Also it highlights the extent to which the British legal and police system had been discredited in the eyes of most Irish people by the autumn of 1920. Above all, attention is drawn to the nub of the police question, that is, that, apart from the totalitarian State, a police force and a system of law and order can be effective only if they are instruments of a generally acceptable form of government.

APPENDIX 4

1 The accuracy of this version was vouched for by ex-Constable Bernard Conway in January 1974.

2   A similar episode occurred at Pomeroy police barracks in 1921 when Constable John (Jack) Staunton, who was on guard duty, allowed local members of the IRA into the barracks between 1–2 a.m. to abscond with arms. For more, see *The Capuchin Annual*, 1976, p. 117.

APPENDIX 5

1   They are to be found among the papers of Major Florence O'Donoghue which are in the National Library.

2   The partisan treatment of Smyth's version of his address by *The Freeman's Journal* probably prompted this fairer presentation of it.

APPENDIX 6

1   This has been compiled from a list drawn up by Head Constable Patrick A. Plover. This list is to be found at the back of an RIC Diary, which was in use in Listowel barracks from 20 June 1918 to 4 June 1920, and which was presented by a son of the former head constable to Listowel Garda Station in September 1969. In finalising the list use has also been made of a record of those who contributed to the Thomas J. McElligott, Patrick J. McGuire, Edward Tarpey Testimonial, and the papers of Jeremiah Mee. I have also had the assistance of ex-Constable Thomas Grennan who was stationed in Listowel police district from December 1919 to 1 November 1920 and in Listowel police barracks from July 1919 to March 1920 and from 3 July to 1 November 1920. Finally, the accuracy of the list has been vouched for by Michael Kelly, who was present on the occasion of the Listowel police mutiny.

I have included the county or place of origin of each man listed. With one exception, none of these policemen attached to the Listowel district was a native of County Kerry, in accordance with the RIC regulation whereby a man was prohibited from serving in his native county. (This regulation sometimes produced anomalies. Thus a man could find himself serving within a few miles of his own home, if that was situated near a county boundary. The corresponding regulation obtaining in the Garda Síochána is more logical. According to it a policeman must be at least thirty miles from his native place, regardless of county boundaries.)

2   Although he was not present in Listowel police barracks on 19 June 1920, as he was out on duty, Constable Michael Lillis later signed the account of the incident which occurred in the barracks on that date.

APPENDIX 8

1   See J. A. Gaughan, *Listowel and its Vicinity*, p. 378.

2   This public house, which was a favourite haunt of members of the RIC at that

time, was run by Kathleen (Kit) Stack, who later became Mrs John (Jack) Lynch.

3 The public house in question belonged to James J. (Jim Joe) Buckley and was the second house from that corner of the Square where the National Bank stood.

4 Active members of the IRA.

5 According to Michael Kelly, he and McNamara spent their last night in Listowel in Kit Stack's and travelled without incident to Dublin on the morning train.

APPENDIX 9

1 State Paper Office, Dáil Éireann Papers, 2/87, item 13.

2 Internal evidence indicates that this letter was written on 27 September.

3 On receiving this letter Collins asked the Irish White Cross to deal with the case, and he forwarded the letter to Thomas J. McElligott with whom he was corresponding at that time about the feasibility of establishing an organisation to look after the interests of resigned and dismissed members of the RIC (cf. State Paper Office, Dáil Éireann Papers, 2/258).

APPENDIX 10

1 For more on the boycott of the RIC, see pp. 400–1 n.2; cf. also I. O., *The Administration of Ireland, 1920*, pp. 275–7.

2 McElligott also prepared this enclosure, that is, No. 1. In finalising it, however, he was assisted by Erskine Childers.

3 It is possible that some of these subsequently found employment. At any rate in his report to the Dáil on 14 August 1921 Dick Cotter stated that ten of the RIC who resigned were helped by the department to find employment and that four had been granted financial assistance, two of these, presumably Kelly and McNamara, being helped to emigrate (Richard Mulcahy papers).

4 See State Paper Office, Dáil Éireann Papers, 2/21, 2/87, 2/161, 2/175 and 2/258; PRO London, CAB 24/132, CP 2523; Dáil Éireann: *Díospóireachta parlaiminte, tuairisc oifigiúil: Parlimentary debates, official report*, vol. 27, col. 688, 22 November 1928; L. Conlon, *Cumann na mBan and the Women of Ireland 1913–25*, p. 87; *The Freeman's Journal*, 25 January 1922; and papers of Thomas J. McElligott.

APPENDIX 11

1 This figure coincides, more or less, with the total number of resigned and dismissed members of the RIC who submitted claims to the Committees of Inquiry of 1922 and 1934 (cf. pp. 290 and 295–6). As is clear from p. 138 this figure represents less than half of the total number of the RIC who resigned or

were dismissed between the beginning of January 1920 and the beginning of March 1921.

2 This figure, the total number of pensions granted by the Committees of Inquiry of 1922 and 1934 (cf. p. 296), does not give a true indication of the number of men who resigned from the RIC for nationalist or other similar reasons. A number of factors such as death, emigration, lack of interest because of other employment, (in the case of the Committee of 1922) involvement with the Republicans during the Civil War, (in the case of the Committee of 1934) the factors mentioned on p. 289, combined to keep the figure of those who received pensions relatively low.

3 The following is the text of a letter, which was written by Collins on 9 February 1922 to the representatives of the resigned and dismissed RIC (1916–21): 'Your suggestion, that the resigned and dismissed men should be dealt with no less generously than the members of the RIC who have continued to serve, has my strong support. At the present moment it is not possible for me to say how the details can be worked out, but I do say that my advice would be always in favour of proper treatment for the men who showed by their actions that they were on the side of Ireland. I think you, personally, are aware that I have always cherished the deepest feelings of regard for these men, and my desire is to translate these feelings into action when I am in a position to do so.' Griffith also replied in the same vein. Moreover, Collins and Griffith in a jointly signed note, which was forwarded through James Crowley, V.S., to the constables in Listowel police barracks following the publication of the story of the Listowel police mutiny in *The Freeman's Journal* of 10 July 1920, had guaranteed that those who resigned from the RIC for patriotic reasons would not regret their decision on financial or other grounds (cf. affidavit written and signed by Michael Kelly and John P. McNamara in 1950).

4 O'Connor was a close friend and admirer of Collins. For more on him, see B. O'Connor, *With Michael Collins*.

5 This occurred mainly in the period between the Anglo-Irish Truce and the Anglo-Irish Treaty. Thus on 21 October 1920 the Police Officers Representative Council was informed that 'in case the negotiations proceed satisfactorily' the active force was to be disbanded on 31 March 1922. However, they were warned that this was not to be communicated to the men. That very night the police were warned officially by cipher: 'situation very critical, notify all ranks, hostilities may be renewed during this week'. Eventually on 25 October an RIC delegation to London was informed by the chief secretary for Ireland, Sir Hamar Greenwood, that: (1) the government meant to settle the Irish question without resort to further hostilities; (2) that the RIC were to remain loyal to the last and would thereby be dealt with generously; and (3) that the force

was to prepare for disbandment, as no hope could be held out of its being transferred to the new Irish government (information taken from the papers of Major Florence O'Donoghue).

Then there was a serious disagreement between representatives of the RIC (in both Northern and Southern Ireland) and the authorities with regard to the terms of disbandment. However, this was, for the most part, resolved by the end of March 1922 (see *Irish Independent*, 30 March 1922).

6   The RIC in the six-county area was, in effect, disbanded on 9 June 1922, its place being taken by the RUC (A. Hezlet, *The 'B' Specials*, p. 73).

7   In the second half of 1928 a number of letters calling attention to the grievances of the resigned and dismissed RIC appeared in the newspapers (cf. for instance, *Irish Independent*, 8, 15 September, 5, 20 November 1928). Letters also appeared in the press at this time from disbanded members of the RIC. Their grievance concerned the failure to wind-up the Constabulary Force Fund – which is to be distinguished from the Widows and Orphans' Fund (cf. pp. 348–9 n.21) – (for three letters on this subject, see *Irish Independent*, 12, 15 September 1928).

8   Liam Price had been OC 5th Battalion, Dublin Brigade, IRA, and also a member of the IRB (information taken from the papers of Major Florence O'Donoghue). For more, see *The Capuchin Annual*, 1970, p. 653 & 1976, pp. 112–17.

9   In fact the terms used were 'no less generously', cf. p. 398 n. 3.

10 The great majority of these applications were from persons who had previously made application to the Committee of Inquiry of 1922 or subsequently to the minister for finance.

11 During the course of this debate, it was stated erroneously that the number of successful applicants to the 1922 Committee of Inquiry was 502 (cf. Dáil Éireann: *Díospóireachta parlaiminte, tuairisc oifigiúil: Parliamentary debates, official report*, vol. 143, col. 1321, 1 December 1953).

12 The resigned and dismissed RIC and DMP (1916–21) were particularly disappointed in 1938. In that year, as a result of the Anglo-Irish agreement, Britain, in exchange for a lump sum of £10,000,000, took over, among other things, liability for the payment of the pensions of the disbanded members of the RIC. Even then, when relieved of the obligation of paying the pensions of some 10,000 former members of the RIC, the Irish government did not rectify the injustice done to the resigned and dismissed men.

It is interesting to note that from *c.*1962, the resigned and dismissed men who were in receipt of pensions from the Irish government were faring better financially than disbanded members of the RIC who were credited with the same years of service and were receiving their pensions from the British government. This arose from the fact that pensions paid by the Irish government were adjusted according to current salaries, whereas those paid by the British government were adjusted according to the cost-of-living index.

(There is a curious parallel between the unjust treatment of resigned and dismissed RIC and DMP (1916–21) by successive Irish governments and the base ingratitude shown by the Irish 'Establishment' to members of the Connaught Rangers who, in protest against British atrocities in Ireland, mutinied at Jullundur and Solon in India, in June-July 1920 (see S. Pollock, *Mutiny for the Cause*, pp. 98–9).)

Much of the information presented above is to be found in Dáil Éireann: *Diospóireachta parlaiminte, tuairisc oifigiúil: Parliamentary debates, official report*, vol. 4, cols 4228–4244, 30 July 1923; vol. 6, cols 817–844, 12 February 1924; vol. 143, col. 1150–1180, 26 November 1953; vol. 143, cols 1319–1332, 1 December 1953; papers of Thomas J. McElligott; *Report of the Committee of Inquiry into resignations and dismissals from the Royal Irish Constabulary, 1934*; and Saorstat Éireann: *Return giving particulars of pensions granted under section 5 of the Superannuation and Pensions Act, 1923, to resigned and dismissed members of the Royal Irish Constabulary*, and the sources already cited.

APPENDIX 12

1   See *Minutes of proceedings of the First Parliament of the Republic of Ireland, 1919–21*, pp. 191–4, 212, 233, 257; *Dáil Éireann: official report*: 16 August–26 August 1921 and 28 February–8 June 1922, pp. 133, 139, 185, 187, 356; *Dáil Éireann: Private sessions of Second Dáil, minutes of proceedings 18 August to 14 September 1921 and Report of debates 14 December 1921 to 8 January 1922*, pp. 17, 19, 68–9, 86; PRO, Minutes (January–April 1922) of the cabinet of the Third Dáil Éireann; State Paper Office, Dáil Éireann Papers, 2/110, 2/261; *The Capuchin Annual*, 1970, pp. 386, 388–9; P. S. O'Hegarty, *The Victory of Sinn Féin*, pp. 49–53, 183–5; C. Younger, *Ireland's Civil War*, pp. 307–9; and information from the late Earnán de Blaghd and Seán McEntee.

ADDENDUM

1   Conclusions of the meetings of the British cabinet, which were held in 1920, are to be found in PRO London, CAB 23/23, 23/37, 23/38; and notes of the two major conferences on the 'Irish Situation' by the cabinet on 23 July and 29–30 December are in CAB 24/109, CP 1693, pp. 445–65, and CAB 23/23, CP 2554, pp. 337–46 respectively.

2   Apart from the above, the British cabinet was left in no doubt in the second half of 1920 as to the dire straits in which members of the RIC then found themselves. Thus in a memorandum, which he circulated to the cabinet on

25 July 1920, Sir John Anderson, joint under-secretary for Ireland, in urging against a policy of 'naked force' in Ireland, wrote:

'That splendid force, the R.I.C., ill-found and inadequately supported, has held together under most adverse circumstances longer and better than those having knowledge of the conditions had any right to expect. Even now it is a most valuable instrument: but its future is, at this moment, in the balance' (PRO London, CAB 24/109, CP 2509). And in a memorandum in the same vein, which he circulated to the cabinet on 11 August 1920, D. M. Wilson, solicitor-general for Ireland, stated: 'Already there have been hundreds of resignations from the police and it is thought by those best qualified to judge that the great majority, if not all, will have resigned by next October unless something is done' (PRO London, CAB 24/110, CP 2522). Moreover, in the weekly intelligence summaries submitted by the director of intelligence to the cabinet between June and September 1920, besides lists of attacks on police barracks, ambushes on police patrols and casualties among the police, the following references were made to the plight of the RIC: *July 1* – 'attempts to intimidate or injure members of the R.I.C. and their families is having a serious effect on the force'; *July 15* – 'the campaign of boycotting directed against the police is more acute'; *August 5* – 'Information has been received from a source believed to be reliable that the campaign of murder directed against the police is to be pursued even more relentlessly this month in the hope of breaking up the force'; *August 12* – 'Sinn Féin is still concentrating on attempts to break up the R.I.C. A Sinn Féin circular has now appeared directing members of clubs to call on the parents of men serving in the force and warn them to try to get their sons to resign, in which case Sinn Féin will get them work or pay their passage to America. Police who resign are to be treated in a friendly manner'; *August 26* – 'During the past week the campaign against the police was intensified'; *September 8* – 'A very bitter feeling exists in police circles because of the liberty allowed to the *Irish Independent* and *The Freeman's Journal* to influence public opinion against men who are only doing their duty. To the baneful influence of these two papers they attribute the murders of their comrades'; *September 16* – 'At a large Sinn Féin meeting in Glasgow the Irish Constabulary were described as hooligans, professional thieves and guttersnipes with bad army records. No decent ex-soldier, it was said, would apply or would be accepted if he did apply, for the government wanted only men to whom murder, looting and arson came easy'; 'Resignations from the R.I.C. are becoming very numerous'; *September 23* – 'The chief efforts of Sinn Féin were still concentrated on the attempt to break up the R.I.C., and boycotting notices signed by local officers of the I.R.A., threatening letters and acts of intimidation towards the parents and families of members of the force were very prevalent' (PRO London, CAB 24/108-111, intelligence reports).

3   Both here and elsewhere this, of course, should be Archbishop Mannix.

4   He was John M. Regan. He joined the RIC as a cadet officer or 3rd class district inspector on 13 March 1909, was promoted 2nd district inspector on 6 August 1910, 1st district inspector on 1 January 1920, and soon afterwards temporary county inspector in Limerick (information from James R. W. Goulden).

5   Cf. I. O., *The Administration of Ireland, 1920*, p. 257.

6   In fact, it was not until September that the British cabinet finally decided on a new Home Rule Bill which, as the Government of Ireland Act, 1920, received the royal assent on 23 November. This act provided for the setting up of two governments and two parliaments in Ireland, one for the six counties which were to form Northern Ireland and the other for the rest of the country, which the act called Southern Ireland.

7   Here, and subsequently, MacMahon is erroneously referred to as Sir James MacMahon. Although MacMahon was offered a knighthood, he did not accept it (information from his daughter, Mrs Mollie Doolin).

SOURCES

The purpose of this list is to give some help to the general reader in search of further information, and to provide initial guidance for the more serious student. All the books and other sources which have been cited are included. Of the books listed some throw light on the RIC in general, but most only deal with it during the present century. No attempt is made to set down a bibliography of the Republican movement. An excellent survey of the material on this subject is to be found on pp. 381–95 of J. B. Bell's, *The Secret Army* (London 1970).

A: MANUSCRIPTS

Down, County, George Murphy
　Register of the White Cross Hotel

Dublin, National Library
　Papers of Major Florence O'Donoghue
　William O'Brien Papers, LO P 114, item 96; P 115, item 122

Dublin, Public Record Office
　Minutes of cabinet of Third Dáil Éireann

Dublin, State Paper Office
　Dáil Éireann Papers

Dublin, Mrs Nora Gallagher
　Typescript statement of Áine bean Eamoinn Ceannt

Dublin, Mrs Eileen Mee Doyle
　Letters to Jeremiah Mee from John P. McNamara, dated 12, 18, and 31 January 1952
　Papers of Jeremiah Mee

Dublin, County, Gerard McElligott
　Contribution book of the Irish branch of the National Union of Police and Prison Officers containing the subscription list of the Thomas J. McElligott, Patrick J. McGuire, Edward Tarpey Testimonial
　Papers of Thomas J. McElligott

Kerry, County, Garda Barracks, Listowel
> RIC Diary used in Listowel police barracks from 20 June 1918 to 4 June 1920

Leitrim, County, John Doonan
> Affidavit on the 'Listowel affair' written and signed by Michael Kelly and John P. McNamara in 1950

London, Public Record Office
> Cabinet Conclusions
> Cabinet Memoranda
> Home Office Papers
> Treasury Blue Notes

B: PUBLISHED WORKS

Adam, H. L., *The Police Encyclopaedia, etc.* 1– (London 1920–)

African Missionary, The, June-July 1957

Allen, G., *The Garda Síochána: policing independent Ireland 1922–82* (Dublin 1999)

American Commission on conditions in Ireland: Interim Report (London 1921)

American Commission: Evidence on conditions in Ireland. Comprising the completed testimony, affidavits and exhibitions presented before the Commission (Washington 1921)

Barry, T., *Guerilla Days in Ireland* (Tralee, n.d.)

——, *The Reality of the Anglo-Irish War 1920–21 in West Cork* (Dublin 1974)

Belfast Newsletter, 29, 30, 31 July, 3, 5, 9, 10 August 1907

Belfast Telegraph, 31 March 1919; 17 June 1920

Brady, C., *Guardians of the Peace* (Dublin 1974)

Breathnach, S., *The Irish Police from the Earliest Times to the Present Day* (Dublin 1974)

Breen, Dan, *My Fight for Irish Freedom* (Tralee 1963)

Broeker, G., *Rural Disorder and Police Reform in Ireland 1812–36* (London 1970)

Camán, An, 15 Aibrean 1933

Capuchin Annual, The, 1970

Carroll, D., *They Have Fooled You Again: Michael O'Flanagan (1876–1942), Priest, Republican, Social Critic* (Dublin 1993)

Conlon, L., *Cumann na mBan and the Women of Ireland 1913–25* (Kilkenny 1969)

Constabulary Gazette, March and April 1919

Cork Examiner, The, 7 August 1920

Cork Weekly Examiner, 17, 24 July, 4 September 1920

Cox, T., *Damned Englishman: a study of Erskine Childers (1870–1922)* (New York 1975)

Critchley, T. A., *A History of Police in England and Wales 900–1966* (London 1967)

Crone, J. S., 'The RIC in literature', *Irish Book Lover,* 12 (1920), pp. 7–9, 29–31

Cronin, M., Durken, M. and Rouse, P., *The GAA: A People's History* (Cork 2009)

Crozier, F. P., *Ireland For Ever* (London 1932)

Cumann Lúthchleas Gael, treoraí oifigiúil (Baile Átha Cliath 1973)

Curtis, R., *The History of the Royal Irish Constabulary* (Dublin 1871)

Dáil Éireann, *Diospóireachta parlaiminte, tuairisc oifigiúil;* Parliamentary debates, official report, 10 October 1922; 30 July 1923; 12 February 1924; 22 November 1928; 26 November, 1 December 1953

Dáil Éireann, *Official Report: 16 August–26 August 1921, and 28 February–5 June 1922* (Dublin 1959)

Daily Chronicle, 19 July 1920

Daily Express (London), 1, 2 August 1920

Daily Herald, 20 July 1920

Daily News, 9, 12, 13, 15 January, 13 July 1920

Davis, R., *Arthur Griffith and Non-Violent Sinn Féin* (Dublin 1974)

Dictionary of National Biography, I–XXII (ed. Sir L. Stephens and Sir Sydney Lee, London 1908–09)

Dictionary of National Biography (ed. J. McGuire and J. Quinn, Cambridge, 2001)

Duggan, G. C., 'The Royal Irish Constabulary', in O. D. Edwards and F. Pyle (eds), *1916: the Easter Rising* (London 1968)

Editor of *Constabulary Gazette* [J. Harding], *The Royal Irish Constabulary: a plea for reform* (Dublin 1907)

Ervine, St John, *Craigavon, Ulsterman* (London 1949)

Evening Echo (Cork), 17 September 1966

Forester, M., *Michael Collins, the Lost Leader* (London 1971)

Freeman's Journal, The, 20 March, 11 April, 16 May, 25 June 1919; 12, 13, 15, 29 March, 10, 12 April, 25 May, 9, 10, 14, 15, 22, 26, 28 July, 12 August, 27 September, 26, 27 October 1920; 10 January, 10 February, 4, 10, 15, 17, 18 March 1921; 25, 26, 28, 30 January 1922; 1 January 1924

Gaelic American, 17 July 1920

Gaelic Athletic Association, Official Guide 1914–15 (Wexford 1914)

Gaire, P. J., *A Brief History of the Diocese of Baker* (Baker City, Oregon, 1966)

Galway Express, 8 November 1919

Gaughan, J. A., *Listowel and its Vicinity* (Cork 1973)

Gillon, S., *The K.O.S.B. in the Great War* (London 1930)

Gleeson, J., *Bloody Sunday* (London 1962)

Greaves, C. D., *Father Michael O'Flanagan, Republican Priest* (London 1954)

Green, G. G., *In the Royal Irish Constabulary* (London 1905)

Gwynn, D., *John Redmond* (London 1932)

Hawkins, R., 'Dublin Castle and the Royal Irish Constabulary', in T. D. Williams (ed.), *The Irish Struggle 1916–1926* (London 1966)

——,'Government versus secret societies: the Parnell era', in T. D. Williams (ed.), *Secret Societies in Ireland* (Dublin 1973)

——, 'An army on police work, 1881–2: Ross of Bladensberg's memorandum', *The Irish Sword* XI (1973)

Hayes-McCoy, G. A., 'The raising of the Connaught Rangers, 1793', *Galway Archaeological and Historical Society Journal 21* (1944)

Healy, T. M., *Letters and Leaders of My Day* (London 1928)

Herlihy, Jim, *The Royal Irish Constabulary 1816–1922* (Dublin 1999)

Hezlet, A., *The 'B' Specials: a history of the Ulster Special Constabulary* (London 1972)

I. O. [Street, C. J. C.], *The Administration of Ireland, 1920* (London 1921)

Iris an Gharda, Eanair 1961–Feabhra 1962

Irish Bulletin, 11 November 1919; 13, 29 July, 19 August, 8, 18 September, 27 October 1920; 18 May 1921

Irish Catholic, 22 February 1919

Irish Independent, 3 October, 1, 20, 27 November, 20, 24, 29 December 1917; 18 January, 21, 22, 28 February, 21 June, 3 September, 20 December 1918; 1, 25, 29 January, 1, 4, 7, 8, 11, 25 February, 6, 21, 28 March, 1, 2, 5, 11, 12, 17, 26 April, 30 May 1919; 15 May, 4, 14, 18 June, 6, 9, 18, 19, 29 July, 5 August 1920; 12 May 1921, 25, 26, 27, 28, 30 January, 30 March 1922; 27 July, 4, 28 August, 8, 12, 15 September, 5, 20 November 1928; 2 February 1953

Irish Labour Party and Trade Union Congress, *Annual Report*, 1919, 1920, and 1921

Irish Monthly, August 1877

Irish Press, 11 July 1936; 18 January 1946

Irish Times, The, 14, 22 May, 18 June, 30 July 1920; 20 May 1961

Irish Volunteer, 19 September 1914

Irish World, and American Industrial Liberator, 31 July 1920

James, D., *The Gore-Booths of Lissadell* (Dublin 2004)

Jeffries, C., *The Colonial Police* (London 1952)

Jones, H. R., *The Policeman's Manual of Sir Andrew Read, K.C.B., C.V.O.* (7th ed., Dublin 1908)

Joyce, P. J., *John Healy, Archbishop of Tuam* (Dublin 1931)

Kerry Champion, 15 September, 8 December 1928

Kerryman, The, 3, 17, 24, 31 July, 27 November 1920

Kerry's Fighting Story, 1916–21, told by the men who made it (Tralee 1947)

Kilfeather, T. P., *The Connaught Rangers* (Tralee 1969)

Kilgannon, T., *Sligo and its Surroundings* (2nd ed., Sligo 1932)

King, C., *The Orange and the Green* (London 1965)

Kipling, R., *The Irish Guards in the Great War*, II (London 1923)

Larkin, E., *James Larkin, Irish Labour Leader 1876–1947* (London 1965)

Larkin, Felix M., *Terror and Discord: the Shemas Cartoons in The Freeman's Journal, 1920–1924* (Dublin 2009)

Leatham, C. W., *Sketch and Stories of the Royal Irish Constabulary* (Dublin 1909)

Leitrim Leader, 15, 22, 29 March, 5, 12, 19, 26 April 1952

Liberty, November 1968; June 1974

Limerick's Fighting Story (ed. J. M. MacCarthy, Tralee, n.d.)

Limerick's Fighting Story, 1916–21, told by the men who made it (Tralee 1948)

Linn, R., *A History of Banbridge* (Banbridge 1935)

Lloyd, C., *Ireland under the Land League* (London 1892)

Longford, Earl of, and O'Neill, T. P., *Eamon de Valera* (Dublin 1970)

Lynch, D., *The I.R.B. and the 1916 Insurrection* (Cork 1957)

Macardle, D., *The Irish Republic* (Dublin 1951)

MacCartan, P., *With de Valera in America* (Dublin 1932)

Mac Carthaigh, M., 'Placenames of Inismurray', *Dinnseanchas*, Meitheamh 1971

MacEvilly, Michael, *A Splendid Resistance: the life of IRA chief of staff Dr Andy Cooney* (Dublin 2011)

MacNeill, E., 'How the Volunteers began', in F. X. Martin (ed.) *The Irish Volunteers 1913–1915; recollections and documents* (Dublin 1963)

Manchester Guardian, The, 29, 30 November, 1 December 1920

Marjoribanks, E., and Colvin, I., *Life of Lord Carson* I–III (London 1932–6)

Marreco, A., *The Rebel Countess* (London 1967)

Martin, F. X. (ed.), *The Irish Volunteers, 1913–15: recollections and documents* (Dublin 1963)

Martin, H., *Ireland in Insurrection* (London 1921)

McInerney, M., *Peadar O'Donnell, Irish Social Rebel* (Dublin 1974)

Milligan, C. D., *History of the Siege of Londonderry 1689* (Belfast 1951)

Minutes of Proceedings of the First Parliament of the Republic of Ireland, 1919–21 (Dublin 1959)

Mitchell, A., 'Thomas Johnson, 1872–1963, a pioneer Labour leader', *Studies* 58 (1969)

——, 'William O'Brien, 1881–1968, and the Irish Labour Movement', *Studies* 60 (1971)

——, *Labour in Irish Politics 1890–1930* (Dublin 1974)

Morning Post, 17 November 1920

Nash, W., *New Zealand: a working democracy* (London 1944)

Neligan, D., *The Spy in the Castle* (Dublin 1968)

New Haven Sunday Register, 13 February 1921

New York American, 9 July 1920

New York Evening Journal, 9 July 1920

New York Times, The, 10 July 1920

New York Tribune, 10 July 1920

New York World, 10 July 1920

O'Brien, C. C., *States of Ireland* (London 1972)

O'Brien, W., *Forth the Banners Go: Reminiscences of William O'Brien* (Dublin 1969)

O'Callaghan, A., *Cork's St Patrick's Street: a history* (Cork 2010)

O'Connor, B., *With Michael Collins in the Fight for Irish Freedom* (London 1929)

O'Doherty, Liam, 'Dublin Brigade Area', *The Capuchin Annual*, 1970

O'Donnell, P., *The Gates Flew Open* (Cork 1965)

O'Donoghue, F., *No Other Law* (Dublin 1954)

——, 'Guerrilla warfare in Ireland, 1919–1921', *An Cosantóir* 23 (1963)

——, *Tomas MacCurtain, Soldier and Patriot* (2nd ed., Tralee 1971)

Óglach, An t-, 29 July 1921, winter 1967

O'Hegarty, P. S., *The Victory of Sinn Féin* (Dublin 1924)

Oibrí imdhala: the distributive worker, An t-, November 1964

O'Kelly, D. J., *Salute to the Gardai, 1922–1958* (Dublin 1959)

Ó Luing, S., *Art Ó Gríofa* (Baile Átha Cliath 1959)

——, *I Die in a Good Cause* (Tralee 1970)

O'Mara, H. (ed.), 'Sensational police developments in Kerry', *Vexilla Regis* (1964)

'One who knows', *Promotion in the Royal Irish Constabulary* (Dublin 1906)

O'Rorke, T., *The History of Sligo: town and county* I-II (Dublin 1890)

O'Shea, B. and White, G., *The Burning of Cork* (Cork 2006)

Pears' shilling cyclopaedia (London 1915)

Pollock, S., *Mutiny for the Cause* (London 1969)

Rebel Cork's Fighting Story, from 1916 to the Truce with Britain (Tralee 1961)

Remembrance ('London Dunne and O'Sullivan Memorial Committee', March 1949)

Report of the Committee of Inquiry into resignations and dismissals from the Royal Irish Constabulary, 1934 (Dublin 1935)

Report of the Irish White Cross (Dublin 1923)

Reynolds News, 25 November, 2, 9, 16, 23, 30 December 1951; 6 January 1952

Rose, P., *The Manchester Martyrs* (London 1970)

Royal Irish Constabulary List and Directory, 1917, 1920

Ryan, D., *Seán Treacy and the Third Tipperary Brigade, IRA* (Tralee 1945)

——, *The Rising: the complete story of Easter Week* (Dublin 1949)

Saorstat Éireann, *Return giving particulars of pensions granted under section 5 of the Superannuation and Pensions Act, 1923, to resigned and dismissed members of the Royal Irish Constabulary* (Dublin 1924)

Sinn Féin Rebellion Handbook, Easter 1916 (Dublin 1917)

Sligo Champion, March 1911; 6 October 1917; 23 February, 2, 9, 30 March 1918; 9, 30 October 1920

Sunday Independent, 27 November 1955

Sunday Press, 26 August 1951; 27 September, 4, 11, 18 October 1953

Sworn to be Free (ed. D. Nolan, Tralee 1971)

Tales of the R.I.C. (London 1921)

Thom, A., *Directory,* 1912, 1920, 1921 and 1922

Times, The, 28 August 1920

Tipperary Star, 1, 29 March 1975

Uí Chonaill, E. [bean], 'A Cumann na mBan recalls Easter week', *The Capuchin Annual,* 1966

United Ireland, 12 August 1882

Wakeman, W. F., *A Survey of the Antiquarian Remains on the Island of Inismurray* (London 1893)

Weekly Freeman, 1 February 1919; 31 July, 21 August, 4, 18 September, 27 November, 4, 11, 18 December 1920; 1, 8, 15 January, 12 February, 21 May 1921; 5 May, 18 August 1923

Weekly News Bulletin, 22 March 1920

Who was Who 1941–50 (4th ed., London 1967)

With the IRA in the Fight for Irish Freedom: 1919 to the Truce (Tralee 1955)

Young Ireland, 3 December 1921

Younger, C., *Ireland's Civil War* (London 1968)

C: PERSONS

Breathnach, Miss Máire

Brennan, Colonel Austin

Conway, Bernard

Cooney, Mrs Frances

de Blaghd, Earnán

Doolin, Mrs Mollie

Dore, Michael

Flynn, Michael J.

Goulden, James R. W.

Grennan, Thomas

Hargaden, Thomas W.
Heraughty, Dr Patrick
Keane, William
Kelly, Sister Mary Pascal
Kelly, Michael
Loughrey, Edward
McBrien, Harold
McCarthy, Michael
McElligott, Denis
McElligott, Gerard
McEntee, Mrs Margaret
McEntee, Seán
Mulcahy, James

Mulvihill, Mrs Ellen
Neligan, Colonel David
Nolan, Daniel
O'Brien, Seamus
O'Carroll, Dr Thomas F.
Riordan, William (Ó Riordain, Liam S.).
Roche, James
Ryan, Mrs Kathleen
Shanahan, Captain Thomas
Stack, Superintendent Gerald
Uí Conaill (née Ryan), Eilís bean
Wilmot, Dr Séamus

Note: I also received information from the relatives of most of those on whom I have written biographical notes.

D: SOUND RECORDING

RTÉ, 18/10, 'Incident at Listowel' (first broadcast on 13 September 1966)

INDEX